T0373621

The TDD Rhythm

The TDD Rhythm:

1. Quickly add a test
2. Run all tests and see the new one fail
3. Make a little change
4. Run all tests and see them all succeed
5. Refactor to remove duplication

Essential TDD Principles

TDD Principle: **Test First**
When should you write your tests? Before you write the code that is to be tested.

TDD Principle: **Test List**
What should you test? Before you begin, write a list of all the tests you know you will have to write. Add to it as you find new potential tests.

TDD Principle: **One Step Test**
Which test should you pick next from the test list? Pick a test that will teach you something and that you are confident you can implement.

TDD Principle: **Isolated Test**
How should the running of tests affect one another? Not at all.

TDD Principle: **Evident Tests**
How do we avoid writing defective tests? By keeping the testing code evident, readable, and as simple as possible.

TDD Principle: **Fake It ('Til You Make It)**
What is your first implementation once you have a broken test? Return a constant. Once you have your tests running, gradually transform it.

TDD Principle: **Triangulation**
How do you most conservatively drive abstraction with tests? Abstract only when you have two or more examples.

TDD Principle: **Assert First**
When should you write the asserts? Try writing them first.

TDD Principle: **Break**
What do you do when you feel tired or stuck? Take a break.

TDD Principle: **Evident Data**
How do you represent the intent of the data? Include expected and actual results in the test itself, and make their relationship apparent. You are writing tests for the reader, not just for the computer.

TDD Principle: **Obvious Implementation**
How do you implement simple operations? Just implement them.

TDD Principle: **Representative Data**
What data do you use for your tests? Select a small set of data where each element represents a conceptual aspect or a special computational processing.

TDD Principle: **Automated Test**
How do you test your software? Write an automated test.

TDD Principle: **Test Data**
What data do you use for test-first tests? Use data that makes the tests easy to read and follow. If there is a difference in the data, then it should be meaningful. If there isn't a conceptual difference between 1 and 2, use 1.

TDD Principle: **Child Test**
How do you get a test case running that turns out to be too big? Write a smaller test case that represents the broken part of the bigger test case. Get the smaller test case running. Reintroduce the larger test case.

TDD Principle: **Do Over**
What do you do when you are feeling lost? Throw away the code and start over.

TDD Principle: **Regression Test**
What's the first thing you do when a defect is reported? Write the smallest possible test that fails and that, once run, will be repaired.

FLEXIBLE, RELIABLE SOFTWARE

Using Patterns and Agile Development

CHAPMAN & HALL/CRC TEXTBOOKS IN COMPUTING

Aims and Scope

This series covers traditional areas of computing, as well as related technical areas, such as software engineering, artificial intelligence, computer engineering, information systems, and information technology. The series will accommodate textbooks for undergraduate and graduate students, generally adhering to worldwide curriculum standards from professional societies. The editors wish to encourage new and imaginative ideas and proposals, and are keen to help and encourage new authors. The editors welcome proposals that: provide groundbreaking and imaginative perspectives on aspects of computing; present topics in a new and exciting context; open up opportunities for emerging areas, such as multi-media, security, and mobile systems; capture new developments and applications in emerging fields of computing; and address topics that provide support for computing, such as mathematics, statistics, life and physical sciences, and business.

Published Titles

Pascal Hitzler, Markus Krötzsch, and Sebastian Rudolph, Foundations of Semantic Web Technologies

Uvais Qidwai and C.H. Chen, Digital Image Processing: An Algorithmic Approach with MATLAB®

Henrik Bærbak Christensen, Flexible, Reliable Software: Using Patterns and Agile Development

CHAPMAN & HALL/CRC
TEXTBOOKS IN COMPUTING

FLEXIBLE, RELIABLE SOFTWARE

Using Patterns and Agile Development

Henrik Bærbak Christensen

CRC Press is an imprint of the
Taylor & Francis Group an **informa** business
A CHAPMAN & HALL BOOK

The cover picture shows the first pyramid ever built, Pharaoh Djoser's step pyramid. It was built around 2600 BC by Djoser's chancellor, Imhotep. Imhotep was the first engineer and architect in history known by name, and he was deified almost 2000 years after his death. Imhotep's ingenious idea was to reuse the existing tomb design of a flat-roofed, rectangular structure, the *mastaba*, and create the royal tomb by building six such mastabas of decreasing size atop one another. You can still admire the pyramid at Saqqara, Egypt, today, more than 4600 years after it was completed. It is a design that has stood the test of time from an architect who was a deified-worthy role model for all who create designs and realize them.

Chapman & Hall/CRC
Taylor & Francis Group
6000 Broken Sound Parkway NW, Suite 300
Boca Raton, FL 33487-2742

Printed in the United States of America on acid-free paper
10 9 8 7 6 5 4 3 2 1

International Standard Book Number: 978-1-4200-9362-9 (Hardback)

Library of Congress Cataloging-in-Publication Data

Christensen, Henrik B.
Flexible, reliable software : using patterns and agile development / Henrik B. Christensen.
p. cm. -- (Chapman & Hall/CRC textbooks in computing)
Includes bibliographical references and index.
ISBN 978-1-4200-9362-9 (hardcover : alk. paper)
1. Computer software--Reliability. 2. Computer software- Development. I. Title. II. Series.

QA76.76.R44C54 2010
005.1--dc22 2009049459

Visit the Taylor & Francis Web site at
http://www.taylorandfrancis.com

and the CRC Press Web site at
http://www.crcpress.com

To my children,
Mikkel, Magnus, and Mathilde

for defining the ultimate purpose
a man can assume...

To my wife,
Susanne

for the greatest in life:
to love and be loved in return...

Contents

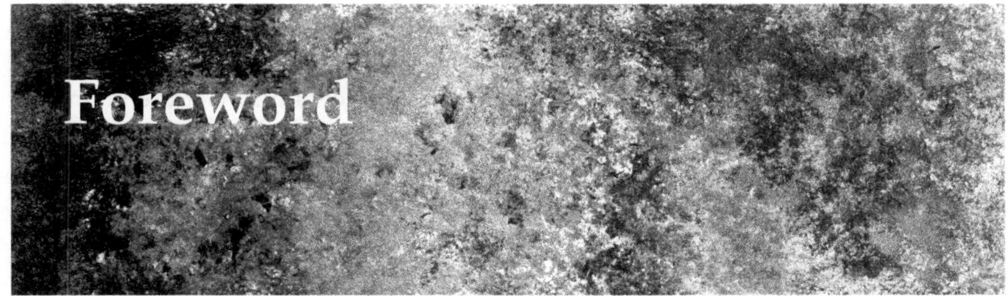

Foreword

by Michael Kölling

Teaching to program well is a hard challenge. Writing a book about it is a difficult undertaking.

The bulk of my own experience in programming teaching is at the introductory level. I see my students leave the first programming course, many of them thinking they are good programmers now. Most of them are not. Only the good ones realise how much they have yet to learn. Learning how to build good quality software is much more than mastering the syntax and semantics of a language. This book is about the next phase of learning they are about to face.

Most academic discussion about the teaching of programming revolves around introductory teaching in the first semester of study, and by far the largest number of books on programming cover the beginners' aspects. Many fewer books are available that cover more advanced aspects—as this one does—and even fewer do it well.

The reason is just that introductory programming is easier to handle, and still so difficult that for many years we—as a teaching community—could not agree how to approach the teaching of modern, object-oriented programming in a technically and pedagogically sound manner. It has taken well over 10 years and more than one hundred published introductory textbooks on learning object orientation with Java alone to get to where we are now: a state where introductory texts are available that are not only a variation of a commented language specification, but that follow sound pedagogical approaches, that are written with learners in mind, that emphasise process over product, and that deal with real problems from real contexts.

For more advanced programming books—usable in advanced programming courses—the situation is less rosy. There is much less agreement about the topics that such a course should cover, and fewer authors have taken the difficult step to write such a book. Many programming books at this level are in character where introductory books were ten years ago: Descriptions of techniques and technologies, written with great emphasis on technical aspects, but with little pedagogical consideration.

This book is a refreshing change in this pattern. This book brings together a careful selection of topics that are relevant, indeed crucial, for developing good quality software with a carefully designed pedagogy that leads the reader through an experience of active learning. The emphasis in the content is on practical goals—how to construct reliable and flexible software systems—covering many topics that every software engineer should have studied. The emphasis in the method is on providing a practical context, hands on projects, and guidance on *process*.

This last point—process—is crucial. The text discusses not only what the end product should be like, but also how to get there.

I know that this book will be a great help for many of my students on the path from a novice programmer to a mature, professional software developer.

—Michael Kölling
Originator of the BlueJ and Greenfoot Environments.
Author and coauthor of the best-selling books
Objects First with Java and
Introduction to Programming with Greenfoot.

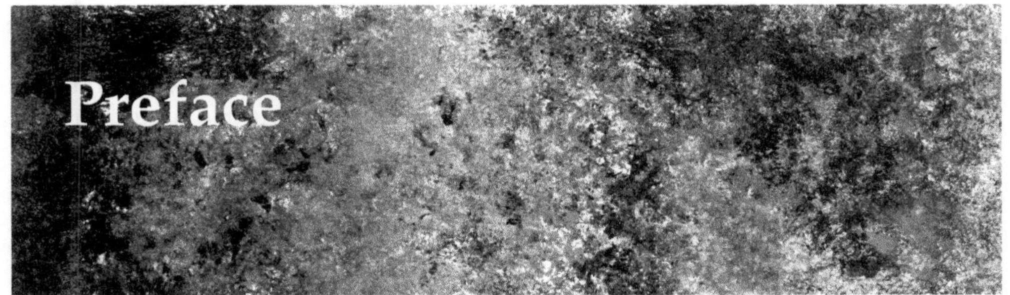

Mostly for the Students...

This is a book about designing and programming flexible and reliable software. The big problem with a book about making software is that you do not learn to make software—by reading a book. You learn it by reading about the techniques, concepts and mind-sets that I present; apply them in practice, perhaps trying alternatives; and reflect upon your experiences. This means you face a lot of challenging and fun programming work at the computer! This is the best way to investigate a problem and its potential solutions: programming is a software engineer's laboratory where great experiments are performed and new insights are gained.

I have tried to give the book both a practical as well as a theoretical and academic flavor. Practical because all the techniques are presented based on concrete and plausible (well, most of the time) requirements that you are likely to face if you are employed in the software industry. Practical because the solutions that I choose work well in practice even in large software projects and not just toy projects like the ones I can squeeze down into this book. Practical because the techniques I present are all ones that have been and are used in practical software development. Theoretical and academic because I am not satisfied with the first solution that I can think of and because I try hard to evaluate benefits and liabilities of all the possible solutions that I can find so I can pick the best. In your design and programming try to do the same: Practical because you will not make a living from making software that does not work in practice; academic because you get a better paycheck if your software is smarter than the competitors'.

Mostly for the Teachers...

This book has an ambitious goal: to provide the best learning context for a student to become a good software engineer. Building flexible and reliable software is a major challenge in itself even for seasoned developers. To a young student it is even more challenging! First, many software engineering techniques are basically solutions to problems that an inexperienced programmer has never had. For instance, why introduce a design pattern to increase flexibility if the program will never be maintained, as is the case with most programming assignments in teaching? Second, real software design and development require numerous techniques to be combined—picking the right technique at the right time for the problem at hand. For instance, to do automated testing and test-driven development you need to decouple abstractions and thus pick the right patterns—thus in practice, automated testing and design patterns benefit from being combined.

This book sets out to lessen these problems facing our students. It does so by *storytelling* (Christensen 2009), by explaining the design and programming *process*, and by using *projects* as a learning context. Many chapters in the book are telling the story of a company developing software for parking lot pay stations and the students are invited to join the development team. The software is continuously exposed to new requirements as new customers buy variations of the system. This story thus sets a natural context for students to understand why a given technique is required and why techniques must be combined to overcome the challenges facing the developers. An agile and test-driven approach is applied and space is devoted to explaining the programming and design process in detail—because often *the devil is in the detail.* Finally, the projects in the last part of the book define larger contexts, similar to real, industrial, development, in which the students via a set of assignments apply and learn the techniques of the book.

A Tour of the Book

The book is structured into nine parts—eight *learning iterations*, parts 1–8, and one *project* part, part 9. The eight learning iterations each defines a "release" of knowledge and skills that you can use right away in software development as well as use as a stepping-stone for the next learning iteration. An overview of the learning iterations and their chapters is outlined in Figure 1. The diagram is organized having introductory topics/chapters at the bottom and advanced topics/chapters at the top. Chapters marked with thick borders cover core topics of the book and are generally required to proceed. Chapters marked with a gray background cover material that adds perspective, background, or reflections to the core topics. The black chapters are the project chapters that define exercises.

For easy reference, an overview of the rhythm and principles of test-driven development is printed as the first two pages, and an index of all design patterns at the last page. In addition to a normal index, you will also find an index of sidebars and key points at the end of the book.

Learning iteration 1 is primarily an overview and introduction of basic terminology that are used in the book. Learning iterations 2 to 5 present the core practices, concepts, tools and analytic skills for designing flexible and reliable software. These iterations use a *story telling* approach as they unfold a story about a company that is producing software for pay stations, a system that is facing new requirements as time passes. Thus, software development techniques are introduced as a response to realistic challenges. Learning iteration 6 is a collection of design patterns—that can now be presented in a terse form due to the skills acquired in the previous iterations. The learning focus of iteration 7 is frameworks which both introduce new terminology as well as demonstrate all acquired skills on a much bigger example, MiniDraw. Learning iteration 8 covers two topics that are important for flexible and reliable software development but nevertheless are relatively independent of the previous iterations.

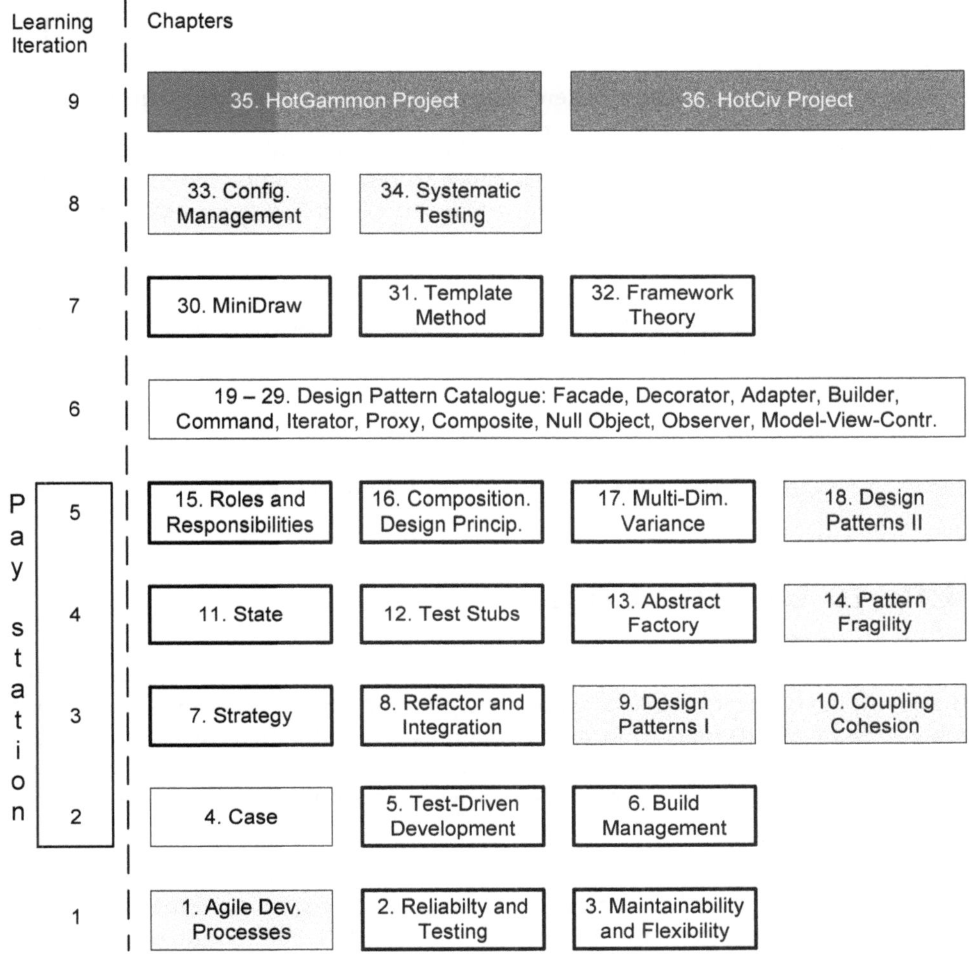

Figure 1: Overview of learning iterations and chapters.

Part 9, *Projects*, defines two large project assignments. These projects are large systems that are developed through a set of assignments covering the learning objectives of the book. Each project is structured into seven releases or iterations that roughly match learning iteration 2 to 8 of the book. Thus by completing the exercises in, say, project HotCiv's iteration on frameworks you will practice the skills and learning objectives defined in the framework learning iteration of the book. If you complete most or all iterations in a project you will end up with a reliable and usable implementation of a large and complex software system, complete with a graphical user interface. The HotGammon project will even include an opponent artificial intelligence player.

Each learning iteration starts with an overview of its chapters, and in turn each chapter follows a common layout:

- *Learning Objectives* state the learning contents of the chapter.
- Next comes a presentation and discussion of the new material usually ending in a section that discusses benefits and liabilities of the approach.

- *Summary of Key Concepts* tries to sum up the main concepts, definitions, and results of the chapter in a few words.
- *Selected Solutions* discusses exercises in the chapter's main text if any.
- *Review Questions* presents a number of questions about the main learning contents of the chapter. You can use these to test your knowledge of the topics. Remember though that many of the learning objectives require you to program and experiment at the computer to ensure that you experience a deep learning process.
- *Further Exercises* presents additional, small, exercises to sharpen your skills. Note, however, that the main body of exercises is defined in the projects in part 9.

Some of the chapters, notably the short design pattern presentations in learning iteration 6, *A Design Pattern Catalogue*, will leave out some of these subsections.

How to Use the Book

This book can be used in a number of ways. The book is written for courses with a strong emphasis on practical software development with a substantial project work element leading all the way to students designing and implementing their own frameworks with several concrete instantiations. The book has been used in semester length, quarter length, and short courses. Below I will outline variations of this theme as well as alternative uses of the book.

Semester lengths project courses. Learning iterations 1–8 of the book are organized to follow a logical path that demonstrates how all the many different development techniques fit nicely together to allow students to build flexible frameworks and discuss them from both the theoretical as well as practical level. Each iteration roughly correlates to two weeks of the course. Topics from iteration 8 need not be introduced last but can more or less be introduced at any time. For instance, it may make sense to introduce a software configuration management tool early to support team collaboration on source code development. The projects in part 9 follow the rhythm of the book and students can start working on these as soon as the test-driven development chapter has been introduced. Alternative projects can be defined, however, consult Christensen (2009) for some pitfalls to avoid.

Quarter lengths project courses. Here the basic organization of the book is still followed but aspects must be left out or treated cursory. Chapters marked by a gray background in Figure 1 are candidates. Depending on the entry level of the students, parts of the *Basic Terminology* part can be cursory reading or introduced as part of a topic in the later iterations—for instance introducing the notion of test cases as part of demonstrating test-driven development, or just introduce maintainability without going into its sub qualities. The build management topic can be skipped and replaced by an introduction to integrated development environments or Ant scripts can be supplied by the teacher, as it is possible to do the projects without doing the build script exercises. The projects in the last part of the book work even in quarter length courses, note however that this may require the teacher to supply additional code to lower the implementation burden. This is especially true for the MiniDraw integration aspect of the framework iteration.

Short courses. Two-three day courses for professional software developers can be organized as full day seminars alternating between presentations of test-driven development, design patterns, variability management, compositional designs, and frameworks, and hands-on sessions working on the pay station case. Depending on the orientation of your course, topics are cursory or optional.

Design pattern courses. Here you may skip the test-driven development aspects all together. Of course this means skipping the specific chapter in part 2, the test stub chapter in part 4, as well as skipping the construction focused sections in the chapters in parts 3 and 4. I advise to spend time on the theory of roles and compositional design in part 5. Optionally part 7 may be skipped altogether and time spent on covering all the patterns present in the catalogue in part 6. The patterns may be supplemented by chapters from other pattern books.

Software engineering courses. Here less emphasis can be put on the pattern catalogue in part 6 and frameworks in part 7 and instead go into more details with tools and techniques for systematic testing, build-management, and configuration management.

Framework oriented courses. Here emphasis is put on the initial patterns from parts 3 and 4 and on the theory in part 5. Only a few of the patterns from part 6 are presented, primarily as examples of compositional design and for understanding the framework case, MiniDraw, in part 7.

Prerequisites

I expect you to be a programmer that has a working experience with Java, C#, or similar modern object-oriented programming languages. I expect that you understand basic object oriented concepts and can design small object-oriented systems and make them "work". I also expect you to be able to read and draw UML class and sequence diagrams.

Conventions

I have used a number of typographic conventions in this book to highlight various aspects. Generally, *definitions* and *principles* are typeset in their own gray box for easy visual reference. I use sidebars to present additional material such as war stories, installation notes, etc. The design patterns I present are all summarized in a single page sidebar (a **pattern box**)—remember that a more thorough analysis of the pattern can be found in the text.

I use typefaces to distinguish class names, role names, and other special meaning words from the main text.

- ClassName and methodName are used for programming language class and method names.

- PATTERNNAME is used for names of design patterns.
- *packagename* is used for packages and paths.
- `task` is used for Ant task names.
- **roleName** is used for the names of roles in designs and design patterns. Bold is also used when new terms are introduced in the text.

Web Resources

The book's Web site, http://www.baerbak.com, contains source code for all examples and projects in the book, installation guides for tools, as well as additional resources. Source code for all chapters, examples, exercises, and projects in the book are available in a single zip file for download. To locate the proper file within this zip file, most listings in chapters are headed by path and filename, like

Fragment: chapter/tdd/iteration-0/PayStation.java

```
public interface PayStation {
```

That is, PayStation.java is located in folder *chapter/tdd/iteration-0* in the zip file. Several exercises are also marked by a folder location, like

Exercise 0.1. Source code directory:
`exercise/iterator/chess`

Permissions and Copyrights

The short formulation of the TDD principles in the book and on the inner cover are reproduced by permission of Pearson Education, Inc., from *Beck, TEST DRIVEN DEVELOPMENT:BY EXAMPLE, © 2003 Pearson Education, Inc and Kent Beck.* The historical account of design patterns in Chapter 9 was first written by Morten Lindholm and published in *Computer Music Journal 29:3* and is reprinted by permission of MIT Press. IEEE term definitions reprinted by permission of Dansk Standard. The *intent* section of the short design pattern overviews in the pattern side bars as well as the formulation of the *program to an interface* and *favor object composition over class inheritance* are reprinted by permission of Pearson Education, Inc., from *Gamma/Helm/Johnson/Vlissides, DESIGN PATTERNS: ELEMENTS OF REUSABLE OBJECT-ORIENTED DESIGN*. Other copyrighted material is reproduced as *fair use* by citing the authors.

Java technology and *Java* are registered trademarks of Sun Microsystems, Inc. *Windows* is a registered trademark of Microsoft Corporation in the United States and other countries. UNIX is a registered trademark in the United States and other countries, exclusively licensed through X/Open Company, Ltd. All other product names mentioned throughout the book are trademarks of their respective owners.

The Inkscape image on page 337 was made by Konstantin Rotkevich and is copyleft under the Free Art Licence. Michael Margold at SoftCollection kindly gave permission to use their Java source code for the LCD display code used in the pay station graphical user interface first introduced in the Facade chapter. Karl Hörnell gave permission to copy the IceBlox game from his web site `www.javaonthebrain.com`. The graphical tile set used for drawing the map in HotCiv is a copy of the neotrident tile set for FreeCiv 2.1.0, released under the GNU public license.

Acknowledgments

The following students have made valuable contributions by pointing out problems in the text or in the exercises: Anders Breindahl, Carsten Moberg Hammer, Emil Nauerby, Jens Peter S. Aggerholm, Jens Bennedsen, Hans Kolind Pedersen, Kristian Ellebæk Kjær, Karsten Noe, Kenneth Sejdenfaden Bøgh, Mads Schaarup Andersen, Mark Sjøner Rasmussen, Marianne Dammand Iversen, Mark Surrow, Martin Norre Christensen, Michael Dahl, Michael Lind Mortensen, Mikael Kragbæk Damborg Jensen, Mikkel Kjeldsen, Morten Wegelbye Nissen, Ole Rasmussen, Peter Urbak, Rasmus Osterlund Feldthaus Hansen, and Søren Kaa. Henrik Agerskov drew the initial graphics for the Backgammon graphical user interface. Ole Rasmussen corrected numerous spelling errors in the second printing.

A special thanks to Finn Rosenbech Jensen for some good discussions, much enthusiasm, and valuable comments. I would like to thank Morten Lindholm Nielsen that contributed to Chapter 9. Jens Bennedsen, Jürgen Börstler, Erik Ernst, Edward F. Gehringer, Klaus Marius Hansen, John Impagliazzo, Michael Kölling, Andrew McGettrick, and Cyndi Rader provided valuable reviews and comments throughout the process. A special thanks to Michael E. Caspersen for getting CRC Press interested in my book. I would also like to thank Alan Apt at CRC Press for being an enthusiastic editor, and to Amy Blalock and Michele Dimont for helping me through the maze of tasks associated with writing a book. My colleagues at Department of Computer Science, Aarhus University , I thank for an inspiring work environment, and the opportunity to spend part of my time writing this book.

Finally, I dedicate this book to my wife, Susanne, and my children, Mikkel, Magnus, and Mathilde. *Home is not a place but the love of your family. . .*

Iteration 1

Basic Terminology

Developing reliable and flexible software is a major challenge that requires a lot of techniques, practices, tools, and analytical skills. In order to evaluate and understand techniques, however, you have to know what the terms *reliable* and *flexible* really means. In the *Basic Terminology* part of the book I will present the terms that are essential for the analyses and discussions in the rest of the book. I will provide small examples in this introduction, but larger and more complex examples will be presented later.

Chapter	Learning Objective
Chapter 1	*Agile Development Processes.* I will focus quite a lot on the *process of programming* in the beginning of the book—that is, the process you go through as you move from the initial requirements and design ideas for a software system towards a high quality program. As time has shown, requirements to software systems change frequently, and I need processes that can cope with that. The objective of this chapter is to present the ideas and values that are fundamental for agile development processes like Extreme Programming, Scrum, and Test-Driven Development.
Chapter 2	*Reliability and Testing.* A major learning objective of this book is to provide you with skills and techniques for writing high quality programs—but what is quality after all? One main aspect is *reliability*: that I can trust my programs not to fail. In this chapter, the objective is learning the terms and definitions that allow us to discuss reliable programs. A central technique to increase reliability is *testing* which has its own set of terms that are also introduced in this chapter.
Chapter 3	*Flexibility and Maintainability.* Another important quality of software today is its ability to adapt to changing requirements at low cost. The objective of this chapter is to introduce the terms and definitions concerning flexibility and maintainability that allow us to discuss these aspects precisely.

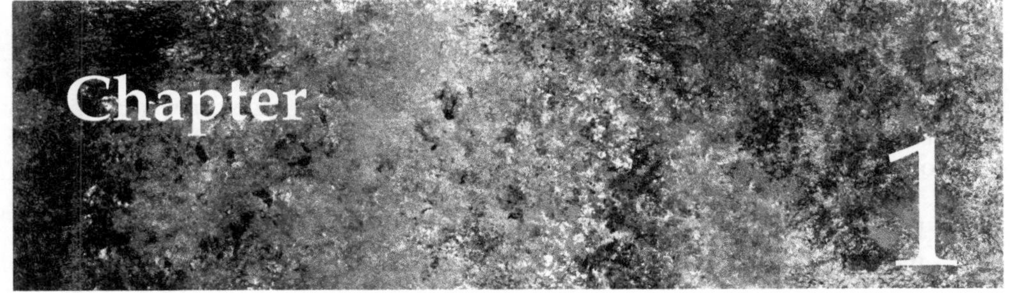

Agile Development Processes

Learning Objectives

In this chapter, the learning objective is an understanding of the main ideas of agile development methods. One particular and influential agile method, namely Extreme Programming, is treated in greater detail. Several of the techniques and practices of Extreme Programming are discussed in great detail later in the book, and this chapter thus primarily serves to create the context in which to understand them.

1.1 Software Development Methods

No matter how you develop software, you apply a certain *software development process*, that is, a structure imposed on the tasks and activities you carry out to build software that meets the expectations of your customer. A software development process must define techniques to deal with activities or steps in development. Such steps will usually include:

- *Requirements.* How do you collect and document the users' and customers' expectations to the software, i.e. what is it supposed to do?
- *Design.* How do you partition and structure the software and how do you communicate this structure?
- *Implementation.* How do developers program the software so that it fulfills the requirements and adheres to the design?
- *Testing.* How do you verify that the executing system indeed conforms to the requirements and users' expectations?
- *Deployment.* How do you ensure that the produced software system executes in the right environment at the user's location?

- *Maintenance.* How do you ensure that the software is corrected and enhanced as defects are discovered by users or new requests for functionality are made?

The amount of rigor in defining processes and tools for these steps vary according to the size of a project: Building aircraft control software in a project with hundreds of developers requires stricter control than a spare time game developed by two friends.

Exercise 1.1: Consider your last project or programming exercise. How was the activities/steps defined, executed, and controlled?

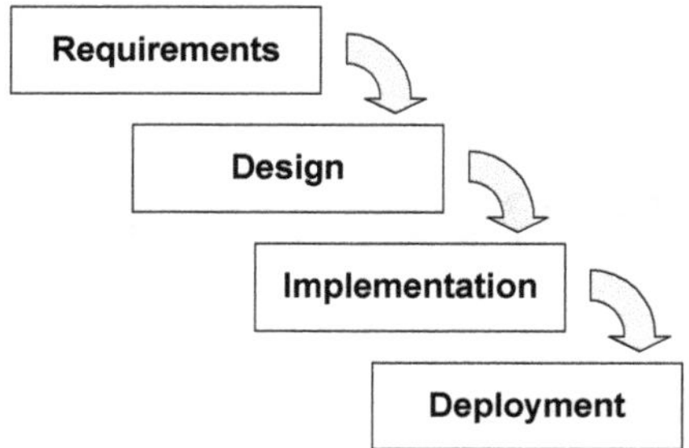

Figure 1.1: Waterfall model.

Over the years researchers and practitioners of software engineering have described and tested a large number of software processes. For many years there was a tendency for them to be heavy-weight, that is, they put much emphasis on strict communication and process rules, on producing large amounts of detailed documentation, and on not beginning one activity before the previous activity had been analyzed and understood in detail. One such model was the **waterfall model**, sketched in Figure 1.1, in which one proceeds from one activity to another in a purely sequential manner: you get all the requirements documented in full detail before you start designing; you do not start implementing before the design is complete, etc. While this process may seem appealing, as it is much cheaper to correct a mistake early in the process, it was quickly realized that perfecting one stage before starting the next was impossible even for small projects. More often than not, requirements and designs are not well understood until a partially working software system has been tested by users. Thus in the waterfall model, such insights discovered late in the phase invalidates a large investment in the early phases. The agile development processes are characterized as lightweight and can be seen as ways to ensure that these insights invalidates as little invested effort as possible.

☞ Find literature or internet resources on some common development models such as *waterfall, cleanroom, spiral model, V-model, XP, Scrum, RUP, etc.*

1.2 Agile Methods

The core of agile methods is expressed in the *agile manifesto*, reproduced here from the agile manifesto web page `agilemanifesto.org`:

> **Manifesto for Agile Software Development**
> We are uncovering better ways of developing software by doing it and helping others do it. Through this work we have come to value:
>
> Individuals and interactions over processes and tools
> Working software over comprehensive documentation
> Customer collaboration over contract negotiation
> Responding to change over following a plan
>
> That is, while there is value in the items on the right, we value the items on the left more.

☞ Find the manifesto on the internet and note that it is "signed" by quite a few people. Several of these people have invented or significantly contributed to the techniques described in this book.

Several points are notable in this manifesto. First of all, it is written by practicing software developers : "by doing it and helping others do it." Next, the agile methods are just as much about *values* as it is about concrete techniques. At present there are quite a few agile methods around: Extreme Programming (XP), Scrum, Crystal Clear, and others; but they share the same core values as expressed in the manifesto. This makes it relatively easy to understand e.g. Scrum once you have understood XP. I will generally use the terminology of XP as the programming process used in this book, *Test-Driven Development*, was invented as part of XP. A final, but central, point is the word "agile." Agile methods value to move towards the defined goal with speed while maintaining the ability to change to a better route without great costs.

Individuals and interactions are emphasized. Agile methods put a lot of emphasis on software development as a team effort where individual's creativity and contribution is central to overall success. Thus forming a good context for individuals and their collaboration is central. Earlier development methods had a tendency to view individuals as "production units" that mechanically produce software code, designs, test plans, etc., and thus little attention was paid to making individuals feel comfortable and more attention paid to documents and processes to control collaboration. Agile methods have suggested a number of practices to ensure that the right decisions are made because people are responsible, want to do the right thing, and have the proper information at hand to make qualified decisions. For instance, attention is paid to how teams are located in buildings: if two teams that are supposed to collaborate are on different floors then they will communicate much less than if located in offices next to each other. And with less communication the risk of misunderstandings and thus defects in the product rise significantly.

Working software. Bertrand Meyer, the inventor of the Eiffel programming language, once said that *"once everything is said, software is defined by code..."*(Meyer 1988). The design may be just right, the UML diagrams beautifully drawn, but if there is no code there is no product and thus no revenue to pay the bills. Agile methods focus on making code of high quality and less on writing documents about the code. The reasoning is that it takes time to write documentation which is then not used to make code. As *individuals and interactions* are emphasized it is much faster and accurate to ask the relevant people than trying to find the information in the documentation. However, it is *working* software that is valued: the code should be of high quality. To this end, *testing* is central: exercising the software to find defects in it. Another central technique to keep the code of high quality is *refactoring*: improving code structure without affecting its functionality. Both techniques are central for this book and discussed in detail later.

Customer collaboration is faster than negotiating contracts. Bjarne Stroustrup, the inventor of the C++ programming language , has said that *"to program is to understand..."* As you implement customer requirements, you get a much deeper understanding of them and spot both ambiguities to be resolved as well as opportunities for improving the final product. If these matters have to go through a long chain of command, *developers ask managers that ask sales people that ask buyers that ask everyday users...*, the feedback loop is too slow. The result is defective or cumbersome software and missed opportunities for a better product. In the vein of focusing on interaction between people, agile methods require customers and users to be readily available for questioning and discussions. A central technique is **small releases** where working but functionally incomplete systems are presented to customers for them to use. These releases are a better starting point for discussing ambiguities and improvement opportunities than long requirement specifications.

Responding to change means that the best route to a goal may be another than that planned at the beginning of the journey. Working in the project means learning and improving the understanding of what best fits the customer—especially as they are integrated in the project as outlined above. Thus an initial plan is important but the plan should be revised as experience accumulates. Maybe the customer thought they wanted feature X but if working with a small release part way into the project shows feature X to be less important but feature Y much more relevant, then why not work on feature Y for the next small release?

1.3 Extreme Programming

One of the first agile methods was **Extreme Programming**, or short **XP**, that received a lot of attention in the beginning of the millennium. XP pioneered many central techniques that are presented in this book and it serves well as an example of an agile method.

1.3.1 Quality and Scope

In the book *Extreme Programming Explained*, Kent Beck (2000) presents a model for software development to explain some of the decisions made in XP. In this model, a software product is controlled by four parameters: *cost*, *time*, *scope*, and *quality*. Cost is basically the price of the product which correlates strongly to the number of people assigned to work on the project. Time is the amount of time to the delivery deadline. Scope is the size of the project in terms of required functionality. Quality is aspects like usability, fitness for purpose, and reliability. These four parameters have a complex relationship, and changing one in a project affects the others. The relationship is, however, not simple. For instance, you may deliver faster (decrease time) by putting additional programmers on a project (increase cost) but doubling the number of programmers will certainly not cut the delivery time in half.

Exercise 1.2: Explain why doubling the number of programmers will likely not cut the time spent on the project in half.

The point made is that often organizations decide the first three parameters (cost, time, scope) and leave the forth parameter (quality) as the only free parameter for developers to control. Typically, the onset of a project is: *We have three months (fix time) to complete the requirements in this specification (fix scope) and this group of eight developers are assigned (fix cost).* As estimates are often optimistic, the developers have no other option than sacrifice quality to meet the other criteria: delivery on time, all features implemented, team size constant. Even still, our software development profession is full of examples of projects that did not deliver in time, did not deliver all features, and went over budget.

Exercise 1.3: Consider a standard design or programming project in a university or computer science school course. Which parameters are typically fixed by the teacher in the project specification?

XP focuses on making *scope* the parameter for teams to control, not quality. That is, the three parameters cost, time, and quality are fixed, but the scope is left open to vary by the team. For example, consider that three features are wanted in the next small release, but after work has started it is realized that there is not enough time to implement them all in high quality. In XP, the customers are then involved to select the one or two most important features to make it into the release. *Two working features are valued higher than three defective or incomplete ones.*

Needless to say, this swapping of the roles of *scope* and *quality* in XP is underlying many of its practices:

- to control and measure quality, *automated testing* is introduced, and made into a paradigm for programming called *test-driven development*. Test-driven development is the learning focus of Chapter 5. To ensure code quality, *refactoring* is integrated in the development process. Refactoring is a learning focus of Chapter 8.
- to control scope, an *on-site customer* is required so the interaction and decisions can be made quickly and without distortion of information. *Small releases* are produced frequently to ensure time is always invested in those features and aspects that serve the users' needs best.

1.3.2 Values and Practices

XP rests upon four central values

- *Communication.* A primary cure for mistakes is to make people communicate with each other. XP value interaction between people: between developers, with customers, management, etc.
- *Simplicity.* "What is the simplest thing that could possibly work?" In XP you focus on the features to put into the next small release, not on what may be needed in six months.

- *Feedback.* You need feedback to know you are on the right path towards the goal, and you need it in a timely manner. If the feature you are developing today will not suit the need of the customer you need to know it today, not in six months, to stay productive. XP focus on feedback in the minutes and hours time scale from automated tests and from the on-site customer, and on the week and month scale from small releases.
- *Courage.* It takes courage to throw away code or make major changes to a design. However, continuing development based on a bad design or fixing defects in low quality code is a waste of resources in the long run.

Based on these values, a lot of practices have evolved. Below, I will describe a few that are central to the practices of programming and the context of this book. It should be noted that XP contains many more practices but these are focused on other aspects of development such as planning, management, and people issues, which are not core topics of this book.

A central technique in XP is **pair programming**. Code is never produced by an individual but by a pair of persons sitting together at a single computer. Each person has a specific role. The person having the keyboard focuses on the best possible implementation at the detailed level. The other person is thinking more strategically and evaluates the design, reviews the produced code, looks for opportunities for simplifications, defines new tests, and keeps track of progress. The pairs are dynamic in that people pair with different people over the day and take turns having the two different roles. To make this work, **collective code ownership** is important: any programmer may change any code if it adds value for the team. Note that this is different from *no ownership* where people may change any code to fit their own purpose irrespective if this is a benefit or not for the team. Collective ownership also force programmers to adhere to the same **coding standards** i.e. the same style of indentation, same rules for naming classes and variables, etc. Pair programming is both a quality and communication technique. It focuses on quality because no code is ever written without being read and reviewed by at least two people; and there are two people who understand the code. And it focuses on communication: pairs teach and learn about the project's domain and about programming tricks. As pairs are dynamic, learning spreads out in the whole team.

Automated testing is vital in XP, and treated in detail in Chapter 2 and 5. Automated testing is testing carried out by the computers, not by humans. Computers do not make mistakes nor get tired of executing the same suite of 500 tests every ten minutes, and they execute them fast. By executing automatic tests on the software system often, the system itself gives feedback about its health and quality, and developers and customers can measure progress. These tests must all pass at all times. To get feedback on the "fitness of purpose" you make **small releases** frequently: once every month, every two weeks, or even daily. A small release is a working, but functionally incomplete, system. At the beginning of a project it may serve primarily as a vehicle to discuss fitness of purpose with the end users and customers; however as quickly as possible it will be deployed into production and used with ever-growing functionality. **Continuous integration** means that the development efforts of each pair programming team are continuously added to the project to ensure that the developed code is not in conflict with that of the other pair teams. Integration testing is one of the learning foci of Chapter 8.

Customers' and users' requirements are captured as **stories** which are short stories about user-visible functionality. These stories are written on index cards and given short headlines, like "Allow stop of video recording after a specified time interval", "Align numbers properly in columns", "Add currency converter tool to the spreadsheet", "Compute account balance by adding all deposits and subtracting all deductions," etc. Finally, they are put on a wall or some other fully visible place. Also each story is estimated for cost in terms of hours to implement. This allows developers and customers to choose those stories that provide the best value for the least cost. Stories should be formulated so they are achievable within a 4–16 hour effort of a pair. Once a pair has selected a story, it is further broken down as will be described in Chapter 5 on test-driven development.

> **Exercise 1.4:** Compare the short outline of XP above with the list of development activities in the start of the chapter. Classify XP practices in that framework: requirements, design, implementation, etc.

XP is a highly **iterative** development process. Work is organized in small *iterations*, each with a well-defined focus. At the smallest level, an iteration may last a few minutes, to implement a simple method in a class. At the next level, it may last from a few hours to a day, to implement a feature or a prerequisite for a feature, and ends in integrating the feature into the product. And at the next level again, the small release defines an iteration, lasting from weeks to a month, to implement a coherent set of features for users to use. It follows that it is also an **incremental** development process: systems are grown piecemeal rather than designed in all detail at the start.

The strong focus in XP on people interactions means it is suited for small and medium sized teams. Large projects with many people involved need more rigor to ensure proper information is available for the right people at the right time. This said, any large project uses a "divide and conquer" strategy and thus there are many small teams working on subsystems or parts of a system and these teams can use XP or another agile method within the team.

1.4 Summary of Key Concepts

A software development process is the organization and structuring of indiviual activities (or steps) in development. Any project must consider and organize activities like requirements, design, implementation, testing, deployment, and maintenance.

Agile methods adhere to the agile manifesto that emphasizes four values: *interacting individuals, working code, collaboration with customers,* and *responding to change.* Extreme Programming is an early and influential agile process. It is lightweight , iterative and incremental. It manifests the agile values in a set of practices many of which have been adopted or adapted in later methods. Key practices are automatic testing, small releases, and continuous integration to ensure timely feedback to developers of both the product's reliability as well as its fitness to purpose. Pair programming is adopted to ensure learning and interaction in the team. Pairs are dynamic and form to implement stories: stories define a user-visible unit of functionality. Stories are written on index cards and usually put on a wall visible to all developers. Each story is estimated for work effort.

Fowler (2005)'s online article *The New Methodology* is a short and easy introduction to agile methods. For further reading on XP, you should consult *Extreme Programming Explained–Embrace Change,* available in a first and second edition, by Beck (2000) and Beck (2005). Another good overview is given in *Extreme Programming Installed* by Jeffries et al. (2001).

1.5 Selected Solutions

Discussion of Exercise 1.2:

Doubling the number of programmers on a project means there is a lot of learning of the domain that has to be made by the new staff before they become productive. The only source of information is usually the existing programmers thus productivity will actually fall for an extended period of time until the new people are "up to speed." More people also mean more coordination and more management which drain resources for the actual implementation effort.

This said, adding more people may in the long run be a wise investment. XP advises to start projects in small teams and then add people as the core system becomes large enough to define suitable subprojects for sub teams to work on.

Discussion of Exercise 1.3:

Well, typical university course design or programming exercises are no different from the culture in industry. Projects specify *time:* "deliver by the end of next month", *cost:* "to be developed in groups of three students", and *scope:* "design and implement feature X, Y, and Z." Thus students typically are left only with the quality parameter to adjust workload.

1.6 Review Questions

Outline the activities or steps that any software development method must include. What is the goal of each activity? Discuss the difference between a waterfall method and an agile method.

What are the four aspects that are valued in the agile manifesto? Explain the argumentation for each of the four aspects.

Describe the model for software development proposed by Kent Beck: what are the four parameters and which are fixed and which are free in many traditional development projects. What parameter does XP propose to fix instead?

Explain the four values in XP. Describe the aspects in key practices such as pair programming, collective code ownership, stories, automated testing, small releases, and continuous integration.

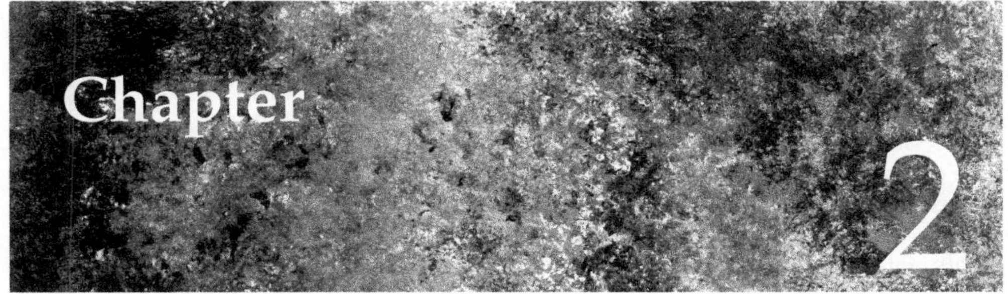

Reliability and Testing

Learning Objectives

Learning to make software *reliable* is important to become a competent and successful developer. Much of this book is devoted to develop the mindset, skills, and practices that contribute to build software that does not fail. The learning objective of this chapter is to develop the foundation for these practices and skills by presenting the basic definitions and terminology concerning reliable software in general, and testing as a technique to achieve it, in particular.

Specifically, this chapter

- Introduces you to the concept of *reliability*.
- Introduces you to definitions in testing terminology: what is testing, a test case, a failure, etc., that are used throughout the book.
- Introduces a concrete Java tool, JUnit, that is a great help in managing and executing automated tests.

2.1 Reliable Software

In the early days of computing, programs were often used by the same persons that wrote them. For instance, a physicist may write a program to help with numerical analysis of the data coming from an experiment. If the program crashed or misbehaved then the damage was rather limited as the program just had to be updated to fix the error. Modern mass adoption of computing has over the last couple of decades changed the requirement for reliable programs dramatically: today the ordinary computer user is not a computer programmer and will not accept software that does not work. Today users expect software to behave properly and *reliability* is a quality to strive for in producing software. Reliability can be defined in several ways but I will generally use definitions from the ISO 9126 (ISO/IEC International Standard 2001) standard.

Definition: Reliability (ISO 9126)

The capability of the software product to maintain a specified level of performance when used under specified conditions.

The central aspect of this definition is ... *to maintain a specified level of performance.* In our setting "performance" is the ability to perform the required functions without failing: letting the users do their work using the software product. Informally developers state that the "system works."

Exercise 2.1: The aspects of the definition that deals with ... *under specified conditions* also have implications. Give some examples of the same software system being considered reliable by one user while being considered unreliable by another because the users have different "specified conditions."

Reliability is one of many qualities a software system must have to be useful. Another quality may be that it must execute fast and efficiently so responses to the users do not take too long, that it must be useable so the users can understand and use the software efficiently, etc. The next chapter discusses "maintainability" as an important quality. However, reliability is a central quality as many other qualities become irrelevant if the software is unreliable e.g. it is of little use that a system responds quickly if the answer is wrong.

Thus reliability is a highly desired quality of software and both the research and industrial communities have produced numerous techniques focused on achieving reliability. Some examples are:

- Programming language constructs. Modern programming languages contain a lot of language constructs and techniques that prevent tricky defects that were common in the early days of machine code and early programming languages. As an example, the original BASIC language did not have local variables, and therefore you could ruin a program's behavior if you accidentally used the same variable name in two otherwise unrelated parts of the program.

- Review. Reviews are more or less formalized sessions where reviewers read source code with the intention of finding defects. Designs and documentation can also be reviewed. Reviews have the advantage that you can find defects in the code that are not visible when executing it. Examples are defects like poor naming of variables, poor formatting of code, misleading or missing comments, etc. The technique's liability is that it is manual and time consuming.

- Testing. Testing is executing a software system in order to find situations where it does not perform its required function. Testing has the advantage that is can to a large extent be automated, but its liability is that it can only detect defects that are related to run-time behavior.

I assume Java or a similar modern object-oriented programming language and therefore get the many reliability benefits these languages have over older languages like C, Fortran, and BASIC. Review is an important technique that can catch many types of defects, but I will not discuss it any further in this book. Testing is a well-known technique but has been revitalized by the agile software development movement, in particular by the test-driven development process. As I will emphasize testing and test-driven development, the rest of this chapter is devoted to the basic terminology and tools that form the foundation for understanding and using these techniques.

2.2 Testing Terminology

I will introduce basic concepts and terminology of testing through a small example. Consider that I am part of a team that has to develop a calendar system. One of my colleagues has developed a class, Date, to represent dates[1], whose constructor header is reproduced below:

Fragment: chapter/reliability/handcoded-test/Date.java

```
public class Date {
  /**
   * Construct a date object.
   * @param year the year as integer, i.e. year 2010 is 2010.
   * @param month the month as integer, i.e.
   *              januar is 1, december is 12.
   * @param dayOfMonth the day number in the month, range 1..31.
   * PRECONDITION: The date parameters must represent a valid date.
   */
  public Date(int year, int month, int dayOfMonth) {
```

Now I have been asked to extend it with a method, dayOfWeek, to calculate the weekday it represents. The method header should be:

Fragment: chapter/reliability/handcoded-test/Date.java

```
  public enum Weekday {
      MONDAY, TUESDAY, WEDNESDAY,
      THURSDAY, FRIDAY,
      SATURDAY, SUNDAY };
  /**
  * Calculate the weekday that this Date object represents.
  * @return the weekday of this date.
  */
  public Weekday dayOfWeek() {
```

How do I ensure that my complex algorithm in this method is reliably implemented? I choose to do so by testing:

Definition: Testing

Testing is the process of executing software in order to find failures.

[1] The java libraries already have such a class. The best path to reliable software is of course to reuse software units that have already been thoroughly tested instead of developing new software from scratch. For the sake of the example, however, I have chosen to forget this fact.

This definition requires we know what a failure is:

Definition: **Failure**

A failure is a situation in which the behavior of the executing software deviates from what is expected.

Thus, if I call this method with a date object representing 19th May 2008, it should return MONDAY, as this date was indeed a Monday.

```
Date d = new Date(2008, 5, 19); // 19th May 2008
// weekday should be MONDAY
Date.Weekday weekday = d.dayOfWeek();
```

If, however, it returns, say, SUNDAY then this is clearly a failure. A failure is the result of a defect:

Definition: **Defect**

A defect is the algorithmic cause of a failure: some code logic that is incorrectly implemented.

Informally, defects are often called faults or "bugs".

☞ Find out why it is called a bug on wikipedia or other internet sources.

In other words, to test I have to define three "parameters": the method I want to test, the input parameters to the method, and the expected output of the method. This is called a *test case*:

Definition: **Test case**

A test case is a definition of input values and expected output values for a unit under test.

A single test case cannot test all aspects of a method so test cases are grouped in test suites.

Definition: **Test suite**

A test suite is a set of test cases.

A short and precise way of representing suites of test cases is in a **test case table**, a table that lists the sets of test cases defining the input values and expected output. In my case, the dayOfWeek method test cases can be documented as in Table 2.1.

A test case may **pass** or **fail**. A test case passes when the computed output of the unit under test is equal to the expected output for the given input values in the test case. If not, the test case fails. The terms are also used for test suites: a test suite passes if all its test cases pass but fails if just one of its test cases does. A failed test is often also referred to as a *broken test*.

I have written the test cases above for testing a single method, but in general, testing can be applied at any granularity of software: a complete software system, a subsystem, a class, a single method... Therefore test cases are defined in terms of the *unit under test*:

Table 2.1: Test case table for dayOfWeek method.

Unit under test: dayOfWeek	
Input	Expected output
year=2008, month=May, dayOfMonth=19	Monday
year=2008, month=Dec, dayOfMonth=25	Thursday
year=2010, month=Dec, dayOfMonth=25	Saturday

Definition: **Unit under test**

A unit under test is some part of a system that we consider to be a whole.

OK, I have made an implementation, I have written my test case table, but the real interesting aspect is to conduct the test. In my case, the Date class is part of a calendar program , and I can do the testing by following a short manuscript like: *"Start the application, and scroll to May 2008. Verify that May 19th is marked as Monday"*. To execute this test and verify that the software does as expected, I have to spend time executing this manuscript manually. This is called manual testing.

Definition: **Manual testing**

Manual testing is a process in which suites of test cases are executed and verified manually by humans.

Usually developers do informal manual testing all the time when developing: add a few lines of code, compile, and run it to see if it "works".

Consider that I have tested the dayOfWeek method and as all tests pass I am confident that the implementation is correct and reliable. Some time later, however, customers complain that the calendar program is too slow when scrolling from one week to another. Our analysis shows that it is caused by the slow algorithm used in the dayOfWeek method—it has to be redesigned to compute weekdays much faster. The question is how I validate that the improved, faster, algorithm is still functionally correct? The answer is of course to repeat all the tests that I made the last time. This process has also its own term:

Definition: **Regression testing**

Regression testing is the repeated execution of test suites to ensure they still pass and the system does not fail after a modification.

One of the reasons that test case tables or other formal documents that outline test cases are important is to serve in regression testing and of course also in the final quality assessment before releasing a software product.

There is a large body of knowledge concerning how to pick a good set of test cases for a given problem: few test cases that have a high probability of finding the defects. Chapter 34 provides an introduction to some of the basic techniques. Until then we will rely on intuition, common sense, and the experience we gain from actual testing.

2.3 Automated Testing

Instead of manual testing, I can utilize my computer to handle the tedious tasks of executing test cases and comparing computed and expected values. I can write a small test program (only the last test case from test case Table 2.1 is shown):

Listing: chapter/reliability/handcoded-test/TestDayOfWeek.java

```
/** A testing tool written from scratch.
*/
public class TestDayOfWeek {
  public static void main(String[] args) {
    // Test that December 25th 2010 is Saturday
    Date d = new Date(2010, 12, 25); // year, month, day of month
    Date.Weekday weekday = d.dayOfWeek();
    if ( weekday == Date.Weekday.SATURDAY ) {
      System.out.println("Test case: Dec 25th 2010: Pass");
    } else {
      System.out.println("Test case: Dec 25th 2010: FAIL");
    }
    // ... fill in more tests
  }
}
```

This simple program shows the anatomy of any program to execute test cases: the unit under test (here dayOfWeek) is invoked with the defined input values, the computed and expected output values are compared and some form of pass/fail reporting takes place. This is *automated testing*:

Definition: Automated testing

Automated testing is a process in which test suites are executed and verified automatically by computer programs.

☞ Download the source code from http://www.baerbak.com and try to run the test. Why does it pass? Please observe that the production code is strictly made to demonstrate testing!

Automated testing requires me to write code to verify the behavior of other pieces of code and this effort results in a lot of source code being produced: code that will be defining the users' product and code that will define test cases that test it. Often we need to distinguish these two bodies of code and I will call them:

Definition: Production code

The production code is the code that defines the behavior implementing the software's requirements.

In other words, production code is what the customer pays for. The code defining test cases, I will call:

Definition: Test code

The test code is the source code that defines test cases for the production code.

Both manual and automated tests have their benefits and liabilities. Manual tests are often quicker to develop (especially the informal ones) than automated tests because the latter require writing code. However, once automated tests have been made it is much easier to perform regression testing compared to manual tests. Second, manual tests are also extremely boring to execute leading to human errors in executing the manual test procedures—or simply not executing them at all. The sidebar 2.1 describes a war story of how it may go. In contrast automated tests can be executed fast and without the problems of incorrect execution.

Exercise 2.2: In some sense automated testing is absurd because I write code to test code—should I then also write code to test the code that tests the code and so on? Or put differently: if a test case fails how do I know that the defect is in the production code and not in the test code? Think about properties that the test code must have for automated testing to make sense.

2.4 JUnit: An Automated Test Tool

Writing the testing program by hand, as I did above, works fine for a very simple example, but consider a system with several hundred classes each with perhaps hundreds or thousands of test cases. In this case you need much better support for executing the large test suite, for reporting, and for pinpointing the test cases that fail. **Unit testing tools** are programs that take care of many of the house holding tasks and let you concentrate on expressing the test cases. In the Java world there are several tools but I will use JUnit 4 in this book. The fundamental concepts and techniques are the same in all the tools so changing from one to another is mostly a matter of syntax.

The test case for the dayOfWeek method can be written using JUnit like this:

Listing: chapter/reliability/junit-test/iteration-0/TestDayOfWeek.java

```
import org.junit.*;
import static org.junit.Assert.*;

/** Testing dayOfWeek using the JUnit 4.x framework.
*/
public class TestDayOfWeek {

  /**
   * Test that December 25th 2010 is Saturday
   */
  @Test
  public void shouldGiveSaturdayFor25Dec2010() {
    Date date = new Date( 2010, 12, 25);
    assertEquals( "Dec 25th 2010 is Saturday",
                  Date.Weekday.SATURDAY, date.dayOfWeek() );
  }
}
```

Sidebar 2.1: SAWOS RVR

I worked a few years in a small company that designed SAWOS systems: Semi-Automatic Weather Observation Systems. These are used in airports by meteorologists to generate reports of the local weather systems to be used by pilots and flight leaders.

One of the important factors when landing an aircraft is RVR: Runway Visual Range. It is the maximal distance at which the bright lamps in the runway can be seen. For instance, RVR = 25 m means you cannot see the lamps until you are only 25 meters away indicating a very heavy fog.

Usually each runway has instruments that measure RVR at both ends of it. Our SAWOS had a display showing the runway with each end colored according to its status ranging from green (no fog) to dark red (heavy fog).

We did not have automated tests and were a bit lazy about the manual ones, so at one time Aarhus airport reported a defect in their SAWOS: They saw a small patch of heavy fog drifting along the runway and when it passed the eastern end of the runway, the display marked the western end with a red color. I had implemented that part and had simply mixed up the assignment of instrument reading to the display and had missed this defect during my own manual testing.

I was on holiday when this defect was reported, but my colleagues fixed it "quick and dirty" as they did not quite understand my design, and sent a new version to Aarhus airport which cleared the problem.

When I returned home I was annoyed by their bug fix as it did not respect my design, so I remade it the "right" way. This change was then sent to the airport some weeks later as part of another software upgrade. Some months later, a technician phoned me and asked why RVR readings once again were showing at the wrong end of the display? I had once again forgotten to run the manual tests...

The first thing to note is the import statements. JUnit is a set of Java classes that you need to import in order to use it. The two imports in the source code listing are all I need for now.

Test cases are expressed as methods in JUnit which makes sense as methods contain code to be executed, just as test cases must be executed. To tell JUnit that a particular method defines a test case you have to mark it using the **@Test** annotation. JUnit will collect all methods with the @Test annotation and execute them, one by one. Thus a set of @Test methods in a class becomes a test suite.

A test case may pass or fail depending on equality between computed and expected value. JUnit provides a set of comparison methods that you must use, all named beginning with assert. In my example, I need to compare the computed weekday from dayOfWeek with the expected value Weekday.SATURDAY. The statement

```
Date date = new Date( 2010, 12, 25);
assertEquals( "Dec 25th 2010 is Saturday",
              Date.Weekday.SATURDAY, date.dayOfWeek() );
```

tells JUnit to compare the expected value (second parameter) with the computed value (third parameter). The first parameter is a string value that JUnit will display in case the test case fails in order for you to better understand the problem. For instance, if the above test fails, JUnit will print something similar to:

Sidebar 2.2: Asserts in JUnit

JUnit contains several assert methods that come in handy. Below I have shown them in their terse form; remember that you can always provide an extra, first, argument of type String that JUnit will print in case a test case fails.

assert	Pass if:
assertTrue(boolean b)	expression b is true
assertFalse(boolean b)	expression b is false
assertNull(Object o)	object o is null
assertNotNull(Object o)	object o is not null
assertEquals(double e, double c, double delta)	e and c are equal to within a positive delta
assertEquals(Object[] e, Object[]c)	object arrays are equal

If a method should throw an exception for a given set of input values, you provide the exception as argument to the @Test annotation. For instance, if method doDivide should throw ArithmeticException in case the second argument is 0:

```
@Test(expected = ArithmeticException.class)
  public void divideByZero() {
    int value = calculator.doDivide(4,0);
  }
}
```

```
java.lang.AssertionError: Dec 25th 2010 is Saturday
     expected:<SATURDAY> but was:<SUNDAY>
```

In all JUnit's assert methods, you may omit the string parameter and only state the comparison, like

```
Date date = new Date( 2010, 12, 25);
assertEquals( Date.Weekday.SATURDAY, date.dayOfWeek() );
```

in which case JUnit prints a less descriptive failure report:

```
java.lang.AssertionError: expected:<SATURDAY> but was:<SUNDAY>
```

The assertEquals method takes two parameters, the expected and the computed value. If the parameters are objects, they are compared using their equals method; if they are primitive types, they are compared using ==. There are other assert methods you can use in your test cases, sidebar 2.2 describes some of them. For a complete list, consult the JUnit documentation on the web.

JUnit does not care about the name of the test case method but test cases are meant to be read by developers and testers so I consider naming important. I like to name my test cases starting with should... as test cases should verify that the unit under test does its job properly. So—dayOfWeek *should* give Saturday for December 25th in 2010.

Now—I have a JUnit test case and the next issue is to execute it to see if it passes or fails. JUnit 4 is a bare-bones tool that is primarily meant to be integrated into development environments like BlueJ (2009) or Eclipse (2009) but it does provide textual

Sidebar 2.3: JUnit Setup

You can download the JUnit framework from the JUnit Web site: `www.junit.org`. I have used JUnit version 4.4 in this book. To compile the JUnit test cases the compiler must know where the JUnit class files are located. You do this by including the provided jar, named `junit-4.4.jar`, on the classpath. This will look like this on Windows:

```
javac -classpath .;junit-4.4.jar *.java
```

Similar, you will need to tell the Java virtual machine to use this jar file when executing:

```
java -classpath .;junit-4.4.jar
  org.junit.runner.JUnitCore TestDayOfWeek
```

You will have to type the above on a single line in the command prompt/shell. If you run on a Linux operating system the ";" must be replaced by ":".

The source code for this chapter as well as compilation scripts for Windows and Linux are provided at the book's web site (http://www.baerbak.com). You need to download the zip archive, unzip it and then you will be able to find the source code in the folders listed above each source code listing. The JUnit jar is provided along with the example code so you do not need to download JUnit unless you want to browse the documentation and guides. The compile script is named "compile.bat" (Windows) or "compile.sh" (Linux bash). The run script is named "run-test.bat" or "run-test.sh".

output. You can find information on running JUnit from a command prompt/shell in sidebar 2.3.

The output of executing the test suite simply looks like this:

```
>java -classpath .;junit-4.4.jar
   org.junit.runner.JUnitCore TestDayOfWeek
JUnit version 4.4
.
Time: 0,031

OK (1 test)
```

JUnit is terse when all test cases pass: it prints a dot for every test case executed and finally outputs OK and some statistics.

OK—I will add another test case from my original test case table. I add a second test method for 25th December 2008 to the TestDayOfWeek class:

Fragment: chapter/reliability/junit-test/iteration-1/TestDayOfWeek

```
@Test
public void shouldGiveThursdayFor25Dec2008() {
  Date date = new Date( 2008, 12, 25);
  assertEquals( "Dec 25th 2008 is Thursday",
                Date.Weekday.THURSDAY, date.dayOfWeek() );
}
```

As my implementation of dayOfWeek is defective and the above test case does not pass, JUnit describes the failure and pinpoints which test case that fails. JUnit is very verbose indeed and I have removed much of the output.

```
>java -classpath .;junit-4.4.jar
   org.junit.runner.JUnitCore TestDayOfWeek
JUnit version 4.4
..E
Time: 0,047
There was 1 failure:
1) shouldGiveThursdayFor25Dec2008(TestDayOfWeek)
java.lang.AssertionError: Dec 25th 2008 is Thursday
    expected:<THURSDAY> but was:<SATURDAY>
      at org.junit.Assert.fail(Assert.java:74)
      at org.junit.Assert.failNotEquals(Assert.java:448)
      at org.junit.Assert.assertEquals(Assert.java:102)
      at org.junit.Assert.assertEquals(Assert.java:323)
      at TestDayOfWeek.shouldGiveThursdayFor25Dec2008(TestDayOfWeek
                                                    .java:27)
      at sun.reflect.NativeMethodAccessorImpl.invoke0(Native Method)
      at sun.reflect.NativeMethodAccessorImpl.invoke(Unknown Source)
 [33 more lines removed here]

FAILURES!!!
Tests run: 2,  Failures: 1
```

Let us dissect the output one piece at a time. The first part is an overview of the test suite

```
JUnit version 4.4
..E
Time: 0,047
There was 1 failure:
```

The time taken to execute the test suite is shown as well as a '.' for every test case run. If a test case fails 'E' is also printed.

Next comes a numbered list of diagnostics information for every failed test case. The first part of the diagnostics name the failed test method, shouldGiveThursday-For25Dec2008, and the test case class, TestDayOfWeek, followed by information about the failed assert:

```
1) shouldGiveThursdayFor25Dec2008(TestDayOfWeek)
java.lang.AssertionError: Dec 25th 2008 is Thursday
    expected:<THURSDAY> but was:<SATURDAY>
```

Here you see the string value that I used as first parameter to the assertEquals followed by expected and computed value. The second part of the diagnostics information is a complete (and unfortunately very long) stack trace. Most of this stack trace is irrelevant, the piece of information you should look for is the method call that is within the test class itself:

```
at TestDayOfWeek.shouldGiveThursdayFor25Dec2008(TestDayOfWeek.java:27)
```

This line is interesting because it contains the line number of the failing assert allowing me to quickly identify the exact spot in the testing code that demonstrates a failure in the production code.

Early versions of JUnit had graphical user interfaces that indicated passing or failing of test suites using a **green bar** (= pass) or **red bar** (= fail). In the Extreme Programming community you will often hear references to the red/green bar terms. JUnit is integrated in several development environments where the graphical bar has been preserved. For instance the above test suite can be run in the Eclipse development environment in which it will show the red bar as well as the same information as I have explained above, see Figure 2.1. Eclipse and other development environments that integrate JUnit have the advantage that double-clicking the stack trace line will open the editor directly on the line with the failed assert statement.

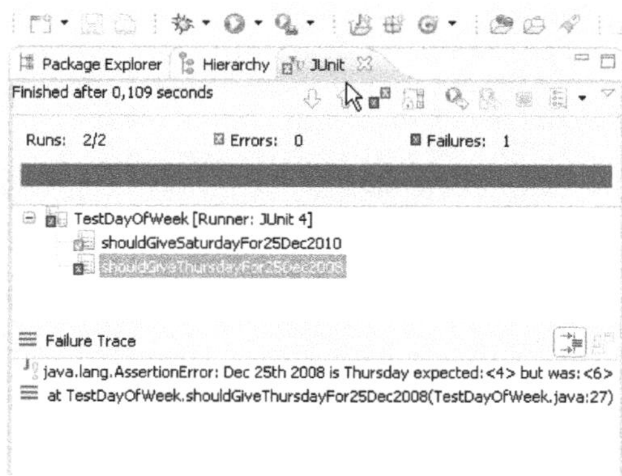

Figure 2.1: The TestDayOfWeek test suite executed by Eclipse.

JUnit has additional features that helps me in organizing large test suites as well as isolating tests so changes to tested objects made in one test case do not influence other test cases. I will introduce these as I need them in the chapters about test-driven development.

2.5 Summary of Key Concepts

Reliability is a very important quality of software and is defined as a *software product's capability to maintain a specified level of performance*. In our setting, "performance" means "do the work it is supposed to do without failing." There are many techniques that increase the reliability of a system, in this book special emphasis is put on *testing*. Testing is *executing software in order to find failures* i.e. situations where the software does not behave as expected. Failures in software are caused by bugs or *defects*, that is, source code that is incorrectly implemented.

A *test suite* is a set of *test cases* that each specify input values and expected output values for a given *unit under test*. If the computed output for the given input does not match the expected output, the test case *fails*, otherwise it *passes*.

When you let software handle the execution of test cases we speak of *automated testing*. JUnit is a Java tool to help you manage, execute, and overview suites of test cases. A test case is defined by a *@Test annotated method* in a Java class. In the test case method you use *assert* methods to compare expected and computed values. JUnit reports diagnostics information when a test case fails, including test case method name and line number for the failed assert method.

The definition of reliability is reproduced from the ISO 9126 standard (ISO/IEC International Standard 2001), other aspects of quality defined by ISO are discussed in the next chapter. *Software Engineering* by Sommerville (2006) provides a comprehensive overview of techniques to achieve reliability including several not covered in this book. There are plenty of books on software testing, personally I can recommend *Practical Software Testing* by Burnstein (2003). A comprehensive and highly practical oriented book is *Testing Computer Software* by Kaner et al. (1993).

2.6 Selected Solutions

Discussion of Exercise 2.1:

Consider a word processor that features "spell checking". Next consider that the implementation of the spell-checking unit contains a defect making spell-checking fail from time to time. Now one user that never uses the spell-checking feature will experience a highly reliable word processor whereas another user that often needs spell checking will find the same system unreliable.

Discussion of Exercise 2.2:

The key property that test code must have is *simplicity!* If the testing code is not simple, then the defects are in the testing code, not in the production code. I generally recommend that you use only very simple programming constructs in testing code: assignments, asserts, and perhaps calling private methods that again only contain simple code. Avoid loops and conditions in your test code if possible and certainly do not use advanced programming like recursion etc. Test case code should be short and easy to read.

2.7 Review Questions

How is reliability defined? What techniques can you use to improve the reliability of software?

How is the following concepts defined: testing, failure, defect, test case, test suite, manual and automatic testing? How are they related? Describe and name the two bodies of source code that is produced when you use automatic testing.

What is JUnit? How do you in JUnit define test cases? Mention some of the asserts that are supplied in JUnit.

2.8 Further Exercises

Exercise 2.3:

A (somewhat strict) format specification for an email address syntax may look like this using BNF notation:

```
<email>      ::= <identifier> @ <identifier> {. <identifier>}
<identifier> ::= letter { letter | digit }
```

The above specification will accept strings like "t12@abc.def.gh" and "john@cs.edu" but not strings like "123@cs.edu" (identifier starting with digit), "john.cs.edu" (no @ character), nor "john@cs-edu" (identifier having other characters than letters and digits).

Consider, as unit under test, a function, isValid, that takes a string as input and computes a boolean value, true if the string obeys the above specification, and false otherwise.

1. Write a test case table with some input values (strings) and expected output of this unit.

Exercise 2.4. Source code directory:
`exercise/reliability/email-address`

The source code directory contains a (highly defective) Java implementation of the email verification method of exercise 2.3 and a template JUnit test case class.

1. Translate the test cases from the previous exercise into JUnit.
2. Write an implementation that passes all tests.

Exercise 2.5:

Consider a function, l, to calculate the number of hours and minutes in a time interval in 24-hour format $(t^{hour}_{start}, t^{min}_{start}, t^{hour}_{end}, t^{min}_{end})$. That is, $l(08, 00, 13, 35)$ should return $(5, 35)$.

1. Generate a test table with test cases.
2. Translate your test cases to JUnit
3. Implement the function l.

Exercise 2.6:

Consider a new method, daysTo, in the Date class, that can calculate the number of days between two dates, for instance:

```
Date d1 = new Date(2009,12,25);
Date d2 = new Date(2010,12,25);
int daysBetween = d1.daysTo(d2);
```

1. Generate a test table with test cases.
2. Translate your test cases to JUnit
3. Implement the daysTo method.

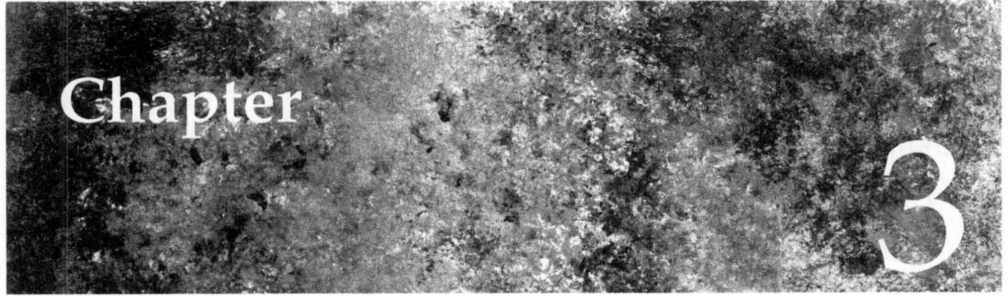

Flexibility and Maintainability

Learning Objectives

One of the main ambitions of this book, as evident from the word *flexible* in the title, is to demonstrate techniques to design and develop software that can easily accommodate change. "Change is the only constant", originally formulated by Greek philosopher Heraclitus, is a quote that has been adopted by the agile community as a truth about software development. Once customers and users begin using a software system they get new ideas for improving it. And the software that handles today's requirements will need to be adopted and changed to handle those of tomorrow. Thus, software must be designed and developed to make it "easy to change."

It turns out that there are many properties that contribute to make software either easy or difficult to change. The learning objective of this chapter is to establish a solid terminology of the different qualities or characteristics that influence ease of change, allowing us to discuss techniques, like design patterns and frameworks, at a more precise level. Specifically, I will introduce the ISO 9126 standard definition of maintainability and the sub qualities it is composed of.

3.1 Maintainability

Let me start by a small code fragment. The code below is correct, it compiles, and it defines a well-known, everyday concept. The main method demonstrates its operations.

Listing: chapter/maintainability/example1/X.java

```
public class X {
  private int y;
  public X() {
    y = 0;
  }
  public int z() {
```

```
    return y;
  }
  public void z1(int z0) {
    y += z0;
  }
  public static void main(String[] args) {
    X y = new X();
    y.z1(200);
    y.z1(3400);
    System.out.println( "Result is "+ y.z() );
  }
}
```

☞ What abstraction does the class represent? What behavior does each method represent?

Can you guess what abstraction it is[1]? The key point here is that the way you name abstractions in source code has profound influence on how easy it is to understand. And code that is hard to understand is next to impossible to change, enhance, and correct.

Next consider the same class X but subject to a novel indentation style.

Listing: chapter/maintainability/example2/X.java

```
public class X{private int y;public X(){y = 0;}public int z(){
return y;}public void z1(int z0){y += z0;}public static void main(
String[] args){X y=new X();y.z1(200);y.z1(3400);System.out.println
("Result is "+ y.z());}}
```

From the point of view of the compiler, this latter version is identical to the first—it is just some white space that has been removed. For a developer, however, it has become incomprehensible. Understanding software requires understanding structure, and proper indentation is a key technique.

Both versions of class X have some qualities and lack other qualities. For instance, the last version of X only require 231 bytes of my hard disk space while the first version takes 314 bytes. This is a substantial difference of 35%. Thus the second version is the "best" when it comes to buying storage. The question is whether this "storage" quality is important or not.

When we discuss software quality we have to be as objective as possible rather than fall into arguments about what is "good" or "bad." The last chapter introduced the ISO-9126 definition for reliability, and I will again take my starting point in this internationally accepted quality model that allows software engineers to more precisely define aspects of quality in their software products.

Definition: **Maintainability (ISO 9126)**

The capability of the software product to be modified. Modifications may include corrections, improvements or adaptation of the software to changes in environment, and in requirements and functional specifications.

[1] You can find an identical class but with proper naming on the website in the same folder as class X.

Basically, maintainability is a *cost measure*. Any software system can be modified (in the extreme case by throwing all the code away and write new software from scratch) but the question is at what cost? Thus the interpretation is that *maintainable software* is software where the *cost of modifying it in order to add/remove/enhance features is low*. Consider the X class above that is difficult to change—it is less maintainable.

Maintainability cannot by nature be a global quality of a given software system in the sense that all parts of the software system can easily be modified for all types of changed requirements. You always have to state in what respect it is maintainable. For instance, an accounting system's source code may have been designed and implemented in anticipation that at some later date it may have to handle different currencies and taxation systems (thus easily modified for use in a new country) but have a fixed graphical user interface (thus difficult to modify for a new operating system).

Exercise 3.1: Give examples of some software systems where maintainability is very important. Give examples where maintainability is not an issue.

3.2 Sub Qualities of Maintainability

A highly maintainable software unit must possess quite a few different qualities and the ISO standard acknowledge this by stating that maintainability is composed of several, finer grained, qualities, as illustrated in Figure 3.1.

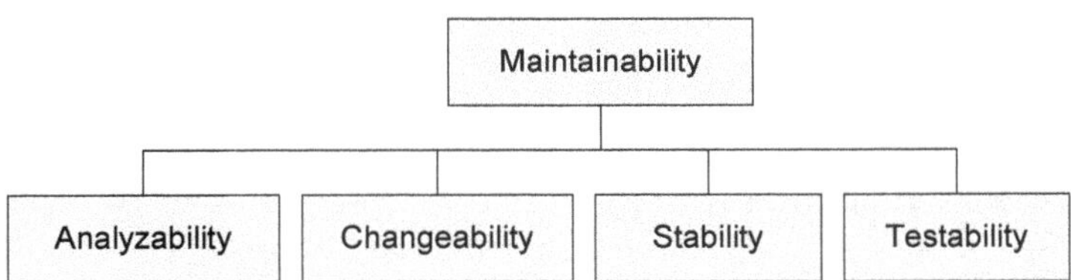

Figure 3.1: Maintainability and its sub qualities.

3.2.1 Analyzability

Definition: Analyzability (ISO 9126)

The capability of the software product to be diagnosed for deficiencies or causes of failures in the software, or for the parts to be modified to be identified.

Analyzability is basically the ability to *understand* software. If I cannot analyze a piece of software, how am I supposed to modify it? Correct it? The problems with class X in the previous section are basically analyzability problems: the methods names z() and z1() do not hint at what behavior they encapsulate and the class name has the same problem. In the second version I cannot even overview the method structure and the code is simply not analyzable.

The ability to read and understand the source code and the structure of our software designs is central to analyzability and I will touch upon it in many places. It will in particular be discussed in Chapter 7, *Deriving Strategy Pattern*, and Chapter 18, *Design Patterns – Part II*.

☞ If you would like to see some real nightmares in analyzability, search the web for *The International Obfuscated C Code Contest*. Here people compete for fun to produce the most unreadable but correct programs in C.

3.2.2 Changeability

Definition: Changeability (ISO 9126)

The capability of the software product to enable a specified modification to be implemented.

Changeability expresses the quality that I can add, modify, or enhance a feature in my system at a reasonable cost. Let me again illustrate this by a simple example. Consider a program to generate and display a rectangular maze. The developers have decided for a 80 column times 25 row maze and have used these constants throughout their program.

Listing: chapter/maintainability/example3/Maze.java

```
public class Maze {
  private boolean[] isWall = new boolean[2000];
  public void print() {
    for (int c = 0; c < 80; c++) {
      for (int r = 0; r < 25; r++) {
        char toPrint = (isWall[r*80+c] ? '#' : ' ');
        System.out.print(toPrint);
      }
      System.out.println();
    }
  }
  public void generate() {
    // generate the maze
  }
}
```

Now consider that the users wants 160 $\times$ 80 mazes instead? Then all occurrences of the constant 80 has to be analyzed in order to evaluate whether it relates to a maze dimension or not (remember, there can be other uses of the constant 80 that are unrelated to the maze size!) and next change those that are related. Also some occurrences are masked and thus difficult to spot, like the constant 2000 in the declaration above that is really 80 $\times$ 25. Of course, in a small example as above it is possible to do, but consider having a 3D graphics engine based on the maze with thousands of lines of code where the constants 80, 25, and 2000 appear in many places. *The changeability of such code is low* as it does not enable a size modification to be implemented reliably.

It is a well-known golden rule in programming never to use *magic numbers* but use named constants. Named constants makes it much easier to change the software to new requirements, like

```
private static final int MAZE_WIDTH = 80;
private static final int MAZE_HEIGHT = 80;
private boolean[] isWall =
  new boolean[MAZE_WIDTH * MAZE_HEIGHT];
```

Changeability basically comes in two flavors. Those aspects of the software that can be changed at compile-time, by modifying the source code, recompile it, and release it; and those aspects that can be changed at run-time, by changing parameters while it is executing. The maze size problem is of course a compile-time change while an example of run-time changeability is your favorite web browser whose "options" dialog contains numerous ways to change its behavior.

Changeability is a central quality in successful software and in particular for software that can be reused. Almost all design patterns are geared towards increasing designs' changeability and I will in particular focus on the quality in Chapter 32, *Framework Theory*.

3.2.3 Stability

> Definition: **Stability (ISO 9126)**
>
> The capability of the software product to avoid unexpected effects from modifications of the system.

As I will emphasize many times, any change to existing software carries a risk of introducing defects: software that has run flawless for years may suddenly stop working properly because some apparently minor change has been made. Software units are often interconnected in subtle ways and changing one unit may lead to failures in other units. As an example, read the war story in sidebar 3.1. Of course we want to minimize this as much as possible, that is, keep the software stability high.

Stability is also a recurring theme in this book and I will advocate the practice to avoid modifying existing code but preferably add features or modify existing ones by other means. Chapters 7, *Deriving Strategy Pattern*, 8, *Refactoring and Integration Testing*, and 16, *Compositional Design Principles*, are in particular focused on stability.

3.2.4 Testability

> Definition: **Testability (ISO 9126)**
>
> The capability of the software product to enable a modified system to be validated.

You may wonder how you can build software you cannot test but it is actually quite easy as the following small example shows. Consider that you are required to build a software system to control chemical processes in a chemical plant. One requirement is that if the temperature measured in a process exceeds 100 degrees Celsius then an alarm must be sounded and some action taken. Consider the following code fragment for this requirement:

Sidebar 3.1: Person Identification in ABC

I once participated in a research project, *Activity Based Computing* (Bardram and Christensen 2007), in which we developed a novel computing platform to support clinicians' complex ways of working in a hospital. In the first design of the platform, we equipped clinicians with RFID tags (small electronic tags that can be sensed by a RFID reader when about half a meter away) that were automatically scanned when they were near a computer thus allowing the computer to quickly log them in and bring up their personal list of ongoing activities. In our design, we had a database where persons were identified by the unique RFID identity string of the tag that they wore. Thus when a tag was scanned it was very easy to look up the person it belonged to.

Later we worked on other aspects of the system and one of our student programmers found that the identity strings used in the database were really weird, so he replaced them with a 10 digit unique person identity number. As the part of the systems he was developing was unrelated to the RFID functionality, and he never used nor tested this part of the system, he never noticed that this seemingly trivial change had serious consequences.

However, we did—during a demonstration for the clinicians! Suddenly none of the fancy functionality to automatically detect and login the physicians and nurses worked. It was not the best time to exclaim: "What? It worked the last time I tried it???" The system design had little stability concerning person identification...

Fragment: chapter/maintainability/example4/Monitor.java

```
public class Monitor {
  private AeroDynTemperatureSensor sensor =
    new AeroDynTemperatureSensor();
  public void controlProcess() {
    while(true) {
      if ( sensor.measure() > 1000.0 ) {
        soundAlarm();
        shutDownProcess();
      }
      // wait 10 seconds
    }
  }
  // rest omitted
```

and consider that class AeroDynTemperatureSensor is the correct implementation that communicate with a temperature sensor from company AeroDyn. The question is how you would test the controlProcess method? If you review the code you will notice that it has a serious defect but how can you demonstrate the failure it will produce at run-time? As the code above is hard wired to the actual sensor, there is no other way than go heating the sensor until it is above 100 degrees Celsius and then notice that the alarm has not been sounded. This is cumbersome and not something you would like to do as part of everyday development. The source code is not very testable.

A major theme of this book is how to make reliable software so techniques to test software and make software testable are central and I will in particular look into it in Chapter 5, *Test-Driven Development*, and Chapter 12, *Test Stubs*.

3.3 Flexibility

A main theme of this book is *flexible software* so I will start by defining what I mean by this term, give a small example, and next consider how it relates to the ISO characteristics.

> **Definition: Flexibility**
>
> The capability of the software product to support added/enhanced functionality purely by adding software units and specifically not by modifying existing software units.

What does this mean? Well, much of this book is about what this really means in a deep way, but to convey a first idea of it, consider your computer system. If for instance you experience that the graphics performance of it is not adequate for the next generation of computer games, then you may buy a better graphics card, open your computer, take out the old graphics card and replace it with the new. You do not do it by cutting wires and start soldering new circuits onto your motherboard. The same goes if you want to add functionality for your computer like being able to digitize and store video: you buy a digital video card and plug it into your machine. Thus, you enhance functionality by adding/replacing units and not by modifying the existing ones. By flexible software, I define software with the same merits—software systems are flexible if they allow adding and/or replacing units of functionality without rewriting and recompiling the existing code.

As a software example, consider that I have developed a point of sales system for customers in the states of California and Nevada. As these two states have different sales taxes, I have programmed a method calculateSalesTax to calculate the tax (2009 values, source: Wikipedia. Local taxes are not considered) to add to the base price of the item, as shown in this code fragment:

Listing: chapter/maintainability/example5/PointOfSale.java

```
public class PointOfSale {
  private State state;
  public double calculateSalesTax(double price) {
    switch (state) {
    case CALIFORNIA: return price * 8.25 / 100.0;
    case NEVADA: return price * 8.10 / 100.0;
    default:
      throw new RuntimeException("Unknown state");
    }
  }
  public enum State {
    CALIFORNIA, NEVADA }
  // rest of functionality omitted
}
```

Next consider that we want to sell the point of sales system in a third state. While the above design for handling sales tax is analyzable, testable, and changeable, it is not flexible. The only way I can add a correct sales tax calculation for a new state is by modifying the existing code, recompile and test it, and finally deploy an updated system to the customer. If the sales tax percentage had been read from a configuration file at system start up instead, then the system had been flexible with respect to this requirement as I could have shipped the existing system to the new customer and just provided a new configuration file with the proper sales tax percentage for the state in question. If a state changes its sales tax then this is also much easier for the point of sales administrators as they just can change the configuration file locally instead of waiting for a new release of the system.

If you require that software can adapt to changing requirements without modifying the production code then you need to employ a special set of design and programming techniques as well as adopt a special mindset. The techniques covered in this book like compositional design, design patterns, and frameworks, are all techniques that focus on the flexibility quality, and treated in particular in Chapters 7, *Deriving Strategy Pattern*, 16, *Compositional Design Principles*, and 32, *Framework Theory*.

Returning to the ISO standard, flexibility can be said to be yet another sub quality of maintainability, and most closely related to changeability. However, changeability does not take a stand point with regards to the way "a specified modification" is implemented—it may be by adding or replacing a new software unit or it may be by modifying an existing one. In contrast *flexibility* does take this stand point and require that no modifications are made.

3.4 Summary of Key Concepts

Maintainability is an important quality aspect of most software products and is defined as the *ability to be modified.* Maintainability is basically a quality that deals with the cost of introducing change: maintainable software means software that is cheap to change, that takes less hours to modify.

Maintainability has sub qualities like *analyzability* (ability to understand), *changeability* (ability to implement specified modification), *stability* (ability to avoid unexpected effects from modifications), and finally *testability* (ability to validate modifications.)

How to write maintainable software is a key focus point in this book. A special case of changeability is a quality that I denote *flexibility*, namely the ability to support modifications purely by adding or replacing software units, in contrast to modifying software units.

Maintainability is just one of the qualities defined in the ISO model. The full model is defined in the ISO/IEC International Standard (2001).

3.5 Selected Solutions

Discussion of Exercise 3.1:

As maintainability is basically a "cost of change" metric, then maintainability is of little relevance for systems that are not required or expected to be changed. Sometimes I write a small program to change some data I have from one format to another. Once the data is converted, then the program is irrelevant, and maintainability is therefore of little importance. Large software systems that live on the market for a long time and where the development is made by many software developers have high requirements to maintainability.

3.6 Review Questions

How is *maintainability* defined? *Analyzability*? *Changeability*? *Stability*? *Testability*? Mention some software systems that do have or do not have these qualities. Argue why they have (or do not have) these qualities. Define *flexibility* and argue for the difference between this quality characteristics and the changeability quality.

3.7 Further Exercises

Exercise 3.2:

Review programs of some complexity that you have written earlier in your career.

1. Analyze each program and argue for the absence or presence of the following capabilities: Analyzability? Changeability? Stability? Testability? Flexibility?
2. Evaluate its maintainability based upon the assessment above.
3. List some program changes that would enhance maintainability. Argue why.

Exercise 3.3. Source code directory:
`exercise/maintainability/iceblox`

Iceblox is a small game in the tradition of early 1980 platform games like Pacman. It is a Java applet meaning it can run in a web browser.

1. Analyze Iceblox and argue for the absence or presence of the following capabilities: Analyzability? Changeability? Stability? Testability? Flexibility?
2. Evaluate its maintainability based upon the assessment above.
3. List some program changes that would enhance maintainability. Argue why.

Iteration 2

The Programming Process

This learning iteration, *The Programming Process,* focuses on two aspects: reliability and the programming process. The key point is that these are fruitfully intertwined in the particular process chosen, namely *test-driven development* that both has a strong focus on ensuring that your program is functionally correct as well as provides a set of concrete techniques that efficiently guide your programming effort. Test-driven development applies to writing programs but defects can also sneak into your system in the compilation and execution phases, especially as our systems grow in size. Here *build management* is a well-known technique to improve reliability and overview in these phases.

To set a realistic stage for these two topics, I will present a concrete case study, a parking pay station, that comes with functional requirements and an initial design. I will then show how the techniques are applied in practice to produce an implementation. The pay station is continuously evolved in the following learning iterations of the book.

Chapter	Learning Objective
Chapter 4	*Pay Station Case.* This chapter presents the case study, the pay station. I will present the initial requirements (they will gradually change in subsequent iterations) and a first and simple object-oriented design.
Chapter 5	*Test-Driven Development.* The learning objective of this chapter is understanding the process of developing software using the test-driven paradigm. This entails learning the rhythm and principles. I will demonstrate them in detail as I develop a reliable implementation of the pay station.
Chapter 6	*Build Management.* The objective is to learn both the underlying theory of build management as well as practical usage for the pay station system.

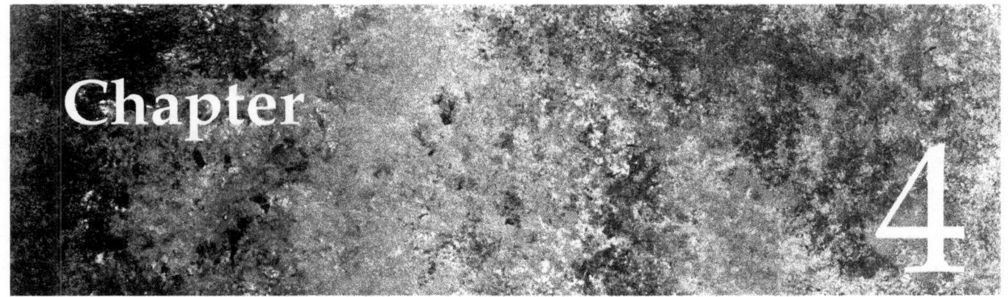

Pay Station Case

Learning Objectives

Very few successful software companies earn their money on producing software for many different types of products. Most companies specialize in a particular domain. In this chapter I will present the domain that becomes a case study for a major part of the book: a pay station system for billing cars on a parking lot. I consider myself as part of a small software development team that has just been contacted by the municipality of Alphatown. Alphatown has asked our team to develop the software for the city's new parking pay stations. The objective of this chapter is stating the basic requirements put forth by Alphatown and an initial design in terms of UML class and sequence diagrams as well as Java interfaces. This design, and the reasons for making it this way, is not argued in detail here but will become apparent later in the book.

The pay station is used in this learning iteration to demonstrate test-driven development and build management. During the following learning iterations it will experience additional and changing requirements which allow us to explore techniques to increase the software's flexibility. In this respect, it is very similar to successful software development where software systems are maintained and enhanced over long periods of time.

4.1 Pay Station Stories

Our small software development company has been asked by the municipality of Alphatown to develop the software to the new pay stations that are going to replace the existing parking meters in the town. The hardware is made by another company thus I concentrate on the software alone. A picture of a real pay station from my hometown Aarhus in Denmark is shown in Figure 4.1. Later, I will develop a graphical user interface for the pay station, see Figure 4.2, where you can push buttons to insert coins, and see the number of minutes parking time in the display.

Figure 4.1: A parking pay station from Aarhus / Denmark.

As is often the case when existing technology is replaced by electronics the requirements are basically to provide the same basic behavior as the old mechanical parking meters. Extreme Programming uses *stories* (see Section 1.3.2) to describe how a software system must behave, so together with the customers I come up with a few stories.

Story 1: Buy a parking ticket. A car driver walks to the pay station to buy parking time. He enters several valid coins (5, 10, and 25 cents) as payment. For each payment of 5 cents he receives 2 minutes parking time. On the pay station's display he can see how much parking time he has bought so far. Once he is satisfied with the amount of time, he presses the button marked "Buy". He receives a printed receipt, stating the number of minutes parking time he has bought. The display is cleared to prepare for another transaction.

Story 2: Cancel a transaction. A driver has entered several coins but realize that the accumulated parking time shown in the display exceeds what she needs. She presses the button marked "Cancel" and her coins are returned. The display is cleared to prepare for another transaction.

Story 3: Reject illegal coin. A driver has entered 50 cents total and the display reads "20". By mistake, he enters a 1-euro coin which is not a recognized coin. The pay station rejects the coin and the display is not updated.

I could come up with more stories, such as administrators that empty the pay station for the cash entered, etc., but the stories above suffice for our learning purposes.

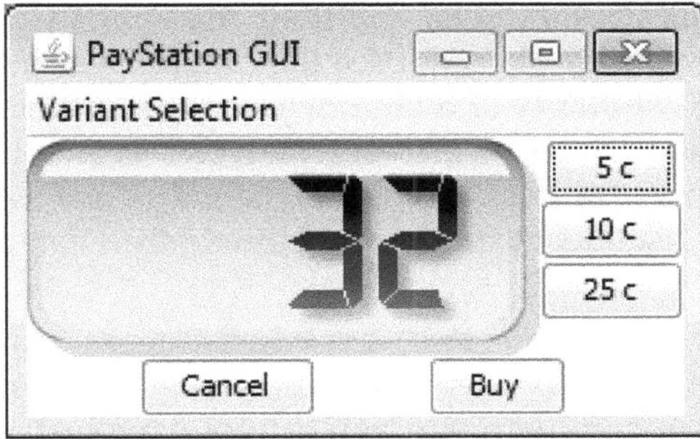

Figure 4.2: A graphical user interface for the pay station.

4.2 Initial Design

The pay station is an example of requiring hardware and software to communicate: for instance the hardware must inform the software every time a new coin has been entered and the software must request the hardware to print a receipt, etc. This interface between the two can get quite complex but is of little relevance to the focus of our discussion: developing reliable and flexible software. Therefore I will take some liberties in order to simplify the design as well as allow for some programming concerns to be addressed.

My initial class design is outlined in the UML class diagram in Figure 4.3. You will find some general observations about how I draw class diagrams in sidebar 4.1. The

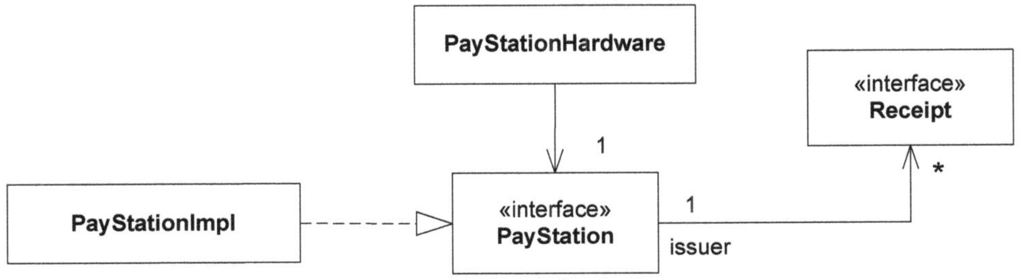

Figure 4.3: Pay station class diagram.

PayStationHardware class encapsulates all hardware related behavior : physical display, coin entry mechanics, etc. The interface PayStation defines the methods that any implementation of the pay station business logic must possess. As is evident from the navigability of the association between the PayStationHardware and the PayStation it is always the hardware that invokes methods on the pay station and not the other way around. The PayStation may produce a number of receipts—as expressed by the Receipt interface. A plausible interaction between the hardware and an implementation of the pay station that mirrors the buy story is outlined in the UML sequence diagram in Figure 4.4 on page 48.

Sidebar 4.1: UML Diagrams in the Book

In my opinion the main advantage of UML class diagrams is the overview they provide: I see the interfaces, classes, and their relations that hint at the collaboration patterns when executing. I do not see the diagrams as a substitute for reading source code, thus I favor clarity and simplicity over completeness. You will therefore seldom see method names or instance variables shown in this book. Methods are the behavioral units of objects, the place where the "action" happens, and this is better shown by UML sequence diagrams. Ultimately, I can and will look into the code.

An issue that my students often raise, is my insisting on drawing associations between interfaces. In Figure 4.3 PayStation and Receipt are associated though both are interfaces. Students complain that you cannot have instance variables in interfaces to implement the association and the diagram is therefore wrong. However, the purpose of diagrams is to *express the intention of the software architect*, not to be a literate copy of the source code. Thus, when I draw an association between PayStation and Receipt I do so to express the intention that *in all possible designs there will always be an association between these two abstractions.* Thus, you would find an implementation of the association in *all* classes implementing these interfaces.

At the code level, I have decided to define two interfaces, PayStation and Receipt, for the central abstractions of the pay station. These must then be implemented by concrete classes, like for instance the PayStationImpl that is already shown in the class diagram. I will later return in great detail to why I have decided to make this distinction, notably in Chapter 16 and 19.

The PayStation interface looks like this:

Listing: chapter/tdd/iteration-1/PayStation.java

```
/** The business logic of a Parking Pay Station.
*/
public interface PayStation {

  /**
   * Insert coin into the pay station and adjust state accordingly.
   * @param coinValue is an integer value representing the coin in
   * cent. That is, a quarter is coinValue=25, etc.
   * @throws IllegalCoinException in case coinValue is not
   * a valid coin value
   */
  public void addPayment( int coinValue )
          throws IllegalCoinException;

  /**
   * Read the machine's display. The display shows a numerical
   * description of the amount of parking time accumulated so far
   * based on inserted payment.
   * @return the number to display on the pay station display
   */
  public int readDisplay();

  /**
   * Buy parking time. Terminate the ongoing transaction and
   * return a parking receipt. A non-null object is always returned.
```

```
   * @return a valid parking receipt object.
   */
  public Receipt buy();

  /**
   * Cancel the present transaction. Resets the machine for a new
   * transaction.
   */
  public void cancel();
}
```

The buy method will return a Receipt which is very simple:

Listing: chapter/tdd/iteration-1/Receipt.java

```
/** The receipt returned from a pay station.
*/
public interface Receipt {

  /**
   * Return the number of minutes this receipt is valid for.
   * @return number of minutes parking time
   */
  public int value();
}
```

Finally, a few notes on some of the minor design decisions:

- Coins are represented by integer values. Other design choices would be to use Java enumeration types or implement a Coin class. I have chosen integers as the code size is smaller and adding a Coin enumeration/class does not add much seen from a learning perspective.
- Validation of coin type is done in the pay station. This would more likely be done in the hardware but by throwing a special exception, IllegalCoinException, I can discuss the special aspects of testing these.
- Integer return type on readDisplay. A more plausible design is to return a string to display that could provide more information to the user but again I have adopted the simpler design in order to make the code as small as possible.
- Cancel does not return the coins. The cancel method only resets the pay station, it does not provide any way of returning coins. Again this is just a simplification of the example to minimize the amount of code to develop.

Now only one problem remains: implementing the classes that form the pay station system. This is the problem I will address in the next chapter.

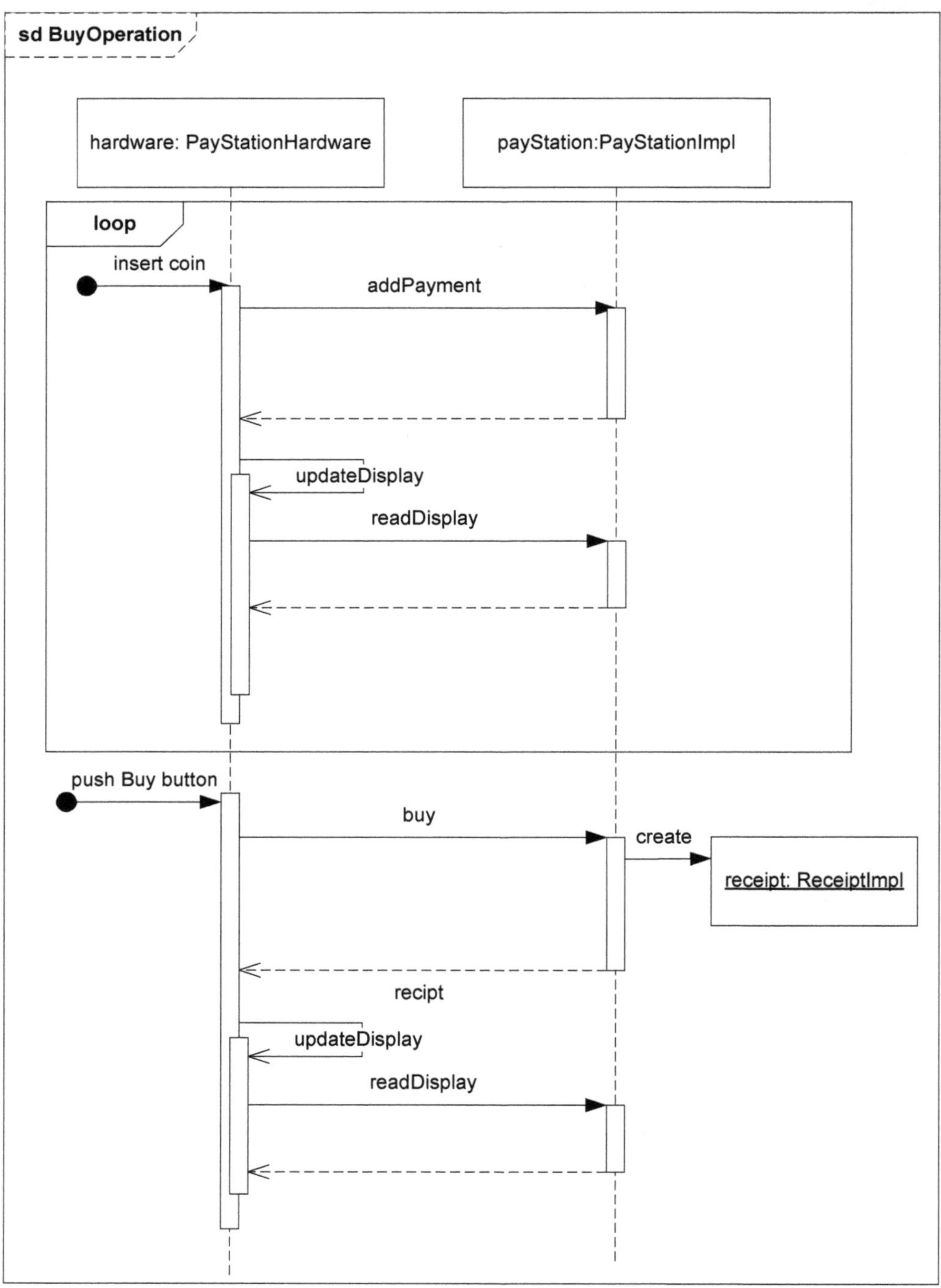

Figure 4.4: Sequence diagram outlining a buy scenario.

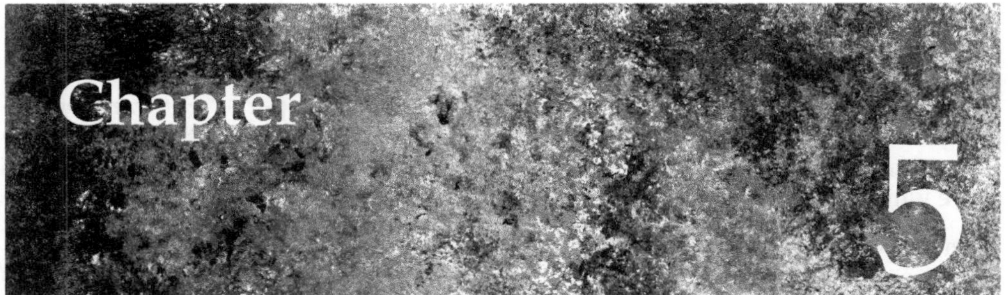

Test-Driven Development

Learning Objectives

Extreme Programming is an agile process for developing software fast. In this chapter the learning objective is to demonstrate a central XP technique, namely *test-driven development*. Test-driven development has a strong focus on crafting reliable and maintainable code: *Clean code that works*. Test cases demonstrate that it *works* while you also constantly restructure your code to make it *clean*.

In this chapter

- You will become familiar with the *rhythm* of test-driven development that drives each iteration, iterations that each have a specific goal namely to add a single feature to the production code.
- You will learn a set of *principles* that form a list of potential actions you can take in each step in the rhythm.
- You will learn the definition of *refactoring* and see some simple example of refactoring the production and testing code.
- You will learn about the liabilities and benefits of a test-driven development process.

I will demonstrate these techniques in practice as I need them to implement the pay station system. Test-driven development is not a question of being able to recite a long list of principles and definitions that you have learned by heart, it is a question of being able to apply them in practice in your program development. Therefore this chapter devotes quite a lot of space to the *devils in the details* at the code level.

5.1 Values of Test-Driven Development

Test-driven development, referred to as *TDD*, is an intrinsic part of *Extreme Programming* that was outlined in Chapter 1. A central point in agile methods is *working software* and TDD most certainly focuses on producing reliable and maintainable software while programming at maximal speed.

There has been a tendency for traditional software development thinking that fixing defects late in a software product's development lifetime is extremely expensive and thus enormous emphasis has been put on the early analysis and design phases. Implementation and coding were seen as "merely" translating the finished design into executable software. Failures in software were often seen as indications that not enough time had been spent on the design. Many seasoned software developers, however, know that this is not the whole truth. Software coding is a learning process that is central in getting to understand both the problem and solution domain. Coding is for software design what experiments are for natural science: A way to ground hypotheses in reality. This does not mean that you should not design—the point is that designs should not stay too long in your head or on your desk before their validity and soundness are tested as computer programs.

This leads to an important point, **speed**. You strive for developing the production code as fast as possible without compromising quality. Speed is not achieved by being sloppy or by rushing, if you want high quality code. On the contrary it is achieved by having a well-structured programming process (the "rhythm") guided by sound principles, by testing design ideas early, and by keeping the code maintainable and of high quality. Another important means to speed is **simplicity** as expressed in one of the mantras of agile development: "Simplicity–the art of maximizing the amount of work not done–is essential." In TDD you implement the code that makes the product work, and no more.

Another central point or value in TDD is to **take small steps**. If a story for the system requires you to add a new class, make relations to it from existing classes, and modify the object instantiation sequence, then you have three steps—at the very least. TDD puts extreme emphasis on taking one, very tiny, step at the time; even if it means writing code that will be removed already in the next step. Why? Because when you try to leap over several steps you usually find yourself falling into an abyss of problems. Before I learned TDD, I have several times found myself in a software quagmire because I have tried to implement a complex feature in a single step. The story usually went along these lines: *After implementing a small part of the feature , I found that some of the implemented functionality was similar to something in another class, therefore I started changing that class so I could use it instead. During that work I discovered a defect that I then began to fix. However, in order to fix it I had to change the internal data structure quite a lot which lead to adding a parameter to a few of the class' methods. Therefore I had to change all the places where these methods were called. During that work I notice that …* After a few days I had made changes in so many places that the system stopped working and I had lost track of why I started all this work in the first place! More often than not I simply had to undo all the changes to get back on track and I learned the value of taking backups very often! In TDD you concentrate on one step at a time—even if it means writing code that will only be used temporarily. Fixing one step and making it work gives confidence and it is easy to return to safe ground if the ideas for the next step turn out to be bad.

A final value is to **keep focus**. You must focus on one step, one issue, at the time. Otherwise code has a fantastic way of detracting your attention so often that you quickly forget the point of the whole exercise. Just look at the story above. So, in my development effort below I will *take small steps* and *keep focus*.

5.2 Setting the Stage

So, I have the specification of the pay station system and some Java interfaces (Chapter 4), I have a computer with some development tools like an editor and a compiler, and I have a need to produce an implementation that satisfies the requirements. As stated in the beginning, I also have a wish not just for any implementation but for a *reliable* implementation. Thus, I need to go from A to B, and TDD is a process that helps me by providing a path between the two points. TDD does so by listing a number of **TDD principles**, strategies or rules that I use to decide what to do next in my programming in order to keep focus and take small steps. The most important rule of them all has given the technique its name:

TDD Principle: **Test First**

When should you write your tests? Before you write the code that is to be tested.

This principle is perhaps a rather surprising statement at first. How do I write the test first, it must mean that I test something that I have not written yet? How do I test something that does not exist? The consequence has historically been that naturally the production code was written first. However, history has also shown that in almost all cases the tests have never been written. I have seen the force to postpone writing tests many times in my own professional life: *"I ought to write some tests, but I feel in a hurry, and anyway it appears to work all right when I run it manually."* However, a few months of working this way and, *Bang*, weird failures begin to surface. Now the defects are tricky to track down because I do not have the small tests that verify the behavior of each small part of the software.

TDD Principle: **Automated Test**

How do you test your software? Write an automated test.

In TDD you run *all* the tests *all* the time to ensure that your last modifications have not accidentally introduced a defect. Therefore manual tests are inadequate because they are too labor intensive. A good unit testing tool is therefore essential, so I ready JUnit (see Section 2.4) for the job of writing my automated tests.

So, I will start the implementation of the pay station by writing JUnit tests and by writing them first. But how do I structure this process? A simple suggestion is:

TDD Principle: **Test List**

What should you test? Before you begin, write a list of all the tests you know you will have to write. Add to it as you find new potential tests.

The test list is a sensible compromise between "moving fast" and "keeping focus." I want to start as soon as possible but I need to maintain a keen eye on what I want to achieve and what the results are. A test list is like a shopping list for the grocery store. It keeps me focused, I don't forget a lot of things, but it does not exclude me from putting some extra stuff in the shopping bag.

Thus, looking over the three stories I developed together with the customer in the previous chapter: *buy a parking ticket*, *cancel a transaction*, and *reject illegal coin*, a first test list may look like this:

- accept legal coin
- 5 cents should give 2 minutes parking time
- reject illegal coin
- readDisplay
- buy produces valid receipt
- cancel resets pay station

If you review the stories you may come up with other suggestions for a test list or may find that this one is too simple. However, the point is to start moving forward fast: arguing over the "best" list does not produce software, it only delays the time when we start producing it. Many issues will automatically arise once we get started implementing test cases and production code. As we program we gain a deeper understanding of the problem and the test list is something that we constantly add to and refine just as a grocery list.

The TDD process consists of five steps that you repeat over and over again: The *TDD rhythm*. The five steps are:

The TDD Rhythm:

1. Quickly add a test
2. Run all tests and see the new one fail
3. Make a little change
4. Run all tests and see them all succeed
5. Refactor to remove duplication

Ideally you try to move through these five steps as quickly as possible while keeping your focus on the implementation job to be done.

5.3 Iteration 1: Inserting Five Cents

Okay, I have the test list with several features to implement (or more correctly: tests of features to write before implementing the features), I have the rhythm, the question remaining is *which test to write first?*

TDD Principle: **One Step Test**

Which test should you pick next from the test list? Pick a test that will teach you something and that you are confident you can implement.

Looking over the list I see some features that are obvious, like for instance *readDisplay* which is probably just returning some instance variable. I do not learn much from choosing that item from the list. A test list often also contains items where I have no clue at all as how to implement. While there are no obviously highly complex items on our pay station test list, still the "buy" item is more complicated as it seems to require several features to be working first. These items are not good candidates either—postpone them until later where your work with the implementation has taught you more about the system and you can rely on more functionality to be present. The *One Step Test* principle tells me to pick a feature that is not too obvious but that I am confident I can implement and thus learn from: I take *one step* forward. Looking over the test list I decide to go for the test "5 cents = 2 minutes parking:" Not too obvious nor too complex.

Step 1: Quickly add a test. To paraphrase this statement in our testing terminology from Chapter 2, I need to write a test case in which the unit under test is the implementation of the pay station in general and the addPayment method in particular; the input value is 5 cents and the expected output is that we can read 2 minutes parking time as the value to be displayed. In JUnit the test case can be expressed like this.

Listing: chapter/tdd/iteration-1/TestPayStation.java

```
import org.junit.*;
import static org.junit.Assert.*;

/** Testcases for the Pay Station system.
*/
public class TestPayStation {

  /**
   * Entering 5 cents should make the display report 2 minutes
   * parking time.
  */
  @Test
  public void shouldDisplay2MinFor5Cents()
          throws IllegalCoinException {
    PayStation ps = new PayStationImpl();
    ps.addPayment( 5 );
    assertEquals( "Should display 2 min for 5 cents",
                  2, ps.readDisplay() );
  }
}
```

Sidebar 5.1 explains how you download, compile, and run the code associated with this chapter.

☞ Study and run the code as you read through this chapter.

Step 2: Run all tests and see the new one fail. We start by compiling production and test code but, of course, the compilation fails! I have not yet provided any class that implements the PayStation interface. Now, I am tempted to start implementing the behavior I want, but TDD tells me to *take small steps.* Therefore, I implement the smallest possible implementation that can compile, even though it is presently functionally incomplete. In practice, it means that all method bodies are empty except those that have a return value: these return 0 or null. Such a minimal implementation is often called a **temporary stub** and in TDD any newly introduced class starts its life as a temporary stub. I will explore and extend the stub concept in detail in Chapter 12.

Sidebar 5.1: Using the Pay Station Code

The source code as well as compilation scripts for Windows and Linux are provided at the book's web site (http://www.baerbak.com). You need to download the zip archive, unzip it and then you will be able to find the source code in the folders listed above each source code listing.

There is a folder for each iteration in this chapter. The contents of the folder show the production and testing code at the *end* of the iteration. Thus the folder *chapter/tdd/iteration-1* contains the code just before iteration 2 starts. There is also a *iteration-0* folder containing the code before the first iteration.

Each directory contains a "compile" script as well as a "run-test" script for respectively compilation and execution of the test cases (.bat for Windows and .sh for Bash shell on Linux). The JUnit jar file is provided in the source folders so there is no installation of JUnit involved. For a discussion of the contents of the scripts, please refer to sidebar 2.3 on page 22.

Listing: chapter/tdd/iteration-0/PayStationImpl.java

```
/** Implementation of the pay station.
*/
public class PayStationImpl implements PayStation {

  public void addPayment( int coinValue )
          throws IllegalCoinException {
  }

  public int readDisplay() {
    return 0;
  }

  public Receipt buy() {
    return null;
  }

  public void cancel() {
  }
}
```

Now, at least, I can compile and is ready to run my test which outputs:

```
JUnit version 4.4
.E
Time: 0,047
There was 1 failure:
1) shouldDisplay2MinFor5Cents(TestPayStation)
java.lang.AssertionError: Should display 2 min for 5 cents
  expected:<2> but was:<0>
     at org.junit.Assert.fail(Assert.java:74)
     at org.junit.Assert.failNotEquals(Assert.java:448)
     at org.junit.Assert.assertEquals(Assert.java:102)
     at org.junit.Assert.assertEquals(Assert.java:323)
     at TestPayStation.shouldDisplay2MinFor5Cents(Test
                                        PayStation.java:20)
  [lines removed here]
```

```
    at org.junit.runner.JUnitCore.main(JUnitCore.java:44)

FAILURES!!!
Tests run: 1,  Failures: 1
```

Returning to our case study, the requirements speak of two minutes parking time for five cents but the production code returns zero. This is hardly surprising considering that our initial method implementation simply returns 0.

Step 3: Make a little change, but what change should I make? TDD provides a principle that always upsets seasoned software developers:

TDD Principle: **Fake It ('Til You Make It)**

What is your first implementation once you have a broken test? Return a constant. Once you have your tests running, gradually transform it.

What? I have to write code that is obviously incomplete? Yes, this principle may seem absurd at first. I will discuss it at length below and as we proceed with the pay station implementation but for now let us just use it. Applying this principle is of course easy—I simply return a constant in the appropriate method in PayStationImpl:

```
public int readDisplay() {
  return 2;
}
```

Step 4: Run all tests and see them all succeed.

```
JUnit version 4.4
.
Time: 0,016

OK (1 test)
```

The passed testcase marks success, progress, and confidence!

Looking over the test list again, I see that I have actually tested quite a few of our initial test cases.

- ~~accept legal coin~~
- ~~5 cents should give 2 minutes parking time.~~
- reject illegal coin
- ~~readDisplay~~
- buy produces valid receipt
- cancel resets pay station

However, you may be concerned at this stage. Our test case passes but surely the production code is incomplete! It will only pass this single test case! And I have apparently wasted time and effort on writing clearly incomplete code that needs to be changed in just a few minutes. This is insane, is it not?

Actually, there are good reasons in this apparent madness. First, the focus of this iteration is *not* to implement a full rate calculation but simply to handle the *5 cents = 2 minutes* entry on the test list. Thus, this *is* the correct and smallest possible implementation of this single test case. Remember the technique is called test-*driven*. If I had begun implementing a complete calculation algorithm then this production code would not have been *driven* into existence by my test cases! This is a key point in TDD:

> **Key Point: Production code is driven into existence by tests**
>
> *In the extreme, you do not enter a single character into your production code unless there is a test case that demands it.*

This leads to the second point, namely that of course the *Fake It* principle can not stand alone, it must be considered in conjunction with the *Triangulation* principle:

> TDD Principle: **Triangulation**
>
> How do you most conservatively drive abstraction with tests? Abstract only when you have two or more examples.

☞ Use Wikipedia or another internet resource to find out what triangulation is in ordinary geometry.

In TDD *Triangulation* states that you must have two, three, or more examples in order to generalize, to *drive an abstraction* like an algorithm or a class into existence. If I had simply started implementing the algorithm for parking time calculations based only on our one test case, odds are that I would have missed something. (Of course, our case is pretty simple here but the principle gets much more valuable when the algorithms are more complex.)

So, I know that I have just introduced *Fake It* code and I know I have to triangulate it away in one of the following iterations. How do I make sure I remember this? This is where the test list comes to my rescue: I simply add a new test case to the test list:

* ~~accept legal coin~~
* reject illegal coin, exception
* ~~5 cents should give 2 minutes parking time.~~
* ~~readDisplay~~
* buy produces valid receipt
* cancel resets pay station
* *25 cents = 10 minutes*

In this iteration 1, the *Fake It* principle has helped me to *keep focus* and *take small steps*! Still, this principle appears odd at first sight, and you need to have applied it a number of times to really appreciate it.

Step 5: Refactor to remove duplication. There appears to be no duplication, so this step is skipped in this iteration.

5.4 Iteration 2: Rate Calculation

Step 1: Quickly add a test. The last iteration left us with production code containing *Fake It* code. Such code should not stay for long and it should certainly not accumulate. I therefore choose the *25 cents = 10 minutes* item as the focus for my next iteration.

The question is how I should express this test case. Two paths come to my mind. One path is to just add more test code into the existing @Test method to produce something like

```
@Test
public void shouldDisplay2MinFor5Cents()
        throws IllegalCoinException {
  PayStation ps = new PayStationImpl();
  ps.addPayment( 5 );
  assertEquals( "Should display 2 min for 5 cents",
                2, ps.readDisplay() );

  ps.addPayment( 25 );
  assertEquals( "Should display 12 min for 30 cents",
                12, ps.readDisplay() );
}
```

The second path is to create a new @Test method in the test class. TDD has a strong opinion concerning the amount of testing done in each method:

TDD Principle: **Isolated Test**

How should the running of tests affect one another? Not at all.

This principle, taken literally, tells me to make another test case to avoid interference between our two test cases. If you first insert 5 cents, and next want to test the amount of parking time given for 25 cents you must test that the display reads 12 minutes because the total amount entered is 30 cents. This interference between the test cases is relatively easy to overlook here, but in the general case things can get complex and you quickly end up in a **ripple effect** in the test cases: it is like dominos—if one falls then they all fall. To see this, consider a situation later in development where some developer accidently introduces a defect so the pay station cannot accept 5-cent coins. In the *Isolate Test* case, then the 5-cent test case would fail and the 25-cent test case would pass. This is a clear indication of what defect has been introduced. In the case where both test cases are expressed in the same test method, however, the whole test method fails. Thus the problems appears worse than it actually is (because apparently both 5 cent and 25 cent entry fails) and also the problem is more difficult to identify (is it a defect in the 5 cent or in the 25 cent validation code?)

Back to our pay station. I write an isolated test for 25 cent parking.

```
@Test
public void shouldDisplay10MinFor25Cents()
        throws IllegalCoinException {
  PayStation ps = new PayStationImpl();
  ps.addPayment( 25 );
  assertEquals( "Should display 10 min for 25 cents",
                10, ps.readDisplay() );
}
```

Step 2: Run all tests and see the new one fail. I get the expected failed tests:

```
1) shouldDisplay10MinFor25Cents(TestPayStation)
java.lang.AssertionError: Should display 10 min for 25 cents
  expected:<10> but was:<2>
  [lines omitted]
  at TestPayStation.shouldDisplay10MinFor25Cents
                                        (TestPayStation.java:32)
  [lines omitted]
```

Step 3: Make a little change. To get the behavior I must introduce a multiplication of whatever amount has been inserted so far. This is not really rocket science, so I come up with:

Fragment: chapter/tdd/iteration-2/PayStationImpl.java

```
1 public class PayStationImpl implements PayStation {
2   private int insertedSoFar;
3   public void addPayment( int coinValue )
4           throws IllegalCoinException {
5     insertedSoFar = coinValue;
6   }
7   public int readDisplay() {
8     return insertedSoFar / 5 * 2;
9   }
```

However, do you notice that this code is also incomplete? As I write the code I realize that I only have test cases that insert a single coin, not two or more. Thus the correct implementation of line 5:

```
insertedSoFar += coinValue;
```

is not driven by any tests yet. I note that I can drive the "+=" by adding yet another item, like *enter two or more legal coins*, to my test list. But even without the summation in the addPayment method I achieve *Step 4: Run all tests and see them all succeed.* Great. Next, let us look at *Step 5: Refactor to remove duplication.* Fowler (1999) defines refactoring as:

Definition: **Refactoring**

Refactoring is the process of modifying and restructuring the source code to improve its maintainability and flexibility without affecting the system's external behavior when executing.

Thus, when I refactor, I change the code but it must behave in the exact same way before and after the code change as seen from the user or some external system. The whole point of the exercise is to "improve its maintainability and flexibility". Recall from Chapter 3 that maintainability and flexibility are qualities that speak of the cost of adding or enhancing the software's features: maintainable code is code that is easy to change. If my code contains duplicated code and the functionality it expresses has to be changed then I have to change in two places. This takes longer time of course but even worse I might forget to make the change in one of the places!

Looking over the production code there seems to be no code duplication, but there is some in the test cases—both contain the object instantiation step:

```
PayStation ps = new PayStationImpl();
```

Merging the two test cases into one to avoid the duplication is not an option as it would not obey *Isolated Test*. Obviously, every test case I may think of will duplicate this line, so a better approach is to isolate the *"object setup"* code in a single place. In testing terminology, such a setup of objects before testing is called a **fixture**. JUnit supports fixtures directly using the @Before annotation.

Listing: chapter/tdd/iteration-2-initial/TestPayStation.java

```
import org.junit.*;
import static org.junit.Assert.*;

/** Testcases for the Pay Station system.
*/
public class TestPayStation {
  PayStation ps;
  /** Fixture for pay station testing. */
  @Before
  public void setUp() {
    ps = new PayStationImpl();
  }

  /**
   * Entering 5 cents should make the display report 2 minutes
   * parking time.
  */
  @Test
  public void shouldDisplay2MinFor5Cents()
          throws IllegalCoinException {
    ps.addPayment( 5 );
    assertEquals( "Should display 2 min for 5 cents",
                  2, ps.readDisplay() );
  }

  /**
   * Entering 25 cents should make the display report 10 minutes
   * parking time.
  */
  @Test
  public void shouldDisplay10MinFor25Cents()
          throws IllegalCoinException {
    ps.addPayment( 25 );
    assertEquals( "Should display 10 min for 25 cents",
                  10, ps.readDisplay() );
  }
}
```

A fixture, a @Before method, is invoked once before every test method so the resulting calling sequence of the above test class will become what I need: setUp(), shouldDisplay2MinFor5Cents, setUp(), shouldDisplay10MinFor25Cents. This is the way JUnit supports the *Isolated Test* principle—each test case is independent from all others.

The last test case contains the assertion assertEquals(10, ps.readDisplay()). Where did '10' come from? It is easy to overview the calculation right now but remember that you may have to look over your test cases three months or two years from now, maybe because some refactoring has made that test case fail. At that time, the 10 may seem like a riddle. In a pressed situation with a deadline coming up, riddles are not what you want to solve, you want your code to work again! The point is yet another rule.

TDD Principle: **Evident Data**

How do you represent the intent of the data? Include expected and actual results in the test itself, and make their relationship apparent. You are writing tests for the reader, not just for the computer.

The '10' is a result of a calculation and instead of giving the answer the test case communicates its intention much better by giving the calculation itself:

```
ps.addPayment( 25 );
assertEquals( "Should display 10 min for 25 cents",
              25 / 5 * 2, ps.readDisplay() );
// 25 cent in 5 cent coins each giving 2 minutes parking
```

This rule especially becomes beneficial when the calculation becomes more complex than in this case. (Beware, though, of blindly copying code fragments containing the calculations from the production code into the test code or the other way around as they may both contain defects!) An alternative is to add a comment outlining the calculation.

I have now made a simple refactoring in the test code but my rhythm is not complete until JUnit has verified that I did not accidentally introduce new defects. I run JUnit again: All pass. It is a success that the new test case passes—however it is just as important that the old one does!

Key Point: All unit tests always pass

At the end of each iteration, all tests must run 100%.

Sometimes in developing more complex software you will add a new test case, modify the existing production code, only to see several other test cases suddenly fail. It is a key point in TDD that those "old" test cases *must* be made to pass before the iteration is considered finished. If you leave the old test cases failing the reliability of your software is of course quickly degrading.

Finally, I strike out the passed test on my test list:

- ~~accept legal coin~~
- reject illegal coin, exception
- ~~5 cents should give 2 minutes parking time.~~
- ~~readDisplay~~
- buy produces valid receipt
- cancel resets pay station
- ~~25 cents = 10 minutes~~
- enter two or more legal coins

5.5 Iteration 3: Illegal Coins

One Step Test tells me to pick an item from my test list that is not too simple, not to complex, and one that I can learn something from. I could go for the buy or cancel operation, or perhaps enter two coins, but I decide to look at illegal coins: my present production code contains no validation of the entered coin values. We do not have that many 17-cent coins around so let us try that. The interface specifies that an IllegalCoinException must be thrown so we must define a test case where the input value is an illegal coin and the expected output is an exception being thrown.

JUnit allows you to specify that a test should throw an exception by giving the exception class as parameter:

Fragment: chapter/tdd/iteration-3/TestPayStation.java

```
@Test(expected=IllegalCoinException.class)
public void shouldRejectIllegalCoin() throws IllegalCoinException {
  ps.addPayment(17);
}
```

Step 2: Run all tests and see the new one fail. The result is of course a broken test:

```
JUnit version 4.4
...E
Time: 0,031
There was 1 failure:
1) shouldRejectIllegalCoin(TestPayStation)
java.lang.AssertionError: Expected exception: IllegalCoinException
  [lines omitted]
FAILURES!!!
Tests run: 3,  Failures: 1
```

Step 3: Make a little change. I have to introduce validation code in method addPayment. My suggestion is to use a switch to define the valid coins:

Fragment: chapter/tdd/iteration-3/PayStationImpl.java

```
public void addPayment( int coinValue )
        throws IllegalCoinException {
  switch ( coinValue ) {
  case 5: break;
  case 25: break;
  default:
    throw new IllegalCoinException("Invalid coin: "+coinValue);
  }
  insertedSoFar = coinValue;
}
```

which leads to *Step 4: Run all tests and see them all succeed.* Three tests passing. Great! So what is my present status? I have test cases for valid and invalid coins. They all pass. I do not have any *Fake It* in the production code. However, the production code is still incomplete. Hopefully you noted the missing case in the switch statement: I do not test for coin value 10 and therefore dimes are presently considered an illegal coin. This is not comparable to the specification from Alphatown. But it demonstrates that a test suite that passes is not the same as reliable software that satisfies all stories and requirements. Testing and test-driven development can never prove the absence of defects, only prove the existence of one. A short story about the truth of this is found in sidebar 5.2. The consequence is that you have to exercise much care when defining test cases so you can convince yourself and ultimately the buyer of your software that your test cases have found as many defects as possible. Yet another principle helps us:

TDD Principle: **Representative Data**

What data do you use for your tests? Select a small set of data where each element represents a conceptual aspect or a special computational processing.

This principle can guide my selection of data. Do not pick several data values that are essentially processed in the same manner. For instance I chose a 17-cent coin as

Sidebar 5.2: Defects in a Plotter Package

I once developed software to make graphical plots for a technical department in a major telephone company. The software operated a pen-based plotter and could plot classic X-Y diagrams. As a feature I added that the creation date of the plot was written in the corner of the plot. I developed this software package for more than a week and it worked fine with all my test data.

However, two problems surfaced later. The first appeared instantly when the technical department tested it: I had tested with X-Y data in the range 0..1000 but the data the technical department needed to plot was in the 10^{-7} range and my software did not handle that well. After fixing this, all worked fine for several weeks—until the package stopped working all together. It took me quite a long time to figure out that the defect was in the code for writing the date in the corner! It turned out that I had started on the package around the 12th in the month and thus for several weeks the date integer had always consisted of two digits! As the date turned to the next month all of a sudden the date only had one digit—and my production code failed on converting the non-existing second digit into a string! Remember the *Representative Data* principle.

illegal coin, , and adding ten extra test cases that try to insert a 3 cent, 42 cent, 5433 cent, etc., do not add much additional confidence in the reliability of the production code. So select a small set of data values. On the other hand your set must not miss values that *do* exhibit a computational difference. This is the case here in which the buy story states that 5, 10, and 25-cent coins are valid and my implementation using a switch treats each coin separately. Thus I need test cases to cover all three types of coins. I remember to keep focus, this iteration is about invalid coins and it is completed, so the way to ensure I remember this observation is to add an item to the test list. In this case I can actually just change one of the existing items:

* ~~accept legal coin~~
* ~~reject illegal coin, exception~~
* ~~5 cents should give 2 minutes parking time.~~
* ~~readDisplay~~
* buy produces valid receipt
* cancel resets pay station
* ~~25 cents = 10 minutes~~
* *enter ~~two or more legal~~ a 10 and 25 coin*

Step 5: Refactor to remove duplication. Looking over the code I find no need for refactoring.

5.6 Iteration 4: Two Valid Coins

I decide to make the last item, *enter a 10 and 25 coin*, on the list my focus for the next iteration. This is because it will allow me both to complete the coin validation functionality as well as drive the summation of inserted payment into existence.

Step 1: Quickly add a test is trivial, I add a shouldDisplay14MinFor10And25Cents method with the proper input and expected values. *Step 2: Run all tests and see the new one fail* provides the answer:

Sidebar 5.3: Test Code Must Obey Production Code Invariants

One nasty experience that some of my students have run into is that their testing code is initially too simple because it relies on the immature production code, the stub code, that always is the initial starting point for a class in TDD. This is best illustrated by example.

Consider our first two iterations of the pay station: accepting a coin and calculating rates. Actually I could have made these iterations by using the value 15 as input parameter to addPayment, and for instance tested the rate calculation by:

```
@Test
public void reallyBadTest() throws IllegalCoinException {
  ps.addPayment( 15 );
  assertEquals( 15/5*2, ps.readDisplay() );
}
```

This would lead to two test cases passing and even to the correct implementation. However, later when I introduce validation of coins, the test case above would suddenly fail and I have to refactor the test case.

An even more subtle example is when the production code behavior is guided by its internal state. As an example, consider implementing a chess program. In chess the white player always moves first. However, if you start your iterations by testing valid and invalid movement for a pawn and happen to use a black pawn then your test cases will pass up until you start implementing the code that handles turn taking. Now your test cases fail because it is not black's turn to move.

The morale is that your testing code must always follow the invariants, preconditions, and specifications of the classes it tests: provide proper and valid parameters, call methods in the correct sequence, etc. Otherwise your test cases will probably break in later iterations.

```
JUnit version 4.4
....E
Time: 0,016
There was 1 failure:
1) shouldDisplay14MinFor10And25Cents(TestPayStation)
IllegalCoinException: Invalid coin: 10
  [...]
```

Step 3: Make a little change is also trivial, inserting the missing case in the switch (line 5) in addPayment.

```
1  public void addPayment( int coinValue )
2          throws IllegalCoinException {
3    switch ( coinValue ) {
4    case 5: break;
5    case 10: break;
6    case 25: break;
7    default:
8      throw new IllegalCoinException("Invalid coin: "+coinValue);
9    }
10   insertedSoFar = coinValue;
11 }
```

When I run the tests again, however, the test again fails but for another reason:

```
JUnit version 4.4
....E
Time: 0,016
There was 1 failure:
1) shouldDisplay14MinFor10And25Cents(TestPayStation)
java.lang.AssertionError: Should display 14 min for 10+25 cents
    expected:<14> but was:<10>
```

This is actually quite typical—that you add a test and then have several mini iterations of adding production code, test fails, modify production code, test still fails, modify, etc., until finally the test case pass. Here, the failed test drives the summation of payment into the production code, the missing "+=". Thus the final code of the iteration becomes:

Fragment: chapter/tdd/iteration-4/PayStationImpl.java

```java
public void addPayment( int coinValue )
        throws IllegalCoinException {
  switch ( coinValue ) {
  case 5: break;
  case 10: break;
  case 25: break;
  default:
    throw new IllegalCoinException("Invalid coin: "+coinValue);
  }
  insertedSoFar += coinValue;
}
```

Step 4: Run all tests and see them all succeed. Four tests pass. Again no need for *Step 5: Refactor to remove duplication.*

* ~~accept legal coin~~
* ~~reject illegal coin, exception~~
* ~~5 cents should give 2 minutes parking time.~~
* ~~readDisplay~~
* buy produces valid receipt
* cancel resets pay station
* ~~25 cents = 10 minutes~~
* ~~enter a 10 and 25 coin~~

Done.

5.7 Iteration 5: Buying (Faked)

OK, now I have enough production in place that I find the item *buy produces valid receipt* is a suitable *One Step Test*. Completing this item also completes the *Buy a parking ticket* story defined in Section 4.1. To remind you, the buy method looks like this

Fragment: chapter/tdd/iteration-5/PayStation.java

```
/**
 * Buy parking time. Terminate the ongoing transaction and
 * return a parking receipt. A non-null object is always returned.
 * @return a valid parking receipt object.
 */
public Receipt buy();
```

The buy method returns an object defined by the interface Receipt. This interface just contains a single method, **int** value(), that returns the number of minutes parking time the receipt object represents.

Step 1: Quickly add a test. Why not try all the three types of coins:

Fragment: chapter/tdd/iteration-5/TestPayStation.java

```
@Test
public void shouldReturnCorrectReceiptWhenBuy()
        throws IllegalCoinException {
  ps.addPayment(5);
  ps.addPayment(10);
  ps.addPayment(25);
  Receipt receipt;
  receipt = ps.buy();
  assertNotNull( "Receipt reference cannot be null",
                 receipt );
  assertEquals( "Receipt value must be 16 min.",
                (5+10+25) / 5 * 2 , receipt.value() );
}
```

I here use another of JUnit's assertions: assertNotNull that tests whether the argument object reference is not null. Thus I first test that we get a receipt object and second that the parking time it represents is correct.

> **Exercise 5.1:** You may observe that if the buy method returns a null reference, then the second assertEquals will report failure. One may argue that the first assertNotNull is then redundant. Argue in favor of having both asserts in the testing code.

I go through *Step 2: Run all tests and see the new one fail.* As I have not made any implementation effort on the buy method, it simply returns null and the output from JUnit is therefore no surprise.

```
1) shouldReturnCorrectReceiptWhenBuy(TestPayStation)
java.lang.AssertionError: Receipt reference should not be null
```

Now, next is *Step 3: Make a little change* but this poses a problem. The buy operation requires two steps: implementing the buy method in PayStationImpl and writing an implementation of the Receipt interface. *Take small steps* races through my head! I need to break this complex problem into two smaller ones that can be done in isolation: getting buy to work and getting receipt to work. The question is: in which order? The buy operation depends upon the receipt implementation, not the other way around, so the most obvious step is to make the receipt work and then go back and get the buy operation in place. Agree?

☞ Take a moment to reflect upon the two ways to go before reading on: A) finish buy and then get receipt to work or B) get receipt to work first, and then go back to the buy operation. What are the benefits and liabilities of each approach?

The answer to this question may at first seem counter intuitive but the arguably best approach is to finish the iteration on the buy test first! You may argue that this is impossible but if you do, then you have not truly appreciated the *Fake It* principle. By using *Fake It* we can break the problem into smaller steps that each can be finished:

1. Keep the focus on the ongoing iteration to get a receipt that reads ((5+10+25) / 5 * 2) minutes by returning a *Fake It* receipt.
2. In the next iteration, implement a proper receipt class.
3. And finally, in an iteration use *Triangulation* to finish the buy operation.

I must remember this analysis by updating my test list to ensure that the fake receipt does not stay in the production code.

* ~~accept legal coin~~
* ~~reject illegal coin, exception~~
* ~~5 cents should give 2 minutes parking time.~~
* ~~readDisplay~~
* buy for 40 cents produces valid receipt
* cancel resets pay station
* ~~25 cents = 10 minutes~~
* ~~enter a 10 and 25 coin~~
* *receipt can store values*
* *buy for 100 cents*

The argument for sticking to the buy operation is *to keep focus* even if it means writing a bit more code in the short run. If you start getting Receipt in place at this moment then you break the focus on the buy iteration and introduce a new focus and therefore a new iteration. This behavior is unfortunately all too well known to seasoned developers: *"In order to fix defect A I must first get method B in place. Implementing method B I find that a new class C would be a good idea. Class C turned out to be quite a bit more complex than I thought and required class D to be refactored. Refactoring it exposed a defect in class E that I had to fix first..."* Before you know it you have spent a week implementing, debugging, testing, and find out that you have completely forgotten *why* all the effort was started in the first place. You have lost focus. And probably introduced code (and defects!) that do not do the original problem any good. It should be avoided.

Now I can finish the "buy for 40 cents" operation by using *Fake It*. An anonymous inner class comes in handy here. If anonymous classes are new to you, you can find a small description in sidebar 5.4.

Fragment: chapter/tdd/iteration-5/PayStationImpl.java

```
public Receipt buy() {
  return new Receipt() {
      public int value() { return (5+10+25)/5*2; }
    };
}
```

Step 4: Run all tests and see them all succeed gives me the comforting signal that all tests pass. No *Step 5: Refactor to remove duplication* this time either.

Sidebar 5.4: Anonymous Classes in Java

Java allows *inner classes*, that is, a class that is defined inside another class.

```
class OuterClass {
    [...]
    class InnerClass {
        [...]
    }
}
```

The normal scoping rules apply so an instance of InnerClass only exists as part of an instance of the OuterClass. A special case is an *anonymous* class which is an inner class declared without naming it. Such an anonymous class is declared simply by defining the method bodies as part of the object creation using new. Thus

Fragment: chapter/tdd/iteration-5/PayStationImpl.java

```
    return new Receipt() {
        public int value() { return (5+10+25)/5*2; }
      };
```

means: *create a new instance of an anonymous class that implements* Receipt *and has this implementation of the* value *method.*

Anonymous inner classes are very handy when using *Fake It* to create a "constant", first, implementation of an interface, as you do not have to create classes in their own Java source code files.

You can consult the *Java Tutorial* at Sun's website for more details on inner classes.

5.8 Iteration 6: Receipt

Fake It should never stay in the production code for long. This requires me to address the *receipt can store values* item. The only method in the receipt is the value() method.

Step 1: Quickly add a test. The receipt must represent a parking time value, so let us express this in a test case. Writing the test case involves a bit of design. value() must return the number of minutes parking time it represents but how does the pay station "tell" the receipt this value? First things first:

TDD Principle: **Assert First**

When should you write the asserts? Try writing them first.

That is, get the assertions in place first and return to the problem of setting up the stuff to be asserted later. First shot:

```
@Test
public void shouldStoreTimeInReceipt() {
  ...
  assertEquals( "Receipt can store 30 minute value",
                30, receipt.value() );
}
```

Where did receipt come from? I have to create it (remember, I am testing Receipt only). How do I do that? I invoke new on the constructor. As receipts are objects whose state should not change after they have been made, it makes good sense to provide the constructor with the minute value directly. I complete the test case:

Fragment: chapter/tdd/iteration-6/TestPayStation.java

```
@Test
public void shouldStoreTimeInReceipt() {
  Receipt receipt = new ReceiptImpl(30);
  assertEquals( "Receipt can store 30 minute value",
                30, receipt.value() );
}
```

Step 2: Run all tests and see the new one fail is this time not indicated by a failed test: it is the compiler that complains loudly:

```
TestPayStation.java:81: cannot find symbol
symbol  : class ReceiptImpl
location: class TestPayStation
    Receipt receipt = new ReceiptImpl(30);
                          ^
1 error
```

Step 3: Make a little change means writing an implementation of the Receipt interface. I often use the convention to name implementation classes with an Impl appended to the interface name, so I create a java source file named ReceiptImpl. Next, I realize that the complexity of ReceiptImpl is very low: it is a matter of assigning a single instance variable in the constructor and return it in the value method. Testing should always be a question of cost versus benefit and with such a straightforward implementation I decide that *Fake It* and *Triangulation* are too small steps. When this is the case use:

TDD Principle: **Obvious Implementation**

How do you implement simple operations? Just implement them.

Consequently, I simply add the new class to the project and introduce all the necessary code in one go:

Listing: chapter/tdd/iteration-6/ReceiptImpl.java

```
/** Implementation of Receipt.
*/

public class ReceiptImpl implements Receipt {
  private int value;
  public ReceiptImpl(int value) { this.value = value; }
  public int value() { return value;}
}
```

Step 4: Run all tests and see them all succeed. The passed tests show we are on track. Again, the code is so small that there is no duplication, so I just update the test list.

- ~~accept legal coin~~
- ~~reject illegal coin, exception~~
- ~~5 cents should give 2 minutes parking time.~~
- ~~readDisplay~~
- ~~buy for 40 cents produces valid receipt~~
- cancel resets pay station
- ~~25 cents = 10 minutes~~
- ~~enter a 10 and 25 coin~~
- ~~receipt can store values~~
- buy for 100 cents

☞ Is one test case enough, only testing with value 30 minutes? Consider the *Representative Data* principle.

5.9 Iteration 7: Buying (Real)

The last iteration ended in a proper implementation of the receipt, so the obvious next choice is to triangulate the proper buy behavior, item *buy for 100 cents.*

Step 1: Quickly add a test:

Fragment: chapter/tdd/iteration-7/TestPayStation.java

```
@Test
public void shouldReturnReceiptWhenBuy100c()
  throws IllegalCoinException {
  ps.addPayment(10);
  ps.addPayment(10);
  ps.addPayment(10);
  ps.addPayment(10);
  ps.addPayment(10);
  ps.addPayment(25);
  ps.addPayment(25);

  Receipt receipt;
  receipt = ps.buy();
  assertEquals((5*10+2*25) / 5 * 2 , receipt.value() );
}
```

which of course leads to *Step 2: Run all tests and see the new one fail.*

At this point you may be concerned with the long list of addPayment method calls. As a programmer, trained to spot opportunities for parameterizing code, you would want to "do something clever" here. Maybe generalize the coin input to make an array of coin values and then make a loop that iterates over the array and call addPayment on each element. Maybe refactor the testing code to make a private method that takes a coin array as parameter and implements the loop.

But there is a problem with this line of thought. Automated test cases are expressed as source code, and we can just as easily make mistakes in the testing code as in the production code. Thus we may ask ourselves the question: *"Why can tests lead to higher reliability when they are simply more code that may contain more defects?"* The answer is that testing only provides value if I keep the tests very simple, evident and easy to read.

TDD Principle: **Evident Tests**

How do we avoid writing defective tests? By keeping the testing code evident, readable, and as simple as possible.

The code complexity of a loop over an array is much higher than the complexity of the simple list of addPayment invocations. You must always consider the complexity in the test code versus the complexity of the code that it is testing. If the testing code is more complex then odds are that defects will be in the testing code. For instance, a simple accessor method like readDisplay is so simple that we will not write a special test case for it (it gets tested in most of the test cases anyway). Test cases should ideally only contain assignments, method calls, and assertions, and you should avoid loops, recursion, and other "complex" structures if possible. Making private (simple) helper methods that can be used from multiple test methods is also OK. For instance, if I later need a test case for entering two dollars, I would refactor the above test case: move the list of addPayment calls into a private method in the test class named e.g. insertOneDollar(), and call it from the shouldReturnReceiptWhenBuy100c method.

Back to the pay station and *Step 3: Make a little change*. I remove the *Fake It* code and introduce a plausible implementation

```
public Receipt buy() {
  return new ReceiptImpl(insertedSoFar * 2 / 5);
}
```

which leads to *Step 4: Run all tests and see them all succeed*.

Finally, *Step 5: Refactor to remove duplication*. Looking over the production code again I discover duplicated code namely:

```
public int readDisplay() {
  return insertedSoFar * 2 / 5;
}
public Receipt buy() {
  return new ReceiptImpl(insertedSoFar * 2 / 5);
}
```

☞ Sketch some plausible designs that remove this duplication.

Two choices that come to my mind are A) to introduce a calculateParkingTime method to be called from both readDisplay and buy or B) introduce an instance variable timeBought that is updated in addPayment to keep track of the amount of parking time bought so far, and used in both readDisplay and buy.

The point is that whatever course taken, I now have several test cases to ensure that my refactoring of the production code does not alter pay station behavior! If I happen to introduce a defect during the implementation then most likely one of my test cases would break and I would have clear indication of what test case and what line number are causing the problem.

I have no strong opinions as to which solution is the better. I choose to introduce an instance variable timeBought that is set in the addPayment method:

Listing: chapter/tdd/iteration-7/PayStationImpl.java

```
/** Implementation of the pay station.
*/

public class PayStationImpl implements PayStation {
  private int insertedSoFar;
  private int timeBought;

  public void addPayment( int coinValue )
          throws IllegalCoinException {
    switch ( coinValue ) {
    case 5: break;
    case 10: break;
    case 25: break;
    default:
      throw new IllegalCoinException("Invalid coin: "+coinValue);
    }
    insertedSoFar += coinValue;
    timeBought = insertedSoFar / 5 * 2;
  }
  public int readDisplay() {
    return timeBought;
  }
  public Receipt buy() {
    return new ReceiptImpl(timeBought);
  }
  public void cancel() {
  }
}
```

and the passed tests tell me that my refactoring was OK: behavior has not changed even though I have made modifications in several methods.

Is this all there is to buying? I look over the original story **Buy a parking ticking** from Chapter 4 and find that there was one additional requirement: the pay station should be cleared and prepared for a new transaction. Presently, payments are simply accumulating from one driver using the station to the next. I put it on the test list:

- ~~accept legal coin~~
- ~~reject illegal coin, exception~~
- ~~5 cents should give 2 minutes parking time.~~
- ~~readDisplay~~
- ~~buy for 40 cents produces valid receipt~~
- cancel resets pay station
- ~~25 cents = 10 minutes~~
- ~~enter a 10 and 25 coin~~
- ~~receipt can store values~~
- ~~buy for 100 cents~~
- *clearing after a buy operation*

5.10 Iteration 8: Clearing after Buy

Step 1: Quickly add a test is done by testing that the display is cleared after a buy—and that doing a following buy scenario behaves as expected. I express this requirement as a test case:

Fragment: chapter/tdd/iteration-8/TestPayStation.java

```
@Test
public void shouldClearAfterBuy()
        throws IllegalCoinException {
  ps.addPayment(25);
  ps.buy(); // I do not care about the result
  // verify that the display reads 0
  assertEquals( "Display should have been cleared",
                0 , ps.readDisplay() );
  // verify that a following buy scenario behaves properly
  ps.addPayment(10); ps.addPayment(25);
  assertEquals( "Next add payment should display correct time",
                (10+25) / 5 * 2, ps.readDisplay() );
  Receipt r = ps.buy();
  assertEquals( "Next buy should return valid receipt",
                (10+25) / 5 * 2, r.value() );
  assertEquals( "Again, display should be cleared",
                0 , ps.readDisplay() );
}
```

Please note that *Isolated Test* does not mean that you have to make a test method for every assert you make. This test case seek to verify that the pay station is properly cleared after one buy scenario has been completed and this entails several aspects: that the display once again reads 0 minutes, that a second adding of payment will properly show number of minutes parking time in the display, and that the resulting receipt from the second buy will indeed show the proper value. Thus in this test case several asserts are required.

Step 2: Run all tests and see the new one fail reports failure as the present code accumulates the inserted amount even over multiple usages:

```
JUnit version 4.4
........E
Time: 0,078
There was 1 failure:
1) shouldClearAfterBuy(TestPayStation)
java.lang.AssertionError: Display should have been cleared
   expected:<0> but was:<10>
   [lines omitted]
```

The *Step 3: Make a little change* is simple as clearing code can be localized to the buy method so I change it to:

Fragment: chapter/tdd/iteration-8/PayStationImpl.java

```
public Receipt buy() {
  Receipt r = new ReceiptImpl(timeBought);
  timeBought = insertedSoFar = 0;
  return r;
}
```

and I achieve *Step 4: Run all tests and see them all succeed*. There is no need for *Step 5: Refactor to remove duplication*.

5.11 Iteration 9: Cancelling

One item left only on the test list.

* ~~accept legal coin~~
* ~~reject illegal coin, exception~~
* ~~5 cents should give 2 minutes parking time.~~
* ~~readDisplay~~
* ~~buy for 40 cents produces valid receipt~~
* cancel resets pay station
* ~~25 cents = 10 minutes~~
* ~~enter a 10 and 25 coin~~
* ~~receipt can store values~~
* ~~buy for 100 cents~~
* ~~clearing after a buy operation~~

Step 1: Quickly add a test, the test case is similar in structure to the one for "clearing after buy", I insert a few coins, cancel, and verify that the display shows 0 minutes.

Fragment: chapter/tdd/iteration-9/TestPayStation.java

```
@Test
public void shouldClearAfterCancel()
        throws IllegalCoinException {
  ps.addPayment(10);
  ps.cancel();
  assertEquals( "Cancel should clear display",
                0 , ps.readDisplay() );
  ps.addPayment(25);
  assertEquals( "Insert after cancel should work",
                25/5*2 , ps.readDisplay() );
}
```

Note again that I am a bit precautious and also verify that adding coins after the cancel works as expected.

Step 2: Run all tests and see the new one fail, yep, quickly on to *Step 3: Make a little change* where I can simply duplicate the clearing code used in the buy:

```
public void cancel() {
  timeBought = insertedSoFar = 0;
}
```

This leads to *Step 4: Run all tests and see them all succeed.* And in *Step 5: Refactor to remove duplication* I obviously have duplicated code: the clearing code. I find that a private method whose responsibility it is to reset the pay station is the proper solution for this problem.

In conclusion, I have now through nine iterations implemented nine test cases that give me high confidence that they cover the requirements put forward by the municipality of Alphatown. Their requirements have been expressed as test cases that I have written first and these have in turn driven the implementation to its final state:

Listing: chapter/tdd/iteration-9/PayStationImpl.java

```
/** Implementation of the pay station.
*/
```

```
public class PayStationImpl implements PayStation {
  private int insertedSoFar;
  private int timeBought;

  public void addPayment( int coinValue )
          throws IllegalCoinException {
    switch ( coinValue ) {
    case 5: break;
    case 10: break;
    case 25: break;
    default:
      throw new IllegalCoinException("Invalid coin: "+coinValue);
    }
    insertedSoFar += coinValue;
    timeBought = insertedSoFar / 5 * 2;
  }
  public int readDisplay() {
    return timeBought;
  }
  public Receipt buy() {
    Receipt r = new ReceiptImpl(timeBought);
    reset();
    return r;
  }
  public void cancel() {
    reset();
  }
  private void reset() {
    timeBought = insertedSoFar = 0;
  }
}
```

After this long chapter I think it is time to list a last but not least important principle.

TDD Principle: **Break**

What do you do when you feel tired or stuck? Take a break.

Programming is a highly demanding, creative, process. If you get too tired when programming then you introduce more defects than you remove and progress is slow or even negative. When you get stuck, then go for coffee, take some fresh air, or chat with your colleagues. Odds are that you have a fresh look and a better idea when you get back.

5.12 The Test-Driven Process

After this long journey in the details, it is time to look at the benefits and liabilities of using a test-driven development process. Some important advantages are:

- *Clean code that works* is a mantra of TDD. TDD aids in writing code that is maintainable (clean) and reliable (works). The reliability aspect is supported by the growing test suite that is run all the time and in which each test case verifies correct behavior of some feature of the production code. The maintainability aspect is supported by the refactoring step in the rhythm that ensure that after each iteration the code is cleaned for duplication or other less maintainable aspects.

- *Fast feedback gives programmer confidence.* The focus is to apply the rhythm's five steps in fast iterations, take small steps, and keep focus. All these contribute to breaking up problems into small, manageable, steps that are more quickly solved. This gives you more confidence as each test that passes is a success and one step closer to finishing your task. Another important advantage is that the location in the production code that is the source of a problem is known: it is almost always the source code added in the present iteration. Thus the time spent on locating a defect is reduced. Contrast this to development processes where there is a time span of weeks between running and testing the code base: you can produce a lot of (untested) code in a week and a defect may be anywhere.

- *Strong focus on reliable software.* A major benefit of writing automated tests is that they become valuable assets that give confidence that our software works as intended even when we make major refactorings. If test cases are not present most developers are simply too afraid to make any dramatic changes in large systems. An old saying is: *"If it ain't broke, don't fix it."* Software development becomes driven by fear of introducing defects. A large suite of high quality tests counters this fear and allows us to quickly assess if a dramatic change will work or not. If 57 test cases of 50,000 break after introducing the change then I am pretty confident that the change is worthwhile to introduce; if 49,000 out of 50,000 break I will think twice before proceeding...

- *Playing with the interface from the client's side.* TDD forces us to write the test first ergo I must write the code that *calls* methods on an object *before* I write the implementation. Therefore you look at the object from the client's point of view (the user of the object) instead of from the server's point of view (the object itself). This counters the force often seen in practice that developers implement all sorts of wonderful behavior that is never used and/or methods that have odd names with weird parameter lists.

- *Documentation of interface and protocol.* Test cases are reliable documentation of a class or a large software unit. They teach you how a class works: what methods it has, the parameters of the methods, and the order in which methods should be invoked, etc. It does not replace higher-level documentation, but maintained test cases are documentation that is not out-of-date and show a class' usage at the most detailed level.

- *No "driver" code.* Early in a project's development life cycle there is often no graphical user interface or any interface at all. Therefore in traditional development small "drivers" are often written: small programs that set up a few objects, call a few methods, and write a bit of output in a shell. Such drivers are seldom maintained and are quickly outdated. In TDD these short-lived programs are replaced by the test cases which in contrast are maintained and keep being an important asset. Thus TDD trades time making driver programs that are of no value in later stages for time making test cases that keep their value throughout the project's lifetime.

- *Structured programming process.* The set of testing principles: *Fake It, Triangulation,* etc.; provides me with a range of possible options to take in the program-

> ming process. I do not have a completely "blank paper" where only the problem statement is given but no clues as how to get the result, instead I have a lot of options. In my own 20-year professional life with programming I have developed intuition regarding "what to do" but it has mostly been "gut-feeling" and therefore communicating what I do now and what I will do next has been difficult. In contrast, the TDD principles form a set of options that I can name, consider, discuss, choose, and apply.

No rose without thorns, however. One issue that often pops up in TDD is that if an interface needs to be changed for some reason then it comes with a penalty as all the test cases that use this interface have to be rewritten as well. This can be quite costly especially if the change is not just syntactically but the logic is changed. Many are tempted simply to dump the test cases—but if you do so then you have also lost your means to ensure that no defects are introduced if you need to refactor. TDD is very strict about this: test cases *must* be maintained. Another issue is the quality of the test cases. They, too, must be refactored and kept small and easily readable to keep their value over time.

The term *driven* in test-driven development is central. The tests *drive* the production code. In its extreme interpretation you must *never* implement any production code that is not driven from the tests. If you find yourself making production code that does more than is warranted by the test cases—then don't! Instead make a note on the test list of a test that *will* require this code and do another iteration.

5.13 Summary of Key Concepts

Test-driven development is a program development process that focuses on writing reliable and maintainable software: *Clean code that works.* TDD is based on the values of *simplicity*, *keep focus*, and *take small steps*. Simplicity is about keeping things simple and avoiding implementing code that is really not needed, while keeping focus and taking small steps are about concentrating on one implementation task at a time and making each small addition work before proceeding.

The TDD process is structured by the five-step *rhythm* that is reproduced in the front inner cover of the book. The rhythm defines an iteration on the software in which one very small feature is added. First you add a new test case to your test suite, a test case that asserts the required or specified behavior of the feature. Next you implement production code until your new test case passes. Finally, you review your code to spot opportunities for refactoring, that is, improving the internal structure of the code to make it more maintainable while keeping the external behavior intact.

During each iteration the *TDD principles* express actions to take, or rules to follow in order to keep your testing and production code reliable and maintainable. The principles are also reproduced on the inner cover.

The benefits of TDD is confidence in your programming effort as you can see all the tests passing, a high focus on reliability and maintainability of your code, and that the rhythm and the principles help you structure your programming process.

The test-driven development technique was invented by Kent Beck and Ward Cunningham. Kent Beck has written a number of excellent books on the topic as well as the larger frame it was invented within: Extreme Programming. The present chapter is highly influenced by the book *Test-Driven Development–By Example* (Beck 2003). Most of the testing principles outlined in this chapter are reprinted from Beck's book with permission.

5.14 Selected Solutions

Discussion of Exercise 5.1:

Tests are written for the programmer and therefore the more information you can get as programmer when a test case fails the better. In this case two things can go wrong: the receipt reference is null or it is valid but the minute contents of the valid Receipt object is wrong. I have added an assert to catch each of these situations to provide as precise information as possible. Otherwise I might try to find a wrong assignment of the minute value while what I should be looking for was a missing object creation.

5.15 Review Questions

Explain the values that TDD is based upon and why.

Describe the steps in the TDD rhythm. Explain the essence and motivation for the following TDD principles: Test, Test First, Test List, One Step Test, Fake It, Triangulation, Obvious Implementation, Isolated Test, Representative Data, and Evident Test. Mention some examples from the pay station where these principles are used.

Explain what refactoring is. How does TDD support you when you refactor code?

5.16 Further Exercises

Exercise 5.2. Source code directory:
`chapter/tdd/iteration-0`

Develop the pay station yourself using the TDD process.

1. Develop it using an alternative path i.e. pick the items from the test list in another order than I have done.

2. Add a method int empty() that returns the total amount of money earned by the pay station since last call; and "empties" it, setting the earning to zero. Implement it using TDD.

Exercise 5.3:

To simulate that you get your coins back when pushing the cancel button, the interface of the cancel method is changed into:

```
/** Cancel the present transaction. Resets the pay station for a
    new transaction.
    @return A map defining the coins returned to the user.
    The key is a valid coin type and the associated value is
    the number of these coins that are returned (i.e. identical
    to the number of this coin type that the user has entered.)
    The map object is never null even if no coins
    have been entered.
*/
public Map<Integer,Integer> cancel();
```

1. Implement the cancel method using TDD.
2. Document your TDD process in a logbook outlining the rhythm, TDD principles used, and final test list.
3. Describe your experience with TDD by outlining benefits and problems encountered. Reflect on your ability to *keep focus* and *take small steps.*

Exercise 5.4. Source code directory:
`exercise/tdd/breakthrough`

Breakthrough is a two-person game played on a 8x8 chessboard, designed by Dan Troyka. Each player has 16 pieces, initially positioned on the two rows nearest to the player, as outlined in Figure 5.1. The winner is the first player to move one of his pieces to the *home row*, that is, the row farthest from the player. Players alternate to take turns, moving one piece per turn. White player begins.

The rules of movement are simple. A piece may move one square straight or diagonally forward towards the home row if that square is empty. A piece, however, may only capture an opponent piece diagonally. When capturing, the opponent piece is removed from the board and the player's piece takes its position, as you do in chess.

1. Develop an implementation of the Breakthrough interface using TDD.
2. Document your TDD process in a logbook outlining the rhythm, TDD principles used, and final test list.
3. Describe your experience with TDD by outlining benefits and problems encountered. Reflect on your ability to *keep focus* and *take small steps.*

Exercise 5.5:

Exercise 2.3 and 2.4 defined a function to verify if an email address is well-formed.

1. Implement the isValid method using TDD.
2. Document your TDD process in a logbook outlining the rhythm, TDD principles used, and final test list.

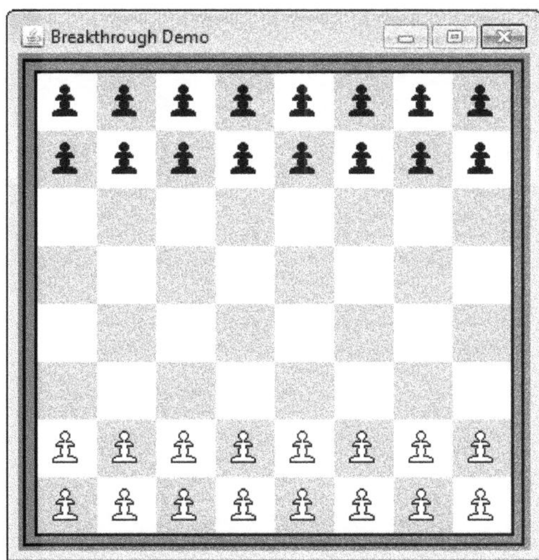

Figure 5.1: Initial position of Breakthrough

3. Describe your experience with TDD by outlining benefits and problems encountered. Reflect on your ability to *keep focus* and *take small steps.*

Note: Even if you use the regular expression library you should adhere to the test-*driven* paradigm: do *not* try to figure out the full regex and then add tests afterwards. Instead, take a simple *one step test* email address, adapt the regex minimally to make it pass, take a more complex email address, make the smallest change to the regex, etc.

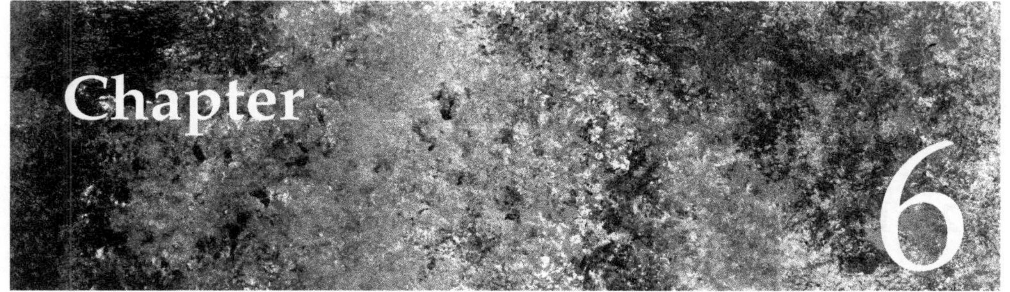

Build Management

Learning Objectives

You have developed a reliable pay station implementation in the last chapter, but your development environment is very limited: just the standard Java tools and some scripts. The purpose of this chapter is for you to learn the basic concepts and techniques of *build management*. Build management tools serve developers well in automating many of the "house-hold" tasks of software development such as compiling, file copy, backup, execution, etc. As example of a concrete tool I will introduce the Apache Ant tool.

A second learning objective is to see how the rhythm of TDD can also be successfully applied in refactoring the development environment: take small steps and keep focus are as important in building Ant scripts as in developing code. Finally, you will learn some design rules for organizing source code in folders and packages.

6.1 New Requirements

Requirements to software systems do not only come from customers, but sometimes from our own development process. The new requirement this time is defined by myself. I do not like the way I compile and execute the pay station software. I have two separate scripts and all they can do is to compile and run the test cases. If I want to add more tasks, such as generating JavaDoc documentation, I have to add more scripts. Also I have to remember to call the scripts in the right order—from time to time I have introduced a new test case but found that JUnit reports that all tests pass even though I guessed that the case test would fail. Often I found that it was because I forgot to compile first. Just like *automated testing* is better than manual tests, so is automated building and execution rather than manual steps I have to remember. So the requirement is: I want a better environment for managing and constructing my pay station system.

Another requirement is to define a suitable package structure. Java, as other modern object-oriented programming languages, allows classes to be grouped into larger, named, units. Packages aid my overview of large software systems and thereby it helps in making software more maintainable.

6.2 Build Management Concepts

So far, I have used a few scripts to call the standard compiler and Java virtual machine supplied as part of the SDK by Sun Microsystems. This works OK for very small software projects but as they grow larger, the task of overviewing this house-holding becomes a problem in itself. As a simple example, the `javac` compiler provided by Sun Microsystems can only recompile source files that reside in the same folder. Thus if you have a project consisting of source code files in thousands of folders just compiling is a major task. Another problem is the dependencies between tasks. As a very simple example the scripts provided for the chapter on TDD are actually not enough—you also need the information that you must call the compile script before the run script. This is obvious for a small project but in large projects the number of dependencies increase and you can easily miss a step if they are done manually.

The standard software engineering solution to repeated, manual tasks is of course a *tool*. Tools in this category are called **build-management tools**. The first one developed that is also still widely used was *make* (Feldman 1979).

> Definition: **Build management**
>
> The process of managing and constructing an executable software system from its parts in a reliable and cost-efficient way.

Note that "parts" may include graphics files, XML, and many other artefacts besides programming language source code. Common to build management tools is that they are tools that read and execute a *build description*.

> Definition: **Build description**
>
> A description of the goals and means for managing and constructing an executable software system. A build description states *targets*, *dependencies*, *procedures*, and *properties*.

A build description is written in a language akin to a programming language. Often I will also call the build description for the *build script*. A build description consists of the constructs mentioned above:

- A **target**. This is the goal that I want, like "compile all source code files."
- A list of **dependencies**. Targets depend upon each other: in order to execute you must first have compiled all source code. Thus the execution target depends upon the compilation target. The build description must provide a way to state such dependencies.

- **Procedures**. The procedures are associated with the targets and describe how to meet the goal of the target, like how to compile the system. For instance the compile goal must have an associated procedure that describes the steps necessary to compile all source files—in this case call *javac* on all files.

- A set of **properties**. Variables and constants are important to improve readability in programming languages, and build descriptions are no different. Properties are variables that you can assign a value in a single place and use it in your procedures.

Below I will demonstrate these concepts in a modern build management tool, Apache Ant (The Apache Software Foundation 2009), that is specifically developed for Java. The task I have set myself is of course to introduce Ant for build management of the pay station software. Introducing Ant means that the present, script based, compilation and execution process is replaced by another. As such I consider it a *refactoring* process: not of the Java source code but of the software production environment. Test-driven development tells me to *keep focus* and *take small steps* by adhering to the *rhythm*. I will demonstrate how these techniques serve me well even though I am not refactoring code but the build environment. Thus I will still write in terms of failed and passed tests but you must interpret them as *passed = all procedures work* and *failed = not all procedures work.*

6.3 Creating the Build Description

OK, I am ready to change the building environment, and TDD advises me to structure the features to introduce by a *Test List*. I want to organize the production code into Java packages and to make targets for compilation and for testing.

* put classes into packages
* make a compile target
* make a testing target

A suitable *One Step Test* is the first one—let us get those classes into a package structure. The Java package declaration provides a way to group classes into a named unit, similar to how a method groups individual statements into a named unit, and classes group methods. As a package groups a set of classes, the name of the package must of course reflect their relationship. For instance, the *javaw.swing* package groups all Java classes that are related to the Swing graphical user interface, *java.io* contains all classes related to input/output, etc.

Java packages are tied to a specific organization of the folder hierarchy, so a class in a package *xx.yy* must be located in a folder *xx/yy* in order for the Java compiler and virtual machine to find it. Thus, to put my present pay station implementation into a package I must

1. define a package structure and corresponding folder structure

2. move my classes (Java files) into this structure

3. add proper package statements to each class

TDD tells me to take small steps and as the analysis above shows, the first item on the test list is actually three steps. So I revise the test list and take one test list item at a time.

* ~~put classes into packages~~
* *define a package structure and corresponding folder structure*
* *move my classes (Java files) into this structure*
* *add proper package statements to each class*
* make a compile target
* make a testing target

6.3.1 Iteration 1: Package Structure

I envision my final pay station system will contain production code for interfacing the hardware, a demonstration graphical user interface, and of course the code that I developed in the previous chapter. I therefore see three major groups of classes that can be put in separate packages. As they are all part of the pay station system I decide to define a package, *paystation*, to contain them all. This leads to a tentative package structure like this.

```
paystation.domain    (core business/domain classes)
paystation.gui       (demonstration graphical user interface)
paystation.hardware (hardware interfacing)
```

As I have only worked on the domain classes, this is my focus here, and I need to create a corresponding folder structure: *paystation/domain*. In Java it is the *classpath* that dictates where the compiler and virtual machine looks for classes in the package structure. To give an example, I could put the source files in *src/paystation/domain* or *source-root/paystation/domain* as long as I remember to tell the Java compiler (and virtual machine) the root of the classpath. From old habits of programming C, I choose to root it in a folder named *src*.

The TDD rhythm outlined in the previous chapter contains the five steps that define each iteration : *Step 1: Quickly add a test, Step 2: Run all tests and see the new one fail, Step 3: Make a little change, Step 4: Run all tests and see them all succeed*, and *Step 5: Refactor to remove duplication*. Essentially I can use the very same rhythm in each of the iterations to make my package structure and Ant description.

In this iteration: *Step 1: Quickly add a test*, I just create the new *src/paystation/domain* folder; *Step 2: Run all tests and see the new one fail*, I compile and execute the compile and test scripts—however they succeed as adding a new folder do not invalidate anything, so no need for *Step 3: Make a little change* and *Step 4: Run all tests and see them all succeed*. Finally, there is also no need for tidying up, so also *Step 5: Refactor to remove duplication* is missing. Done. I can strike out the item *define a package structure and corresponding folder structure* from the test list.

☞ I recommend that you review the code for each iteration in the *chapter/build-management/* folder as you read through this chapter.

6.3.2 Iteration 2: Moving Classes

The obvious next item on the test list is *move my classes (Java files) into this structure.* In *Step 1: Quickly add a test,* I move the Java source code files but leave the scripts and the JUnit jar file in the root.

Step 2: Run all tests and see the new one fail, when I execute the compile script it fails, complaining that no .java files are found. *Step 3: Make a little change,* I modify the compile script to find the java source files in the proper folder:

Listing: chapter/build-management/iteration-2/compile.bat

```
javac -classpath .;junit-4.4.jar src/paystation/domain/*.java
```

getting me to *Step 4: Run all tests and see them all succeed,* as the compile executes cleanly ("the test case passes").

I have the same problem with the run-test script that complains that the TestPayStation class is not found. Thus I modify that script as well by stating the proper classpath[1].

Listing: chapter/build-management/iteration-2/run-test.bat

```
java -classpath src/paystation/domain;junit-4.4.jar^
 org.junit.runner.JUnitCore TestPayStation
```

Both scripts now execute cleanly after the classes have been moved and the iteration ends by overstriking the item on the test list.

6.3.3 Iteration 3: Adding Package Statements

So far I have only moved source code files around, I haven't actually changed the package structure. The item *add proper package statements to each class*'s *Step 1* requires me to add a simple package statement in each and every .java file in package *paystation.domain.*

```
package paystation.domain;

[original contents here]
```

The *Step 2* result is that the compile script still executes cleanly but the run-test script fails throwing a NoClassDefFoundError exception stating that TestPayStation has a wrong name. This is because the run-script invokes JUnit on TestPayStation but due to the newly introduce package statement, it has found paystation.domain.TestPayStation. The *Step 3* remedy is to change the classpath setting in the run-script:

Listing: chapter/build-management/iteration-3/run-test.bat

```
java -classpath src;junit-4.4.jar org.junit.runner.JUnitCore^
 paystation.domain.TestPayStation
```

[1]The caret symbol, ^, in the listing is a way to write two lines that are considered one line by the command line processor.

And I arrive at *Step 4: Run all tests and see them all succeed.* I am done with this iteration and I note the result on the test-list.

* ~~put classes into packages~~
* ~~define a package structure and corresponding folder structure~~
* ~~move my classes (Java files) into this structure~~
* ~~add proper package statements to each class~~
* make a compile target
* make a testing target

6.3.4 Iteration 4: Compile Target

Finally, the item *make a compile target* forces me to get rid of the compile and testing scripts and write a build description in the Ant format instead. Ant build descriptions (or "Ant buildfiles") are written in XML.

> ☞ If Ant is not installed on your system, you can find an installation guide on the book's web site, http://www.baerbak.com.

You may tell Ant which buildfile to use but if you do not, it will assume your buildfile is named `build.xml` and I will adhere to this convention. The smallest *Step 1* I can make in this situation is to make a minimal build file and make Ant run it. Ant requires that the build file defines a **project** and at least one target so I will make a "see-that-it-works" target in the pay station project. So I edit *build.xml* to contain:

```
<project name="PayStation" default="help" basedir=".">

  <target name="help">
    <echo>
Pay station build management.
    </echo>
  </target>

</project>
```

The project tag must enclose all targets, tasks, properties, etc., in the project. The attributes specify the project's name, the default target to execute, and finally the folder that Ant uses as root for all processing. Thus, I have defined the `help` target as default and Ant will process with the present folder, ".", as the root.

> ☞ You can find the final build description in Section 6.3.10 on page 96 as reference.

The `help` target, in turn, is defined by a target tag. Inside this tag, I must define the procedure i.e. all the tasks that must be executed to fulfill the target. Ant comes with a long list of build-in tasks that serve most things you want to do when managing a project, many of which are presented shortly. The first example is the `echo` task that simply prints the text inside the tags.

It is time to validate my minimal ant buildfile: I invoke Ant in a shell

```
ant
```

and the reply is:

```
Buildfile: build.xml

help:
     [echo] Pay station build management.

BUILD SUCCESSFUL
Total time: 0 seconds
```

Ant lists the targets that it executes, namely help, and I can see that the echo task was executed. Alas, this first test passes.

However, it is compiling the pay station source code that I am interested in. Ant has a `javac` task that will do the job. Unlike the command line `javac` that you get from Sun Ant's javac task compiles a complete source tree at a time. The javac task has a long list of attributes that you can set and I will only treat a few essential ones here. My first shot at a compile target is:

```
<target name="build-src">
  <javac srcdir="src">
  </javac>
</target>
```

I have to tell the `javac` task the root of the source code folder, the *srcdir* parameter. Note that this is another target than `help` so in order to make Ant execute it I must supply it as parameter when I invoke Ant from my shell:

```
ant build-src
```

and in *Step 2: Run all tests and see the new one fail,* I get a very long list of complaints

```
Buildfile: build.xml

build-src:
    [javac] Compiling 6 source files
    [javac] src\paystation\domain\TestPayStation.java:3:
       package org.junit does not exist
    [javac] import org.junit.*;
  [...]
```

In *Step 3: Make a little change,* I need to set the classpath to include the JUnit jar. Ant is a versatile tool and has a long story which means that you can actually tell the `javac` task the classpath in numerous ways. I will only show the most flexible one which includes introducing a nested `classpath` element.

```
<target name="build-src">
  <javac srcdir="src">
    <classpath>
      <pathelement location="junit-4.4.jar"/>
    </classpath>
  </javac>
</target>
```

Inside the `classpath` tags you list all elements of the classpath. Here, I only need the JUnit jar. Upon executing the target again I see that I am at *Step 4: Run all tests and see them all succeed*:

```
Buildfile: build.xml

build-src:
    [javac] Compiling 6 source files

BUILD SUCCESSFUL
Total time: 1 second
```

I got Ant to compile the source files and even get a count of how many files were compiled. As an extra validation, I can run the old run-test script and it still executes the JUnit test cases cleanly.

You may wonder, however, if I have gained anything over the simpler compile script in the previous iteration. It turns out that Ant actually performs an important processing for me, and I can see it by invoking the `build-src` once again:

```
Buildfile: build.xml

build-src:

BUILD SUCCESSFUL
Total time: 0 seconds
```

The compilation is quicker and Ant does not report any files being compiled! Why? Because Ant recursively scans the folder hierarchy and only compiles source files that have no corresponding .class file or if the class file is older than the .java file. In my case, no compilation is made at all as I did not change any source code files, and Ant only spends time to perform this analysis, not to perform any compilation. Another advantage is that Ant works transparently on common operating systems using the same syntax. Thus, even in this simple case, Ant helps in two important respects: A) it compiles entire source trees in one operation and B) it compiles source files only if it is necessary making compilation much speedier for large systems.

One last thing remains: I like all my Ant buildfiles to have the `help` target as default. This target should print a list of the build description's most important tasks along with a short explanation. This is a great help to the developers as it serves as a reminder of "what can I do." Thus I update the `help` target so it produces the following:

```
Buildfile: build.xml

help:
     [echo] Pay station build management.
     [echo] Targets:
     [echo]   build-src: Builds production code.

BUILD SUCCESSFUL
Total time: 0 seconds
```

The last aspect of the rhythm is *Step 5: Refactor to remove duplication*. As the old compile script is now "duplicated code," it is obsolete and I delete it as a cleaning up step. One more item can be removed from the list:

- ~~put classes into packages~~
- ~~define a package structure and corresponding folder structure~~
- ~~move my classes (Java files) into this structure~~
- ~~add proper package statements to each class~~
- ~~make a compile target~~
- make a testing target

6.3.5 Iteration 5: Running the Tests

The last item on the list is to run the tests. (While I will keep using the steps of the rhythm, I will no longer write them in full in the text.) Not surprisingly, Ant has a predefined task `java` that invokes the Java virtual machine on a class. `java` has numerous attributes that allows me to configure the virtual machine. As in the run-test script I really only need to supply two parameters namely the Java program to run (org.junit.runner.JUnitCore) and the test case class to execute (TestPayStation). This leads to the following new target `test`:

```
<target name="test">
  <java classname="org.junit.runner.JUnitCore">
    <arg value="paystation.domain.TestPayStation"/>
    <classpath>
      <pathelement location="junit-4.4.jar"/>
    </classpath>
  </java>
</target>
```

This time I have remembered to set the classpath. Fortunately both the `java` and `javac` use the same classpath syntax. I run the `test` target and—it fails?

```
Buildfile: build.xml

test:
     [java] JUnit version 4.4
     [java] Could not find class: paystation.domain.TestPayStation
```

What happened? Well, I forgot to provide the classpath for the pay station code itself. This is quickly remedied by updating the classpath attributed: adding another `pathelement` (line 5) pointing to the root of the new package structure.

```
1  <target name="test">
2    <java classname="org.junit.runner.JUnitCore">
3      <arg value="paystation.domain.TestPayStation"/>
4      <classpath>
5        <pathelement location="src"/>
6        <pathelement location="junit-4.4.jar"/>
7      </classpath>
8    </java>
9  </target>
```

Finally the `test` target executes cleanly and JUnit reports that all test cases pass.

Am I done? Not quite, one of the most important aspects is missing: When I run the tests I would like Ant to ensure that all source files have been compiled first! Otherwise I may make a change or a new test case, forget to compile, and then run the test cases to see a false "all tests pass" as it is the unmodified .class files I am running. You say that the `test` target *depends* upon the `build-src` task. To test that Ant does not handle this correctly at present, you can simply delete a .class file and try to execute the `test` target: JUnit complains loudly.

I need to tell Ant the dependency between the two targets. You do that in Ant by specifying the depended-on target in the *depends* attribute (line 1):

```
<target name="test"  depends="build-src">
  <java classname="org.junit.runner.JUnitCore">
    <arg value="paystation.domain.TestPayStation"/>
    <classpath>
      <pathelement location="src"/>
      <pathelement location="junit-4.4.jar"/>
    </classpath>
  </java>
</target>
```

If I delete one or all .class files and execute the `test` target (without compiling first) I get:

```
Buildfile: build.xml

build-src:
    [javac] Compiling 1 source file

test:
     [java] JUnit version 4.4
     [java] ......
     [java] Time: 0,094
     [java]
     [java] OK (9 tests)
     [java]

BUILD SUCCESSFUL
Total time: 1 second
```

That is, Ant notes that `test` depends upon `build-src` and execute this first. The `build-src` procedure analyzes the .java and .class files and only recompiles the missing file. Next, the `test` target is run. The dependency graph here is simple but as more targets are added it can become quite complex. Ant will complain if you happen to define a circular dependency like A depends-on B and B depends-on A.

It is time for step 5 of the rhythm—to refactor. I note several things: first, I can delete the run-test script, and second, the `classpath` property is duplicated code in the buildfile. Also the source code directory path *src* is written as a "magic constant" appearing several times in the buildfile. An Ant buildfile is code and I want to keep the analyzability and maintainability high so I want to get rid of this duplication.

The run-test script can simply be deleted, now that I have the new `test` target. To remove the duplication of the *src* constant I use **properties** in Ant: the ability to define a variable in one place and use it several other places. You define a variable by the `property` tag:

```
<property name="source-directory" value="src"/>
```

and usage of the variable is indicated by `${source-directory}`. The result is the refactored targets (lines 2 and 13 are changed), that both execute as intended.

```
1  <target name="build-src">
2    <javac srcdir="${source-directory}">
3      <classpath>
4        <pathelement location="junit-4.4.jar"/>
5      </classpath>
6    </javac>
7  </target>
8
9  <target name="test" depends="build-src">
10   <java classname="org.junit.runner.JUnitCore">
11     <arg value="paystation.domain.TestPayStation"/>
12     <classpath>
13       <pathelement location="${source-directory}"/>
14       <pathelement location="junit-4.4.jar"/>
15     </classpath>
16   </java>
17 </target>
```

Finally, there is the "almost" duplicated classpath. To handle a classpath as a property, Ant uses **path-like structures** and the ability to make **references**. It is similar to properties that you define once and may reference in many other places. The syntax is unfortunately a bit different from normal properties. Definitions are made by defining a `path` property and assign it a name by the `id` attribute (that are unlike normal properties *not* put into curly braces):

```
<path id="class-path">
  <pathelement location="${source-directory}"/>
  <pathelement location="junit-4.4.jar"/>
</path>
```

Next I can replace the duplicated classpath in my targets by referring to this path (lines 3 and 10 are changed):

```
1  <target name="build-src">
2    <javac srcdir="${source-directory}">
3      <classpath refid="class-path"/>
4    </javac>
5  </target>
6
7  <target name="test" depends="build-src">
8    <java classname="org.junit.runner.JUnitCore">
9      <arg value="paystation.domain.TestPayStation"/>
10     <classpath refid="class-path"/>
11   </java>
12 </target>
```

Execution shows that this refactoring also has not changed the behavior of the tasks and is thus successful.

* ~~put classes into packages~~
* ~~define a package structure and corresponding folder structure~~
* ~~move my classes (Java files) into this structure~~
* ~~add proper package statements to each class~~
* ~~make a compile target~~
* ~~make a testing target~~

I have now reached the goals that I originally set myself. However, Ant (and build management tools in general) can do much more than these simple tasks so I will devote the next few iterations on showing some very helpful features. For space reasons I will not reproduce the test list here for these iterations.

> **Exercise 6.1:** Actually Ant has a built-in `junit` task. It is classified as an optional task because the task requires libraries to be installed that are not part of the main distribution. Study the Ant documentation and rewrite the `test` target to use the `junit` task instead of calling JUnit directly.

6.3.6 Iteration 6: Separate Build Tree

If you run the `build-src` target and look in the *src/paystation/domain* folder, you will see both the .java and .class files. Thus, the folder structure contains two different (but of course highly related) aspects of my pay station system: the source code aspect and the bytecode aspect. I do not like to see them mixed because it lowers my overview of the project. I like to browse and overview the source code Java files as they are directly related to the classes that I constantly read and edit. The bytecode files, on the other hand, are only interesting for the virtual machine, and simply clutter my overview of the source code. The answer to this problem is to put the bytecode files in a separate folder structure.

> **Key Point: Separate source and build tree**
>
> *The output from the compilation process (bytecode) should be stored in a separate folder tree (the build tree) to increase the overview of the source code (the source tree).*

This build tree must of course have the same subfolder hierarchy as the source tree in order for the virtual machine to understand the package structure—but the root folder should be different. I like to put bytecode files in a build tree rooted in a folder called *build*. I can tell the `javac` task to use this folder as the destination root folder, using the `destdir` attribute (line 5):

```
1  <property name="build-directory" value="build"/>
2  [...]
3  <target name="build-src">
4    <javac srcdir="${source-directory}"
5      destdir="${build-directory}">
6      <classpath refid="class-path"/>
7    </javac>
8  </target>
```

When I execute it, however, I am informed that the *build* directory does not exist. I must tell Ant to create this directory and ensure that this is done before the compilation. In build management terminology I must create a new task (I will call it `prepare`) and set a dependency to it.

```
<target name="prepare">
  <mkdir dir="${build-directory}"/>
</target>
<target name="build-src" depends="prepare">
  <javac srcdir="${source-directory}"
    destdir="${build-directory}">
    <classpath refid="class-path"/>
  </javac>
</target>
```

If you browse the root folder after having invoked `build-src` you will see two folders, *src* and *build*, and Java source files are in the former while bytecode files are in the latter. I have achieved a much better overview and normally need not look into the *build* folder at all.

Finally, I have to fix the `test` target as it no longer can find any bytecode files. I have to update the classpath that before referred to the *src* root folder and now instead must refer the *build* folder (line 2):

```
1 <path id="class-path">
2   <pathelement location="${build-directory}"/>
3   <pathelement location="junit-4.4.jar"/>
4 </path>
```

I execute `test` and the JUnit tests are now executed correctly. Having all the bytecode files in a single folder makes it very simple to `clean` the project, that is, to ensure that the next building will indeed recompile all source files:

```
<target name="clean">
  <delete dir="${build_directory}"/>
</target>
```

A `clean` comes in handy as there are situations where Ant's way of recompiling gives a false positive, i.e. report a correct compile where there indeed is a failure. The most common situation is that you remove a Java class from your system, but unfortunately forget to remove a reference to it in another class. In this case, Ant will not discover and report a failed compilation because the .class file still exists in the *build* folder. Remember, Ant `javac` will produce a class file if the .class file is missing or out of date, it never removes .class files.

Key Point: Rebuild everything after package structure changes

Make it a habit to rebuild everything from scratch every time you remove classes or rearrange source code in the package structure.

6.3.7 Iteration 7: Make JavaDoc Documentation

Ant also makes it easy to generate the JavaDoc for the pay station system using the built in `javadoc` task. I will put the documentation into a folder named name *javadoc*:

```
[...]
<property name="javadoc-directory" value="javadoc"/>
 <[...]
<target name="javadoc" depends="prepare">
  <javadoc
    packagenames="paystation.*"
    destdir="${javadoc-directory}"
    sourcepath="${source-directory}"
    windowtitle="Pay station system">

    <classpath refid="class-path"/>
  </javadoc>
</target>
```

Exercise 6.2: Which *Obvious Implementation* changes do you have to introduce in the `prepare` and `clean` targets?

The attributes of the `javadoc` task defines the packages to document (here *paystation* and subpackages), the path to the source code files and the destination output directory. I can now browse the JavaDoc by using my web browser on *javadoc/index.html*. Done!

I am a bit disappointed however. The JavaDoc also include the JUnit test class: TestPayStation. I do not want the test cases to lower the overview and readability of the JavaDoc that is supposed to document the production code, not the test code. *Clean code that works* can be translated to *clean documentation that can be read.*

Actually, I could use some aspects of Ant to make it avoid the test classes but there is another way that enhances overview even more: I can split the source tree into two: a production code tree and a test code tree. I will do that in the next iteration.

6.3.8 Iteration 8: Separate Production and Test Tree

The Java package structure only fixes the structure of class names below a root: class *paystation.domain.TestPayStation* must be located in a folder with a *paystation/domain/TestPayStation* structure. However, the *paystation* folder can be located anywhere as long as I set the proper source and classpath attributes in the `javac` and `java` tasks.

I can use this to my advantage and increase the folder overview and analyzability by splitting the source code tree into two. I will keep the production code tree in the *src* root folder but I will move the test code into another *test* root folder. Another advantage of this is that when it comes to shipping a system to my customers I of course only want it to contain production code, not testing code. By keeping the testing code in a separate tree I can simply avoid compiling this tree when making the final software release.

Key Point: Separate production code and test code tree

The production source code and the testing source code should be stored in separate folder trees. This increases your ability to locate appropriate source code files and makes it easy to make a customer release without test code.

This requirement involves a bit of folder refactoring: making a *test* folder with the proper substructure and a move of the test case classes there. The resulting structure is shown in Figure 6.1.

Figure 6.1: Splitting the production and test code.

As always after a step, I test it, here by executing the `test` target. It fails. Only 5 files are compiled and the TestPayStation cannot be found by the java virtual machine.

☞ Take a moment to consider why this is so before reading on.

The problem is that the source files in the new source code tree are not compiled. I solve this by introducing yet another compile target namely one to compile the test tree:

```
[...]
<property name="test-source-directory" value="test"/>
[...]
<target name="build-test" depends="build-src">
  <javac srcdir="${test-source-directory}"
    destdir="${build-directory}">
    <classpath refid="class-path"/>
  </javac>
</target>
```

Note that I keep *build* as the destination folder thus it is only the source code folder that is split whereas the bytecode folder contains all the .class files.

> **Exercise 6.3:** Why does `build-test` depend upon `build-src`? Would it not be OK to make it depend upon `prepare` only? Change the dependency to find out why it does not work. You have to `clean` and then `build-test` to see the failure.

Now the old `build-src` target compiled all source code files in the project but has now been replaced by *two* targets that must be referenced in dependency lists. This is unfortunate for the standard reasons: I may forget to list it, specifications are duplicated, etc. I therefore define a new target `build-all`:

```
<target name="build-all" depends="build-src,build-test"/>
```

and add a description of it to the `help` target.

I finally have to change the dependencies of the targets that execute to state that they rely on a full compile as for instance:

```
<target name="test" depends="build-all">
  ...
```

Now the `test` target and all it depends upon works. If you run the `javadoc` target you will see that it now only lists production code classes as the `javadoc` task only refers to the production code source tree.

Done. However, one thing nags me. When I look in the project root folder I see the `build.xml` file but also the jar files. I like the improved overview of having libraries in a special library folder.

6.3.9 Iteration 9: Library folder

Now I create a folder, *lib*, in the project root folder and move the JUnit jar file there. Because I will only identify jar file using a property definition in the build description, the change to make everything work again is small (note that because Ant works across all modern computing platforms I can use the UNIX "/" as a directory separator; Ant will automatically convert to the relevant separator on the platform it is running on):

```
<property name="junit-jar" value="lib/junit-4.4.jar"/>

<path id="class-path">
  <pathelement location="${build-directory}"/>
  <pathelement location="${junit-jar}"/>
</path>
```

Done. No more items on the test list nor on my mind.

6.3.10 The Final Build Description

The resulting Ant description from the iterations.

Listing: chapter/build-management/iteration-9/build.xml

```
<!-- Build file for the Pay Station case study
-->
<project name="PayStation" default="help" basedir=".">

  <property name="source-directory" value="src"/>
  <property name="test-source-directory" value="test"/>
  <property name="build-directory" value="build"/>
  <property name="javadoc-directory" value="javadoc"/>

  <property name="junit-jar" value="lib/junit-4.4.jar"/>

  <path id="class-path">
    <pathelement location="${build-directory}"/>
    <pathelement location="${junit-jar}"/>
  </path>

  <target name="help">
    <echo>
Pay station build management.
```

```
  Targets:
    build-src: Builds production code.
    test:      JUnit test production code.
    clean:     Removes all bytecode.
    javadoc:   Generate JavaDoc.
    </echo>
  </target>

  <target name="clean">
    <delete dir="${build-directory}"/>
    <delete dir="${javadoc-directory}"/>
  </target>

  <target name="prepare">
    <mkdir dir="${build-directory}"/>
    <mkdir dir="${javadoc-directory}"/>
  </target>

  <target name="build-src" depends="prepare">
    <javac srcdir="${source-directory}"
      destdir="${build-directory}">
      <classpath refid="class-path"/>
    </javac>
  </target>

  <target name="build-test" depends="build-src">
    <javac srcdir="${test-source-directory}"
      destdir="${build-directory}">
      <classpath refid="class-path"/>
    </javac>
  </target>

  <target name="build-all" depends="build-src,build-test"/>

  <target name="test"  depends="build-all">
    <java classname="org.junit.runner.JUnitCore">
      <arg value="paystation.domain.TestPayStation"/>
      <classpath refid="class-path"/>
    </java>
  </target>

  <target name="javadoc" depends="prepare">
    <javadoc
      packagenames="paystation.*"
      destdir="${javadoc-directory}"
      sourcepath="${source-directory}"
      windowtitle="Pay station system">

      <classpath refid="class-path"/>
    </javadoc>
  </target>

</project>
```

6.4 Additional Ant Tasks

Ant comes with a lot of built-in tasks that covers many aspects of managing a large project: there are tasks to copy files, do version control, zip files, make jar files, upload files to webpages, and send e-mails. Below I will shortly outline some core activities.

6.4.1 Copying Resource Files

Modern software systems have graphical user interfaces and as such need a lot of auxiliary files to be deployed besides pure executable code: icons, sounds, graphic files, configuration files, etc. As a simple example, the MiniDraw framework (discussed in the *Frameworks* part of the book) requires that all graphics files are stored in a special folder, named *resource*, inside the *build* folder. To ensure these files are up-to-date, a `copy` task in Ant can copy the files into their proper position in the *build* folder.

```
<target name="copy-resource" depends="prepare">
  <copy todir="${buildDirectory}/${resourceDirectory}" >
    <fileset dir="${resourceDirectory}">
      <include name="*.gif"/>
    </fileset>
  </copy>
</target>
```

The copy task copies to the destination folder mentioned in the `todir` attribute and the files to copy are defined by a `fileset` tag. As you can guess, the file set has an elaborate structure to allow expressing wildcards.

6.4.2 Making a Backup

Backups are important. As most people I too learned it the hard way, losing about one month's work on a system because I used a wrong filename in a copy command. For small projects, a `zip` can do the trick (a version control system as described in Chapter 33 is a better choice for anything of even mild importance).

```
<target name="backup" depends="mkdir_backup">
  <zip zipfile="${backup}/backup.zip"
    update="true">
    <fileset dir="${basedir}">
      <include name="${src}/**"/>
      <include name="${test}/**"/>
      <include name="build.xml"/>
      <include name="${resource}/**"/>
      <include name="diary.txt"/>
    </fileset>
  </zip>
</target>
```

Note that zip also uses the fileset tag to define source files. The "**" defines the full recursive folder structure.

Exercise 6.4: The target above overwrites the same zip file, `backup.zip`, every time. Rewrite the target above so the backup file is named by the current date, like "20090319.zip". Hint: Look at the `TStamp` task.

6.4.3 Making a Jar Archive

Java systems are normally packaged into jar files which are little more than a zip archive file. Ant has therefore a `jar` task that can package a full build tree into a jar file.

```
<target name="mkdir_deploy">
   <mkdir dir="${deploy}"></mkdir>
</target>

<target name="jar"
  depends="clean,mkdir_deploy,build_src">
  <jar jarfile="${deploy}/${jarname}" basedir="${build}"/>
</target>
```

6.5 Analysis

What does build management tools do for me that I could not do using scripts? The theoretical answer is of course that ordinary scripts could have done the same thing. In practice, however, build management tools are tailored for software development and thus automate many otherwise tedious details. The result is development that is easier and more reliable. A main feature is the analysis of dependencies between tasks that ensures that all required steps are executed. Sidebar 6.1 describes how Ant is used to keep track of all the complex aspects of the production of this book.

An important benefit of using a build tool is that a lot of knowledge that is otherwise often tacit knowledge is now carefully described in the build description. In a research project I was once involved in, we had a client-server system with a large code base and a lot of development activity by many programmers. If you had not been active in the project for a week, it was almost certain that the name of the executable had changed as had the server and client setups. Thus I spent a lot of wasted time just to find out how to start the server or set up the topology. After introducing Ant I could instead simply browse the target list and quickly it became even more simple as we agreed on target names like `run-server` etc. Even if a lot of renaming was made of the server name, this was the task that would start it. Thus, build descriptions are good documentation of the production environment. This also holds in a teaching context: you can ship your full development environment in a zip file to your teacher or your team members and they are able to compile and run your project "out-of-the-box" if only you agree upon the names of the targets.

Key Point: Build descriptions becomes management documentation

Build descriptions documents how the system is built as well as describe related house-hold tasks in a single place for easy reference.

Sidebar 6.1: Ant Processing of This Book

This book is typeset using LaTeX that is an old but reliable text processing system. One of the aspects that show LaTeX's age is the way you use it—it is basically a compilation system. You write the text in standard text files using any text editor you like and you format your text using the LaTeX "typesetting language" . For instance the source code of the start of the "Analysis" section in this chapter looks like this:

```
\section{Analysis}

What does build management tools do for me that
I could not do using scripts? The theoretical answer
```

To produce PDF you "compile" the source code using the `pdflatex` compiler. The LaTeX toolbox includes programs to generate the table of contents, index, and bibliography. In addition this book refers to a lot of source code that is generated into two formats: one without class headers for inclusion in the printed book and one with class headers to be published on the web site. Thus, just as a software program, there are lots of house-holding tasks to perform, and a lot of dependencies to keep track of. All these details are handled by Ant, I only type `ant book` to produce the latest version.

On the downside, Ant is a big tool with a lot of built in tasks, each with a large set of attributes. It therefore takes quite some time to learn and unfortunately similar abstractions are often called different things. You saw one example in that the `javac` and `javadoc` tasks use different names for the source folder attribute. Another liability, in my opinion, is that XML is verbose and tedious to read and write.

I have used the ideas and the rhythm inherent in TDD to refactor the pay station system from its original script based environment to a much more advanced environment based on Ant. While some aspects of TDD cannot be applied, for instance, I do not have automated tests but must rely on manual verification, it is still the underlying rhythm of TDD (formulate small requirement, change to make it work, refactor) that I have applied to keep focus and take small steps. And you want reliable build management just as much as you want reliable programs.

6.6 Summary of Key Concepts

Agile and iterative software development rely on production and test code being compiled and executed over and over again at short intervals. It is therefore important that these repetitious tasks are automated as much as possible to avoid human errors and to increase speed. Build management tools are important tools to organize and execute these "house hold" tasks of software development.

All build tools are defined in terms of similar concepts even though their concrete syntax may vary. Build tools take a build description as input parameter and executes tasks defined therein. Typical tasks define compilation, execution, resource copy, directory manipulation, and other relevant activities in the development process. Build descriptions are written in special languages. These languages contain constructs to define properties, procedures, dependencies, and targets. The target is a name for a certain activity you want performed, like "compile everything". A given target is defined in terms of a procedure that, like a programming language procedure, states what to do and in which sequence. Properties are variables that can be declared once and used in several places in the procedures. Finally, procedures are often dependent upon each other, for instance before you may execute a program it has to have been compiled. This can be expressed as a dependency between the execution and the compilation target.

Apache Ant is a build management tool oriented towards the Java world. The Ant build description, often called a build file or build script, is formatted in XML. It contains a large set of built in tasks that can be used in procedures. Typically Ant tasks understand typical programming activities, like for instance the `javac` task can compile all files in a source code tree as a single action.

The rhythm and the principles of test-driven development have been developed for source code production. However, you can use the very same rhythm of (define small requirement, make it work, refactor) inherent in TDD when you want to modify the production environment.

Maintainability is also a function of the production environment. Having a build script aids in itself as you have a single place, the build description, that shows the recipe for building the system. Second, some key points further increase overview, like separating the production and test code trees, and ensuring that compilation output is put in a separate build tree.

6.7 Selected Solutions

Discussion of Exercise 6.1:

The `junit` task requires some jar files to be installed and the proper classpath set up. Fortunately these are of course the JUnit jar files that I have already available, and the classpath I have also set up in the iteration. This means that conversion is straightforward.

<classpath refid="class-path"/>

```
<target name="test" depends="build-all">
  <junit printsummary="yes">
    <test name="paystation.domain.TestAll"/>
    <classpath refid="class-path"/>
  </junit>
</target>
```

The "printsummary" parameter tells Ant to print some statistics on the test run:

```
test:
    [junit] Running paystation.domain.TestAll
    [junit] Tests run: 16, Failures: 0, Errors: 0,
                      Time elapsed: 0,094 sec

BUILD SUCCESSFUL
```

Discussion of Exercise 6.3:

The test case code depends upon the production code but not the other way around: for instance the Receipt interface is referenced many times in the TestPayStation class. Thus if I first do ask Ant to `clean` and next to `build-test` then the bytecode file for Receipt is missing in the *build* folder and I get a compilation error. Therefore `build-src` must be executed before `build-test`.

6.8 Review Questions

What is the purpose of a build management tool? Explain the following concepts used in build management tools: Targets, dependencies, procedures, and properties. Mention examples of each concept as they are implemented in Apache Ant. What are the benefits and liabilities of using Ant over using scripts?

Explain the similarities and differences between refactoring source code and refactoring the software production environment? Explain how the TDD rhythm can be applied in this refactoring process.

Describe the benefits of separating the build tree from the source tree. What are the benefits of separating the production and test code tree?

6.9 Further Exercises

Exercise 6.5. Source code directory:
`chapter/build-management/`

Walk in my footsteps and develop the Ant build script in a number of iterations.

Exercise 6.6. Source code directory:
`exercise/tdd/breakthrough/`

Refactor the development environment for the breakthrough production and test code (exercise 5.4) to use the Ant build management tool. Use the *rhythm* and *take small steps.*

1. Develop Ant targets to compile production and test code and execute your developed tests.
2. Refactor your targets to split the source and build tree, and further split the source tree into a production code and test code tree.
3. Use Ant to create JavaDoc for the production tree code.

Exercise 6.7:

Add a new target, `make-jar`, to the build script that generates a `paystation.jar` jar file. The jar file must contain production code only, not testcode.

Note that you cannot execute this jar file but you can verify the contents by running the jar command line tool directly, for instance

```
jar tvf paystation.jar
```

This will list the files in the jar file.

Exercise 6.8:

Ant allows files to be modified during copy. This can be used to set values in configurations files that are read by a program. For instance consider a system that reads the address of a server from an XML file containing a tag like:

```
<server>
  www.baerbak.com
</server>
```

However, during testing you may want to run both client and server on the local machine, `localhost`, but it is really tedious to manually change the string in the XML configuration file. Ant can look for strings delimited by @ in a file while copying and replace them with the value of Ant properties.

```
<server>
  @server_name@
</server>
```

1. Use the `filter` and `copy` tasks in Ant to copy a file with the above XML tag and replace the placeholder string with the value "www.baerbak.com".

Iteration 3

The First Design Pattern

This part of the book, *The First Design Pattern*, is a gentle introduction to design patterns. The path, however, is over how to handle variability in your production code when two different customers want *nearly* the same system but have minor divergences in requirements. I will also demonstrate how to introduce a design pattern by refactoring an existing design, which brings us around yet another area of testing.

Chapter	Learning Objective
Chapter 7	*Deriving Strategy Pattern.* You will learn four different techniques to handle variable behavior in the production code. Each of these are thoroughly analyzed. One of them, the compositional design approach, is an instance of the STRATEGY pattern.
Chapter 8	*Refactoring and Integration Testing.* We need to introduce the STRATEGY pattern in our production code and this chapter is about how to use TDD to do this refactoring. The refactored design allows me to introduce the concepts of integration testing and system testing.
Chapter 9	*Design Patterns – Part I.* This chapter is a historical account of patterns. It also discusses the writing template and key aspects that all patterns must describe.
Chapter 10	*Coupling and Cohesion.* Here the focus is two important metrics that correlate to design patterns and how maintainable your software is.

Deriving Strategy Pattern

Learning Objectives

Our pay station system has successfully been deployed in Alphatown. However, a new customer, Betatown, wants to buy our system but has another requirement on how rates are calculated. The learning objective of this chapter is twofold. First you will learn several different solutions to this problem and see their respective benefits and liabilities. Second, you will learn that one of the solutions, the *compositional* one, is actually the STRATEGY pattern. You will also see a special process, that I denote the ③-①-② process, in action for the first time.

During my analysis a lot of new concepts and principles will be presented. Do not worry too much if you do not get all the fine points as I will return to these principles and concepts many times during the rest of the book.

7.1 New Requirements

The pay station software has been a great success. The Alphatown municipality is satisfied. Rumors start to spread about this fantastic piece of software and before long we are facing the nightmare of all developers: new requirements! We are contacted by the municipality of the neighbor town Betatown.

As is often the case they want *"exactly the same, but with one minor change."* They want another rate policy. Betatown has had problems with cars staying too long at the parking lots so they require a *progressive rate* according to the following scheme:

1. First hour: \$1.50 (5 cents gives 2 minutes parking)
2. Second hour: \$2.00 (5 cents gives 1.5 minutes)
3. Third and following hours: \$3.00 per hour (5 cents gives 1 minute)

Note that this specification divides the time spent on the parking lot into three intervals in minutes, $[0;60]$, $]60;120]$, and $]120;\infty[$, in which the cost per minute change between 2.50, 3.33, and 5 cents. This way there is an economic benefit from using a parking lot as little as possible.

But—I am facing a challenge. I have to maintain and support software running in two different towns but most of the software's behavior is exactly the same. I am also faced with exciting business possibilities: why should it stop with only two towns? If I come up with a flexible solution that will allow me to provide whatever rate policy a town wants quickly and reliably, my product will clearly have a competitive edge!

☞ Spend some time considering how you would approach this problem before reading on. Do not try to come up with a single solution, but instead present as many different solutions as possible and for each consider their benefits and liabilities.

7.2 One Problem – Many Designs

Let me start by stating the problem more rigorously.

Problem (formulation 1): We need to develop and maintain two variants of the software system in a way that introduces the least cost and defects.

This statement directly reflects my wish for reliable and flexible software. Looking closer at the code I discover that the part of the source code that must be changed is almost surgically small:

Fragment: chapter/tdd/iteration-9/PayStationImpl.java

```
1  private int timeBought;
2
3  public void addPayment( int coinValue )
4          throws IllegalCoinException {
5    switch ( coinValue ) {
6    case 5: break;
7    case 10: break;
8    case 25: break;
9    default:
10     throw new IllegalCoinException("Invalid coin: "+coinValue);
11   }
12   insertedSoFar += coinValue;
13   timeBought = insertedSoFar / 5 * 2;
14 }
15 public int readDisplay() {
16   return timeBought;
```

The only change in the Alphatown software to make it Betatown software is the single statement, line 13, that has to be replaced by another set of statements. Such a point in the source code that I need in two (or more) different variants is termed:

Definition: Variability point

A variability point is a well-defined section of the production code whose behavior it should be possible to vary.

So, another way to formulate the problem is:

> **Problem (formulation 2):** How do I introduce having two different behaviors of the rate calculation variability point such that both the cost and the risk of introducing defects are low?

This question has many different possible answers. Here I will concentrate on four classes of solutions that are feasible in modern object-oriented languages and all widely used in practice.

1. *Source tree copy proposal:* I simply make a copy of all the source code. In one copy I maintain the Alphatown variant and in the other the Betatown variant.
2. *Parametric proposal:* I introduce a parameter that defines the town the software is running in: either Alphatown or Betatown. I only have one copy of the production code but at appropriate places (in my concrete case: in the rate calculation variability point) the code branches on this parameter to give the behavior required.
3. *Polymorphic proposal:* I can subclass the PayStationImpl and override a method that calculates the rate.
4. *Compositional proposal:* I can describe the variable behavior, rate calculation, in an interface and have classes implementing each concrete rate calculation policy. I then let the pay station call such a rate calculation object instead of performing the calculation itself.

I will treat each of these proposals in depth in the following sections.

7.3 Source Tree Copy Proposal

The probably oldest way of reusing code is based on the fact that software is expressed in *text*. Thus if a programmer faces a challenge that is very similar to something he has already solved, he can simply copy that source code text and modify it to solve the new challenge. This kind of software reuse is often called **cut'n'paste reuse**.

Thus, as I have the source code in a source code folder tree I can simply make a copy of that tree, rename the root of the tree to, say, Betatown, and overwrite the rate calculation code with the proper algorithm for the progressive rate. Figure 7.1 shows a plausible folder structure before and after a source code folder copy: the original Alphatown source code (a) is simply copied and renamed (b). As I develop code in a test-driven way, I will also copy the test cases. In my case, most of the test cases have to be rewritten because almost all of them rely on the rate policy, but in the general case, only a few test cases may have to be changed.

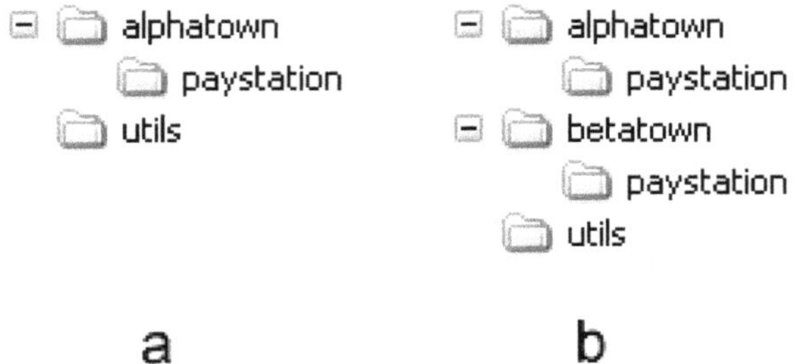

Figure 7.1: Source tree copy proposal.

This solution proposal has several obvious benefits.

- *Speed.* It is quick! It is a matter of a single copy operation, modify the test cases and let it drive the production code changes, and you are ready to ship it to the customer. This is probably *the* main reason that it is encountered so often in practice.
- *Simple.* The idea is simple and easy to explain to colleagues and new developers.
- *No implementation interference.* The two implementations do not interfere with each other. For instance, if you happen to introduce a defect in the Betatown implementation it is guaranteed that it will have no implications on the Alphatown implementation.

However, the proposal has some severe limitations. In the long run this proposal is often a real disaster because it leads to the **multiple maintenance problem**. To appreciate this problem consider a situation where I have also sold the pay station solution to some other customers, Gammatown and Deltatown and that they also only differ in the way parking time prices are calculated. Then I have four different source trees that only differ in the implementation of the behavior of single source code line number 13 in PayStationImpl. Now consider a situation in which you want to introduce a next generation pay station that can keep track of its earning: a new method amountEarned defines the responsibility of telling how much money a pay station has earned since it was last emptied.

> ☞ Spend a few minutes considering how you would introduce this new behavior in all four implementations before reading on.

There is no real easy way out of that: you have to implement the same test cases and exactly the same production code in all four source trees. This is repetitive and tedious at best, and highly prone to errors. If this is not bad enough, consider a situation where a defect is detected in this new behavior. Then the defect also has to be removed in all four code trees, one by one.

Practice shows that over time the contents of the code trees even begin to evolve into completely different directions, often because different people work on each copy and use slightly different techniques. Thus the commonality of the production code

Sidebar 7.1: Source Tree Copying in SAWOS

The SAWOS system, introduced in sidebar 2.1, existed in several variants, one for each airport in Denmark (being a small country this means less than ten). I had invested great effort in avoiding the multiple maintenance problem on the production code that dealt with the core domain namely meteorological reports. Thus I came up with a design that allowed me to keep only one production code base and handle variations by adding classes. However, I found that the most easy way to handle the initialization and configuration code (including the main method) was to keep separate directories, one for each airport, and live with the copy problem in these few source files. The development environment we used and its idea of "projects" also made it natural to go this way.

However, SAWOS evolved and many programmers participated in its development. When I left the company the setup and configuration code had grown into about 20 source code files containing 425 KB code (roughly 13,000 lines of code) and these were now maintained in eight different copies. Any defect or new requirement that was realized by code in these parts had to be analyzed and potentially coded in each of the eight copies. It required extreme care to do this properly. I usually made a change work in one airport's software and when my manual testing told me it worked I would then copy the changes to the source code of the other airport. Even a simple mistake as misunderstanding what file from what airport I was looking at in the editor could introduce defects—you get quite dizzy of looking at nearly identical source code in eight copies!

replicas begins to erode and they drift apart. It becomes more and more difficult to apply the same defect removal techniques on all variants, and after a while it is more or less like maintaining a set of completely different applications: the analysis must be made anew for each copy even for the same defect! This of course makes the maintenance costs very high.

To sum up, the source tree copy proposal is quick but very dangerous. A short war story about source tree copy can be found in sidebar 7.1.

7.4 Parametric Proposal

Another solution is to use an **if** statement that selects the proper code block to execute based upon which city the code is running in. A parametric proposal represents a plausible and often used solution. Looking again over the price calculation code:

```
[...]
timeBought = insertedSoFar * 2 / 5;
```

it is obvious that we simply enclose it in an if statement where the code above gets executed in the Alphatown variant and something different in the Betatown variant.

As the requirement follows the town in question it is natural to invent a town parameter:

```
public class PayStationImpl implements PayStation {
  [...]
  public enum Town { ALPHATOWN, BETATOWN }
  private Town town;

  public PayStationImpl( Town town ) {
    this.town = town;
  }
  [...]
}
```

and then introduce the variability handling in the addPayment method (lines 11–15):

```
1  public void addPayment( int coinValue )
2          throws IllegalCoinException {
3    switch ( coinValue ) {
4    case 5:
5    case 10:
6    case 25: break;
7    default:
8      throw new IllegalCoinException("Invalid coin: "+coinValue);
9    }
10   insertedSoFar += coinValue;
11   if ( town == Town.ALPHATOWN ) {
12     timeBought = insertedSoFar * 2 / 5;
13   } else if ( town == Town.BETATOWN ) {
14     [the progressive rate policy code]
15   }
16 }
```

Exercise 7.1: Showing the solution before having written the test cases is of course not a TDD approach. Outline a plan of the iterations involved in a test-driven development process: What problem would you address first, what test cases would you look at and in which order? Next, use TDD to develop the parametric proposal.

A concrete pay station object of course has to have its town attribute set in order for it to behave correctly. Thus the setUp method must be rewritten in the JUnit test case:

```
public void setUp() {
  ps = new PayStationImpl( PayStationImpl.Town.ALPHATOWN );
}
```

Note that a parametric proposal can come in "many shapes", for instance you can parameterize a system in many different ways: accept a parameter as argument when starting the program, reading the parameter from a property file, accessing a key-value in the registry, reading from a database, using conditional compilation in C-type languages, etc., but they all basically follow the same principle as I have outlined here.

7.4.1 Analysis

Analyzing this proposal reveals that it has several advantages. The benefits are:

- *Simple.* Conditionals are easy to understand and often one of the first language constructs introduced to new learners of programming. Thus the parametric idea is easy to describe to other developers.
- *Avoids the multiple maintenance problem.* There is only one code base to maintain for both Alphatown and Betatown. Thus a defect in common behavior can be fixed once and for all. As argued above most of the pay station's production code is identical for both towns and this will therefore make bug fixing less expensive and less prone to errors. Also new features for the pay station that both towns can benefit from is also less costly to develop as only one production code base is affected by added code and new tests.

The proposal, however, has also some liabilities most of which deal with long term maintainability. I will list them here and go through them in greater detail below.

- *Reliability concerns.* The new requirement is handled by *change by modification* that has a risk of introducing new defects.
- *Analyzability concerns.* As more and more requirements are handled by parameter switching, the production code becomes less easy to analyze.
- *Responsibility Erosion.* The pay station has, without much notice, been given an extra responsibility.

Reliability concerns. One liability of the parametric solution compared to the source tree copy proposal is that I have to *change in the existing production code* that is already released and operational in Alphatown. Thus there is a risk that I introduce defects in the software for Alphatown even though my intention is only to make the software run in Betatown as well. Defects are not introduced into production code by spontaneous creation—they are introduced because developers physically modify the source code text. As a logical consequence, the less I ever modify a class, the higher is the probability that it will remain free of defects. This is an important concept that I will call:

> **Definition: Change by modification**
>
> *Change by modification* is behavioral changes that are introduced by modifying existing production code.

My automated test cases, of course, reduce the risk of introducing defects compared to a situation where I am relying on manual, sporadic, or even no testing. Still, tests can only show the presence of defects, never that they are absent.

The main problem with the parametric proposal compared to the next two proposals, polymorphic and compositional, is that any new rate structure requirement forces me to modify the code over and over again. The problem is that *I must change pay station code every time a new rate model must be implemented.* That is, when Gammatown wants to buy our pay station but asks for a third kind of rate structure I have no options but to modify the implementation for the third time.

```
[...]
if ( town == Town.ALPHATOWN ) {
  timeBought = insertedSoFar * 2 / 5;
} else if ( town == Town.BETATOWN ) {
  [BetaTown implementation]
} else if ( town == Town.GAMMATOWN ) {
  [GammaTown implementation]
}
```

When Deltatown wants to buy the pay station, I have to change the code the fourth time, and so on. Thus, any such new requirement is associated with the risk of introducing defects, and the necessary cost of avoiding them: testing, code reviewing, etc. The polymorphic and compositional proposals, described later, can to a large extent avoid this problem.

Analyzability concerns. Analyzability (see page 31) is the capability of the software to be diagnosed for defects. This property is of course closely related to a developer's ability to understand the code that he or she reads. At this point in time, there is only a single *if-else* that is quite obvious. My concern is if the number of cases starts growing as I hinted at in the previous section. If I need to handle a large set of variants using switches, then it becomes difficult to "see the forest for all the trees." If the amount of variant switching code, all the ifs, outnumbers the code associated with the stated requirements, the rate calculations, then analyzability suffers greatly. This problem is commonly referred to as **code bloat**: code that is unnecessarily difficult to read, long, or slow. I will return to this point in later chapters when the number of variants has grown.

Responsibility Erosion. The last problem is not as much a code issue as it is an issue regarding how we design and "think" software. One major problem with the parametric proposal is that it sneaks in another responsibility into our pay station. I will discuss the concept of "responsibility" at great length in later chapters but let us just think of responsibility as "something that the pay station is required to do."

The original Alphatown pay station's responsibilities are described in the interface and designed as:

PayStation (as-designed)

- Accept payment
- Calculate parking time
- Handle transactions (buy, cancel)
- Know time bought, earning
- Print receipt

But looking over our parameterized code we discover that another responsibility has sneaked in without much attention:

PayStation (as-built)

- Accept payment
- Calculate parking time
- Handle transactions (buy, cancel)
- Know time bought, earning
- Print receipt
- **Handle variants of the product**

Sidebar 7.2: Conditional Compilation in GCC

The GNU Compiler Collection (GCC 2009) is a collection of open source compilers for a number of languages, most prominent C and C++ as they were the origin of the project. GCC is able to compile the set of supported languages to a large set of operating systems and CPUs: it must cope with a large set of variations. GCC is written in C and has inherited the C tradition of handling variations by using preprocessor directives. For instance if a certain variable is only interesting for some compiler variant then you can set a variable like `HAVE_cc0` to either true or false and then the preprocessor will feed the compiler with source code depending on switches in the code, like:

```
static int
combine_instructions (rtx f, unsigned int nregs)
{
  rtx insn, next;
#ifdef HAVE_cc0
  rtx prev;
#endif
```

will either have or not have the declaration `rtx prev;` compiled into the executable.

I did a count on release 4.1.1 of GCC and there are a total of 4079 lines with an #ifdef in the source code. The `HAVE_cc0` alone is switched upon in 83 places in 22 different source files.

A study by Ernst et al. (2002) showed that about 8.4% of the source code lines on average in 26 Unix software packages written in C were preprocessor directives.

Thus, the pay station now "does something more" than it was originally designed for. Just as with code bloat this problem also has a tendency to sneak in on your design without you really noticing. But it is a bad tendency because it drives your design towards a procedural design where a large class seems to suck up all functionality in the system as it does all the decision making and processing. This phenomenon is also often met in practice—it is called **The Blob** or *The God class* (Brown et al. 1998). Such classes are difficult to understand, to modify, and to reuse. My advice is to keep track of the responsibilities each object has, keep the number small, and be very careful about introducing code that sneaks in additional responsibilities.

7.5 Polymorphic Proposal

The underlying theme of this book is the object-oriented paradigm, so it is obvious that I must consider using one of the most prominent features of OO languages: polymorphism and subclassing.

Subclassing lets me define a subclass and override methods. Thus to introduce a new way of calculating the rate I can override the addPayment method. Unfortunately, this would also force me to duplicate the coin type checking code and I have already discussed the negative consequences of the multiple maintenance problem. Therefore my proposal is to encapsulate the rate calculation by invoking a protected method, calculateTime (see Figure 7.2 and line 11 in the listing below). This method (lines 18–20) can then be overridden in a subclass PayStationProgressiveRate.

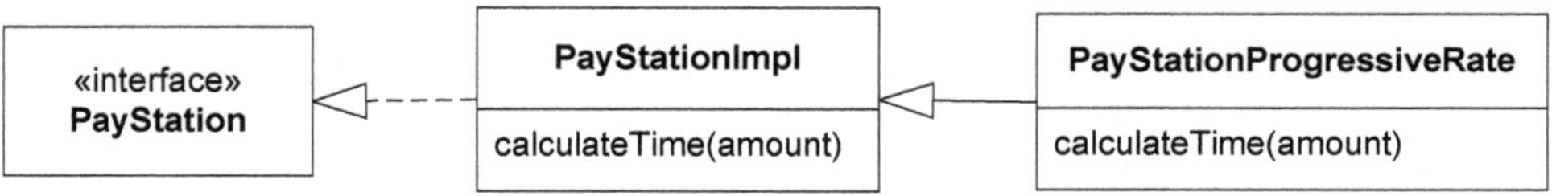

Figure 7.2: Subclassing proposal for new rate calculation.

```
1  public void addPayment( int coinValue )
2          throws IllegalCoinException {
3    switch ( coinValue ) {
4    case 5:
5    case 10:
6    case 25: break;
7    default:
8      throw new IllegalCoinException("Invalid coin: "+coinValue);
9    }
10   insertedSoFar += coinValue;
11   timeBought = calculateTime(insertedSoFar);
12 }
13 /** calculate the parking time equivalent to the amount of
14     cents paid so far
15     @param paidSoFar the amount of cents paid so far
16     @return the parking time this amount qualifies for
17 */
18 protected int calculateTime(int paidSoFar) {
19   return paidSoFar * 2 / 5;
20 }
```

Note that this is a refactoring. The external behavior has not changed but the internal structure has improved with respect to the upcoming addition of code to handle an additional rate structure. Once I get this Alphatown refactoring working as indicated by all test cases passing, I can implement the Betatown subclass.

Exercise 7.2: Outline a plan over iterations for a test-driven development of the polymorphic proposal. Next, develop the polymorphic proposal using TDD.

7.5.1 Analysis

Analyzing this proposal shows me that it is an improvement in many ways compared to the parametric proposal. Below I summarize benefits and liabilities for easy reference before explaining the details. To summarize the benefits, they are:

- *Avoid multiple maintenance problem.* I only have one code base which is a good property as already argued.
- *Reliability concern.* The production code has once and for all been prepared for any new rate policy to be required later.

- *Code analyzability.* This proposal does not suffer from code bloat, you have to read less code to understand a variant.

But in summary the proposal has a fair number of liabilities:

- *Increased number of classes.* Every new rate policy will introduce a new subclass.
- *Inheritance relation spent on single type of variation.* I cannot use the inheritance relation to handle other types of variation.
- *Reuse across variants difficult.* It turns out to be cumbersome to reuse the algorithms defined by one variant in another.
- *Compile-time binding.* The binding between the particular rate policy and the pay station is defined at compile time.

Let us look at these benefits and liabilities in more detail.

Reliability concern. As with the parametric solution I have to modify the production code: I have to introduce both a definition and a call of the calculateTime method, and I have to move code from the addPayment method into the new calculateTime method. The question is then: is the polymorphic solution just as bad as the parametric? The answer is *no*. There is namely one big difference. The modification can be considered the *last* with regards to new requirements to rate calculation. To see why, consider that Gammatown requires a third rate policy, different from the two I have already implemented.

☞ Take a moment to consider how you would implement the 3rd unique rate policy requirement in the polymorphic proposal.

The advantage is that it can be implemented *without* any changes to class PayStationImpl. It only requires *adding a new subclass*. And this applies to all new rate structure requirements that we can think of: Any new requirement adds a class, it does not modify any existing ones. I will term this way of handling change:

Definition: **Change by addition**

Change by addition is behavioral changes that are introduced by adding new production code instead of modifying existing.

Change by addition is important, because I have no fear of introducing defects in existing products as they do not use any of the code I have added. Consider for a second that you have a large system that can be configured for 50 different product variants. Next consider that you must add a variant number 51. Which strategy would make you feel most confident that the existing 50 variants still behave correctly: Strategy 1: by adding a new class (which, of course, is only used in the new variant 51), or strategy 2: by modifying several existing classes? Well, strategy 1 has no risk of introducing defects in existing products while strategy 2 certainly has...

Another way of characterizing *change by addition* that you may come across is the **open/closed principle**. This principle says that software should be open for extension but closed for modification. Meyer (1988) is generally credited as having originated the term, however his focus (being in the golden days of object-oriented inheritance) was on the polymorphic approach.

Analyzability. The polymorphic proposal does not suffer from code bloat. In contrast to the parametric proposal where new rate requirements lead to ever increasing conditionals inside the same class the structure of addPayment is defined once and for all. Thus when I in the future get the 43rd unique requirement for a rate structure I can safely make a new variant without touching any of the code that is currently running in the pay stations of Alphatown.

Also, the change the new requirement has introduced is nicely localized in a single class which makes it easy to spot. As the two products are now handled by separate classes instead of by conditional statements there is no code bloat.

However, the proposal also has its fair share of liabilities:

Increased number of classes. If there is a large number of rate algorithms that I must support, it will directly lead to a large number of classes—one for each rate policy. Thus the developer has to overview a large set of classes in his development environment that could potentially be overwhelming and confusing, especially to new developers on the project. You may argue that I have traded *complexity in the code* with *complexity in the class structure*.

Inheritance relation spent on single type of variation. Java and C# only support single inheritance of implementation: a class can only have one superclass. Here I have "wasted" this scarce resource on one particular type of variation, namely variations in the rate structure. This is obvious from the somewhat odd name that I gave the subclass: PayStationProgressiveRate. It sounds a bit disturbing, does it not? I have coded the theme of variation, rate structure, directly into the class name???

Customers often demand variations across different aspects of the product. Maybe some customers want another type of information printed on the receipt, maybe some request that the parking expiration time is displayed instead of minutes parking time bought, maybe others require that each buy transaction is logged into a database, etc. Supporting many customers' different requirements may lead to a subclass called PayStationProgressiveRateDatabaseLoggingHourMinuteDisplayOptionMobilePhone-Payment. Of course, this sounds like a joke, but the point is that single inheritance is not a good option for supporting several types of variations. I will return to this problem in the next section, and give a theoretical treatment of it in Chapter 17.

Reuse across variants difficult. The polymorphic solution also begins to fail when it comes to making combinations of previously coded solutions. Consider that Gammatown wants to buy our pay station and want a rate structure similar Alphatown's during weekdays but similar to Betatown's during weekends. The problem is that I have already written the two rate calculation algorithms—some of it in the original PayStationImpl and some in PayStationProgressiveRate and I of course do not want to duplicate code as it leads to the multiple maintenance problem.

Exercise 7.3: Consider how you would support this demand using the polymorphic proposal.

The bottom-line is that it is actually a bit cumbersome to support this demand and any solution will require quite a bit of refactoring and modification to the existing source code. I will treat this problem in detail in Chapter 11.

Compile-time binding. The relation between a superclass and a subclass is expressed explicitly in the source code: I directly write

```
public class PayStationProgressiveRate extends PayStationImpl
```

This means that the object instance that results from a **new** PayStationProgressiveRate() can never over its lifetime change the way that it calculates the rate. *It cannot change behavior at run-time.*

☞ Is this also the case for the source code copy and parametric proposals?

Consider a request from our Betatown costumer that they are disappointed with the rate structure and prefer to use that of Alphatown after all. If I look at the objects that actually execute out in the pay stations then in the parametric solution I could actually make this change at run-time: all it takes is to set the town variable in the pay station object to a new value. This is not so for the polymorphic proposal: the object can never change behavior. If I insist on a run-time change, I would have to delete the object and replace it with a new instance with the PayStationImpl class. The problem may seem a bit absurd for the pay station case. Most likely the software will be shut down for maintenance in order to make such a change anyway. However, in many other types of software the ability to change behavior while running is desirable.

The bottom-line is that inheritance is a static binding that is inflexible when it comes to making behavioral changes while programs execute. If this is not important, I of course have no problem in this respect. However, often it *is* important that software can change behavior while executing.

7.6 Compositional Proposal

The fourth proposal I denote *compositional* as it composes behavior: it lets objects *collaborate* so their *combined* effort provide the required behavior—instead of letting a single abstraction struggle with doing it all by itself as was the case with both the parametric and polymorphic solution. This "combined effort" viewpoint is one of the primary aims of this book and requires a special mind set when designing software and thinking in terms of software. However, as I will argue in this section, once it is understood and applied it is extremely powerful and will help you design very flexible object-oriented software.

But—I will start the analysis in a somewhat different place. Let us look at the *responsibilities* that our original pay station has.

PayStation

- Accept payment
- Calculate parking time based on payment
- Know earning, parking time bought
- Print receipts
- Handle buy and cancel transactions

Any class implementing the PayStation interface is free to provide concrete behavior as long as these responsibilities are met. We can see that all the rate requirements I have introduced so far only deals with one of the responsibilities on the list, namely the item: *Calculate parking time based on payment*. Neither Alphatown, Betatown, nor Gammatown have defined requirements that require me to change behavior associated with the four other responsibilities: *Accept payment*, *Know earning, parking time bought*, etc.

This important analysis tells me why the source-tree copy and parametric proposals have the property that I have to modify code instead of add code: as the code that handles the parking time calculation responsibility is completely handled by the very same abstraction that also serves the other responsibilities I have no other option but to modify it.

So: What do we do about that? The compositional answer is to *divide the responsibilities over a set of objects and let them collaborate*. That is: I move the responsibility *Calculate parking time based on payment* away from the pay station abstraction itself and put it into a new abstraction whose only purpose in life is to serve just this one responsibility. I will describe this abstraction and its responsibility by an interface and I end up with the UML class diagram in Figure 7.3 where the responsibilities are marked in the class box. Thus the variability point will look something like (the code will be treated in detail in the next chapter):

```
[...]
insertedSoFar += coinValue;
timeBought = someOtherObject.calculateTime(insertedSoFar);
```

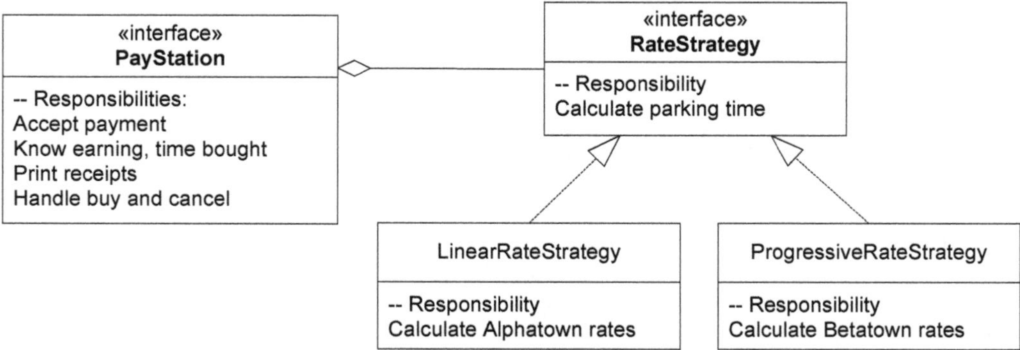

Figure 7.3: Dividing the responsibilities between two abstractions.

The Alphatown variant will use one particular implementation (LinearRateStrategy) of this interface that implements the old linear rate policy, while the Betatown variant will use another (ProgressiveRateStrategy) that implements the new rate requirements. The interaction between the pay station object and the rate strategy object

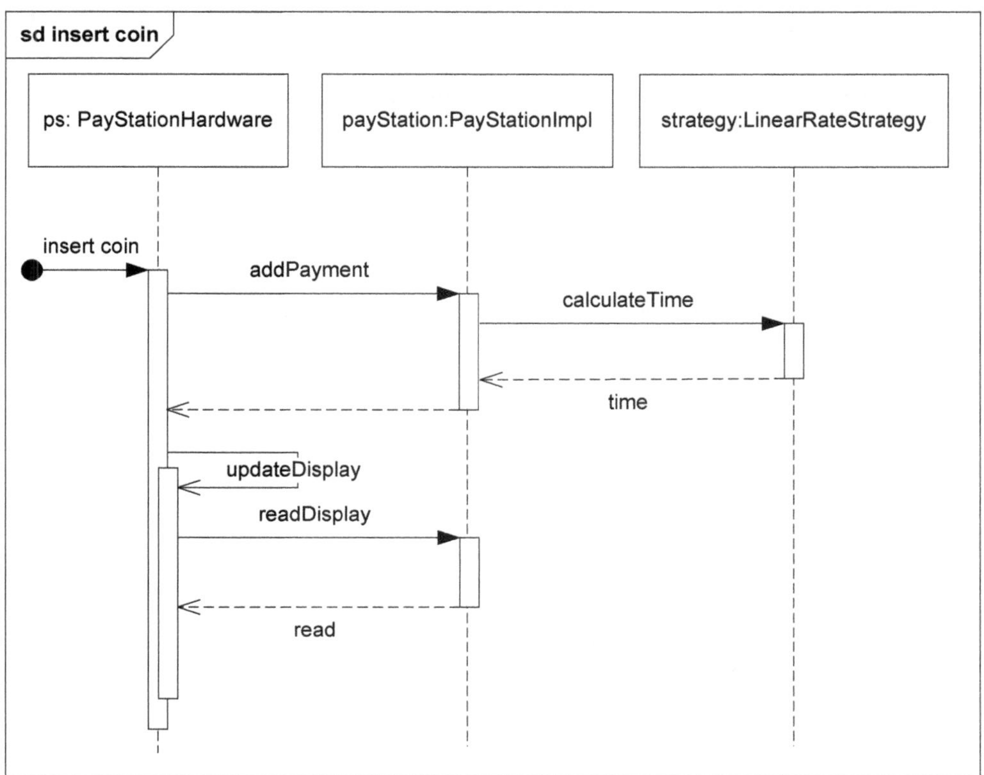

Figure 7.4: Delegating rate calculation to a delegate.

is seen in Figure 7.4. The overall behavior of the pay station when accepting coins becomes a *combined* effort between the pay station implementation and the object implementing the rate calculation. That is, instead of one object being involved in handling a request, two objects collaborate to achieve the desired behavior. This is called delegation.

Definition: **Delegation**

In delegation, two objects collaborate to satisfy a request or fulfill a responsibility. The behavior of the receiving object is partially handled by a subordinate object, called the **delegate**.

In the pay station, rate calculation is delegated to the rate calculation object. I often call this delegation based way of getting work done for *let someone else do the dirty job!* I have called the interface RateStrategy because objects implementing it are defining a certain strategy for calculating rates. As you will see shortly, there is also another reason for the name.

7.6.1 Analysis

The compositional proposal has a number of nice properties with regards to reliability and flexibility. I will outline benefits and liabilities in an overview form here for easy reference and discuss each point in depth below.

Benefits:

- *Reliability.* The pay station has been refactored once and for all with respect to rate calculations, and new rate structures can be handled only by adding more classes.
- *Run-time binding.* The binding between the pay station and its associate rate calculation can be changed at run-time.
- *Separation of responsibilities.* Responsibilities are clearly separated and assigned to easily identifiable abstractions in the design.
- *Separation of testing.* As the responsibilities have been separated I can actually test rate calculations and core pay station functionality independently.
- *Variant selection is localized.* The code that decides what particular variant of rate calculation to use is in one spot only.
- *Combinatorial.* We can introduce other types of variability without interfering with the rate calculation variability.

Liabilities:

- *Increased number of classes and interfaces.* The number of classes and interfaces has grown in comparison to the original design.
- *Clients must be aware of strategies.* The selection of which rate policy to use is no longer in the pay station but still someone has to make this decision. Variant selection is moved to the client objects.

Reliability. The compositional proposal has the property that new functionality is defined by *change by addition* instead of *change by modification*. Thus the advantages that I described in the analysis of the polymorphic proposal are valid here as well.

Run-time binding. The compositional proposal defines a run-time binding between the pay station and its rate calculation behavior: if we want a particular pay station instance to perform rate calculations in another way it is simply a matter of changing the object reference rateStrategy—just as simple as changing the value of the town variable in the parametric proposal. Note, however, that this is possible because the rate strategies do not store any state information. In the general case, strategies can be changed at run-time if they are stateless.

Exercise 7.4: Sketch the design changes and implementation changes that are necessary in order to allow the pay station to change rate structure while it is executing.

Separation of Responsibilities. Responsibilities are clearly separated and expressed in interfaces. This has several implications.

First, it counters the tendency towards "The Blob". Instead of one object trying to get everything done by itself, two objects have divided the work into manageable parts and each take on a more specific assignment: *"You make the rate calculations, and I will handle accepting coins and making the transaction."*

Second, it is clearer where a defect is located. Defects *do* make it into the final product and when those bug reports start ticking in from the users, a clear division of responsibilities is the first guideline for locating it: *"They say the rate calculation is wrong, thus it must be in the RateStrategy implementation there is a defect"* or *"No problem with the rate calculations, so the defect cannot be in the RateStrategy implementation."*

Third, it provides more readable and navigable source code when responsibilities are clearly stated and expressed. You know what kind of behavior is associated with interfaces and implementing classes—and these are distinct objects in your class browser and file structure. Contrast this to the parametric proposal where *all* behavior—variant selection, coin acceptance, rate calculation—is mixed up in the same class.

Separation of testing. I now have two interfaces with two implementing classes. This allows me to test the two implementations independently. I will elaborate on this point in detail in Chapter 8.

Variant selection in one place only. There is no place in the source code that deals with deciding the rate policy to use—the pay station object simply delegates rate calculations to whatever RateStrategy object it is configured with. Contrast this with the parametric proposal where there is code associated with the decision both at the initialization point (the town parameter in the constructor call) and in the pay station code (the conditionals in the rate calculation code).

You say that the decision is **localized** in the code. The opposite situation, when the decision is not localized, is problematic as you have to look in many different places in your code to make a change, and chances are that you overlook one or a few of these places. It is also difficult to ensure that a change is applied consistently.

I also note that the decision of what rate calculation to use is made during the initialization of the pay station object, that is, early in the program's lifetime and "near" the program's main method. This way all the setup of the system is grouped in the same part of the code. This also leads to code that is more easy to read and understand.

Combinatorial. I have not used implementation inheritance in the compositional proposal. Thus the generalization/specialization relation is still "free" to be used. The main benefit of the combinatorial proposal is that it does not get in the way of varying other types of behavior. I can apply the same compositional technique to vary, say, the coin values that are accepted. I will return to this important property in depth later in the book.

There are some liabilities as well.

Increased number of classes and interfaces. A concern is the introduction of a new interface, RateStrategy, as well as the two implementing classes. Thus the number of source files that a developer has to overview grows which has a negative impact on analyzability. I will discuss how to counter this effect in Chapter 18.

Clients must be aware of strategies. If the selection of which concrete RateStrategy instance to use is made in the pay station object itself, then this solution is no better than the parametric one: you end up with conditional statements in the pay station production code itself. Thus the pay station object must be told which rate strategy object to use. Thus the client object (typically the one that instantiates the pay station object) has to know about RateStrategy. This can also make it more difficult for a developer to overview the system.

7.7 The Compositional Process

The last proposal, the compositional proposal, is actually an example of using the STRATEGY pattern. Before I describe STRATEGY, let me sum up the line of reasoning that lead to it. The argumentation went along these lines:

- *I identified some behavior that varied.* The rate calculation behavior of the pay station is variable depending on which town the station is located in. Furthermore I can expect this behavior to be variable for new customers that buy the pay station.
- *I stated a responsibility that covered the variable behavior and encapsulated it by expressing it as an interface.* The RateStrategy interface defines the responsibility to *calculate parking time* by defining the method calculateTime.
- *I get the full pay station behavior by delegating the rate calculation responsibility to a delegate.* Now the pay station provides its full behavior as a result of collaboration between itself and an object specializing in rate calculations, either an instance of LinearRateStrategy or ProgressiveRateStrategy.

I will call this three step line of reasoning the ③-①-② process. The numbers refer to three principles for flexible design that were originally stated in the introduction to the first book on design patterns, *Design Patterns: Elements of Reusable Object-Oriented Software* (Gamma et al. 1995). In this book the principles are numbered 1–3 but they are applied in another order: The ③-①-② process first applies the third principle (find variability), then the first (use interface), and finally the second (delegate), hence the reason that I have chosen this odd numbering. I will discuss these principles in great detail in Chapter 16.

This collaboration mind set is a fruitful one in object-oriented design and is actually familiar to everybody working in a company, a public institution, or living in a family. Work is done by coordinating the collaboration of different people with different competences and skills. One person cannot perform all tasks but has to delegate responsibility and work to others. A person having too many concrete tasks to do leads to stress, making errors, and poor performance. *Objects are no different...*

7.8 The Strategy Pattern

The ③-①-② process and the ideas of identifying, encapsulating, and delegating variable behavior has resulted in a design with a number of desirable properties—and some liabilities of course. The resulting design is actually an example of the design pattern STRATEGY. STRATEGY is a pattern that addresses the problem of encapsulating a family of algorithms or business rules, and allows implementations of these algorithms to vary independently from the client that uses them. In our case, the business rule is calculation of rates.

The STRATEGY pattern's properties are summarized in the design pattern box 7.1 on page 130. The format used is explained in more detail in Chapter 9. An important aspect of any design pattern is the list of benefits and liabilities of using it to solve your particular design problem. The design pattern box only lists a few keywords but the discussion above is of course the comprehensive version of this.

7.9 Summary of Key Concepts

Often behavior in software systems must come in different variants. The requirements for these variants may stem from customers that have special needs (like the new customer of our pay station system), from us wanting to be able to run (and sell) a system on various operating systems or using various hardware and software configurations, or from the development team itself that needs to execute the system in "testing mode" and/or without actual hardware connected. The points in the production code that must exhibit variable behavior in different variants are called *variability points*. Variants can be handled in different ways but they are all basically variations over four different themes:

- *Source code copy solution.* You copy parts of or the entire software production code and simply replace the code in the variability points.
- *Parametric solution.* You enter conditional statements around the variability points. The conditions branch on a configuration parameter identifying the configuration.
- *Polymorphic solution.* You encapsulate the variability points in instance methods. These can then be overridden in subclasses, one for each required variant.
- *Compositional solution.* You encapsulate the variability points in a well-defined interface and use delegation to compose the overall behavior. Concrete classes, implementing the interface, define each variant's behavior.

Often compositional solutions arise from a line of design thinking that is called the ③-①-② process in this book. It consists of three steps: first you *identify some behavior that needs to vary.* You next abstract the behavior into *a responsibility that covers the variable behavior and express it as an interface.* Finally, you *use delegation to compose the full behavior.*

The STRATEGY pattern is a compositional solution to the problem of supporting variations in algorithms or business rules. The algorithm is encapsulated in an interface and the client delegates to implementations of this interface.

The first comprehensive overview of design patterns was the seminal book by Gamma et al. (1995). The *intent* sections of design pattern boxes in this book are in most cases literate copies from this book and reproduced with permission. The ③-①-② process is inspired by Shalloway and Trott (2004).

7.10 Selected Solutions

Discussion of Exercise 7.3:

The problem is that there are no elegant solutions! I will discuss a set of potential solutions in detail in Section 11.4 but all of them turn out to be rather clumsy.

Discussion of Exercise 7.4:

As the calculation of rates is delegated to an instance implementing the RateStrategy interface, all you have to do is to change the stored reference to refer to a new instance that implements another rate calculation algorithm.

7.11 Review Questions

Outline the four different proposals to support two products with varying rate structure: What is the idea, what coding is involved? Explain what a variability point is.

What are the benefits and liabilities of the source tree copy proposal? The parametric proposal? The polymorphic proposal? The compositional proposal?

What is *change by addition*? What is *change by modification*?

What are the three steps, ③ ① and ②, involved in the compositional proposal process?

What is the STRATEGY pattern? What problem does it address and what solution does it suggest? What are the objects and interfaces involved? What are the benefits and liabilities?

7.12 Further Exercises

Exercise 7.5:

The reputation of our reliable and flexible pay station has reached Europe and Denmark and a Danish county wants to buy it. However, it should accept Danish coin values and of course use an appropriate rate structure. The requirements are:

- Danish coins have values: 1, 2, 5, 10, and 20 Danish kroner.
- 1 Danish krone should equal 7 minutes parking time.

1. Use the ③ ① ② process to identify and design a compositional solution to the coin type aspect that needs to vary in our pay station product.
2. Another Danish county wants also to buy our system but they want another rate policy: 1 Danish krone should equal 6 minutes parking time, however if the car stays for more than 2 hours then a krone only buys 5 minutes parking time. Analyze if this requirement will affect any code that was introduced by the above requirement. Can the two types of requirements, rate policy and coin validation, be varied independent of each other?

Exercise 7.6:

A software shop wants to produce a calendar application for the international market. One important requirement is the ability for the calendar to mark public holidays for the given country in the calendar, for instance by giving public holidays a different background color in a graphical week overview.

Sketch how this requirement could be handled by the four different proposals for handling variability. Consider that the calendar must handle at least US, UK, French, and Danish public holidays, and allow easy integration of other nations' public holidays.

[7.1] Design Pattern: Strategy

Intent Define a family of business rules or algorithms, encapsulate each one, and make them interchangeable. Strategy lets the algorithms vary independently from clients that use it.

Problem Your product must support variable algorithms or business rules and you want a flexible and reliable way of controlling the variability.

Solution Separate the selection of algorithm from its implementation by expressing the algorithm's responsibilities in an interface and let each implementation of the algorithm realize this interface.

Structure:

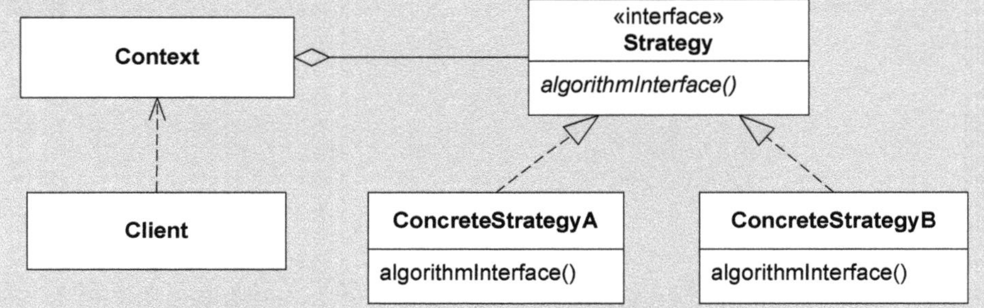

Roles **Strategy** specifies the responsibility and interface of the algorithm. **ConcreteStrategies** defines concrete behavior fulfilling the responsibility. **Context** performs its work for **Client** by delegating to an instance of type **Strategy**.

Cost - Benefit The benefits are: *Strategies eliminate conditional statements.* It is an *alternative to subclassing.* It facilitates *separate testing* of **Context** and **ConcreteStrategy**. Strategies may be changed at run-time (if they are stateless).

The liabilities are: *Increased number of objects. Clients must be aware of strategies.*

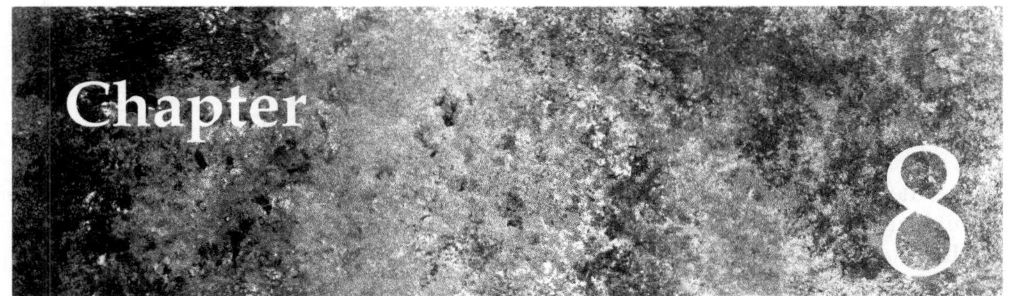

Refactoring and Integration Testing

Learning Objectives

Updating the pay station design with the STRATEGY pattern also pose a challenge. In this chapter you will learn a *small steps* approach to refactoring as well as see the *Triangulation* principle in action on a more complex problem. As the system is now composed of three parts, two rate strategies and one pay station, you will also learn about the different levels in testing and the difference between unit and integration testing in particular.

8.1 Developing the Compositional Proposal

How should I introduce the Betatown rate structure? At the onset I have two options.

- Write test cases that tests the behavior of Betatown rate structure and get the new compositional design as well as the rate calculation algorithm in place.
- Refactor the existing pay station to use a compositional design first for Alphatown. Next write test cases and algorithm for the Betatown rate structure.

The mantra of TDD is *take small steps* because all too often we overestimate the steps we can take without falling. The first approach is a single, large, step while the second is two, smaller, steps. TDD tells me to follow the latter strategy.

So I define an initial test list

∗ refactor Alphatown to use a compositional design
∗ handle rate structure for Betatown

8.1.1 Iteration 1: Refactoring

Thus the challenge facing me is to refactor the pay station design in a way that I am confident that I have not introduced any defects in the process.

The important punch line here is: *I already have the Alphatown test cases* that can minimize the risk that I accidentally introduce defects while refactoring the design. The JUnit test cases for Alphatown's rate structure are written without any assumptions of the underlying pay station implementation—they only assume the PayStation interface.

I identify the following plan of steps that I will likely pursue:

i Introduce the RateStrategy interface.

ii Refactor PayStationImpl to use a reference to a RateStrategy instance for calculating rate (test to see it fails.)

iii Move the rate calculation algorithm to a class implementing the RateStrategy interface.

iv Refactor the pay station setup to use a concrete RateStrategy instance.

Step i) Introduce a RateStrategy interface: I introduce a suitable interface RateStrategy that expresses the responsibility for calculating parking time:

Listing: chapter/refactor/iteration-1/src/paystation/domain/RateStrategy.java

```
package paystation.domain;
/** The strategy for calculating parking rates.
*/
public interface RateStrategy {
  /**
   return the number of minutes parking time the provided
   payment is valid for.
   @param amount payment in some currency.
   @return number of minutes parking time.
   */
  public int calculateTime( int amount );
}
```

Step ii) Refactor to delegate to a RateStrategy object: I play it safe and start by running the old test cases. JUnit reports all tests pass.

The TDD rhythm is a bit different here, because we do not start by adding a new test but by modifying the production code—still the movement from the failed to passed tests is essential.

Now a RateStrategy instance has to perform the parking time calculation in the pay station—thus I introduce a reference as an attribute in the PayStationImpl:

```
public class PayStationImpl implements PayStation {
  private int insertedSoFar;
  private int timeBought;

  /** the strategy for rate calculations */
  private RateStrategy rateStrategy;
  ...
```

and modify the addPayment method in its rate calculation variability point (line 11):

```
1  public void addPayment( int coinValue )
2        throws IllegalCoinException {
3    switch ( coinValue ) {
4    case 5:
5    case 10:
6    case 25: break;
7    default:
8      throw new IllegalCoinException("Invalid coin: "+coinValue);
9    }
10   insertedSoFar += coinValue;
11   timeBought = rateStrategy.calculateTime(insertedSoFar);
12 }
```

This change does compile but now most tests fail. I of course have to create a concrete RateStrategy instance somewhere. I can do this in numerous ways, but let us start by discussing two approaches: a) define a setRateStrategy method in the PayStation and call it with an appropriate object reference in the test setup; b) add a RateStrategy parameter to the pay station constructor and set this when constructing the pay station in the test setup.

Option a) is the more flexible one as it allows us to invoke the setRateStrategy even at run-time to change behavior of the pay station. However, it has two major drawbacks. First, a programmer could forget to invoke the method and thus leave the pay station with a null reference which makes it vulnerable to defective behavior. Second, it requires us to add another method to the PayStation interface—a method that has little to do with the pay station's stated responsibilities. Option b) on the other hand *forces* a programmer to consider the RateStrategy parameter: if he or she forgets it, the compiler will complain! It is always better to make the compiler check things for us rather than rely on our own discipline. The downside of the constructor approach is that we cannot change the RateStrategy reference after the pay station has been created. By combining the two approaches the best of both worlds can be made: Ensuring a valid RateStrategy as well as allow changes at run-time. However, we will introduce option b) only to keep the code short.

I change the setup in the test case class:

```
public void setUp() {
  ps = new PayStationImpl( new LinearRateStrategy() );
}
```

and I have to change the constructor

```
/** Construct a pay station.
    @param rateStrategy the rate calculation strategy to use.
*/
public PayStationImpl( RateStrategy rateStrategy ) {
  this.rateStrategy = rateStrategy;
}
```

Compiling it of course complains that there is no LinearRateStrategy. So, I apply *Fake It* by quickly defining a stub:

```
public class LinearRateStrategy implements RateStrategy {
  public int calculateTime( int amount ) {
    return 0;
  }
}
```

Now it compiles but of course the test fails. The final piece of the puzzle is to change the stub LinearRateStrategy into a real implementation: the old rate calculation code is put into place.

```
public class LinearRateStrategy implements RateStrategy {
  public int calculateTime( int amount ) {
    return amount * 2 / 5;
  }
}
```

Tests pass—Done! I have now completed the refactoring: the external behavior is the same as before as evident by the running test cases, but the internal structure of the production code has been altered and is now much better prepared for the Betatown rate structure requirement. This leads to a key point when a new feature or requirement to an existing system requires a design change:

> **Key Point: Refactor the design before introducing new features**
>
> *Introduce the design changes and refactor the system to make all existing test suites pass* before *you begin implementing new features.*

If you try to develop the new features *and* the design changes required to support them in a single iteration, then you *lose focus* and end up *taking too large steps.* During the refactoring, the existing test cases are your lifeline that tells you when your refactoring is a success.

> **Key Point: Test cases support refactoring**
>
> *Refactoring means changing the internal structure of a system* without changing its external behavior. *Therefore test cases directly support the task of refactoring because when they pass you are confident that the external behavior they test is unchanged.*

This is an important point and a major reason that developers are convinced to make the extra effort of test-first development: the investment in the test cases pays back many fold when you dare making even radical changes of your software system.

Returning to the plan I laid out—what happened to *step iii)* and *step iv)*? Reviewing the steps I envisioned I now see that I took another path: By using *Fake It* I actually took *step iv)* before *step iii).* You will often experience that opportunities will present themselves as you work that leads to better paths. It is like rock-climbing: You look at the rock and decide a feasible path but it is during the climb that you can really assess whether the plan is good or needs refinement. The point is that the plan is still important to make in advance but should not dictate every move as long as you work towards the goal.

* ~~refactor Alphatown to use a compositional design~~
* handle rate structure for Betatown

8.1.2 Iteration 2: First Hour

Based on the refactored production code I can now turn my attention to the new rate requirement. The first thing is that I want to avoid mixing up the Alphatown and Betatown test cases. The test cases are my software reliability lifeline: if the set of test cases becomes unmanageable and unreadable I am in trouble. It is therefore wise to separate the test cases for the two cities into distinct classes and thus source code files.

I keep my old Alphatown test cases and introduce a new test case source file, TestProgressiveRate, specifically for the test cases that test the progressive rate policy calculations. Of course, I also need to tell JUnit to execute the new test cases by supplying the new test case class as argument. In Ant I simply do this by adding a second argument (line 4 added to the existing `test` target):

```
1  <target name="test"  depends="build-all">
2    <java classname="org.junit.runner.JUnitCore">
3      <arg value="paystation.domain.TestPayStation"/>
4      <arg value="paystation.domain.TestProgressiveRate"/>
5      <classpath refid="class-path"/>
6    </java>
7  </target>
```

Now, for the test cases to be defined, I remember to *take small steps*. The Betatown rate structure actually consists of a series of distinct computations. I therefore rewrite my test list to allow taking small steps.

* ~~refactor Alphatown to use a compositional design~~
* First hour = $ 1.50
* Second hour = $ 1.50 + $ 2.0
* Third hour = $ 1.50 + $ 2.0 + $ 3.0
* Fourth hour = $ 1.50 + $ 2.0 + 2 * $ 3.0

Let us go for the simple one first: *First hour = $ 1.50*. I start by *Step 1: Quickly add a test* introducing my first test case in the new JUnit test case class. Also I have to configure the pay station with a ProgressiveRateStrategy.

Fragment: chapter/refactor/iteration-2/test/paystation/domain/TestProgressiveRate.java

```
@Before
public void setUp() {
  ps = new PayStationImpl( new ProgressiveRateStrategy() );
}

/** Test a single hour parking */
@Test public void shouldDisplay60MinFor150cent()
        throws IllegalCoinException {
  // First hour: $1.5
  ps.addPayment( 25 ); ps.addPayment( 25 );
  ps.addPayment( 25 ); ps.addPayment( 25 );

  ps.addPayment( 25 ); ps.addPayment( 25 );

  assertEquals( 60 /*minutes*/, ps.readDisplay() );
}
```

This code, however, does not compile as there is no implementation of ProgressiveRateStrategy. I could introduce a minimal test stub and thereby get a successful compilation but a failed test, but I realize that the first hour rate calculation is actually *Obvious Implementation* because it is identical to that of Alphatown's rate policy. The first iteration of the rate policy calculation is therefore simply:

Listing: chapter/refactor/iteration-2/src/paystation/domain/ProgressiveRateStrategy.java

```
package paystation.domain;
/** A progressive calculation rate strategy.
*/
public class ProgressiveRateStrategy implements RateStrategy {
  public int calculateTime( int amount ) {
    return amount * 2 / 5;
  }
}
```

As a result all test cases now pass which means I am already at *Step 4: Run all tests and see them all succeed.*

Actually, I always get suspicious if a test case passes the first time, and you should be concerned too. Often the test case passes for the wrong reason. A recurring reason is forgetting to add the @Test annotation to the test method! Or introducing a new test class but forgetting to make JUnit execute it. One suggestion is to temporarily add a `assertTrue(false);` at the end of the test case method and execute the suite! If the suite does not fail now you know that it was due to the test case not being executed.

Key Point: Ensure that your tests actually execute

Test cases that are not executed does not improve our software's reliability. A simple trick to get that safe feeling in your stomach is to temporarily make the test case fail on purpose. If you do not see the test suite fail, then you have somehow forgotten to add it properly to the suite of executing tests.

Adding the ProgressiveRateStrategy leads to the compositional design in Figure 8.1 that I have been aiming at.

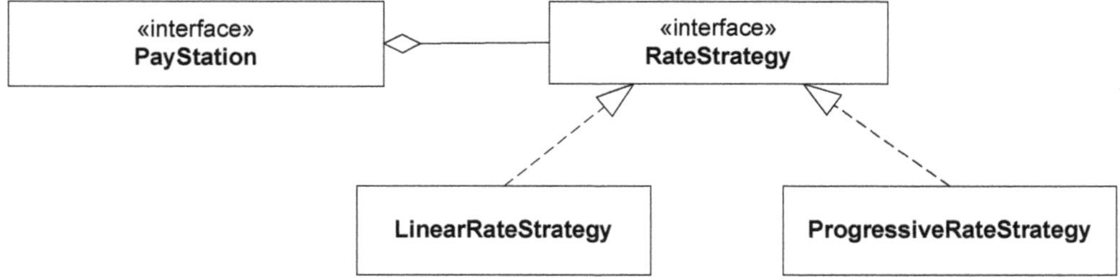

Figure 8.1: Compositional proposal for handling variants of rate calculation.

Step 5: Refactor to remove duplication. Is there any code duplication? Actually there is. The first hour rate is the same for the two towns and thus the calculation code is duplicated in both concrete implementations of the RateStrategy interface. Should I do something about that? Here, as always, I must weigh the cost of the duplication with the cost of removing it. And removing it would introduce more complexity than it would remove. A final thought is that the overlap in algorithms in the two towns is likely a coincidence which also weighs against trying to come up with a way to remove the duplication.

☞ Come up with some proposals to avoid duplicating the code.

However, another duplication concern is in the testing code. I have quite a few ps.addPayment(25); statements. Looking over the next test cases I realize that they will contain even more of these and lead to a large amount of duplicated code. So I decide to reduce the clutter that the long lists of payment statements will generate. I must keep the *Evident Tests* principle so making a loop is not the obvious path; but a private method is a readable and simple approach. So I refactor the test case implementation:

Fragment: chapter/refactor/iteration-2.5/test/paystation/domain/TestProgressiveRate.java

```
/** Test a single hour parking */
@Test public void shouldDisplay60MinFor150cent()
        throws IllegalCoinException {
  // First hour: $1.5
  addOneDollar();
  addHalfDollar();

  assertEquals( 60 /*minutes*/, ps.readDisplay() );
}

private void addHalfDollar() throws IllegalCoinException  {
  ps.addPayment( 25 ); ps.addPayment( 25 );
}
private void addOneDollar() throws IllegalCoinException {
  addHalfDollar(); addHalfDollar();
}
```

JUnit tells that all tests pass, and I am finished with this iteration.

* ~~refactor Alphatown to use a compositional design~~
* ~~First hour = $ 1.50~~
* Second hour = $ 1.50 + $ 2.0
* Third hour = $ 1.50 + $ 2.0 + $ 3.0
* Fourth hour = $ 1.50 + $ 2.0 + 2 * $ 3.0

8.1.3 Iteration 3: Second Hour

Note how Betatown has a rate structure that demands a somewhat complex algorithm. This is where the *Triangulation* principle shows it strength! I simply add new test cases until I am certain that all aspects of the algorithm is complete. At the moment I have a single test case that covers only the algorithm's ability to correctly compute the first hour's rate. Thus the natural next triangulation step is to add a test case for the second hour calculation, update the production code algorithm to correctly handle that case, and so on. Thus *Step 1: Quickly add a test*, the next requirement *Second hour: $2.00* I express as a test case (while remembering *Evident Data*):

Fragment: chapter/refactor/iteration-3/test/paystation/domain/TestProgressiveRate.java

```
/** Test two hours parking */
@Test public void shouldDisplay120MinFor350cent()
        throws IllegalCoinException {
  // Two hours: $1.5+2.0
  addOneDollar();
  addOneDollar();
  addOneDollar();
  addHalfDollar();

  assertEquals( 2 * 60 /*minutes*/ , ps.readDisplay() );
}
```

giving *Step 2: Run all tests and see the new one fail*: "expected: 120 but was: 140".

Step 3: Make a little change. The purpose of the ProgressiveRateStrategy is to implement the progressive rate algorithm—after a bit of pen-and-pencil work with the numbers I come up with:

Fragment: chapter/refactor/iteration-3/src/paystation/domain/ProgressiveRateStrategy.java

```
public int calculateTime( int amount ) {
  int time = 0;
  if ( amount >= 150 ) { // from 1st to 2nd hour
    amount -= 150;
    time = 60 /*min*/ + amount * 3 / 10;
  } else { // up to 1st hour
    time = amount * 2 / 5;
  }
  return time;
}
```

leading to *Step 4: Run all tests and see them all succeed.* No need for a *Step 5: Refactor to remove duplication.*

* ~~refactor Alphatown to use a compositional design~~
* ~~First hour = $ 1.50~~
* ~~Second hour = $ 1.50 + $ 2.0~~
* Third hour = $ 1.50 + $ 2.0 + $ 3.0
* Fourth hour = $ 1.50 + $ 2.0 + 2 * $ 3.0

8.1.4 Iteration 4: Third and Following Hours

The rest of the items on the test list are simply further applications of the *Triangulation* principle: drive the implementation of the algorithm by introducing more test cases. I will leave these as an exercise.

Exercise 8.1: Make the TDD iteration(s) to complete the progressive strategy implementation.

8.1.5 Iteration 5: Unit and Integration Testing

Testing is advocated in Extreme Programming and in the present book as one feasible path to strengthen software's reliability. By factoring out the rate calculation responsibility in a new abstraction I have also made it possible to factor out the testing: I can test the rate policy algorithms independent of the rest of the pay station behavior.

To see how this works, I can refactor the test class for the progressive rate calculation algorithm and in the fixture simply declare a RateStrategy instance directly and let the test cases exercise that instead of the full pay station.

Fragment: chapter/refactor/iteration-5/test/paystation/domain/TestProgressiveRate.java

```
public class TestProgressiveRate {
  RateStrategy rs;

  @Before public void setUp() {
    rs = new ProgressiveRateStrategy();
  }
```

The result turns out to be shorter and easier to read. For instance, compare the two hour parking cost for Betatown below with the original on page 137:

Fragment: chapter/refactor/iteration-5/test/paystation/domain/TestProgressiveRate.java

```
  @Test public void shouldGive120MinFor350cent() {
    // Two hours: $1.5+2.0
    assertEquals( 2 * 60 /*minutes*/ , rs.calculateTime(350) );
  }
```

I simply avoid all the method calls to insert coins. Once all the tests pass I am confident that the progressive rate algorithm is correct.

One issue remains, though. Do I test the configured Betatown pay station anywhere? No, actually I do not: the TestPayStation class tests all the behavior of the pay station and as it is configured with the LinearRateStrategy it is testing the Alphatown configuration. However, it is only the ProgressiveRateStrategy implementation that is tested in TestProgressiveRate.

In general, you distinguish between different levels of testing. Generally, three levels are identified:

Definition: Unit test

Unit testing is the process of executing a software unit in isolation in order to find defects in the unit itself.

Definition: Integration test

Integration testing is the process of executing a software unit in collaboration with other units in order to find defects in their interactions.

Definition: System test

System testing is the process of executing the whole software system in order to find deviations from the specified requirements.

Thus the testing levels represent both a difference in scale: going from the individual class or unit to the whole system; as well as difference in viewpoint: going from the developer's viewpoint to the user's viewpoint.

You cannot in general conclude that a system as a whole is tested even though you have thoroughly tested all its parts, nor can you conclude that all parts are thoroughly tested based upon a thorough test of the system as a whole. Therefore testing at all levels is important.

To give an example, I have unit tested the pay station with the LinearRateStrategy and I have unit tested the Betatown rate policy—however, I might configure the Betatown final pay station with the wrong rate strategy. Testing that they are properly integrated is therefore important. In my case, I can make a Betatown integration testing by adding a test case using the Betatown configuration and make sure to test in where its special rate policy appears, for instance in the two hour range:

Fragment: chapter/refactor/iteration-5/test/paystation/domain/TestPayStation.java

```
@Test
public void shouldIntegrateProgressiveRateCorrectly()
        throws IllegalCoinException {
  // reconfigure ps to be the progressive rate pay station
  ps = new PayStationImpl( new ProgressiveRateStrategy() );
  // add $ 2.0: 1.5 gives 1 hours, next 0.5 gives 15 min
  addOneDollar(); addOneDollar();

  assertEquals( "Progressive Rate: 2$ should give 75 min ",
                75 , ps.readDisplay() );
}
```

To give an example of a unit that may contain defects even though the enclosing system has been thoroughly tested, consider a class that implements methods that are never called by the system (but may later be called when the class is reused in another system), or methods that are called with a limited range of parameter values (say, void foo(int x) is only called with positive values but there is a defect in the algorithm for negative values).

8.1.6 Iteration 6: Unit Testing the Pay Station

I showed how the ProgressiveRateStrategy could be independently unit tested. In this section I will show how you can go one step further and actually unit test the pay station itself independent of the rate strategy chosen. As it is now, much of the test cases for the pay stations behavior, such as buy and cancel, is dependent on the particular Alphatown rate. However, I can actually simplify the testing of the pay station by defining a RateStrategy implementation that is *extremely* simple:

Listing: chapter/refactor/iteration-6/test/paystation/domain/One2OneRateStrategy.java

```
package paystation.domain;
/** A simple one cent = one minute rate strategy for simplifying
    unit testing the pay station.
*/
public class One2OneRateStrategy implements RateStrategy {
  public int calculateTime( int amount ) {
    return amount;
  }
}
```

Essentially, I have defined a "one cent equals one minute parking" strategy. Now, I can use this rate structure calculation when I make the test cases for the pay station's behavior that is not related to rate calculations—the simple one-to-one relation between number of entered cents and parking time in minutes makes it less likely that I make errors in the expected output of my tests, for instance review the following testing code:

Fragment: chapter/refactor/iteration-6/test/paystation/domain/TestPayStation.java

```
@Test
public void shouldAcceptLegalCoins() throws IllegalCoinException {
  ps.addPayment( 5 );
  ps.addPayment( 10 );
  ps.addPayment( 25 );
  assertEquals( "Should accept 5, 10, and 25 cents",
                5+10+25, ps.readDisplay() );
}
```

This initiative works in favor of software reliability.

☞ Consider what TDD testing principles this refactoring is using.

I have located the One2OneRateStrategy in the test code folder hierarchy: it is only for testing purposes and is not part of the production code.

Key Point: Keep all testing related code in the test tree

Implementations of delegates that are only used for testing purposes should be stored in the testing tree. This way you avoid cluttering the production code with classes that are not part of the deployed system. It also lets you make deployment files (like jar files) that contain no more code than necessary for the production system.

The result of this improved analyzability of the pay station testing code is that there is no longer any testing of the LinearRateStrategy. I therefore have to introduce a unit testing of it.

Listing: chapter/refactor/iteration-6/test/paystation/domain/TestLinearRate.java

```
package paystation.domain;

import org.junit.*;
import static org.junit.Assert.*;

/** Test the linear rate strategy.
*/
public class TestLinearRate {
  /** Test a single hour parking */
  @Test public void shouldDisplay120MinFor300cent() {
    RateStrategy rs = new LinearRateStrategy();
    assertEquals( 300 / 5 * 2, rs.calculateTime(300) );
  }
}
```

Exercise 8.2: Why have I only made a single test for the linear rate policy?

Am I done now? No, I still must do integration testing of the Alphatown pay station. I make yet another test case class TestIntegration and tests the integration between the pay station and the rate strategies.

Listing: chapter/refactor/iteration-6/test/paystation/domain/TestIntegration.java

```
package paystation.domain;

import org.junit.*;
import static org.junit.Assert.*;

/** Integration testing of the configurations of the pay station.
*/
public class TestIntegration {
  private PayStation ps;

  /**
   * Integration testing for the linear rate configuration
   */
  @Test
  public void shouldIntegrateLinearRateCorrectly()
          throws IllegalCoinException {
    // Configure pay station to be the progressive rate pay station
    ps = new PayStationImpl( new LinearRateStrategy() );
    // add $ 2.0:
    addOneDollar(); addOneDollar();

    assertEquals( "Linear Rate: 2$ should give 80 min ",
                  80 , ps.readDisplay() );
  }
  /**
   * Integration testing for the progressive rate configuration
   */
  @Test
  public void shouldIntegrateProgressiveRateCorrectly()
          throws IllegalCoinException {
    // reconfigure ps to be the progressive rate pay station
    ps = new PayStationImpl( new ProgressiveRateStrategy() );
    // add $ 2.0: 1.5 gives 1 hours, next 0.5 gives 15 min
    addOneDollar(); addOneDollar();

    assertEquals( "Progressive Rate: 2$ should give 75 min ",
                  75 , ps.readDisplay() );
  }

  private void addOneDollar() throws IllegalCoinException {
    ps.addPayment(25); ps.addPayment(25);
    ps.addPayment(25); ps.addPayment(25);
  }
}
```

I also take the opportunity to move the Betatown integration testing into this test class to keep logically related test cases in the same class. Of course, introducing these new test classes requires an update of the build script (lines 4–6 are changed.)

Fragment: chapter/refactor/iteration-6/build.xml

```
1  <target name="test" depends="build-all">
2    <java classname="org.junit.runner.JUnitCore">
3      <arg value="paystation.domain.TestPayStation"/>
```

```
      <arg value="paystation.domain.TestLinearRate"/>
      <arg value="paystation.domain.TestProgressiveRate"/>
      <arg value="paystation.domain.TestIntegration"/>
      <classpath refid="class-path"/>
    </java>
  </target>
```

To sum up my refactoring iteration has included

- Introducing a rate policy One2OneRateStrategy that makes the pay station testing code more readable.
- By necessity introduced testing of the LinearRateStrategy in a new test class TestLinearRate.
- Updated the build script to execute the newly introduced test class.
- Added a test class for the integration testing.
- And of course updated the build script again.

Now, this is a lot of steps—in the concrete work I have *taken smaller steps* than described here and run the test suite after each small step. Still, there has been some investment of effort in this iteration, and one may question if the gain is worth it. I have improved analyzability of the pay station test cases and separated unit tests and integration tests into separate test case classes but the downside has been the many required changes. These all risked introducing defects in the testing code. In a project where the focus was on software development and not on teaching as it is in this book I would probably have postponed this refactoring to see if I could have avoided the cost.

8.1.7 Iteration 7: JUnit Test Suite

The last iteration of this chapter is just to demonstrate JUnit's syntax for building suites. This feature becomes increasingly relevant when you have a large set of test cases covering many packages. I will show it here even though it is a bit of an overkill for our small set of test classes. Again annotations are used to define suites. As a Java class is used to aggregate a set of test methods, you can make a suite as an aggregate of a set of test classes, similar to how folder structures are organized in a file system. The JUnit Suite class can be populated with an array of test classes using its SuiteClasses annotation. Remember that you get a reference to a class in Java by appending ".class" to a class name, like e.g. `TestPayStation.class`. JUnit's standard runner will expect a test class with methods, so in order for it to execute a set of classes with test methods, you have to reconfigure it—again using an annotation @RunWith. Admittedly, the syntax becomes a bit weird, but you can see the result below.

I prefer to define JUnit test suites in a test class that I always call TestAll. It contains a suite of all test cases within the package that it is located in. By having this name I always know where to find the suite definitions.

Listing: chapter/refactor/iteration-7/test/paystation/domain/TestAll.java

```
package paystation.domain;

import org.junit.runner.RunWith;
import org.junit.runners.Suite;

@RunWith ( Suite.class )
  @Suite.SuiteClasses(
    { TestPayStation.class,
      TestLinearRate.class,
      TestProgressiveRate.class,
      TestIntegration.class } )

/** Test suite for this package.
*/
public class TestAll {
  // Dummy - it is the annotations that tell JUnit what to do...
}
```

Note the array that lists all test classes. As a suite can consist of other suites I can make a TestAll at the *paystation* package level that makes a suite of all the TestAll classes in subpackages. This way a complex recursive testing suite can be built and invoked by just asking JUnit to execute the root package TestAll class. A final change is to adjust the build script to invoke the TestAll suite instead.

Fragment: chapter/refactor/iteration-7/build.xml

```
<target name="test" depends="build-all">
  <java classname="org.junit.runner.JUnitCore">
    <arg value="paystation.domain.TestAll"/>
    <classpath refid="class-path"/>
  </java>
</target>
```

8.1.8 Overview of the Iterations

At this stage, I have been through seven iterations. Several of these iterations were not planned initially, but made as opportunities arose in my work. The iterations were:

1. I refactor to introduce a rate strategy, make all existing test cases pass to ensure the refactoring is reliable.
2. I triangulate the first hour rate calculation into the rate algorithm.
3. I triangulate the second hour rate.
4. I triangulate the third and following hours rate.
5. I discover that the rate strategies can be tested as separate software units, and refactored the test cases for the Betatown's rate algorithm to become a unit test. All this to improve analyzability of the test code.
6. I discover that the analyzability of the pay station test code can be improved by introducing a simple rate strategy. Refactored these test cases. Introduced integration testing of the pay station with the individual rate strategies.
7. I introduce the JUnit annotations for handling test suites.

8.1.9 Testing Levels in XP

After these iterations our test suite includes both unit testing, the individual rate strategies and the pay station, as well as integration testing, the whole pay station configured with proper rate strategies. But what about the system testing level? In our case study, the integration and system testing level overlap. This is because the pay station system is so small and only include a few classes. In larger systems, the system testing level does not necessarily overlap with the integration testing level. As an example, a system that consists of four subsystems (think Java packages with 10–20 classes in each) may have integration testing of the interactions between subsystems. These will focus on the interactions themselves. The system level testing, however, will focus on the system returning the proper answers or doing the proper actions to enable users to do their job efficiently. Thus the former test cases stem from an analysis of the interactions while the latter from an analysis of usage situations. In the pay station case, the integration test case found in iteration 5 came from my worry that the Betatown pay station was not configured correctly. Due to the small size of the system, however, you can see that all the actions a user may do to the system are already covered by our set of test cases and no additional system testing cases are needed.

In XP the system testing level is called **functional testing**. Functional tests are still automated tests, just like the unit tests, but they are defined and written in close collaboration with the customer. Unit tests must run at 100% all the time, but this is not so for the functional tests. Rather each small release of the system will generally increase the number of functional tests passing but some will fail due to the features not being free of defects or implementation work simply not begun yet. Being an agile and incremental process, the suite of functional tests also starts out small in the beginning of the project and grows until the project is concluded.

8.2 Summary of Key Concepts

The introduction of the Betatown variant allowed us to explore a number of different techniques and key points. Two key points are that you should *refactor your design first, and only introduce new features second* and you can *use your test cases to verify refactorings*. In this way, you keep focus and take small steps, and the risk of introducing defects are minimized.

The *Triangulation* principle was introduced in a previous chapter but it showed its potential here: I used triangulation to drive the implementation of the Betatown rate algorithm—inventing new test cases that would add more and more parts to the algorithm implementation.

The compositional design allowed me to *test the rate policy in isolation*. I did not need the pay station code. The term *unit testing* denotes testing a software unit in isolation while *integration testing* denotes testing that units collaborate correctly. I could improve analyzability of the pay station unit testing code by configuring it with a simplified rate policy explicitly developed for this purpose. The final level of testing is *system testing* that denotes testing the whole system as seen from the users' and requirements specifications' perspective. In XP this level is called *functional testing* and in contrast to unit tests they do not run at 100% until the project is concluded.

Finally, JUnit supports defining test suites as collections of test classes using the @RunWith and @Suite annotations.

8.3 Selected Solutions

Discussion of Exercise 8.1:

You will find the resulting production and test code in iteration 5 onwards.

8.4 Review Questions

Argue for the benefits of refactoring the design before introducing new functionality. Argue and exemplify how developed test cases support the refactoring process.

Define the concepts *unit, integration* and *system testing*. What is *functional testing* in XP?

Describe the considerations involved when deciding to put an implementing class in either the production or test source code tree. Describe the techniques used to define suites of test cases.

8.5 Further Exercises

Exercise 8.3:

Walk in my footsteps: develop the Betatown variant of the pay station using the compositional approach while maintaining the Alphatown variant.

Exercise 8.4:

In exercise 7.5 you designed a compositional proposal for allowing the pay station to either accept US or Danish coins.

1. Introduce your design by refactoring the existing pay station system.
2. Use TDD to implement the variant that can handle Danish coins and the Danish rate policy.
3. Review your test cases and classify them as either unit or integration tests.
4. Refactor your test cases so unit and integration tests are separated into distinct test classes.

Exercise 8.5:

In exercise 5.4 and 6.6 the game of Breakthrough was defined and implemented. Consider that we want to support new rules for how the pawns are moved and captured.

1. Design a STRATEGY based design for handling variants with respect to how pawns are moved and captured.
2. Refactor your production and test code to support your new design.
3. Invent a new movement rule and implement it using your improved design.

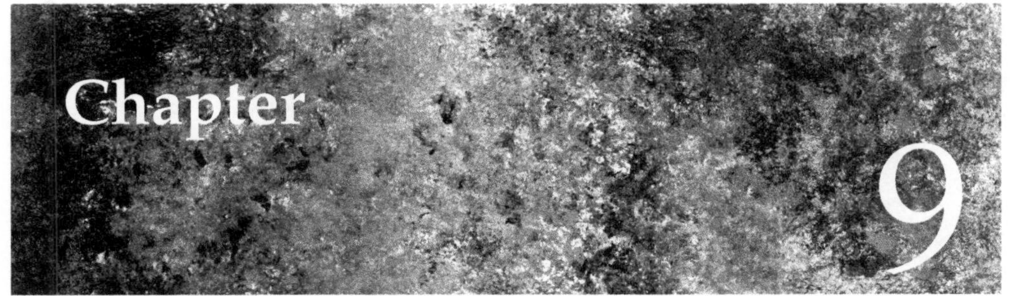

Design Patterns – Part I

with Morten Lindholm Nielsen

Learning Objectives

So far, I have discussed a design pattern from the viewpoint of solving a problem, analyzing benefits, and studying the programming associated. The learning focus of this chapter is the historical and conceptual aspects of design patterns—the theory of patterns. Two different definitions of patterns will be presented that each represents different aspects of the design pattern concept.

9.1 The History of Design Patterns

The origin of the term "design pattern" can be traced back to the book *Notes on the Synthesis of Form*, written by American architect Christopher Alexander (1964). Alexander examined what he thought to be a new foundation for architectural design, namely that of achieving a "good fit" between form and context. This is exemplified in Figure 9.1: plus or minus symbols on the figure indicate whether the constraints have a positive agreement or are in conflict. To illustrate these concepts, he considered the task of designing a kettle. On one hand, there are constraints regarding the physical shape (the "form") the designer must keep in mind: the kettle must hold water, it must be possible to drain it without scalding oneself, it should be convenient to fill, etc. On the other hand, there are equally important constraints regarding the context of use: should it be designed for gas, electricity, or an open fire? And what about manufacturing? It should be inexpensive to produce and easy to assemble. A design that achieves a "good fit" is a design in which all the constraints are taken into consideration and have been balanced against each other.

Alexander originally strove to create a "science of design" by using mathematics to analyze the various elements, or "forces," that influence the solution to the design

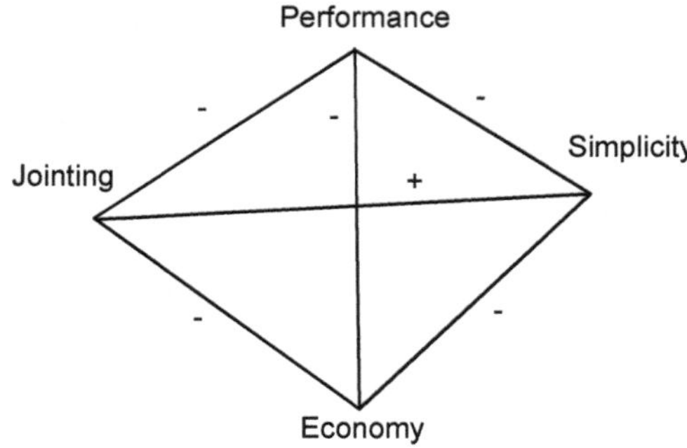

Figure 9.1: Christopher Alexander's explanation of forces.

problem. With this approach, he hoped to overcome the growing complexity of design problems. His analysis of forces later evolved into what is now called "design patterns." During the 1970s, Alexander and colleagues published three books in which they applied the pattern concept to the design of houses and urban plans (see Alexander et al. (1975), (1977), and (1979)). In his books, Alexander orders the patterns by size, beginning with the largest down to the smallest. The largest of the architectural patterns applies to a region, and the smallest applies to some construction detail. Each pattern is connected to the other so that no pattern becomes isolated. The total of all the patterns grows into a "pattern catalogue" to be used as a design tool. This term involves the interrelation between different patterns, where the larger-scale patterns are constructed from smaller-scale patterns. A house is built using small patterns, houses are then clustered following larger patterns, and finally, the relation between towns is laid out according to the largest patterns. Alexander writes his patterns in a specific way which has become the generally accepted format and is therefore known as the Alexandrian Form of pattern writing.

9.2 The Purpose of Patterns

The first question is what problem patterns attempt to solve. The answer is complexity. Alexander noted in 1964 that the modern world has become increasingly more complex and that no modern individual, no matter how capable, can hold all current knowledge. The consequence is the proliferation of specialists, each knowledgeable in a certain area. His observation was that the world, and thus also design activities, have accelerated. Consequently, there is a shorter and shorter time span to complete designs. He then used these two observations to comment on the (to him) apparent lack of quality in modern architecture. To do that, he first had to define what quality is in architecture, or more generally in design. It proved more difficult than he anticipated, because quality in anything is difficult to express verbally. It is not easy to say what characteristic of an object or house that makes it possess quality; it is easier to tell when something does not. It might have a "wrong" shape or lack harmony in some way. Alexander's definition of quality thus became a negating definition, and he named the concept a "quality without a name."

This brings us to his second observation, that of speed. Alexander found that some houses of age had this "quality without a name"—the same quality he also found in palm-leaf huts and Polynesian architecture. He found the reason to be rooted in the cultures that built these houses: they were premodern, and their techniques evolved slowly over time. Therefore, when a house was built and there was something about it that did not look "right," the wrong feature was not included in the next house to be built. If a scarf was woven and the pattern did not please, the pattern was not used again. It follows that quality is the result of a historic process in which the odd designs were culled and the pleasing designs were elaborated. Quality is viewed as an emerging concept. It was refined to a degree where even a small alteration disrupted the balance between the various elements affecting the design. The design converged on perfection—a perfect match between form and context.

The central question for Alexander became how to achieve this perfect match, the good fit, when the designer was constrained by lack of knowledge and a shortage of time. Initially, he tried to solve this problem by using mathematics and logic, but later on, his development of the pattern concept to describe interrelating parts of the design proved more fruitful.

The fact that patterns describe interrelating parts of the design leads to a recursive use of patterns (i.e., using a pattern to describe a part of another pattern). Alexander saw this as one of the great advantages of his approach, and he called this use a "pattern language"—a language for speaking about design in terms of patterns consisting of other patterns. This also reflects the structure of the books he wrote, in which large-scale patterns describing the layout and placement of towns are themselves divided into smaller-scale patterns describing neighborhoods and still smaller-scale patterns dealing with the construction of houses and rooms.

Following Alexander's development of the ideas behind patterns, it is helpful to see a pattern as a communicative device used to convey knowledge among designers about problem solving and design. The pattern itself is an open-ended structure that, by itself, does not force a specific design into the debate, but rather hints at relevant possibilities, taking surrounding structures into consideration.

9.3 Patterns as a Communication Device

Another aspect of using patterns in interpersonal communication is the implicit transfer of knowledge that takes place when a person is introduced to patterns. Because the pattern itself encompasses knowledge that former designers have found to be well-founded, the act of learning a pattern presents a special case of learning from the "masters." New ideas are not presented as monolithic solutions but rather in the context of the elements (forces) that may influence how the resulting design may deviate from the actual described solution. Combined with the notion of using pattern languages, this constitutes knowledge transfer, in a way more systematic and encompassing than the presentation of singular, optimal solutions. This communication aspect of pattern fits well with what has become the one-liner description of what a pattern is:

> *A solution to a problem in a context.*

The idea of using patterns in architecture did not catch on, and, during the 1980s, the idea apparently was disavowed by architects. In another community, however, the patterns concept started to generate interest, namely in the computer science and software engineering camp. In the mid to late 1980s, rumors about "patterns" were heard at conferences on software design.

In 1987, Kent Beck and Ward Cunningham presented the first paper on patterns at a software engineering conference (Beck and Cunningham 1987). Beck and Cunningham describe the results of developing a small pattern language with the goal of guiding novice Smalltalk programmers in creating applications. Over the next few years, interest in patterns was growing, and in 1995, the seminal book *Design Patterns: Elements of Reusable Object-Oriented Software* was published (Gamma et al. 1995)[1]. This book brought the term *design pattern* into mainstream use in software development, and it is still considered an essential book on patterns.

Many other books and articles describing additional patterns have been published, but Gamma et al. (1995) remains one of the most influential books on software design of that period. Gamma et al. defined patterns for software as:

> Definition: **Design pattern (Gamma et al.)**
>
> Patterns are descriptions of communicating objects and classes that are customized to solve a general design problem in a particular context.

This definition still stands. The idea was contagious and spread to other fields. In software design, it has been more successful than in any other field we know of.

A defining characteristic of patterns is that one does not invent them; one finds them. A pattern must have proven its worth in real life, and it must have done so more than once. As a rule of thumb, a pattern is not really considered a pattern until it has been verified as a recurring principle, a solution that is general and powerful enough to have been used several times and solved problems in existing systems. A so-called "rule of three" is often used in selecting patterns. A solution must be observed at least three times in different systems before it should be considered a pattern.

9.4 The Pattern Template

As described above, patterns are written according to a specific format or template. In other words, they can be interpreted as a *particular prose form* as emphasized by a definition by Beck et al. (1996):

> Definition: **Design pattern (Beck et al.)**
>
> A design pattern is a particular prose form of recording design information such that designs which have worked well in the past can be applied again in similar situations in the future.

[1] In the community the four authors became known as the *Gang of Four* (or *GoF*) so you may hear the book referenced by its nickname "the GoF book".

Authors generally use slightly different templates but they all share common characteristics and have to include:

- **Name.** A pattern has a name that allows us to remember it and communicate with other pattern literates. The name should be short and descriptive of the problem it addresses.
- **Problem.** The problem it addresses must be described, often using examples from real software projects.
- **Solution.** The solution the pattern proposes is described. In a software context this is often done using prose as well as diagrams that show the static and dynamic structure of the software. These diagrams are not to be copied literally but must be viewed as templates for the final solution.
- **Consequences.** Patterns represent solutions that have trade-offs. The benefits and liabilities must be described in order for a developer to make a qualified judgement whether to apply the pattern or not.

In addition to these items, the template used in the design pattern boxes in this book also contains:

- **Intent.** The intent tries to describe the problem as well as the solution in one or two sentences. The intent sections used in this book are generally verbatim copies of those defined in the original book by Gamma et al.
- **Roles.** The pattern structure is a template for object structure and collaboration. This section names each participant or role in the pattern solution.

9.5 Summary of Key Concepts

Design patterns are deeply inspired by the work of Christopher Alexander on building architecture. Alexander wanted to convey high quality solutions to architectural challenges to designers that were constrained by lack of knowledge and a shortage of time. His work led him to propose a pattern language: a set of interrelated patterns ranging from large-scale patterns describing layout of towns right down to small-scale patterns dealing with the construction of rooms. A main benefit of these patterns were as communication devices where designers could learn from the masters.

In late 1980, the software engineering community took on the idea that ultimately led to the first, seminal, design pattern catalogue *Design Patterns: Elements of Reusable Object-Oriented Software* (Gamma et al. 1995). In it, the authors define a design pattern as *descriptions of communicating objects that solve a design problem in a particular context.* Another definition is given by Beck et al. which focuses on design patterns as a *prose form*. This has led to a common template for describing patterns that at least includes *its name*, the *problem* it addresses, the *solution* it proposes, and finally the *consequences* of applying the pattern.

9.6 Review Questions

Where does the idea of patterns come from? Who invented the first pattern language? Name some of people who brought the pattern idea into software design.

Describe the key elements in the design pattern definitions by Gamma et al. as well as that of Beck et al. Are design patterns invented or discovered? Why? Describe the elements in the template for describing design patterns, and explain why they are required.

9.7 Further Exercises

Exercise 9.1:

Discuss the similarities and differences between a design pattern and an abstract algorithm, like for instance a sorting algorithm described in pseudo-code.

Exercise 9.2:

Describe some advantages of designing and implementing software design with a knowledge of patterns compared to the situation where you do not have this knowledge.

Exercise 9.3:

Discuss the two different definitions of design patterns introduced in this chapter. Explain why they are not in conflict with each other.

Exercise 9.4:

Review the STRATEGY design pattern, defined in pattern box 7.1 on page 130, in the light of the various definitions of design patterns. What aspects of the pattern box does each definition emphasize?

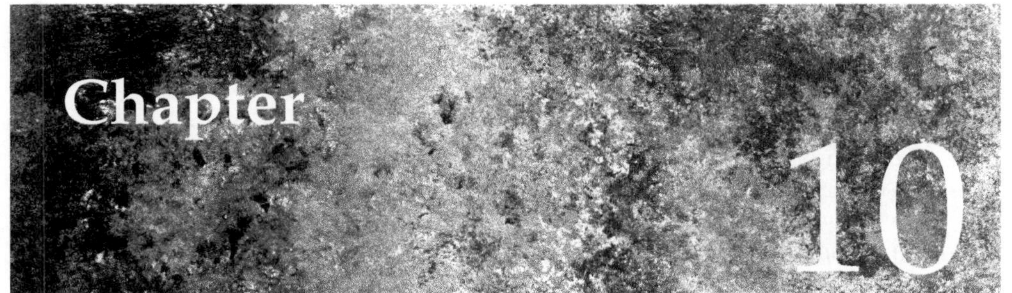

Coupling and Cohesion

Learning Objectives

Underlying almost all design patterns is a wish for maintainability and flexibility. The objective of this chapter is to introduce two qualities that are relatively easy to judge or measure in our code: *coupling* and *cohesion*. These two qualities are interesting because if I achieve high cohesion and low coupling then maintainability and reliability increase. I will also present a concrete rule, *law of Demeter*, that aims at getting low coupling.

10.1 Maintainable Code

Chapter 3, *Flexibility and Maintainability*, introduced the ISO definition of maintainability, its subqualities, and argued that maintainability measures cost of software change. Furthermore, *flexibility* was defined as a special case of changeability, namely the capability to add/enhance functionality purely by adding software units. The coding practice *change by addition, not by modification* is of course a means to achieve flexible software.

The question is what does maintainable code look like? The problem with the definition of maintainability is that it is not operational: it does not tell me how to write maintainable software. It merely tells me a label, *not very maintainable*, to put on my source code when I later discover it is highly expensive to modify to accommodate my customer's new idea. Of course, I want some more operational concepts, concepts that I can readily apply *while* I am programming in order to keep the code maintainable. And fortunately there are. In the next sections, I will cover some central qualities that are closely linked to source code and therefore relatively easy to measure or judge, and that have a huge impact on how maintainable the system will become.

10.2 Coupling

Definition: Coupling

Coupling is a measure of how strongly dependent one software unit is on other software units.

As usual, a *software unit* may be of any granularity: classes, subsystems, packages, even individual methods in a class.

Dependencies between software units come in many forms. In an object-oriented language several types of dependencies come to our mind: methods in a class are coupled by their dependency on the class' instance variables, and classes are coupled as they have relations with each other. Such relations may at the code level be in the form of object creation, method calls to another class, receiving an object as parameter in a method call, etc. Dependencies also exist between packages, when a class in one package calls a method in a class in another, etc. Common to these is that they are directly visible in our source code and you can make tools to find them and thus measure the coupling.

However, dependencies can be much more subtle and less directly visible in the code. This is the reason, you have to review the unit and subjectively judge the degree of coupling, as tools can only find some of the couplings between software units.

Exercise 10.1: List dependencies between software units that exist but are not described by method calls, object references, or other constructs that are easily spotted in the code.

Consider two packages whose dependencies are programmed in two different ways as outline in Figure 10.1. In the left side (a) the *system.gui* package contains two classes that depends on two, respectively three, classes in the *system.domain* package. Thus a change in the dark gray class in the lower package will most likely induce changes to be made in three other classes, those marked light gray in the figure. For instance, a method signature may have to be changed in the dark gray class which means that all places in the light gray classes where the method is called has to be reviewed and analyzed to make the classes compile again. Even worse, if a developer on the domain code team responsible for the *system.domain* package makes changes to what a method does in the dark gray class but does not change any method signature, he may remember to tell his colleague working on the light gray class within the same package, but perhaps he does not tell the GUI team down the hallway. Having strong test cases may catch such changes in the contract, but still effort has to be invested in making the light gray classes work correctly again. The packages have *tight* or *high* coupling; and high coupling lowers maintainability.

High coupling also impacts reliability in a negative way, as any defect or even just changed behavior introduced in the dark gray class may create undesirable effects and maybe defects in all classes depending on it. Thus even a small change in the class may lower reliability in many dependent classes. Also a class that depends on a lot of other classes becomes harder to read and understand again increasing the likelihood of introducing defects. Finally, a class that has many dependencies is harder to reuse in another context.

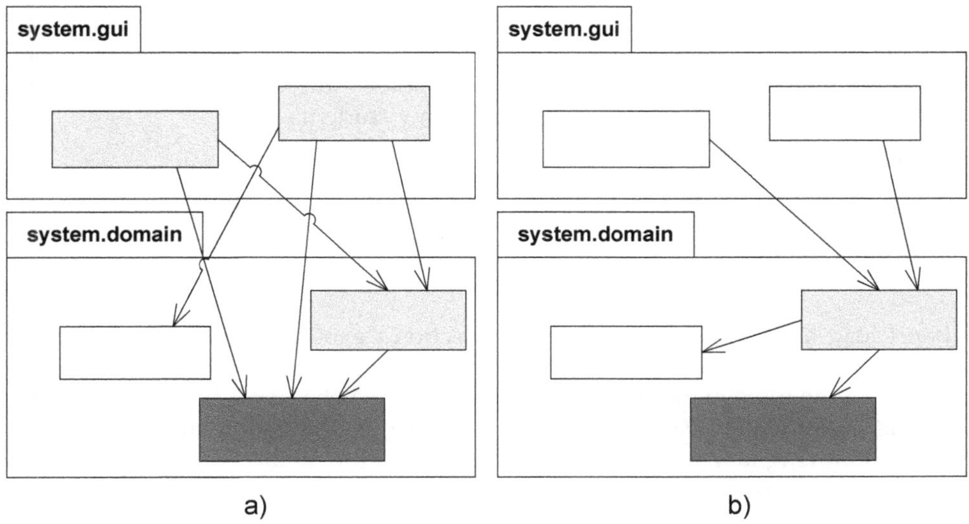

Figure 10.1: Tight (a) and low (b) coupling.

The implementation shown on the right side (b) of the figure shows the same two packages and the same number of classes, but attention has been paid to lower the coupling between classes. Thus only one class directly depends on the change marked class. The two classes in the upper package only depend on a single class in the lower package, in essence this class encapsulates the package (which is in fact the FACADE pattern, discussed in Chapter 19.) The packages have *weak* or *low* coupling.

Weak coupling generally works in favor of maintainable and reliable software. Maintainable because the change in the change marked class only has implications in a single dependent class—thus the effort to review, recode, debug and test is lower compared to the tight coupled version. And the side-effects and defects introduced in the dark gray class ideally only have reliability consequences for the single dependent class. It is only the interplay between these two classes that we must ensure the reliability of. Thus weak coupling also works towards more reliable software. And, a class with few dependencies is easier to reuse and make to work in a new software context.

10.3 Cohesion

Definition: **Cohesion**

Cohesion is a measure of how strongly related and focused the responsibilities and provided behaviors of a software unit are.

Cohesion is a term that basically means "being organized". Consider that all clean clothes of a family with a couple of children are stored in one big pile. It would take ages to find a pair of trousers and a pair of matching socks. Instead, if each member of the family has his or her chest of drawers, and each drawer contains one or two types of clothes, finding what to put on today is easy. High cohesion means placing the same type of clothes together in the same drawer. In software, it means software units should have just a few closely related responsibilities. As an example consider this remove method in a collection that one of my students wrote:

```
public void remove(Item i) {
  if ( list.isEmpty() ) {
    System.out.println(''The list is empty, cannot remove'');
  }
  [ remove behavior implemented here ]
}
```

When I read a class that must act as a collection I expect to see methods like add, and remove, and these names convey a lot of understanding of the behavior they provide. In the remove method above, however, the behavior is that of removing an item *and* occasionally printing something! These two behaviors are absolutely not related: removing items and printing. The name of the method does not adequately convey what it actually does. Cohesion is low.

Cohesion is a quality to strive for at all granularities. As an example of cohesion at the package level, consider the following two Java packages, organized by two different principles:

- Package *ABCClasses*: Contains all classes whose names begin with either the letters A, B, or C in my flight reservation system.
- Package *SeatBooking*: All classes related to booking a seat on a plane in my flight reservation system.

Clearly, package *ABCClasses* has low cohesion: it may contain all types of functionality and there is no clear relation between the responsibilities it serves. In contrast, package *SeatBooking* has high cohesion as seat booking embodies a small set of clearly defined responsibilities and the package provides behavior for just that and nothing else.

> **Exercise 10.2:** Find an example of a high cohesion and a low cohesion package in the Java libraries.

High cohesion also contributes towards reliability and maintainability. Cohesive software units greatly increases the analyzability of software, the capability to find defects or parts to be modified, just as the organized approach for storing clothes allows us to find socks quickly. If a software unit has too many responsibilities it will get changed too often. If a class only implements a single feature it will change much less frequently, thus increasing stability.

Of course, you must keep your balance. Cohesive software does not mean software where every class only has one method, and every package only one class. In the pay station case, I started out with a cohesive abstraction, represented by the PayStation interface, but it had five–six responsibilities. However, they all were highly related to the "concept of being a pay station". When need arose, it was refactored to introduce the rate strategy which is of course also very focused.

Cohesion and responsibility are two sides of the same coin per definition. Therefore the discussion on roles, responsibilities, and behavior in Chapter 15 is intimately related to the concept cohesion.

10.4 Law of Demeter

A very concrete rule that addresses coupling is the law of Demeter first formulated by Lieberherr and Holland (1989). This rule states

Definition: Law of Demeter

Do not collaborate with indirect objects.

To illustrate what "indirect" and "direct" objects means, let me start with an example. Consider that the Dean of the Faculty of Science is worried about low intake of students at the Department of Computer Science. The department is organized with a head of department that is assisted by several committees which in turn are also headed by a person. One of these committees is the Teaching Committee which is responsible for the webpages that provide information for future students interested in computer science. The actual editing of the webpages is performed by a secretary. As the webpages are confusing and badly written at the moment, one plausible action to take is to improve them. So the question is what action should the dean take? One highly infeasible action is to ask the department head to tell him who is the head of the teaching committee, and next ask him or her about who is the secretary responsible for updating the public relations web pages, and finally tell the secretary detailed instructions about what to change. In pseudo code this action would look something like this:

```
getHeadOfDepartment(CS).getHeadOfCommitte(Teaching).getSecretary().
  changeSection(webpage, section, newText);
```

This is absurd in any organization. The CEO or manager does not have the time to tell each individual employee what to do in detail several times a day. The feasible action of the dean is to tell the department head to make the necessary actions to increase student intake, and leave for him to decide what to do down the chain of command.

```
getHeadOfDepartment(CS).increaseStudentIntake();
```

In the terminology of law of Demeter, the department head is a *direct object* while the secretary is an *indirect object*, and the law states that the dean should talk to his department head, not to the secretary nor to the head of the teaching committee. The rule is also known as *Don't Talk to Strangers* (Larman 2005) which perhaps more directly expresses what the rule is about.

In a software context, there is another reason that talking to strangers is a bad idea. In the first pseudo code line, the dean object actually has to know no less than three interfaces: the interface of the department head, the teaching committee head, and the secretary. Consider that some developer changes the signature of method changeSection in the secretary interface: change the parameter list, change the method name, or similar. This would then require a rewrite of the code line in the dean class and regression testing after the change. The same argument applies for changes in the interface for committee heads. Thus the classes become highly coupled. In the second pseudo code line there are only a coupling between two classes, a change in the secretary interfaces does not ripple up into the dean class. Coupling is much lower.

The law can be restated in more operational terms by defining which objects are not strangers.

In a method, you should only invoke methods on

- this
- a parameter of the method
- an attribute of this
- an element in a collection which is an attribute of this
- an object created within the method

While formulated as a law, it is rather a good design rule that may be broken if good reasons exist.

10.5 Summary of Key Concepts

Coupling and cohesion are two qualities that are relatively easy to judge in our code and as they are highly related to maintainability, they are important to consider in practical development. *Coupling* is a measure of the degree of dependency of one software unit to other units. If a unit has many dependencies it is termed *high or tight coupling*. If a unit has high coupling then it is less maintainable as there are many sources that can force a change to the unit. *Cohesion* is a measure of how closely focused the behaviors of a unit is—how well defined its responsibility is. If a unit has a narrow and well defined responsibility it has *high cohesion* and is more maintainable. The reason is that it is easier to locate the relevant unit to modify in case of a defect or requirement update. The *law of Demeter* is a rule of thumb that, if followed, lowers coupling in deep dependency graphs. It states that software code should not collaborate with indirect objects.

10.6 Selected Solutions

Discussion of Exercise 10.1:

The indirect dependencies between units are often the most devilish when it comes to software defects. They are difficult to track down and you are often puzzled when they first appear. And the compiler has no chance of helping you out.

Typical indirect dependencies include: Sharing a common global variable, relying on entries in operating system registries or environment variables, relying on a common file format that units read or write, relying on a specific order of initialization, relying on a specific database schema, relying on specific port numbers or IP addresses, etc. All these create coupling between units in a system but are much less visible couplings than direct object references.

The list is very long and in a development team it can be quite difficult to ensure that everybody understands all couplings between units. The war story in sidebar 3.1 is a good example of a coupling that was hidden from one team developer. It is also an example of an unfortunate coupling that should have been avoided by the other developers.

Discussion of Exercise 10.2:

Classic examples from the Java libraries are java.util that has low cohesion as all sorts of different classes with little or nothing in common are grouped into this package: it contains collection classes, calendar classes, etc. The javax.swing package is highly cohesive as only Swing related GUI components are packaged here.

10.7 Review Questions

Define what coupling is and how to achieve weak and tight coupling.

Define what cohesion is and how to achieve low and high cohesion.

Describe the relationship between coupling and cohesion and software reliability and maintainability.

Describe the law of Demeter and its implications. What is its relation to the coupling and cohesion properties?

10.8 Further Exercises

Exercise 10.3:

Discuss the design patterns you have learnt with respect to coupling and cohesion. Do they increase or decrease coupling? Cohesion? Argue why.

Exercise 10.4:

On page 141 is given a key point: *Keep All Testing Related Code in the Test Tree.* Reformulate this key point using the concepts of coupling and/or cohesion.

Exercise 10.5. Source code directory:
`chapter/refactor/iteration-7`

The final iteration of the pay station system exhibits a complex folder, package, and class structure. Analyze the organization with respect to coupling and cohesion. Consider at least: the contents of the source code and test code tree and the organization and grouping of test cases into separate test classes.

Iteration 4

Variability Management and ③-①-②

The emphasis in the *Variability Management and* ③-①-② learning iteration is on how the ③-①-② process applied to some concrete requirements to our pay station leads to flexible software, and in the process derives some new design patterns and testing techniques.

Chapter	Learning Objective
Chapter 11	*Deriving State Pattern.* A new requirement requires us to reuse the two rate policies already developed but in a combination. The ③-①-② process provides a solution to this variability problem and the result is the STATE pattern.
Chapter 12	*Test Stubs.* This time the requirement is from ourselves: we need to increase the testability of the pay station. Here you will apply ③-①-② to develop a test stub, and along the way learn the terminology and impliciations.
Chapter 13	*Deriving Abstract Factory.* Yet another requirement is handled by ③-①-② and the result is ABSTRACT FACTORY.
Chapter 14	*Pattern Fragility.* Design patterns are implemented using ordinary programming techniques. However, if you are not careful in your programming effort, many of the benefits of a pattern are lost. Here you will learn some of the pitfalls.

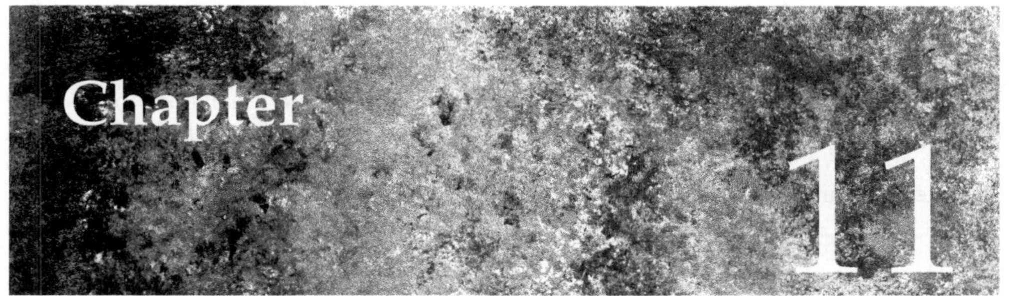

Deriving State Pattern

Learning Objectives

Structuring software systems using a compositional approach has many benefits and here I will demonstrate how it elegantly supports reuse. The learning objective of this chapter is in particular to analyze how the polymorphic and compositional proposals cope when faced with a requirement that combines existing solutions. A major outcome is to demonstrate how the compositional proposal leads to the STATE pattern. Finally, you will see the problems of doing test-driven development when the production code uses resources that are not under direct testing control.

11.1 New Requirements

I have been contacted by a new municipality, Gammatown. They want "almost the same" pay station but with a small twist. They would like to have different rate structures during weekdays and during weekends as they would like people to stay for only shorter intervals during the weekends to increase the number of people that visit the town's shops during Saturday opening hours[1].

They require:

- *Weekdays:* The linear rate structure that is used in Alphatown.
- *Weekends:* The progressive rate structure that is used in Betatown.

Obviously, this requirement provides opportunities for a lot of software reuse as I have already designed and programmed both the rate calculation algorithms in question.

[1]Some towns instead offer free parking during weekends—it does not matter much as the learning objective is to handle altering between rate policies over the week.

11.2 One Problem – Many Designs

Basically I can address this new requirement with the same means as I have done before. I now have three different products to support and they each differs only in a very small fraction of the production code. The question here is the technique to handle this variation.

My options for the production code are:

- *Source tree copy proposal:* Make a copy of the existing source code tree, name it Gammatown and make the alternate coding there. In this case the rate calculation algorithm will contain copies of code from both the Alphatown and Betatown rate algorithms.
- *Parametric proposal:* I add a new Gammatown clause to all relevant switches in the pay station production code.
- *Polymorphic proposal:* I make a subclass of PayStation that can perform the particulars of Gammatown's rate calculation.
- *Compositional proposal with a few if's:* I use my compositional proposal, but introduce a switch in the pay station that selects the proper rate strategy depending on the day of the week.
- *Compositional proposal:* I provide the resulting behavior by composing it, letting object collaboration instead of letting a single one do all the work.

The analysis with regards to the source copy tree proposal as well as the parametric proposal has been sufficiently dealt with in the STRATEGY pattern chapter. The techniques and thus the analyses are the same and I will not repeat the arguments here.

> **Exercise 11.1:** Sketch or program the parametric proposal. Analyze benefits and liabilities of the parametric proposal, and compare with the analysis in the STRATEGY pattern chapter.

The polymorphic and compositional proposals, however, pose special problems and the analysis is thus worthwhile. But before that I must discuss the tests that may drive the process.

11.3 TDD of Alternating Rates

The TDD rhythm states that I must write the tests first. For the Gammatown requirement the only added behavior is the weekend-or-not selection of rate calculation. The rate calculation algorithms themselves have already passed their tests.

It turns out that this is a tricky requirement to test because the pay station's behavior depends upon something that is not under the direct control of our test cases! Remember, a test case is defined as a set of input for a unit under test as well as the expected output. Using the table format, I can write an Alphatown test case like this:

Unit under test: Rate calculation	
Input	Expected output
pay = 500 cent	200 min.

The translation into a JUnit test case is easy as you have already seen. When the unit under test is the pay station in Gammatown then there is an additional input parameter, namely the day of week, and a test case must of course include this additional parameter.

Unit under test: Rate calculation	
Input	Expected output
pay = 500 cent, day = Monday	200 min.
pay = 500 cent, day = Sunday	150 min.

The problem is that the day of week is not a parameter to neither the pay station nor the rate calculation algorithm and I can therefore not define a JUnit test that expresses the test cases above.

Day of week is an example of an **indirect input parameter**. This input parameter is defined by the computing environment, by the clock in the operating system. The Java libraries can of course read the operating system clock by the class java.util.GregorianCalendar. The production code:

```
private boolean isWeekend() {
  Date d = new Date();
  Calendar c = new GregorianCalendar();
  c.setTime(d);
  int dayOfWeek = c.get(Calendar.DAY_OF_WEEK);
  return ( dayOfWeek == Calendar.SATURDAY
           ||
           dayOfWeek == Calendar.SUNDAY);
}
```

is a method that returns true if the present day is either Saturday or Sunday.

So, the question is how can I proceed using TDD? I can see several options but none of them are very good.

- I run the linear rate tests during normal work days but have to come in during the weekend to test that the Gammatown pay station uses the progressive rate. This is not what you would call automated testing. Another manual procedure is to set the date on my computer to an appropriate day before running the test case which is also a manual procedure.
- I write some script or procedure to set the date from within the testing code. This may seem like a feasible path but it is actually poor because the Ant build system depends upon the clock in order to recompile properly. Thus the likely result is that the build system fails. Also setting the clock will interfere with clock synchronization software which is standard in modern operating systems.
- I refactor the production code to accept a Date object instead of retrieving one by itself. This is actually not a solution because the pay station must continually request a new date as time passes. Thus it cannot simply receive one when it is instantiated.

This date example is an instance of a more general problem, namely how we can get external resources, like the clock, external hardware and sensors, random-number generators, and others, under direct testing control. I will in Chapter 12 discuss an improved and general way of handling external resources.

For now, however, I will continue the discussion of the production code challenges and simply assume that I do manual testing of the Gammatown pay station.

11.4 Polymorphic Proposal

The question is how can I use polymorphism to reuse the two existing and reliable rate algorithms? Let us for a moment forget the compositional design, based on the STRATEGY pattern that I have introduced in the previous chapters, and let us consider how things would have looked like if I had adopted the polymorphic approach for handling Alphatown and Betatown's rate policies. Conceptually, what I want is a class that inherits behavior from both Alphatown's pay station class as well as Betatown's pay station subclass. Thus a class diagram like that in Figure 11.1 comes to mind.

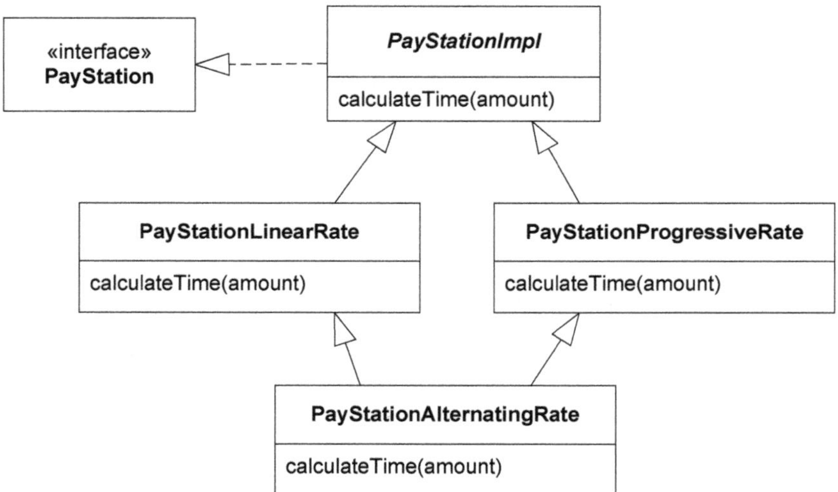

Figure 11.1: Multiple inheritance solution.

In the diagram, I have taken the liberty to refactor the previous polymorphic solution discussed in Section 7.5 a bit: I have introduced an abstract class handling most of the pay station's responsibilities and furthermore defined two subclasses that each fills in the missing rate calculation behavior. Next, I have defined the combined rate strategy as a subclass with both these as superclasses.

You can do this in languages that support *multiple inheritance of implementation* like C++. (If you are not familiar with the difference between inheritance of interface and inheritance of implementation, a short outline is given in sidebar 11.1.) However, modern object-oriented languages like Java and C# have removed the support for having more than one superclass with implementation. The reason is that practice

Sidebar 11.1: Interface and Implementation Inheritance

A class actually defines two things: the interface of objects instantiated from it; and the behavior when methods are called. Thus it combines *specification* as well as *implementation*. An interface, known in Java and C#, on the other hand is only a declaration of the specification, as no implementation is allowed.

When you make a subclass you inherit both the interface as well as the implementation. However, you run into some subtleties when you introduce multiple inheritance—that is if your subclass has two or more superclasses.

The first problem is what `super` means. super.foo() calls the superclass' foo() method but what then if you have multiple superclasses? C++ solves this as you have to indicate which superclass you mean by writing its name like

```
time = LinearRateStrategy::calculateTime(amount);
```

The problem is now that you have high coupling between the subclass and the superclass: you are actually not invoking a method in your superclass but have hard-wired a call to a specific class in the class hierarchy. Thus if you change the inheritance hierarchy you introduce some really weird defects.

Other languages have experimented with constructs that allow you to specify in which order superclass methods are called. Experience showed that this gave rise to defects that were even more tricky to find and remove. Yet another attempt is to rename methods in one superclass path but then a developer has to remember two different names for the same method and select the proper one depending on which class it is programmed in.

Java and C# has removed this problem all together by simply removing the possibility of inheriting multiple implementations: you can only have one superclass. However, the possibility of inheriting just the specification, the interface, is a powerful tool and fully supported. Thus you can write

```
public class Foo extends Bar implements X, Y, Z {
  public void calculate() { ... }
```

Note that Bar, X, Y, as well as Z may define the calculate method but there is never any conflict or misinterpretation of what calculate is. In Foo calling super.calculate() in calculate can mean only one thing, namely Bar's calculate; and a declaration like

```
  private Z myZ = new Foo();
```

is fine as the Foo instance of course provides the calculate behavior.

has shown such a construct to open a can of worms of problems: The code is difficult to understand and often leads to odd defects that are difficult to find.

The bottom line is that in Java and C# we cannot do this but have to make a subclass with a single superclass. The question is then how to reuse the implementation we already have in the linear and progressive rate strategy classes. The problem has no "nice" solution actually. I can identify several possibilities but they are all pretty bad (you can find an overview of all four solutions, side by side, in Figure 11.2 on page 173):

1. *Cut'n'paste in a subclass of* PayStationImpl. I make a PayStationAlternatingRate subclass of PayStationImpl and copy the source code of the two algorithms directly into it.

2. *Cut'n'paste in a subclass of* PayStationLinearRate. Then I only need to cut'n'paste the progressive rate calculation as the other is available by a call to the superclass.

3. *Move the two rate algorithm implementations up as protected methods in the superclass.* I can now define a direct subclass and it simply calls the respective two algorithms as they are accessible in the superclass.

4. *Making a pay station with two pay stations inside.* I make a subclass and inside of it I can instantiate one of each type to handle the calculations.

Below I will treat each solution.

1: Direct subclass. One approach is simple cut'n'paste reuse by defining a subclass PayStationAlternatingRate inheriting directly from the abstract PayStationImpl. In this I simply paste the code fragments defining the algorithms from the two other classes. This of course works but I now have duplicated code and thus the multiple maintenance problem—not across source tree copies but across classes that contain copies of identical code fragments. In my case these fragments are so small that it is unlikely that I identify defects, but consider the case where the two rate algorithms had been large and complex. Code duplication leads to maintenance problems and better solutions exist.

2: A sub-subclass. If I define the PayStationAlternatingRate as a subclass of, say, PayStationLinearRate then I can access the linear rate calculation directly in the code by a call to the superclass:

```
public class PayStationAlternatingRate
  extends PayStationLinearRate {
  [...]
  private int calculateTime( int amount ) {
    int time;
    if ( isWeekend() ) {
      [Paste progressive calculation code here]
    } else {
      time = super.calculateTime( amount );
    }
    return time;
  }
}
```

Thus I avoid "half" of the code duplication as any changes or defects removed in the linear strategy algorithm will automatically be reflected. Still, the asymmetry is odd. Why is it this superclass that is chosen and not the other? And I still have the multiple maintenance problem. The bottom line is that I have an odd design that reflects an arbitrary design decision that still has a major problem. Not good...

3: Superclass rate calculations. I can push the rate calculation algorithms up into the superclass PayStationImpl in two separate, protected, methods like

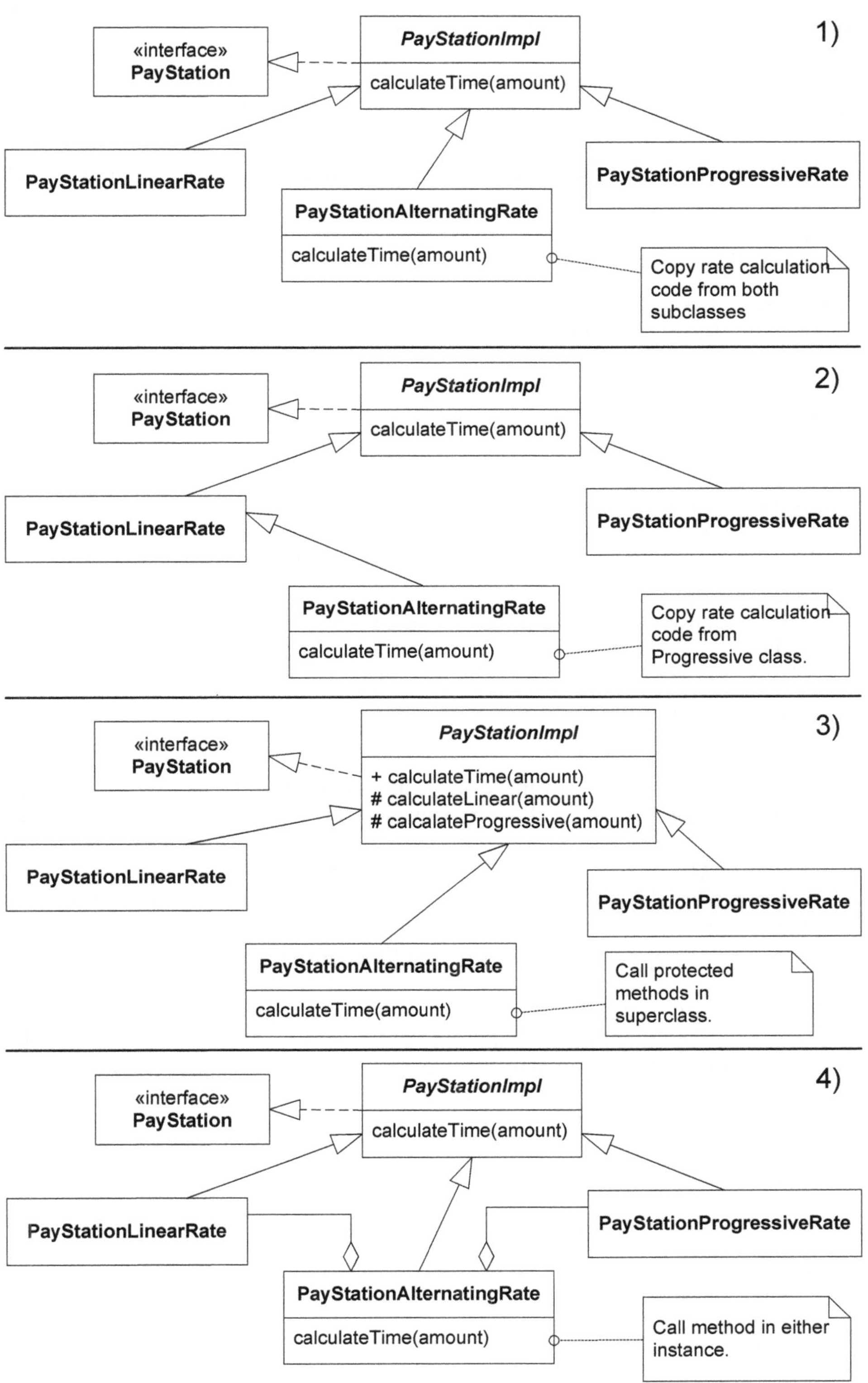

Figure 11.2: Four polymorphic proposals for reusing rate algorithms.

```
public class PayStationImpl implements PayStation {
  [...]
  protected int calculateLinearTime( int amount ) { [...] }
  protected int calculateProgressiveTime( int amount ) { [...] }
}
```

Then the two concrete pay stations for Alphatown and Betatown can call up into the superclass:

```
public class PayStationLinearStrategy
  extends PayStationImpl {
  [...]
  protected int calculateTime( int amount ) {
    return super.calculateLinearTime( amount );
  }
  [...]
}
```

The new Gammatown pay station then becomes:

```
public class PayStationAlternatingRate
  extends PayStationImpl {
  [...]
  protected int calculateTime( int amount ) {
    int time;
    if ( isWeekend() ) {
      time = super.calcProgressiveTime( amount );
    } else {
      time = super.calcLinearTime( amount );
    }
    return time;
  }
```

By doing this I avoid code duplication! This solution may seem appealing but it represents a dangerous path in the long run as you will see in the exercise below.

> **Exercise 11.2:** Analyze this proposal's long term maintainability. Consider a scenario where we sell products to a large set of towns with many different rate structure requirements. Also consider whether such changes are supported by *change by addition* or *change by modification.*

4: Pay station with pay stations inside. One other solution that I can come up with is to instantiate PayStationLinearRate and PayStationProgressiveRate objects within the PayStationAlternatingRate object. Then this combination object can delegate rate calculation to these objects. Something like:

```
public class PayStationAlternatingRate
  extends PayStationImpl {
  private PayStation psLinear, psProgressive;
  [...]
  private int calculateTime( int amount ) {
    int time;
    if ( isWeekend() ) {
      time = psProgressive.calculateTime( amount );
    } else {
      time = psLinear.calculateTime( amount );
    }
    return time;
  }
```

This solution also has no code duplication. One thing nags me a lot, though. Conceptually, I have a pay station that now contains two other pay stations inside of it. This is conceptually wrong—you do not build pay stations like that. It is the rate calculation algorithms I am interested in reusing, not complete pay stations. Even at the machine level this solution appears strange as memory is used on three pay station objects of which the instance variables of two of them will never be used—not a major technical concern given the vast amount of memory in modern machines but still it points to a problem in this design.

11.5 Compositional + Parametric Proposal

Now, let me return to the compositional design from the strategy pattern chapter. As I have this design and the associated code, it is tempting simply to throw a condition into the pay station to switch on the rate strategy to use. The rationale is that Alphatown's pay stations are simply pay stations that use the same linear rate strategy both in weekends and during weekdays.

While it appears simple at first it quickly becomes a bit awkward to keep all three products intact. I wind up with an implementation like

```
public class PayStationImpl implements PayStation {
  [...]
  /** the strategy for rate calculations */
  private RateStrategy rateStrategyWeekday;
  private RateStrategy rateStrategyWeekend;

  /** Construct a pay station. */
  public PayStationImpl( RateStrategy rateStrategyWeekday,
                         RateStrategy rateStrategyWeekend ) {
    this.rateStrategyWeekday = rateStrategyWeekday;
    this.rateStrategyWeekend = rateStrategyWeekend;
  }
  public void addPayment( int coinValue )
          throws IllegalCoinException {
    [...]
    if ( isWeekend() ) {
      timeBought = rateStrategyWeekend.calculateTime(insertedSoFar);
    } else {
      timeBought = rateStrategyWeekday.calculateTime(insertedSoFar);
    }
  }
  [...]
  private boolean isWeekend() {
  [...]
  }
}
```

and the testing code for Alphatown then becomes:

```
  public void setUp() {
    ps = new PayStationImpl( new LinearRateStrategy(),
                             new LinearRateStrategy() );
  }
```

I have several objections to this proposal. First, of course, I modify existing code which is generally a bad idea. Not only is the pay station implementation code changed but even worse I have to change all the testing code and all other code that instantiates pay stations as the constructor signature has been changed. This is a change with a lot of ripple effect.

Second, the pay station constructor signature is simply weird and inconsistent for Alphatown and Betatown. Why provide *two* rate structures when only one is needed? Even worse, the instantiation of Alphatown pay stations is influenced by a requirement from another town! I have no encapsulation of the pay station and the solution suffers weak cohesion.

Third, I have added yet another responsibility to the pay station, namely *Determine weekend or not* that was not a part of the original design. This is one step towards making the pay station a blob object. It has sneaked in without much notice, and it has nothing to do with the abstraction of a pay station at all. It contributes to low cohesion indeed.

My conclusion: This is a terrible solution.

11.6 Compositional Proposal

In a previous chapter, I introduced the ③-①-② process so let us try to crank the handles of it again and see what comes out this time.

③ *I identify some behavior that varies.* The rate calculation behavior is what must vary for Gammatown and this we have already identified.

① *I state a responsibility that covers the behavior that varies and encapsulate it by expressing it as an interface.* The RateStrategy interface already defines the responsibility to *Calculate parking time* by defining the method calculateTime.

② *I compose the resulting behavior by delegating the concrete behavior to subordinate objects.* This is the point that takes on a new meaning concerning the Gammatown requirement: its rate calculation behavior can be achieved by combining the two I have already developed.

In my mind, the key to understand compositional design is to think of *collaboration!* If I view my existing design not as objects but metaphorically as a company with employees I see a "specialist worker" that has specialized in calculating linear rates and one that has specialized in progressive rate calculations. The pay station "company" also has an employee that collects money and every time he gets a new coin, he asks the associated specialist worker to calculate the minutes of parking time that he should display. He delegates this task to the rate calculation specialist in the team. The point here is that the pay station employee (alas the PayStationImpl object) does not himself choose which rate calculation specialist to use... He has simply been put in a team where there is a specialist responsible for doing these calculations—it is the "management" that has defined the team (alas the parameter given in the constructor when the pay station object was created).

Thus, the compositional way to handle this is to realize that we already have the two required specialists in rate calculation in our company. However, we do not want our pay station employee to be overburdened of choosing which one to use. Instead we simply create a team to perform the calculation instead. The team of course consists of the two specialists and then we hire a coordinator to decide which specialist should make the calculation. Officially, he is the guy responsible for calculating rates but instead of doing it himself he simply asks one of his two team mates to make it. The actual behavior required is teamwork instead of individual effort. Also note that the behavior of the coordinator is very simple: he looks at the calendar and based upon whether it is weekday or not he asks the proper specialist.

The pay station employee thus does "business as usual". He receives a coin and asks the assigned person to calculate parking time. In the Gammatown case, this is the coordinator that delegates the calculation. Once he has received the answer from the specialist, he returns it to the pay station employee. Indeed, many persons are involved but each person's task is small, well-defined, and easy to understand. The complex behavior arises from the way people collaborate, not because one person performs a complex task.

Objects are no different. Objects provide behavior that match a set of responsibilities and collaborate to get the work done. As long as each object fulfills its responsibility it does not matter how it does it: all by itself, by asking other objects for help, by requesting data from a database, by communicating with a server on the internet, etc. Complex behavior arises from making simple objects collaborate.

Key Point: Object collaborations define compositional designs

When designing software compositionally, you make objects collaborate to achieve complex behavior.

The resulting design is shown in Figure 11.3. I have defined a AlternatingRateStrategy class that implements the RateStrategy interface, and objects of this class aggregate two rate strategy objects: one for weekend calculations and one for weekdays.

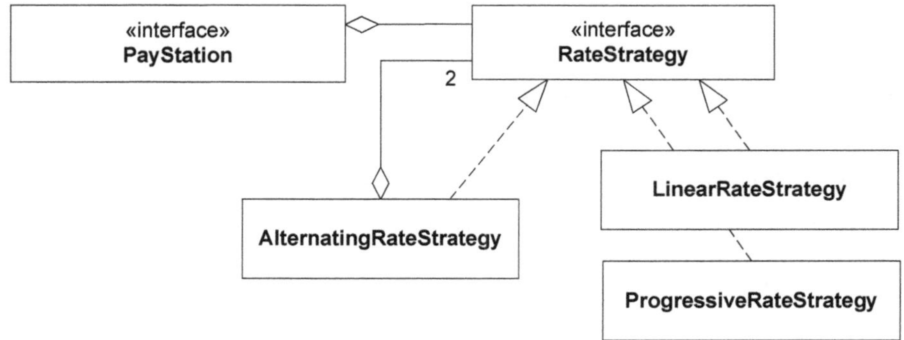

Figure 11.3: Rate calculation as a combined effort.

The required code is very simple as the only addition to the production code is the AlternatingRateStrategy class: *Change by addition, not by modification!*

11.7 Development by TDD

The important problem of getting an external resource (such as the system clock) under automated testing control presents an important design challenge that I will deal with in Chapter 12. Until I get these techniques in place, I will make the testing semi-automatic : add a special Ant target `test-weekday` for testing the Gammatown variant during normal working days, and `test-weekend` for weekend testing. I would then have to set the clock to a normal working day and run the `test-weekday` tests and next set it to a weekend day and run the `test-weekend` tests.

I will leave the development as an exercise. My own iterations look like this.

- *Iteration 1: Weekday.* In this iteration, I add the `test-weekday` target, a TestGammaWeekdayRate test case class that tests a AlternatingRateStrategy and has a single *Representative Data* test case for the linear rate during weekdays. As it fails due to a missing AlternatingRateStrategy I create it, add the first linear rate subordinate object and delegate the calculation to it if it is not weekend. *Step 4: Run all tests and see them all succeed* but only because I actually made this iteration on a Wednesday!
- *Iteration 2: Weekend.* Next, I add the `test-weekend` target, I set the clock to next Sunday, add a TestGammaWeekendRate and finally *Triangulate* the implementation of the rate policy.
- *Iteration 3: Integration.* Integration testing poses some special problems that I will discuss in Chapter 12.

The resulting rate policy implementation becomes

Listing: chapter/state/compositional/iteration-2/src/paystation/domain/AlternatingRateStrategy.java

```
package paystation.domain;

import java.util.*;

/** A rate strategy that uses the State pattern to vary behavior
    according to the state of the system clock: a linear rate
    during weekdays and a progressive rate during weekdends.
*/
public class AlternatingRateStrategy implements RateStrategy {
  private RateStrategy
    weekendStrategy, weekdayStrategy, currentState;
  public AlternatingRateStrategy( RateStrategy weekdayStrategy,
                                  RateStrategy weekendStrategy ) {
    this.weekdayStrategy = weekdayStrategy;
    this.weekendStrategy = weekendStrategy;
    this.currentState = null;
  }
  public int calculateTime( int amount ) {
    if ( isWeekend() ) {
      currentState = weekendStrategy;
    } else {
      currentState = weekdayStrategy;
    }
    return currentState.calculateTime( amount );
```

```
  }
  private boolean isWeekend() {
    Date d = new Date();
    Calendar c = new GregorianCalendar();
    c.setTime(d);
    int dayOfWeek = c.get(Calendar.DAY_OF_WEEK);
    return ( dayOfWeek == Calendar.SATURDAY
             ||
             dayOfWeek == Calendar.SUNDAY);
  }
}
```

Note that I have divided the calculateTime method into two behavioral parts. First, I decide what state the rate strategy object is in, either the current state is weekend processing or weekday processing. Next, the rate is calculated by delegating to the selected rate strategy object. I could have written this shorter, but as the analysis next shows, this is an example of the STATE pattern, and I have written the code to emphasize this.

The configuration of the pay station then becomes a matter of providing the relevant strategies for weekdays and weekends:

```
  public void setUp() {
    RateStrategy rs =
      new AlternatingRateStrategy( new LinearRateStrategy(),
                                   new ProgressiveRateStrategy() );

    ps = new PayStationImpl( rs );
  }
```

Exercise 11.3: Consider what happens if a driver is entering coins while the time changes over midnight from Friday to Saturday.

11.8 Analysis

What are the properties of the compositional proposal? The benefits are:

- *Reliability.* I have not touched *any* existing production code! The pay station implementation is untouched, as is both rate calculation strategy implementations. I am thus confident that my new Gammatown product will have no effect on the production software for Alphatown and Betatown. Furthermore, I have met a new requirement by *change by addition, not by modification* and thus only have one single new class, AlternatingRateStrategy, that I must question the reliability of. Its complexity is low and I can do semi-automatic testing of it so I am confident. But I have admittedly no fully automated testing of it. I must return later to solve this reliability issue.

- *Maintainability.* The implementation is simple and straight forward—except perhaps for the calendar checking code, but this code is required in all solutions. It is much easier to maintain code that you understand.

- *Client's interface consistent.* A very important aspect of this proposal is that the pay station's use of rate calculation objects is unchanged. It has stayed the same even in the face of a new complex requirement. Complex and simple rate calculations are treated uniformly.
- *Reuse.* I have once and for all written the strategy to handle weekday/weekend variations. A new town that is interested in this behavior but with other concrete rate calculations for the respective two periods of time is a simple matter of configuration in the constructor call.
- *Flexible and open for extension.* The present solution is open for new requirements by *Change by addition.* This is in contrast to a parametric solution where the pay station's production code would have to be modified to support new states.
- *State specific behavior is localized.* All the behavior that is depending on the state of the system clock is encapsulated in the AlternatingRateStrategy. As the only aspect of the Gammatown requirements that relates to system time is indeed the rate calculation it is the right place. To put it in other words, the cohesion is high.

Some of the liabilities:

- *Increased number of objects.* This is the standard problem with compositional design namely that it introduces more classes and objects. Knowing your patterns, as described in Chapter 18, is a way to reduce this problem.

11.9 The State Pattern

In the discussion above I once again used the ③-①-② process as I did when I discovered the STRATEGY pattern. This time it was in particular the ② part that I elaborated upon: *thinking collaboration.* Instead of the AlternatingRateStrategy doing all the calculations itself it *delegated* the concrete rate calculations to delegate objects and itself concentrated on the task of deciding which delegate to use depending on the clock. This perspective on AlternatingRateStrategy is focused on how it fulfills its responsibility but let me turn the table and instead look at what it appears to do seen from the pay station's perspective. In essence, the pay station sees an *object that behaves differently depending on its internal state*: is it in its weekend state or is it in its weekday state? This formulation is exactly the intent of the STATE pattern: *Allow an object to alter its behavior when its internal state changes.* The STATE pattern is summarized in design pattern box 11.1 on page 185.

The state pattern defines two central roles: the **context** and the **state**. The context object delegate requests to its current state object, and internal state changes are affected by changing the concrete state object. In my pay station case, the AlternatingRateStrategy is the context while LinearRateStrategy and ProgressiveRateStrategy are state objects. It should be noted that the structure of the STATE pattern (see the pattern box on page 185) is more general than the structure in the pay station: in the pay station, the context object also implements the state interface but this is not always the case. Also the new state is "calculated" each time the calculateTime method is invoked which is also not a requirement of the pattern.

An important observation is that the STATE pattern structurally is equivalent to the STRATEGY pattern! Look at the UML class diagrams for the two patterns: they are alike. This is not surprising as it is the same compositional design idea, the ③-①-② process, that leads to both. So, the interesting question is why do we speak of two different patterns? The answer is that it is two different *problems* that this compositional structure is a solution to. STRATEGY's intent is to handle *variability of business rules or algorithms* whereas STATE's intent is to provide *behavior that varies according to object's internal state*. The rate policy is a variation in business rules used by Alphatown and Betatown, hence the STRATEGY pattern. The problem of Gammatown in contrast is to pick the proper behavior based upon the pay stations internal state, the clock, hence the STATE pattern.

Key Point: Design patterns are defined by the problems they solve

It is the characteristics of the problem a design pattern aims to solve, its intent, that define the proper pattern to apply.

11.10 State Machines

The STATE pattern is a compositional way of implementing **state machines**. State machines are seen in many real life and computational contexts and describe systems that change between different states as a response to external events. A classic and simple case is a subway turnstile that grants access to a subway station only when a traveler inserts a coin. A transition table shows how the turnstile reacts and changes state:

Current State	Event	New State	Action
Locked	Coin entered	Unlocked	Unlock arms
Unlocked	Person passes	Locked	Lock arms
Locked	Person passes	Locked	Sound alarm
Unlocked	Coin entered	Unlocked	Return coin

That is, the turnstile can be in one of two states: "Locked" and "Unlocked" and it changes state depending on the events defined in the table, like entering a coin or passing the arms. The state change itself has an associated action, like sounding the alarm, unlocking the turnstile arms, etc. The STATE pattern can be used to implement the state machine behavior. The turnstile class simply forwards the "coin" and "pass" events to its state object, while the locked and unlocked state objects take appropriate action as well as ensure state changes. An example implementation is shown in Figure 11.4 on page 186.

The state pattern does not dictate which object is responsible for making the state change: the context object or the concrete-state objects. In my pay station case, the only right place to put the state changing code is in the context object, AlternatingRateStrategy: putting it in the concrete state objects, LinearRateStrategy and ProgressiveRateStrategy, would make them incohesive and make them malfunction in a Alphatown/Betatown setting. However, in many state machines it is the individual concrete-state object that knows the proper next state. In this case the concrete-state objects must of course have a reference to the context object in order to tell it to change state.

11.11 Summary of Key Concepts

It is a recurring situation that a requirement for behavior is a combination of behavior already developed. In such a case, reusing the existing code becomes important. In this chapter I have analyzed the polymorphic proposal and it turns out that it is very difficult to achieve a satisfactory design. The polymorphic variants suffer from either code duplication or low cohesion. The code duplication is partly due to the lack of multiple implementation inheritance in modern object-oriented languages like Java and C#; however even the multiple inheritance solution suffers from low maintainability. One of the low cohesion solutions often seen in practice leads to a design where behavior and methods that is actually unique to the subclasses nevertheless bubbles up into an ever growing (abstract) superclass that therefore suffers low cohesion.

The compositional proposal, based upon the ③-①-② process, provides a cleaner way by suggesting to *compose complex behavior from simpler behaviors.* An often useful metaphor is to consider software design as a company or organization consisting of coordinators and specialists that collaborate to get the job done. In the same vein the corner stone of compositional design is *objects that collaborate.*

In the concrete pay station case, the resulting design is an application of the STATE pattern. The STATE pattern describes a solution to the problem of *making an object change behavior according to its internal state.* In the pay station case, the rate calculation changes behavior according to the state of the system clock. The STATE pattern defines two roles, the **context** and the **state** role and require the context object to delegate all state dependent requests to the current state object. The context changes state by changing the object implementing the state role and thus appears to change behavior. Often it is the context itself that changes the state object reference, but it can also be some of the concrete state objects that do it. The STATE pattern is often used to implement *state machines.*

11.12 Selected Solutions

Discussion of Exercise 11.2:

The problem with this solution is that if we want to be consistent in the way we handle new rate requirements (and consistency is the way to keep your code understandable) then the abstract superclass just grows bigger and bigger as it fills up with rate calculation methods. You get *method bloat* in the superclass. This is also a tendency that is often seen in practice. The result is a class with lower cohesion as it contains methods unrelated to itself.

A superclass bloated with methods that are not relevant for itself but only for a large set of subclasses is less understandable. And—new rate requirements will lead to *change by modification* in the superclass.

There is also a risk that it becomes a junk pile of dead code. Consider that "FortyThreeTown" no longer uses our pay station product. Maybe I remember to remove the pay station subclass that was running there, but do I also remember to remove the methods in the superclass that are no longer used in any product?

Discussion of Exercise 11.3:

In the current proposal, it is the time of the last entered coin that dictates the rate policy used. So if the driver starts entering coins on Friday but ends on a Saturday it is the weekend rate policy that is used for the full amount.

11.13 Review Questions

Describe the problems associated with testing the Gammatown requirement of rate calculation based upon the day of week.

Outline the benefits and liabilities of a polymorphic proposal to handle Gammatown's requirement.

Outline the benefits and liabilities of a proposal that uses a conditional statement in the pay station to determine which rate strategy object to use.

Outline the fully compositional proposal: What are the steps in the ③-①-② process and what is the resulting design? Outline benefits and liabilities of this proposal.

What is the STATE pattern? What problem does it address and what solution does it suggest? What are the roles involved? What are the benefits and liabilities?

11.14 Further Exercises

Exercise 11.4:

Compare the STRATEGY and STATE pattern and identify similarities and differences between them. You should include aspects like the structure (interfaces, classes, and relations), intent, roles, and cost-benefits.

Exercise 11.5. Source code directory:
`exercise/state/alarm`

A simple digital alarm clock has a display, showing "hour:minute", and three buttons marked "mode", "+" and "–". Normally the display shows the time. By pressing "mode" the display instead shows the alarm time and allows setting the alarm hour by pressing "+" or "–" to increase or decrease the hour. Pressing "mode" a second time allows changing the minutes, and pressing a third time returns the display to showing the time. That is, the alarm clock can be in one of three states: "display time", "set alarm hour", and "set alarm minute" state.

The hardware buttons of the clock invoke methods in the AlarmClock interface:

Listing: exercise/state/alarm/AlarmClock.java

```
/** Interface for a simple alarm clock.
*/
public interface AlarmClock {
  /** return the contents of the display depending on the
   * state of the alarm clock.
```

```
   * @return the display contents
   */
  public String readDisplay();

  /** press the "mode" button on the clock */
  public void mode();

  /** press the "increase" (+) button on the clock */
  public void increase();

  /** press the "decrease" (-) button on the clock */
  public void decrease();
}
```

To demonstrate how the interface works, consider the following (learning) test where the present time is "11:32" and the alarm set to "06:15".

```
  @Test
  public void shouldHandleAll() {
    // show time mode
    assertEquals( "11:32", clock.readDisplay() );
    // + and - has no effect in show time mode
    clock.increase();
    assertEquals( "11:32", clock.readDisplay() );
    clock.decrease();
    assertEquals( "11:32", clock.readDisplay() );
    // switch to set hour mode
    clock.mode();
    assertEquals( "06:15", clock.readDisplay() );
    clock.increase(); // increment hour by one
    clock.increase();
    clock.increase();
    assertEquals( "09:15", clock.readDisplay() );
    // switch to set minute mode
    clock.mode();
    clock.decrease();
    clock.decrease();
    clock.decrease();
    clock.decrease();
    clock.decrease();
    assertEquals( "09:10", clock.readDisplay() );

    // go back to show time mode
    clock.mode();
    assertEquals( "11:32", clock.readDisplay() );
    // remembers the set alarm time.
    clock.mode();
    assertEquals( "09:10", clock.readDisplay() );
  }
```

1. Sketch a STATE pattern based design for implementing the state machine.
2. Implement the production code. You may "fake" the time (like the clock always being "11:32") but the alarm time must be setable.

[11.1] Design Pattern: State

Intent Allow an object to alter its behavior when its internal state changes.

Problem Your product's behavior varies at run-time depending upon some internal state.

Solution Describe the responsibilities of the dynamically varying behavior in an interface and implement the concrete behavior associated with each unique state in an object, the state object, that implements this interface. The context object delegates to its current state object. When internal state changes occur, the current state object reference is changed to refer to the corresponding state object.

Structure:

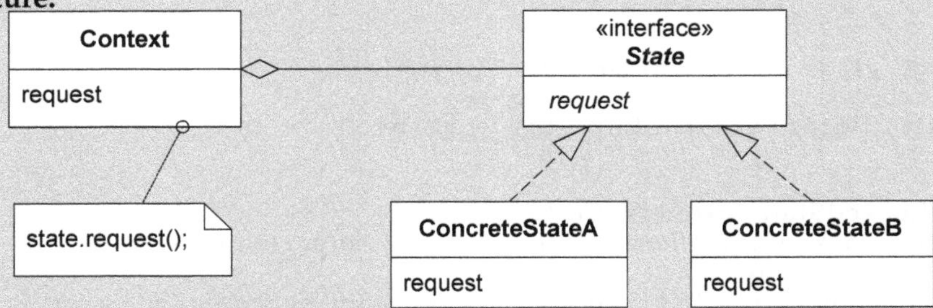

Roles **State** specifies the responsibilities and interface of the varying behavior associated with a state, and **ConcreteState** objects define the specific behavior associated with each specific state. The **Context** object delegates to its current state object. The state object reference is changed whenever the context changes its internal state.

Cost - Benefit *State specific behavior is localized* as all behavior associated with a specific state is in a single class. It *makes state transitions explicit* as assigning the current state object is the only way to change state. A liability is the *increased number of objects and interactions* compared to a state machine based upon conditional statements in the context object.

Listing: chapter/state/turnstile/TurnstileImpl.java

```
/** State pattern implementation of a subway turnstile.
*/
public class TurnstileImpl implements Turnstile {
  State
    lockedState = new LockedState(this),
    unlockedState = new UnlockedState(this),
    state = lockedState;
  public void coin() { state.coin(); }
  public void pass() { state.pass(); }

  public static void main(String[] args) {
    System.out.println( "Demo of turnstile state pattern" );
    Turnstile turnstile = new TurnstileImpl();
    turnstile.coin();
    turnstile.pass();
    turnstile.pass();
    turnstile.coin();
    turnstile.coin();
  }
}

abstract class State implements Turnstile {
  protected TurnstileImpl turnstile;
  public State(TurnstileImpl ts) { turnstile = ts; }
}

class LockedState extends State {
  public LockedState(TurnstileImpl ts) { super(ts); }
  public void coin() {
    System.out.println( "Locked state: Coin accepted");
    turnstile.state = turnstile.unlockedState;
  }
  public void pass() {
    System.out.println( "Locked state: Passenger pass: SOUND ALARM" );
  }
}
class UnlockedState extends State {
  public UnlockedState(TurnstileImpl ts) { super(ts); }
  public void coin() {
    System.out.println( "Unlocked state: Coin entered: RETURN IT");
  }
  public void pass() {
    System.out.println( "Unlocked state: Passenger pass");
    turnstile.state = turnstile.lockedState;
  }
}
```

Figure 11.4: Example implementation of turnstile state pattern.

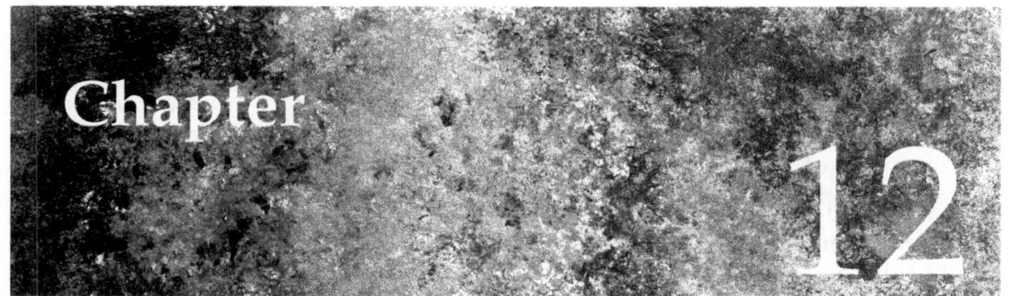

Test Stubs

Learning Objectives

A result of the design developed in the last chapter was the identification of a major problem, namely how to get the pay station rate policy under automated testing control when it depends upon the system clock. The focus of this chapter is for you to learn the terminology for *test stubs* and see how they help us in our quest to automate testing as much as possible. This chapter

- Defines a new requirement demanding that all rate strategies are under fully automatic testing control.
- Analyzes the present production and testing code in order to isolate the problem.
- Identifies the problem as one of controlling the *input* values to a unit under test, and defines terminology, *direct* and *indirect input*, to describe the problem.
- Discusses ways to handle indirect input and classifies them as yet another example of handling variability.
- Develops the compositional proposal by using the ③-①-② process and refactoring the pay station production code.

12.1 New Requirement

The present solution for testing Gammatown's rate policy is not fully automated as it requires me to pick one of two different test targets, one for weekends and one for weekdays. Moreover I have to set and reset the system clock in order to verify the behavior. My new requirement is to make as much as possible of this verification automated by JUnit testing code.

12.2 Direct and Indirect Input

In the last chapter I identified the system clock as an indirect input parameter. So before I discuss a plausible solution I will dwell a bit on the problem from a more abstract point of view as it is something you run into all the time in testing and test-driven development.

Abstractly I can describe the relation between production and testing code like in Figure 12.1. In this UML communication diagram, the numbered lines represent method calls between objects, executed in the sequence shown by the numbers. The JUnit test object symbolize the JUnit testing code that first sets up the production code, next exercises it, and finally verifies that its output matches the expected output. The testing code exercises a particular part of the production code, the *unit under test* shown as the UUT object. The right hand object, denoted DOU, symbolizes units of the production code that the UUT depends upon, and is explained in detail below.

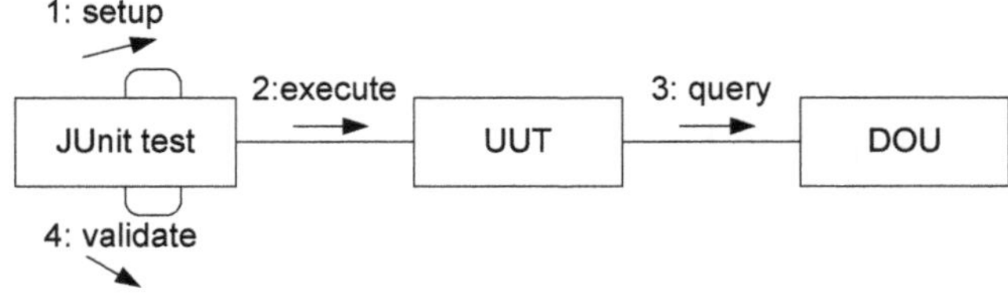

Figure 12.1: The relation between test and production code.

In our concrete context the setup, exercise and verify code was (for weekdays):

chapter/state/compositional/iteration-2/test/paystation/domain/TestGammaWeekdayRate.java
```
@Test public void shouldDisplay120MinFor300cent() {
  RateStrategy rs =
    new AlternatingRateStrategy( new LinearRateStrategy(),
                                 new ProgressiveRateStrategy() );
  assertEquals( 300 / 5 * 2, rs.calculateTime(300) );
}
```

Now, a test case must state all the input parameters

Input	Expected output
pay = 500 cent, day = Monday	200 min.
pay = 500 cent, day = Sunday	150 min.

This allows us to classify input into two categories.

Definition: Direct input

Direct input is values or data, provided directly by the testing code, that affect the behavior of the unit under test (UUT).

Definition: Indirect input

Indirect input is values or data, that cannot be provided directly by the testing code, that affect the behavior of the unit under test (UUT).

In my example, the payment of 500 cent is direct input (it is a parameter to the method), while the day of week is indirect (I cannot provide the method with this value.) Note that input is not required to be direct parameters to a method to be classified as direct input, the only qualifying property is the ability of the testing code to *somehow* provide the proper values. For instance an object's instance variables may be direct input if there are methods available that allows the testing code to set their values.

Indirect input stems from units that our UUT depends upon. These are called depended-on units (DOU):

> Definition: **Depended-on unit**
> A unit in the production code that provides values or behavior that affect the behavior of the unit under test.

Control and data flows both from the UUT towards the DOU as it calls methods in the DOU and back when the DOU returns values or invoke methods in the UUT. In our Gammatown example, the UUT is the Gammatown AlternatingRateStrategy instance which depends upon a DOU, the Java library behavior to compute whether it is weekend or not.

Armed with this analysis I can restate my problem: *How can I ensure that the DOU returns the values (indirect input) that are specified in my test case during testing — and the real values during normal execution?*

12.3 One Problem – Many Designs

The new problem statement certainly sounds like something that I have already analyzed: How do I vary software behavior? I may do it using several proposals:

- *Parametric proposal:* I define some boolean instance variable in the pay station that defines whether the production code is in testing or normal mode. I can switch on this parameter in the AlternatingRateStrategy. Of course I also have to make an instance variable that tells which day it is. This variable is then never used in normal operation.
- *Polymorphic proposal:* I can subclass the AlternatingRateStrategy into an TestingAlternatingRateStrategy that overrides the isWeekend method, and provide the pay station with an instance of this class instead. This class must of course also be told which day to return.
- *Compositional proposal:* I use the ③-①-② process to identify, encapsulate, and delegate to the behavior that is variable.

I of course favor the compositional solution for all the same reasons that you have already seen and will therefore focus on the compositional proposal.

12.4 Test Stub: A Compositional Proposal

The ③-①-② process:

③ *I identify some behavior that varies.* It is basically the behavior defined by the isWeekend() method that is variable.

① *I state a responsibility that covers the behavior that varies by an interface.* I will define an interface WeekendDecisionStrategy containing the isWeekend() method.

② *I compose the desired behavior by delegating.* Again, this is the real principle that brings the solution: I simply let the AlternatingRateStrategy call the isWeekend() method provided by the WeekendDecisionStrategy to find out whether it is weekend or not. I can then make implementations that either returns a preset value (for testing) or uses the operating system clock (for production usage).

This is another application of the STRATEGY pattern.

Exercise 12.1: Provide the arguments why this is a STRATEGY pattern and not a STATE pattern.

Thus the class diagram will look like in Figure 12.2.

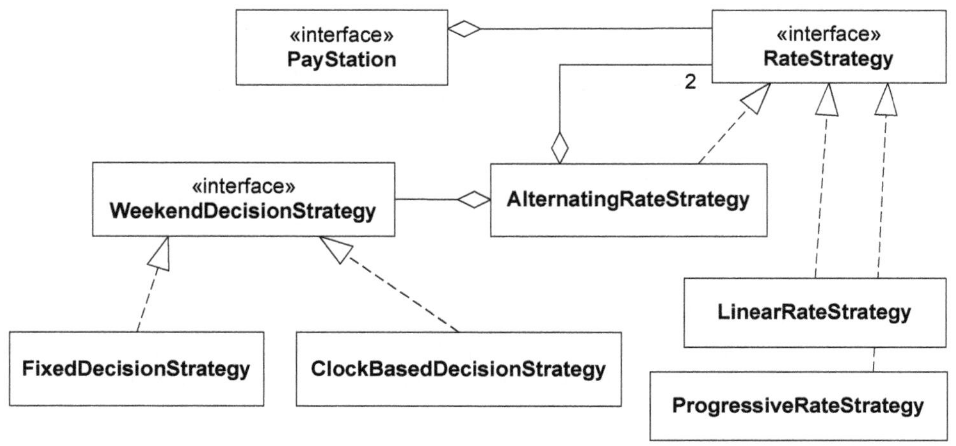

Figure 12.2: Adding a strategy to decide whether it is weekend or not.

Returning to the problem from the testing point of view, I have actually replaced the real depended-on unit with a *test stub*:

Definition: Test stub

A test stub is a replacement of a real *depended-on unit* that feeds indirect input, defined by the test code, into the *unit under test*.

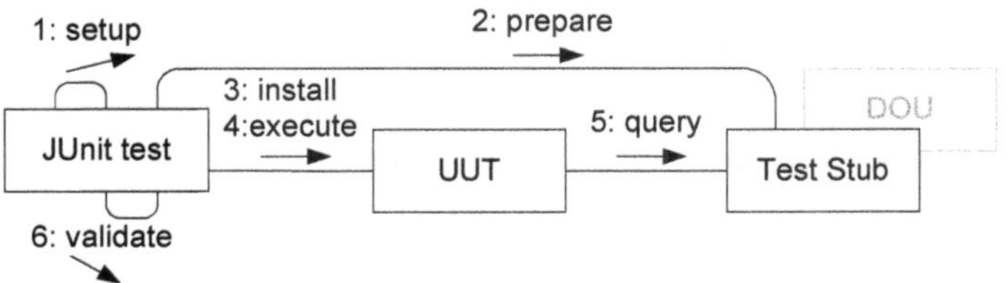

Figure 12.3: Test Stub replacing the DOU.

A test stub has the exact same interface as the DOU but normally only returns values that have been set by the testing code, as shown in Figure 12.3. Here the test code prepares the stub (usually by creating it and setting what it should return), next installs it into the UUT, and finally execute the tests.

Thus, to test the AlternatingRateStrategy for its weekend processing I will provide it with a WeekendDecisionStrategy whose isWeekend() method is set to return whatever value the testing code has set.

Key Point: Test stubs make software testable

Many software units depend on indirect input that influence their behavior. Typical indirect input are external resources like hardware sensors, random-number generators, system clocks, etc. Test stubs replace the real units and allow the testing code to control the indirect input.

Note that the ability to use test stubs hinges on the UUT's ability to collaborate with the stub instead of the real depended-on unit. That is, it is not possible if the UUT itself creates the DOU or in other ways are tightly coupled to it.

The term *test stub* is often used to denote any test-oriented replacement. However, you can classify stubs more precisely according to their use. Sidebar 12.1 describes such a classification.

Exercise 12.2: In Chapter 8, I introduced a special rate strategy, One2OneRateStrategy, to isolate testing of the pay station from the testing of the rate calculation. Review this design in the light of the test stub terminology introduced. What software units in the pay station design match the terms above?

12.5 Developing the Compositional Proposal

As when I introduced the RateStrategy I first go through a refactoring phase. When all tests again pass on the refactored design I concentrate on introducing the test stub.

Sidebar 12.1: Classifying Test Stubs

Meszaros (2007) suggests a more detailed classification of stubs based upon their intended use. He defines **test double** as the general concept, and identifies these classes:

- *Test stub:* A double whose purpose it is to feed indirect input, defined by the test case, into the UUT.
- *Test spy:* A double whose purpose it is to record the UUT's indirect output for later verification by the test case.
- *Mock object:* A double, created and programmed dynamically by a mock library, that may both serve as a stub and spy.
- *Fake object:* A double whose purpose is to be a high performance replacement for a slow or expensive DOU.

A good example of a spy is TDD development of a control system for a robot. Such system should issue the proper commands in the right sequence for the robot's different motors but verifying correctness by watching the robot move is of course not automatic testing. Here, spies can replace each motor and record the control system's issued commands to verify its behavior.

Mock objects are doubles that are created dynamically by a mock library based upon an interface. This way you avoid writing the test stub code which increase your speed when developing code that introduces *Fake It* objects. However, the mocks have to be told what to return and what sequence of method invocations to expect and this programming can turn out to be quite cumbersome. A good presentation of mocks is given by Freeman, Mackinnon, Pryce, and Walnes (2004).

Fake objects are often used to replace a database. A database is comparatively slow to query and update, and it is expensive to reset it to an initial state to allow *Isolated Test*. A fake object may be implemented as a simple in-memory map that returns a limited set of fixed values for queries.

12.5.1 Iteration 1: Refactoring

Refactoring is of course supported by the already developed test cases and I follow the same plan as I did in the STRATEGY chapter:

- Introduce the new interface.
- Refactor the existing AlternatingRateStrategy to take instances of this interface as parameter in the constructor. See that it compiles but the tests fail.
- Refactor the existing design to make all test cases pass again. This will require introducing the ClockBasedDecisionStrategy.

As the refactoring process is similar to the one I went through in Section 8.1.1 I will leave out the details.

12.5.2 Iteration 2: Test Stub

I can now introduce the test stub that I name FixedDecisionStrategy. The implementation is *Obvious Implementation*.

Listing: chapter/test-stub/iteration-2/test/paystation/domain/FixedDecisionStrategy.java

```
package paystation.domain;

import java.util.*;

/** A test stub for the weekend decision strategy.
*/

public class FixedDecisionStrategy
        implements WeekendDecisionStrategy {
  private boolean isWeekend;
  /** construct a test stub weekend decision strategy.
   * @param isWeekend the boolean value to return in all calls to
   * method isWeekend().
   */
  public FixedDecisionStrategy(boolean isWeekend) {
    this.isWeekend = isWeekend;
  }
  public boolean isWeekend() {
    return isWeekend;
  }
}
```

☞ Why is this implementation located in the test folder?

Now for the first time, the testing of Gammatown's rate strategy for *both* weekday and weekend pass as the test stub can now provide the UUT with the proper indirect input. Thus a test case for the week day testing

Input	Expected output
pay = 300 cent, day = Wednesday	120 min.

can be rephrased

Input	Expected output
pay = 300 cent, day-type = weekday	120 min.

and directly expressed in my JUnit test case:

Fragment: chapter/test-stub/iteration-2/test/paystation/domain/TestGammaWeekdayRate.java

```
@Test public void shouldDisplay120MinFor300cent() {
  RateStrategy rs =
    new AlternatingRateStrategy( new LinearRateStrategy(),
                                 new ProgressiveRateStrategy(),
                                 new FixedDecisionStrategy(false));
  assertEquals( 300 / 5 * 2, rs.calculateTime(300) );
}
```

The direct input is given as parameter to calculateTime while the indirect input by the test stub. Now I can run both weekday and weekend tests at any time. As there is now no need for the separate test targets I can add an item to my test list so I remember to refactor the tests to make the structure of the Gammatown tests similar to that of Alphatown and Betatown.

12.5.3 Iteration 3: Refactoring Tests

This step entails

- Making a TestAlternatingRate, moving all Gammatown rate policy test cases here, and deleting the two old test case classes.
- Modifying TestAll so it includes the new test cases.
- Removing the special test targets from the build script.

These are pretty trivial steps and I will not dwell on the details. However, I note that an important issue remains: *integration testing*.

12.5.4 Iteration 4: Integration Testing

Integration testing is defined as validating the interaction between software units, and here I need to test that the pay station is indeed configured with the proper rate strategy. To verify that the pay station is indeed a Gammatown pay station I will actually have to add two test cases: one in which the pay station is configured with the AlternatingRateStrategy which again is configured to use the test stub, FixedDecisionStrategy, telling it is a weekday; and one in which the latter tells it is a weekend day.

However, when I look into the TestIntegration class I see the existing two integration test cases that I developed earlier for Alphatown and Betatown, and the question is what increased reliability I get for the cost of making the additional test cases.

> ☞ Take a moment to review the TestIntegration code and evaluate if there are any additional interactions that a pay station configured with the Gammatown rate strategy will test over the interactions already tested by the two other test cases.

My conclusion is that I get very little return on my investment in coding time. The two existing integration tests verify that the pay station indeed interact correctly with the rate strategy object that is passed as parameter in its constructor. Then why should it not interact properly with the rate strategy of Gammatown? Therefore I conclude that additional integration testing of this interaction is a waste of time.

> **Exercise 12.3:** Actually, this argumentation can be tied to one of the testing principles that was presented in Chapter 5. Evaluate the various TDD principles, find the one that matches the argumentation, and argue why it matches.

Sidebar 12.2: Wind Computation Testing in SAWOS

Data on wind is essential for aircraft pilots during landing and take-off. Therefore the SAWOS system (see page 20) calculated a *two minute mean* wind value that averaged the wind direction and wind speed in the last two minute interval. Wind direction calculations were especially tricky as the valid interval is between 0 and 360 degrees where 0 degrees is due north, 90 degrees is due east, etc. However, if the wind is in north then the set of readings vary from 0 to perhaps 358, back to 0, to 3, etc., so a trivial summation and average algorithm is incorrect. Obviously, we could not wait for the weather to be correct in order to test the computations, so we developed a test stub that could be instrumented with a set of wind data readings, and configured the wind computation object with this instead of the real wind sensor.

Later we reused the test stub (and those developed for all the other types of sensors: temperature, humidity, clouds, RVR, ...) for demonstration purposes where the SAWOS system ran on a stand-alone computer without any sensors attached. This allowed us to go through the first acceptance tests by the customer at our premises.

12.6 Analysis

So, what have I achieved in this exercise? First, I have increased the fraction of the production code under testing control, and the testing is fully automatic. At the start of this iteration, I had three different test targets and some only worked on specific days. Now, all test cases are again run as a single suite. Second, the main point of this exercise, of course, is the *test stub* concept. Test stubs allow us to replace "real" software units (the *depended on units*) with surrogates that can be instrumented by our testing code to provide the proper *indirect input values*. And third, the process of defining the test stub demonstrates how a strong focus on testing goes hand in hand with compositional design and the ③-①-② process.

It is difficult to introduce test stubs if the behavior that provides the indirect input is not well encapsulated. The ③-①-② process is basically all about solving this problem and tells me to do it by abstracting and expressing the behavior by defining an interface and by using delegation.

You may argue that my solution is overly complex for such a minor problem as testing a single `if` statement in a single method. And of course you are right. The key point is that the technique becomes much more valuable once the size and complexity of the problem grows, so take the simple Gammatown pay station problem as a vehicle for demonstrating the technique in practice. Consult sidebar 12.2 for a realistic case of using stubs.

However, this iteration also has its weaknesses. There are no more any specific test cases for the real production code implementation of the isWeekend method. Let us consider a situation where I have actually coded a defect into the ClockBasedDecisionStrategy that leads to failures. My refactored test cases will not expose this failure and thus the defect may go undetected until our Gammatown customer starts complaining. From this perspective, the refactored solution I have now is automatic, yes, but the quality of the test is slightly lower as the old manual tests *did* test the real clock based behavior. The bottom-line is that you can drive automatic testing to a certain point and no further, and the key is to have as little code as possible left for manual or system testing. *The fewer lines of code, the lesser the risk of having defects is.* In our case, only the simple isWeekend method in the ClockBasedDecisionStrategy has to be manually tested.

It is also important to note that I rely on the Java library code to perform as specified. I do not make test cases to test get(Calendar.DAY_OF_WEEK), or stub the GregorianCalendar class. Testing is about getting as much reliability as possible with the least possible effort, and I do not think the investment in testing Java library implementation will find any defects, and therefore is a waste of time.

12.7 Summary of Key Concepts

The basic idea of unit testing is to execute a specific software unit (the *unit under test*, UUT) with specific input values and verify that the computed output match the expected output. The input can be classified as either *direct* or *indirect* input. Direct input is values that the testing code can directly control, typically by passing values as parameters in method calls. Indirect input is values that are provided by other software units that the unit under test depends upon (*depended-on units*, DOUs). Often it is difficult or impossible for the testing code to force these depended-on units to provide specific values relevant for the particular test.

In this case, these units should be replaced by *test stubs* i.e. test specific software units that have the same interface but can be programmed by the testing code to provide specific indirect input. This makes automated testing feasible.

The requirement that a certain type of input, the indirect input, should be able to stem from two different sources is basically a variability requirement, and the ③-①-② process can be applied. This means that the indirect input should be encapsulated by an interface and that the production code should use delegation to request the indirect input.

A typical example of using test stubs is to encapsulate external resources like random-number generators, hardware sensors, etc. In this case, there will often be some code that cannot be verified by automated tests, namely the code that do the actual hardware handling, random-number generation, etc. The key point is to make this portion of the code as small as possible. Manual and system testing should be employed to ensure the reliability of these code sections.

Test stubs have been used throughout computing history and as such one of those "tricks of the trade" that everybody is supposed to know about but is seldom discussed in depth in literature. Its prominent role in test-driven development has changed this somewhat and I can recommend "xUnit Test Patterns: Refactoring Test Code" by Meszaros (2007).

12.8 Selected Solutions

Discussion of Exercise 12.1:

The structure of object relations in STRATEGY and STATE are identical. However, their *intent* are different. STATE is to *Allow an object to alter its behavior when its internal state changes*. In contrast the intent of STRATEGY is *Define a family of business rules or algorithms, encapsulate each one, and make them interchangeable*. The former speaks of behavior based on state, the latter of interchangeable algorithms. Here the question is what algorithm to use to calculate if it is weekend, hence it is the STRATEGY pattern.

Discussion of Exercise 12.2:

One2OneRateStrategy can also be classified as a test stub. The unit under test was the pay station and the rate strategy was the depended-on unit that this test stub ease the testing of. In this case, though, the reason for the stub was not that the indirect input (the calculated minutes) was not under testing control, but that the verification code, the asserts, was easier to write and maintain. In this light, we can state that the rate calculations were "altered" by the testing code for the purpose of easing the verification.

Discussion of Exercise 12.3:

I find that it is the *Representative Data* principle at work. The basic testing challenge is if the pay station interacts with the proper rate strategy object. The *Representative Data* principle states that I should use a small set and that each element should represent a particular aspect or a particular computational processing. In this case, there is no particular computational processing associated with the Gammatown rate policy that is not already demonstrated by the two other test cases.

12.9 Review Questions

Explain the difference between *direct input* and *indirect input*. Why is direct input not always simply values to be provided by method parameters?

Explain the terms *depended-on unit* (DOU) and *unit under test* and their relations to each other and to the test case code.

Explain what a *test stub* is: what is its purpose and how does it programmatically serve this purpose?

Relate how the use of test stubs relate to the ③-①-② process and the compositional proposal for handling variable behavior.

12.10 Further Exercises

Exercise 12.4:

In a computer game the program typically validates that the user moves his pieces correctly, and testing correctness of this algorithm is of course important. Many games rely on throwing dice or other random behavior to determine the number of positions a piece may move.

1. Describe a design that allows testing the move validation algorithm in a die based game using a stub that encapsulate the die throwing algorithm. Describe the design using class and sequence diagrams.

2. Define a Java interface for the die throwing algorithm, and define two implementations: one that uses Java's random libraries to make real random die values in the range 1 to 6; and a second that can be set by JUnit testing code.

Exercise 12.5. Source code directory:
`exercise/test-stub/sevensegment`

The hardware producer of a *seven segment LED display* provides a very low-level interface for turning on each of the seven LED (light-emitting diode) segments on or off, see Figure 12.4.

Figure 12.4: Seven segment LED showing 0.

Listing: exercise/test-stub/sevensegment/SevenSegment.java

```
/** Defines the contract for a seven segment LED display.
*/

public interface SevenSegment {
  /** turn a LED on or off.
   * @param led the number of the LED. Range is 0 to 6. The LEDs are
   * numbered top to bottom, left to right. That is, the top,
   * horizontal, LED is 0, the top left LED is 1, etc.
   * @param on if true the LED is turned on otherwise it is turned
   * off.
  */
  void setLED(int led, boolean on);
}
```

Clearly, this is cumbersome in practice, so it is much better to define an abstraction that can turn on and off the proper LEDs for our ten numbers 0 to 9:

Listing: exercise/test-stub/sevensegment/NumberDisplay.java

```
/** The interface to a seven segment LED that displays numbers 0-9.
*/

public interface NumberDisplay {
  /** display a number on a seven segment.
   * @param number the number to display.
   * Precondition: number should be in the range 0 to 9.
  */
  void display(int number);
}
```

1. Sketch how a TDD process, based upon automated testing and no visual inspection of the seven segment display, can develop a reliable implementation of NumberDisplay.

2. Classify the developed test stub according to the classification defined in sidebar 12.1.

3. Use TDD to develop an implementation of NumberDisplay.

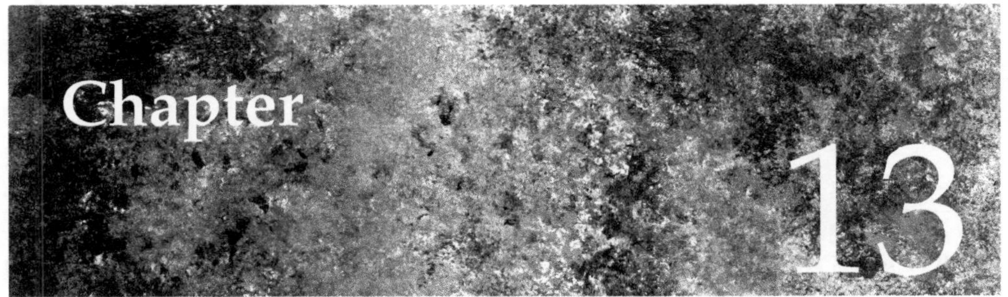

Deriving Abstract Factory

Learning Objectives

New requirements are the reality of successful software development—and this time it has to do with *creating* objects. In this chapter, the objective is to establish the ABSTRACT FACTORY as a solution to the problem of creating variable types of objects. As was the case in the introduction of the two preceding design patterns, another objective is to show how this pattern also comes naturally from a compositional design philosophy. However, this time you will see that blindly following the ③-①-② process do not necessarily provide the best solution—you have to analyze the result and constantly refactor to optimize the design.

In this chapter, I will also spend some time on the actual refactoring to introduce the ABSTRACT FACTORY and the associated code, as it is a more complex design pattern compared to STRATEGY and STATE and people often misunderstand it or implement it incorrectly.

13.1 Prelude

So far, I have not spent much attention on the Receipt class—its responsibility is simply to know its value in minutes parking time. In this chapter, I will add another relevant responsibility to the receipt class, namely the ability to print some kind of visual representation of itself.

Receipt
• know its value in minutes parking time • print itself

For the sake of simplicity, I will introduce a very simple scheme for printing, namely a single method:

```
public void print(PrintStream stream);
```

A PrintStream from the Java libraries allows character only printing, so a visual design of a parking receipt is here simply:

```
--------------------------------------------------
-------   P A R K I N G   R E C E I P T    -------
              Value 049 minutes.
            Car parked at 08:06
--------------------------------------------------
```

A more fancy graphical design would perhaps have been more appealing, but the principle is the same with a character based output medium.

For manual testing, I can pass the System.out print stream instance to a receipt object's print method and then manually inspect what gets printed. Fortunately, the Java IO libraries also provides the ByteArrayOutputStream that you can print to. This class is a stream that writes to a byte array that can then be converted to a string. Therefore I can use this to write automated tests of the print method.

Exercise 13.1: Sketch or program a JUnit test case for testing the print method. You should use the ByteArrayOutputStream and in order to "chunk" the resulting string into an array of individual lines you can use the following code:

```
ByteArrayOutputStream baos = new ByteArrayOutputStream();
PrintStream ps = new PrintStream(baos);
// let the receipt print itself
receipt.print(ps);

// get the string printed to the stream
String output = baos.toString();
// split the string into individual lines
String[] lines = output.split("\n");
```

13.2 New Requirements

Change is the only constant in software development. Betatown would like to make some statistics on the receipts that parking meter checkers come across. To do this they require us to print a *bar code* on the receipts so the parking meter checkers can simply scan all receipts they see, instead of manually writing down data.

Thus I am faced with a new challenge: one of the products must issue a special type of receipts, different from standard receipts. Of course, developing software to print real bar codes is out of the scope of the present book, and my interest is in the way our pay station can reliably and flexibly issue different types of receipts. Thus in my treatment the actual implementation will only print a *Fake It* bar code like

```
--------------------------------------------------
-------   P A R K I N G   R E C E I P T    -------
              Value 049 minutes.
            Car parked at 08:06
||  ||||| | || ||| || ||  ||| | || |||| | || ||||
--------------------------------------------------
```

That is, an extra line is added to the printed receipt that consists of a set of "|" and space characters.

13.3 One Problem – Many Designs

The above requirement conceptually boils down to having two different implementations of the Receipt interface as outlined in Figure 13.1. In the diagram I have made a small refactoring, namely to rename the present implementation named ReceiptImpl to StandardReceipt.

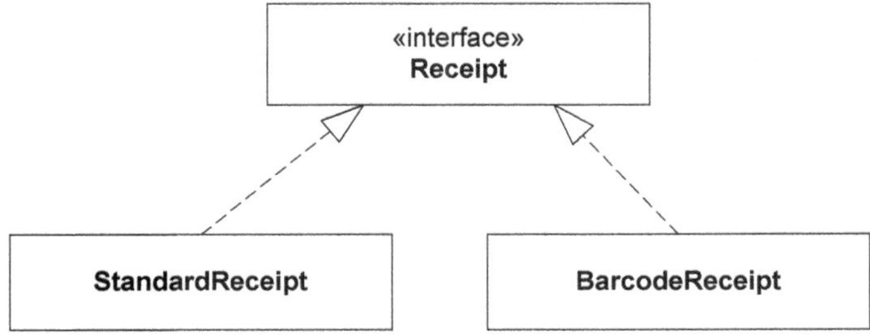

Figure 13.1: New types of Receipts.

Note that this requirement is independent of the previous requirements concerning rate calculations. I can therefore make a configuration table, see Table 13.1, that outlines how pay stations should be configured for the present three towns, stating the type of rate calculation and type of receipt that the town has required.

Table 13.1: The three different configurations of the pay station.

	Variability points	
Product	**Rate**	**Receipt**
Alphatown	Linear	Standard
Betatown	Progressive	Barcode
Gammatown	Alternating	Standard

The new requirement can of course be handled with all the same proposals as we have already analyzed in the strategy and state chapters: by source code copy, by parameterization, by polymorphism, and by a compositional approach. The argumentation is well-known by now, and I will therefore concentrate on the compositional proposal.

Exercise 13.2: Table 13.1 shows the configurations of the pay station but only the production variants (those that are in operation in the different towns). Update the table to show all variants, including those in the testing code.

13.4 A Compositional Proposal

In this section, I will crank the handles of the ③-①-② machine once again and come up with a compositional solution. However, be warned that this first attempt will be flawed. Nevertheless, I will detail this failed attempt as it is important to understand *why* it fails: you appreciate good designs better if you are exposed to less good designs.

So, my first attempt goes like this:

- ③ *I identify a behavior that needs to vary.* The printing of receipts is the behavior that needs to vary. As receipts are objects in the pay station software, the verb "print" is actually the same as "instantiation": it is the way I instantiate Receipt objects that needs to vary. In Alphatown and Gammatown the pay station should instantiate StandardReceipt objects while it should instantiate BarcodeReceipt objects in the Betatown configuration.
- ① *I state a responsibility that covers the behavior and express it as an interface.* One plausible way was to define a ReceiptIssuer interface whose responsibility it is to issue receipts, that is create Receipt objects. This responsibility is at present handled by the pay station so this would also remove one responsibility from it.
- ② *I compose the resulting behavior by delegating to subordinate objects.* The pay station should ask the receipt issuer to instantiate the receipt instead of doing it itself.

This leads to a design shown in Figure 13.2.

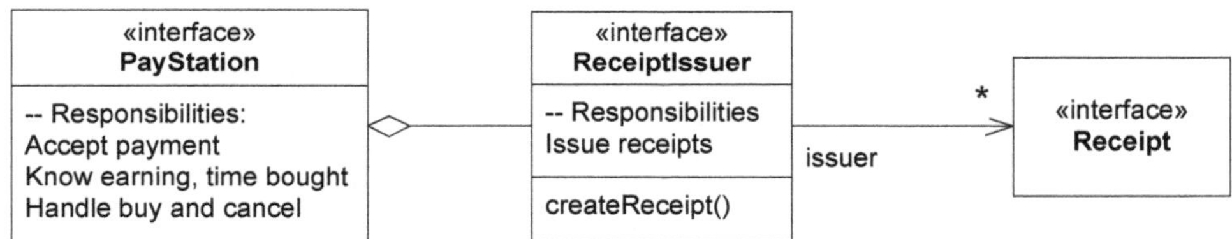

Figure 13.2: Factoring out the receipt issuing responsibility.

Something nags me though. Do I really need this additional ReceiptIssuer abstraction? If I look at the original design in Figure 4.3 on page 45, it has quite a lot of similarity with the way I handled varying the rate calculations. In the original design, I have a pay station object that is associated with a receipt object; and in the strategy chapter I have a pay station associated with a rate strategy. Why can't I simply provide the pay station with the receipt types to issue; just as I provided the pay station with the rate calculation strategy to use? Something along the lines of configuration the Betatown pay station like this:

```
PayStation ps
  = new PayStationImpl( new ProgressiveRateStrategy(),
                        new BarcodeReceipt() );
```

This would do the trick, would it not? And it certainly would simplify the design a lot compared to the above one with the extra ReceiptIssuer class.

> ☞ Spend a few minutes considering what the difference is between issuing receipts and calculating rates before reading on. Looking into the code should provide you with a clue.

It turns out that the situation is quite different and I cannot apply a STRATEGY pattern for receipts. The reason is found in the source code for PayStationImpl's buy method:

Fragment: chapter/abstract-factory/iteration-0/src/paystation/domain/PayStationImpl.java

```
public Receipt buy() {
  Receipt r = new ReceiptImpl(timeBought);
  reset();
  return r;
}
```

The big problem is the **new** statement! The pay station does not just *use* a receipt object as is the case with the rate strategy; it *creates* a receipt object. Each receipt is unique and has its own value of parking time. Therefore it does not make sense to provide the pay station with a single receipt object during construction as it cannot use this object to create new ones[1]. Second, the code that instantiates the pay station above does not compile. The ReceiptImpl constructor takes an argument, namely the number of minutes parking time to print on the receipt. This again highlights the difference between the pay station using an object versus creating new objects.

If I introduce an intermediate object, like ReceiptIssuer, I instead delegate the responsibility of creating receipts to it and can avoid the problem.

13.4.1 Iteration 1: Refactoring

OK, let me try to figure out if the design based on a ReceiptIssuer is a feasible path. I will confront it with reality: quickly develop it and see if it feels right, and be prepared to backtrack if it turns out bad before the costs get too high.

Test-driven development tells me to take small steps, and as was the case earlier, the best path is to refactor the existing design to introduce the new design and make all test cases pass, and next introduce the new bar code receipt.

* refactor to introduce ReceiptIssuer
* add bar code receipts to Betatown.

The present fixture in TestPayStation looks like this:

Fragment: chapter/abstract-factory/iteration-0/test/paystation/domain/TestPayStation.java

```
PayStation ps;
/** Fixture for pay station testing. */
@Before
public void setUp() {
  ps = new PayStationImpl( new One2OneRateStrategy() );
}
```

Thus, according to my design, I must configure it with an issuer object:

[1] I should mention that Java does provide a number of techniques to do this anyway. The clone() method defined in Object would allow me to get a new receipt object that I could change the state in and then use. This is actually the PROTOTYPE design pattern.

```
PayStation ps;
/** Fixture for pay station testing. */
@Before
public void setUp() {
  ps = new PayStationImpl( new One2OneRateStrategy(),
                           new StandardReceiptIssuer() );
}
```

But—this design worries me quite a bit. The reason is that the *configuration responsibility* is assigned two *different* objects. The client code that defines the pay station (like setUp() above) is responsible for configuring the pay station with the proper rate calculation strategy to use. The responsibility of creating the proper receipt types to issue, however, is handled by the receipt issuer. It is "all configuration behavior" but handled by two different objects and thus in disjoint portions of the code. This is again potentially dangerous because a developer that needs to modify a given configuration may more easily miss the point that he or she should review and potentially change in *two* different places—for all the same reasons that I made against handling variable behavior using a parametric proposal. Therefore this solution is not very cohesive.

> ☞ Read the definition of cohesion and rephrase the argumentation above in terms of the cohesion property.

As I aim for a maintainable solution, it is important to achieve high cohesion and therefore I do not like the way things are moving. I see no other way but to undo the implementation and rethink my design. This is actually also the essence of a testing pattern so I do a small sidestep into TDD and present it.

TDD Principle: **Do Over**

What do you do when you are feeling lost? Throw away the code and start over.

The cost is not high here as I have barely begun designing any code. The difficult aspect of this testing pattern is applying it when you have spent three hours coding and it does not go well. You inclination is to "keep your investment". This pattern says it is better to view the three hours as an experiment that has taught you how *not* to do it and use this new knowledge to make a much better design!

Back to the "two ways of creating objects". I have to rethink the responsibilities. I really would like that one object alone is responsible for creating *all* objects that are related to the pay station configuration. I would like to define a responsibility *To make objects* and collect all object creation in a single place. Such an abstraction is often called a *factory*:

PayStationFactory
• Create receipts • Create rate strategies

Thus I would get a cohesive design: *"Aha, a problem with object creation? I know where to look—in the factory."* Concrete factories then instantiate appropriate objects for each pay station product as shown on Figure 13.3. Armed with this new design proposal, I can once again start the refactoring iteration using a test list

* ✱ refactor to introduce PayStationFactory
* ✱ add bar code receipts to Betatown

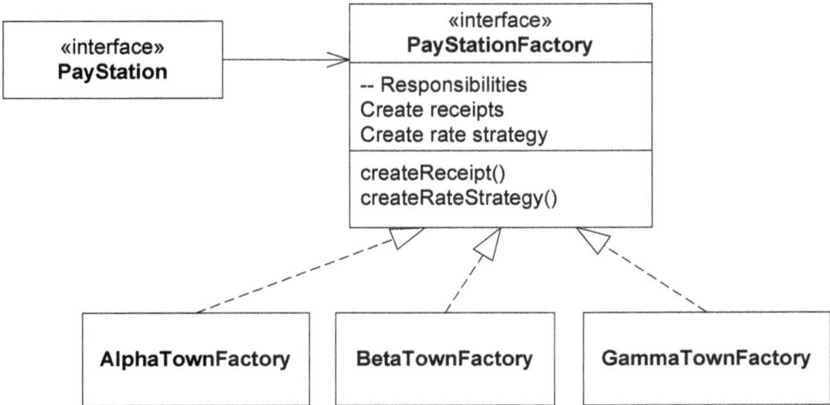

Figure 13.3: Factory handles object instantiation.

13.4.2 Iteration 1: Refactoring (Do Over)

I will make a special factory, named TestTownFactory, that configures the pay station to operate with the One2OneRateStrategy and StandardReceipt, as this is what all the test cases in the TestPayStation class assumes.

Fragment: chapter/abstract-factory/iteration-1a/test/paystation/domain/TestPayStation.java

```
  PayStation ps;
  /** Fixture for pay station testing. */
  @Before
  public void setUp() {
    ps = new PayStationImpl( new TestTownFactory() );
```

This, of course, does not compile. I therefore introduce the factory interface:

Listing: chapter/abstract-factory/iteration-1a/src/paystation/domain/PayStationFactory.java

```
package paystation.domain;
/** The factory for creating the objects that configure
    a pay station for the particular town to operate in.
*/

public interface PayStationFactory {
  /** Create an instance of the rate strategy to use. */
  public RateStrategy createRateStrategy();

  /** Create an instance of the receipt.
   * @param the number of minutes the receipt represents. */
  public Receipt createReceipt( int parkingTime );
}
```

and a TestTownFactory class that simply returns null objects to get to *Step 2: Run all tests and see the new one fail.*

Listing: chapter/abstract-factory/iteration-1a/test/paystation/domain/TestTownFactory.java

```
package paystation.domain;
/** Factory for making the pay station configuration
    for unit testing pay station behavior.
```

```
*/
class TestTownFactory implements PayStationFactory {
  public RateStrategy createRateStrategy() {
    return null;
  }
  public Receipt createReceipt( int parkingTime ) {
    return null;
  }
}
```

Huhh—it still does not compile? Ahh, of course, I need to refactor the PayStationImpl to use the factory. Something like:

```
public class PayStationImpl implements PayStation {
  [...]
  /** the strategy for rate calculations */
  private RateStrategy rateStrategy;
  /** the factory that defines strategies */
  private PayStationFactory factory;

  /** Construct a pay station.
      @param factory the factory to produce strategies and receipts
  */
  public PayStationImpl( PayStationFactory factory ) {
    this.factory = factory;
    this.rateStrategy = factory.createRateStrategy();
    reset();
  }
  [...]
  public Receipt buy() {
    Receipt r = factory.createReceipt(timeBought);
    reset();
    return r;
  }
  [...]
}
```

Compiling—still fails... The integration tests in TestIntegration still use the old constructor. I silence both test cases by configuring the pay station with the test town factory:

```
ps = new PayStationImpl( new TestTownFactory() );
```

Again this is terribly wrong, but I *keep focus* on getting everything to compile. I know that the integration tests will not pass before I get the proper factories for Alphatown and Betatown working, so there is absolutely no fear in my mind that I will forget these fake configurations—the failed tests will tell me.

Compilation success. Good feeling.... However, seven test cases fail. No wonder, as the create methods of the factory just returns null. The change is *Obvious Implementation*:

Listing: chapter/abstract-factory/iteration-1b/test/paystation/domain/TestTownFactory.java

```
package paystation.domain;
/** Factory for making the pay station configuration
    for unit testing pay station behavior.
*/
class TestTownFactory implements PayStationFactory {
```

```
  public RateStrategy createRateStrategy() {
    return new One2OneRateStrategy();
  }
  public Receipt createReceipt( int parkingTime ) {
    return new StandardReceipt(parkingTime);
  }
}
```

I am moving forward—only two tests fail now. The integration tests! To make these pass, I need to make the proper factories for Alphatown and Betatown. Again, obvious implementation, for instance the one for Betatown:

Listing: chapter/abstract-factory/iteration-1b/src/paystation/domain/BetaTownFactory.java

```
package paystation.domain;
/** Factory to configure BetaTown.
*/
class BetaTownFactory implements PayStationFactory {
  public RateStrategy createRateStrategy() {
    return new ProgressiveRateStrategy();
  }
  public Receipt createReceipt( int parkingTime ) {
    return new StandardReceipt(parkingTime);
  }
}
```

(Remember, adding the proper bar code receipt is the next iteration.) Great, all tests now pass. However, it appears to me that I still have not made a factory for the Gammatown configuration. The old argumentation was that the interaction between Gammatown's rate strategy and the pay station was already well tested, but I have added complexity by introducing the factory, and I of course also need to implement the factory for Gammatown. However, this is not the purpose of the refactoring iteration, so I note it on the test list.

* ~~refactor to introduce PayStationFactory~~
* add bar code receipts to Betatown
* test the Gammatown configuration

13.4.3 Iteration 2: Unit Test Barcode Receipts

Looking at the test list item *add bar code receipts to Betatown* I realize that it contains two iterations: unit testing the new bar code receipt, and next integration testing that the Betatown pay station actually delivers the proper type of receipts. I note the last aspect on the test list to be done in a later iteration.

As stated in the introduction, the bar codes on Betatown's receipts are not real bar codes, merely an additional line added to the receipt to make it different from the standard receipt. I will therefore not dwell on this iteration, but refer you to the source code for the iteration.

Exercise 13.3: If you study the production code for iteration 2 you will notice that I have used a parametric proposal to handle the two variants of the receipts: standard and bar code. Sketch the design for handling the variation using a compositional approach, analyze benefits and liabilities, and argue why a parametric solution is better in this special case.

13.4.4 Iteration 3: Integration Tests

I still have no test cases that tests that for instance the Gammatown pay station is actually configured properly—and as a result no tests that drive the development of Gammatown's factory. This is the purpose of this iteration. I will, however, only describe the steps abstractly and leave the TDD process to you or you may find the outcome in the chapter's source code folders.

Opening TestIntegration I note that the original integration tests for Alphatown and Betatown actually only test that the proper rate strategies are used. They must be updated to validate that also the proper receipts are issued. It is not the focus of this iteration, so I note it on the test list.

In my TDD process for Gammatown, I make a test case that tests both that the proper rate strategy is used as well as the proper type of receipt is issued. Next, I use the failed test case to introduce the GammaTownFactory. Note that I once again face the problem of choosing between testing the production code Gammatown variant based on the system clock or the stub-based one with a test controlled "clock". You can see my choice and the argumentation in the source code.

13.4.5 Iteration 4: City Configurations

Finally, the integration test for both Alphatown and Betatown lacks tests that validate that they issue the right type of receipts. I augment these integration tests with the validation code. During this process I discover that I can refactor the testing code to avoid duplication of the code that verifies the type of receipt issued. Also the names of the test cases are updated to reflect the type of test.

During this iteration, I discover that I had actually configured Betatown with a standard receipt! Tests are good...

13.5 The Compositional Process

Even though the initial attempt at using the ③-①-② process lead me into a less cohesive design, the resulting design is nevertheless the same principles applied, and the result is the ABSTRACT FACTORY pattern. The line of thought was:

- ③ *I identified some behavior, creating objects, that varies between different products.* So far products vary with regards to the types of receipts and the types of rate calculations.
- ① *I expressed the responsibility of creating objects in an interface.* PayStationFactory expressed this responsibility.
- ② *I let the pay station delegate all creation of objects it needs to the delegate object, namely the factory.* I can define a factory for each product variant (and particular testing variants), and provide the pay station with the factory. The pay station then delegates object creation to the factory instead of doing it itself.

If you look over the production code that is common to all pay station variants, you will see that it *only* refers to, and collaborates with, delegates through their interfaces. In no place does it create objects, cast references to concrete types, nor declare instance variables by a class type. Therefore, it does not depend on concrete types at any level. As argued, this leads to a low coupling and this principle is so important that it has received its own term.

Definition: Dependency inversion principle

High level modules should not depend upon low level modules. Both should depend upon abstractions. Abstractions should not depend upon details. Details should depend upon abstractions. (Martin 1996)

Rephrasing the definition for our case, it states that the pay station code shared by all variants (the "high level modules") should not depend on the variant's implementation (the "low level modules"), but only on interfaces (the abstractions).

Of course, some part of the code then has to make the actual binding, i.e. tell the high level modules the actual low level modules to communicate with. This binding process also has a name:

Definition: Dependency injection

High-level, common, abstractions should not themselves establish dependencies to low level, implementing, classes, instead the dependencies should be established by injection, that is, by client objects. (Fowler 2004)

In our case, the factory object is asked to create concrete objects to be used by the pay station, thus the factory injects the dependencies. Dependency injection is central in frameworks as discussed in Chapter 32.

13.6 Abstract Factory

The intent of the ABSTRACT FACTORY is to *Provide an interface for creating families of related or dependent objects without specifying their concrete classes.* In our pay station case, it is the family of objects that determines the variant of our pay station product. The general structure and condensed presentation of the pattern is given in design pattern box 13.1 on page 217. The central roles in abstract factory is the **client** that must create a consistent set of **products**. In our case, the client is the pay station and the products are receipts and rate strategies. Instead of creating the products itself, the role **abstract factory** does it. In the classic design pattern book, *Design Patterns: Elements of Reusable Object-Oriented Software* (Gamma et al. 1995), the two previous design patterns, STRATEGY and STATE, are classified as *behavioral* design patterns while ABSTRACT FACTORY is classified as *creational*. The intention of creational patterns is of course to *create objects*. Behavioral patterns deal with variability in the behavior of the system and the use of state and strategy in the pay station are clear examples of this.

The benefits of using an abstract factory in our designs are:

- *Low coupling between client and products.* There are no new statements in the client to make a high coupling to particular product variants. Thus the client only communicates with its products through their interface.
- *Configuring clients is easy.* All you have to do is to provide the client with the proper concrete factory. In our case, the pay station is configured simply by passing the proper pay station factory object during construction.
- *Promoting consistency among products.* Locality is important in making software easy to understand and maintain. The individual factories encapsulate the pay station's configuration: To review how a Betatown configuration looks like, you know that the place to look for it is in BetaTownFactory—and no other place. Thus any defects in configuration are traceable to a single class in the system. And as you are not required to look and change in five or ten different places in your code in order to make a configuration, the risk of introducing defects is substantially lessened.
- *Change by addition, not by modification.* I can introduce new pay stations product types easily as I can add new rate strategies and new receipt types, and provide the pay station with these by defining a new factory for it. Existing pay station code remains unchanged giving higher reliability and easier maintenance. Note, however, this argument is only true when it comes to introducing new *variants* of the existing rate strategies and receipt types! See the liability discussion below...
- *Client constructor parameter list stays intact.* Even if I need to introduce new products in the client, the client's constructor will still only take a single factory object as its parameter. Compare this to the practice of adding more and more configuration parameters to the constructor list.

Of course, ABSTRACT FACTORY has liabilities, some of which should be well known to you by now.

- *It introduces extra classes and objects.* Compared to a parametric solution where decision making is embodied in the client code I instead get several new interfaces and classes and thus objects: the factory interface as well as implementation classes. Therefore the pattern requires quite a lot of coding—you should certainly not use it if you only have a single type of product.
- *Introducing new aspects of variation is problematic.* The problem with abstract factory is that if I want to introduce new aspects that must be varied (logging to different vendor's databases, accepting other types of payment, etc.) then the abstract factory interface must be augmented with additional create-methods, and all its subclasses changed to provide behavior for them. This is certainly *change by modification.*

A classical example of the use of abstract factory is the Java AWT graphical user interface toolkit. A major problem for Java is that it runs on a variety of platforms including Windows, Macintosh, and Unix. However, AWT allows you to write a graphical user interface form (a dialog with text fields, radio buttons, drop-down list boxes, etc.) that will run on all the supported platforms. Thus to instantiate an AWT button the Java run-time library has to make a decision whether to create a Win32 button, a Mac button, or a Unix windows manager button; to instantiate a list box is has to make a similar decision; etc. Thus, the source code could be thick with zillions of if-statements—but it is all handled elegantly by an ABSTRACT FACTORY. The AWT code delegates any instantiation request for a graphical user component to its associated factory. The factory has methods for creating buttons, list boxes, radio buttons, text fields, etc. Each concrete factory, one for Win32, one for Mac, etc., then creates the proper graphical component from each platform's graphical toolbox.

In this light, it is also fair to say that the use of a factory to create the rate strategy in the pay station is sort of a special case because it only happens initially in contrast to receipts that are created continuously. Usually, abstract factory is considered the solution to the "continuous creation" problem. Still, it makes sense to group all object creation responsibility into a single abstraction as I have done in the pay station.

13.7 Summary of Key Concepts

Object-oriented systems need to create objects. However, when you strive to make a loosely coupled design you face the problem that the new statement expresses the tightest coupling possible: you once and for all bind an object reference to a particular concrete class.

```
Receipt r = new StandardReceipt(30);
```

While the first part of this statement Receipt r is loosely coupled as you only rely on the interface type Receipt the exact opposite is true for the right hand side of the assignment. The creational pattern ABSTRACT FACTORY provides a compositional solution to the problem of loosening the coupling between a client and the concrete products it needs to create, by delegating the creation responsibility to an instance of a factory. Furthermore the factory becomes a localized class responsible for configuration leading to a design that promotes consistency among products. A liability of the pattern is that it is somewhat complex and requires quite a lot of coding.

This chapter also showed that the ③-①-② process should not be used mechanically without considering the resulting design's cohesion and coupling. Always consider how the existing design could be refactored in such a way that the overall compositional design has high cohesion and low coupling. In our case, the creation of rate strategies had to be included in the analysis.

13.8 Selected Solutions

Discussion of Exercise 13.1:

```
/** Test that the receipt's show method prints proper info */
@Test public void shouldPrintReceiptsCorrectly() {
  Receipt receipt = new ReceiptImpl(30);
  // Prepare a PrintStream instance that lets me inspect the
```

```
    // data written to it.
    ByteArrayOutputStream baos = new ByteArrayOutputStream();
    PrintStream ps = new PrintStream(baos);
    // let the 30 minute print itself
    receipt.print(ps);

    // get the string printed to the stream
    String output = baos.toString();
    // split the string into individual lines
    String[] lines = output.split("\n");
    // test to see that the receipt consist of five lines
    assertEquals( 5, lines.length );
    // test parts of the contents
    assertEquals( "---", lines[0].substring(0,3) );
    assertEquals( "---", lines[4].substring(0,3) );
    assertEquals( "P A R K I N G", lines[1].substring(9,22) );
    // test the receipt's value
    assertEquals( "030", lines[2].substring(22,25) );
    // test that the format of the "parking starts at" time
    // is plausible
    String parkedAtString = lines[3].substring(28,33);
    assertEquals( ':', parkedAtString.charAt(2) );
    // if the substring below is not an integer a
    // NumberFormatException is thrown which will
    // make JUnit fail this test
    Integer.parseInt( parkedAtString.substring(0,2) );
    Integer.parseInt( parkedAtString.substring(3,5) );
  }
```

This is a plausible test case for print, but a major problem with this test code is that it is longer than the corresponding production code thus there is a high probability that the defects are in the testing code.

Discussion of Exercise 13.2:

The testing code includes also the use of the One2OneRateStrategy, and the testing of Gammatown actually includes an additional dimension of variance, namely the choice of strategy to determine if it is weekend or not. Therefore a complete table will include these aspects.

	Variability points		
Product	**Rate**	**Receipt**	**Weekend**
Alphatown	Linear	Standard	–
Betatown	Progressive	Barcode	–
Gammatown	Alternating	Standard	Clock
PayStation unit test	One2One	Standard	–
Gammatown rate unit test	Alternating	–	Fixed

Here "–" means that the selection is not applicable.

Discussion of Exercise 13.3:

The only difference in the two receipt types is in one additional line printed. A compositional approach would encapsulate the responsibility of outputting this line in an interface and use delegation to print it. Something along of the following line embedded in the receipt's print method:

```
[...]
stream.println("                Car parked at "+nowstring);
additionalInfoPrinter.print(stream);
stream.println("------------------------------------------------");
```

One concrete implementation would then print nothing and the other print the bar code. The problem I see with this solution is that I do not see viable future variations: what is the obvious new requirement for something new to print? And with only two variations, the parametric solution:

```
[...]
stream.println("                Car parked at "+nowstring);
if ( withBarCode ) {
  stream.println("|| ||||| | || ||| || ||  ||| | || |||| | || ||||");
}
stream.println("------------------------------------------------");
```

is much shorter and does not require additional interfaces and implementation classes. If, at a later time, new requirements pop up with regards to this variability point, I would consider refactoring this design.

13.9 Review Questions

Why can't the pay station simply take a receipt object as parameter in the constructor and use this; like it did with the rate strategy?

What is the ABSTRACT FACTORY pattern? What problem does it address and what solution does it suggest? What are the roles involved? What are the benefits and liabilities?

Argue why ABSTRACT FACTORY is an example of using a compositional design approach.

Define the *dependency inversion principle* and *dependency injection* and why they are considered important principles. Argue how it relates to the use of the factory object in the pay station case.

13.10 Further Exercises

Exercise 13.4:

Walk in my footsteps. Develop the new product variant that has a new receipt type with a (fake it) bar code.

Exercise 13.5:

In the present design, each new combination requires at least one new class, namely a new instance of the PayStationFactory. Thus, if 24 product combinations are required, there will be 24 factories.

Outline a number of different techniques to avoid this multitude of factories. For each describe benefits and liabilities.

Exercise 13.6:

The first graphical user interface for Java was the Abstract Window Toolkit or AWT. AWT allowed graphical applications to be written once and then allowed to run on multiple computing platforms: Macintosh, Windows, and UNIX Motif. A central challenge for AWT was thus to couple the AWT abstractions to the concrete graphical elements of the underlying platform. That is, the statement:

```
java.awt.Button b = new java.awt.Button(''A Button'');
```

must create a button object that in turn creates a Win32 button when running on the windows platform; or creates a Mac toolkit button on the Mac OS; etc.

Sketch how the implementation of java.awt.Button may use an ABSTRACT FACTORY to create the proper buttons depending on the platform.

Note: The complete solution to this problem is complex and requires several of the design patterns mentioned in part 6, so focus on the ABSTRACT FACTORY aspect only.

[13.1] Design Pattern: Abstract Factory

Intent Provide an interface for creating families of related or dependent objects without specifying their concrete classes.

Problem Families of related objects need to be instantiated. Product variants need to be consistently configured.

Solution Define an abstraction whose responsibility it is to create families of objects. The client delegates object creation to instances of this abstraction.

Structure:

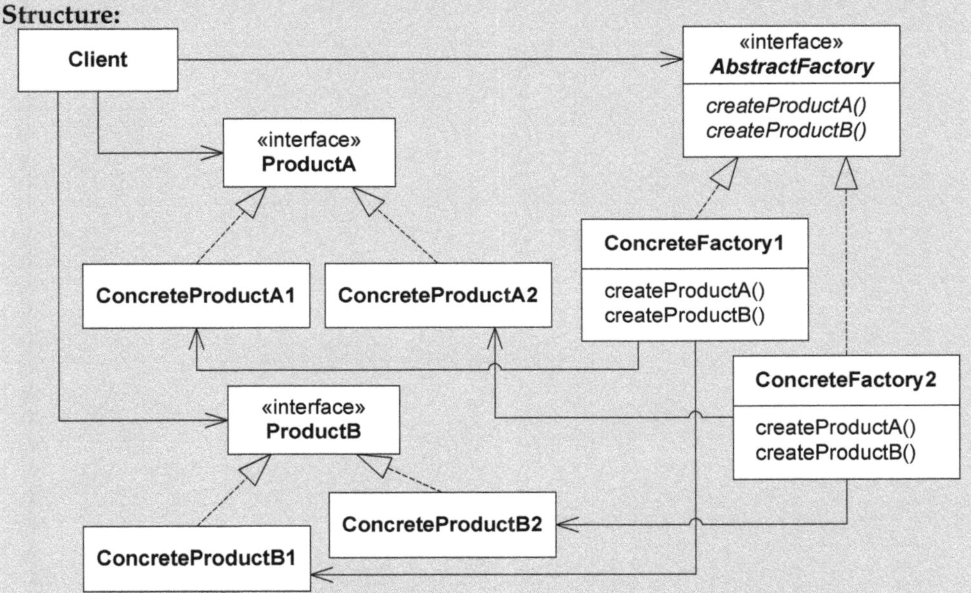

Roles **Abstract Factory** defines a common interface for object creation. **ProductA** defines the interface of an object, **ConcreteProductA1**, (product A in variant 1) required by the client. **ConcreteFactory1** is responsible for creating **Products** that belong to the variant 1 family of objects that are consistent with each other.

Cost - Benefit *It lowers coupling between client and products* as there are no new statements in the client to create high coupling. *It makes exchanging product families easy* by providing the client with different factories. *It promotes consistency among products* as all instantiation code is within the same class definition that is easy to overview. However, *supporting new kinds of products is difficult*: every new product introduced requires all factories to be changed.

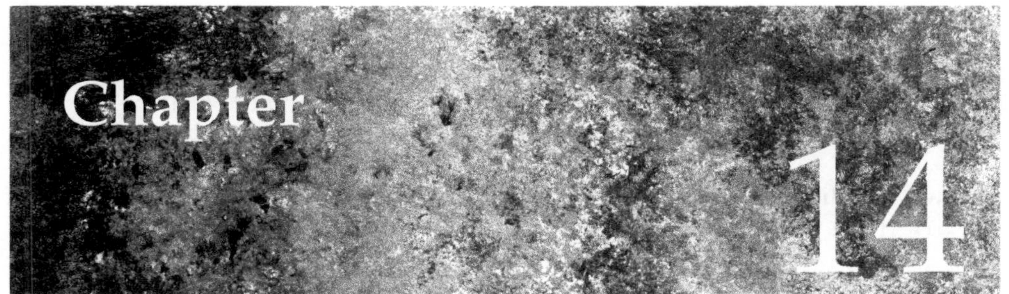

Pattern Fragility

Learning Objectives

Naturally, design patterns must be implemented in our production code: they are not just fancy ideas of software designers. The objective of this chapter is to highlight the importance of *getting the implementation right* as I will demonstrate how even small errors may cripple the advantages a pattern was supposed to have. I will also provide a small (and by no means complete) set of mistakes that occur in practice.

14.1 Patterns are Implemented by Code

Design patterns organize and structure code in a particular way. The structure is both in terms of the static aspects of the architecture, division of code into classes and interfaces, as well as the dynamic aspects, assigning responsibilities and defining object interactions. The reason I use a certain design pattern to structure my code is that software engineering knowledge and experience has shown that this particular structure has a certain balance between benefits and liabilities that my analysis shows is the appropriate one for the design problem I am tackling.

The bottom line is that applying design patterns is not a goal in itself—patterns are means to achieve a certain balance of qualities in my software. Most design patterns focus on maintainability and flexibility, especially those defined in the original GoF book. I do not get flexible software by writing in the documentation that I have used the STRATEGY pattern nor do I get it from naming one of my classes LinearRateStrategy. I get it because the structure and interactions between objects at run-time obey those rules that are set forward by the STRATEGY pattern. The consequence is that you should pay great attention to detail when you introduce design patterns into your designs or make use of those introduced by others. Otherwise you may easily "amputate" the pattern which leaves you with all the liabilities and none of the benefits. I call this *pattern fragility*:

Definition: Pattern fragility

Pattern fragility is the property of design patterns that their benefits can only be fully utilized if the pattern's object structure and interaction patterns are implemented correctly.

Below I will discuss some of the coding mistakes that may invalidate the benefits of the STRATEGY pattern as an example.

14.2 Declaration of Delegates

A primary purpose of many design patterns is to strengthen flexibility and reusability by allowing a particular object that answers a given request to be replaced by another, like the pay station that can interact with several different instances of RateStrategy.

This means declarations must be written in terms of *interfaces* instead of concrete classes. If a programmer accidentally declares an object by its concrete class the flexibility property is essentially lost. Consider the following example from the pay station. If I am working intensively on the Betatown pay station I may write the declaration of the rate strategy in the PayStationImpl as:

```
public class PayStationImpl implements PayStation {
  [...]

  /** the strategy for rate calculations */
  private ProgressiveRateStrategy rateStrategy;

  [...]
}
```

instead of declaring the delegate object by its interface type:

```
public class PayStationImpl implements PayStation {
  [...]

  /** the strategy for rate calculations */
  private RateStrategy rateStrategy;

  [...]
}
```

If you develop without automated tests or if you do not run the Alphatown and Gammatown test cases then your development will proceed fine. The problem is, however, that the pay station implementation is no longer flexible—it is hardwired to Betatown's rate strategy. Essentially the simple declaration mistake has removed all benefits of the STRATEGY pattern but sadly retained all its liabilities: more interfaces and classes to consider, and more objects in play.

Key Point: Declare delegate objects by their interface type

Declare object references that are part of a design pattern by their interface type, never by their concrete class type.

☞ Compare this discussion with the dependency inversion principle on page 211.

14.3 Binding in the Right Place

As argued above, the declaration of the delegate must be in terms of the interface to support flexibility. Essentially, this is the way to ensure loose coupling: the coupling relation between the pay station and the rate strategy is weak because the pay station only assumes the contract / the interface. However, the coupling must be made at some time: a concrete rate strategy object must be instantiated and associated with the pay station implementation. Care must be exercised to make this association in the proper place just as the declarations must be made with care. Consider the following pay station implementation code fragment I have seen students write:

```
public class PayStationImpl implements PayStation {
  [...]
  public void addPayment( int coinValue )
          throws IllegalCoinException {
    switch ( coinValue ) {
    case 5:
    case 10:
    case 25: break;
    default:
      throw new IllegalCoinException("Invalid coin: "+coinValue);
    }
    insertedSoFar += coinValue;
    RateStrategy rateStrategy = new LinearRateStrategy();
    timeBought = rateStrategy.calculateTime(insertedSoFar);
  }
  [...]
}
```

Again, no test case for Alphatown with its linear rate policy will fail. The system is behaviorally correct. But the pay station implementation is no longer flexible with respect to new rate policies, it is hardwired to the Alphatown's policy. I have none of the pattern's benefits but all of its liabilities.

From an abstract perspective, the problem here is that the PayStationImpl code is shared by all pay station products. It is specifically designed for flexibility. It therefore must only be weakly coupled to its delegate objects, like the rate strategy and receipt type. The direct instantiation in the above code makes a tight coupling and invalidates the implementation's flexibility and generality. The binding, i.e. the instantiation of delegate objects, must be made somewhere of course but it cannot be done in a part of the code that is reused across all product variants.

> ☞ This is actually the *dependency injection* principle (page 211). Read this principle again and argue how it relates to the outlined problem.

The question then is where should the binding be made? Well, the obvious answer is that it must be in the part of the code that is product specific. In the pay station system I started out instantiating the proper rate strategy in the testing code and then passed it on in the pay station's constructor. Later I refactored to use an abstract factory. The latter I find a good solution because it is highly cohesive: an object whose only responsibility is to create the proper delegates for a specific configuration.

Key Point: Localize bindings

There should be a well-defined point in the code where the creation of delegate objects to configure the particular product variant is put.

ABSTRACT FACTORY and other creational patterns are obvious units that have the configuration and binding responsibility. Typically, configuration and binding may also be part of the "main" unit of the code, that is, the part that executed first when a system starts, like in the main method of Java programs, the JFrame constructor of Swing applications, etc.

In some patterns, the binding is the issue of the pattern. For instance the STATE pattern's intent is altering the binding. Still, it is important that you make a careful analysis of which object that makes the binding and make it explicit.

14.4 Concealed Parameterization

Let me assume that the mistake I showed in the previous section has somehow survived unnoticed in my production code. The instantiation of the LinearRateStrategy directly in the addPayment method works fine for Alphatown and no new releases of the software have been made for Betatown and Gammatown for ages. Suddenly one of the colleagues of my team has to dig out the old code again because Betatown has requested some changes. Now she realizes that PayStationImpl does not work properly for Betatown anymore. She has not really worked with the pay station code before, and is not very well trained in design patterns—and Betatown wants the new software update urgently. In a situation like this, parameterization may easily sneak in:

```
public class PayStationImpl implements PayStation {
  [...]
  public void addPayment( int coinValue )
          throws IllegalCoinException {
    switch ( coinValue ) {
    case 5:
    case 10:
    case 25: break;
    default:
      throw new IllegalCoinException("Invalid coin: "+coinValue);
    }
    insertedSoFar += coinValue;
    RateStrategy rateStrategy;
    if ( town == Town.ALPHATOWN ) {
      rateStrategy = new LinearRateStrategy();
    } else if ( town == Town.BETATOWN ) {
      rateStrategy = new ProgressiveRateStrategy();
    }
    timeBought = rateStrategy.calculateTime(insertedSoFar);
  }
  [...]
}
```

The solution is behaviorally correct. All test cases pass. The design is terrible of course as it disables the benefits of the compositional design and introduced a parametric design instead. The result is the worst of two worlds: we got all the added complexity and added objects of the compositional design and all the *change by modification* of the parametric design.

> **Key Point: Be consistent in choice of variability handling**
>
> *Decide on the design strategy to handle a given variability and stick to it.*

This does not mean that you should handle all variability by a compositional approach. It simply means you must handle one specific variability consistently with the same technique. For instance while I generally favor compositional designs I did choose a parametric design for handling the "bar code or not" variability of the receipts as outlined in Section 13.4.3.

14.5 Avoid Responsibility Erosion

Software grows with the users' requests: *Software changes its own requirements.* Minor requests are often handled by minor "fixes" to the production code. The problem is that many "minor" fixes over a long period of time have a distinct tendency to erode the design. It is often termed *software aging* or *architectural erosion*. The bad decision to mix compositional and parametric design in the previous section is a typical example of erosion.

A particular type of erosion is that some object of a particular variant needs to do a bit extra compared to the other variants. This "extra" may be handled by adding an additional method. As a contrived example, let me state a really weird requirement from Gammatown that the receipt should include a text explaining how the rate was calculated. I may therefore add another method to AlternatingRateStrategy:

```
public class AlternatingRateStrategy implements RateStrategy {
  [...]
  public int calculateTime( int amount ) {
    if ( decisionStrategy.isWeekend() ) {
      currentState = weekendStrategy;
    } else {
      currentState = weekdayStrategy;
    }
    return currentState.calculateTime( amount );
  }

  public String explanationText() {
    if ( currentState == weekdayStrategy ) {
      return [the explanation for weekday];
    } else {
      return [the explanation for weekend];
    }
  }
}
```

Because this method is defined in the subtype and not in the RateStrategy interface I cannot simply invoke this method but must check the object type before using it:

```
if ( rateStrategy instanceof AlternatingRateStrategy ) {
  AlternatingRateStrategy rs =
    (AlternatingRateStrategy) rateStrategy;
  String theExplanation = rs.explanationText();
  [use it somehow]
}
```

This way the compositional design is again moving towards a parametric design where the object's type becomes the parameter to switch upon. Therefore there is the danger that the design creeps towards a parametric one.

An alternative is to move the explanationText method up into the RateStrategy interface. It is better as I avoid the object type switching code but now I am in the process of adding responsibilities to the rate strategy role. It is defined as a rate calculator but now it also must handle human readable text. It may be the proper decision but make it based on an analysis instead of just making it happen by accident.

Key Point: Avoid responsibility erosion

Carefully analyze new requirements to avoid responsibility erosion and bloating interfaces with incohesive methods.

14.6 Discussion

One interesting observation is that all the above examples of coding uses the STRATEGY pattern at a superficial glance: there is the context object, the strategy interface, and the concrete strategy objects. The devil is in the detail. One mistaken declaration, a new statement in the wrong place, a quick-and-dirty parameterization, and the pattern benefits are nevertheless lost. The examples above are *not* examples of using the STRATEGY pattern because its intent has been lost in coding mistakes.

Above I have talked about how coding practices or mistakes may invalidate the benefits of patterns. *Patterns are fragile.* It is therefore important that the programmers that handle the code with design patterns are well trained: know the patterns, know the roles and interaction patterns they involve, and know the implications of how they are coded.

14.7 Summary of Key Concepts

Design patterns manifest themselves in our code. While they do have some inherent benefits in terms of maintainability and reliability, these benefits are easily destroyed by coding mistakes. Such mistakes usually appear because people do not deeply understand the patterns but they can also appear because of carelessness. The problem about such coding errors is that the liabilities remain, like an overhead of interfaces, classes and objects, but the benefits are gone.

Some common problems are forgetting to declare instance variables by their interface type; making bindings to delegate objects in the common/shared implementation; or accidentally mixing different design strategies for handling variability.

14.8 Review Questions

How is *pattern fragility* defined and what does the concept cover? Name some mistakes in code that spoil the benefits of design patterns.

Iteration 5

Compositional Design

The primary focus of the preceding learning iterations has been on concrete requirements that I solved by analysis and by hinting at some underlying principles. In this learning iteration I will focus on defining these principles rigorously and extend our vocabulary regarding compositional design. This will allow me to explain the list of design patterns in the next part, the pattern catalogue, easily as they are simply applications and variations of the principles.

Chapter	Learning Objective
Chapter 15	*Roles and Responsibilities.* I will discuss three different perspectives on what object-oriented design and programming is. The point is not to nominate one as superior, rather they each build upon the other to form a deeper understanding of object-oriented design. Next, I will define and discuss the concepts of behavior, responsibility, roles, and protocol that are central to the responsibility centered perspective that is central in designing flexible systems.
Chapter 16	*Compositional Design Principles.* The seminal design pattern book, *Design Patterns: Elements of Reusable Design*, described a small set of principles that show up on almost all design patterns. In this chapter, I describe the principles and show how I have already applied them in the form of the ③-①-② process.
Chapter 17	*Multi-Dimensional Variance.* Returning to the pay station and a new requirement, I will define the combinatorial explosion problem that is handled elegantly by compositional designs but poorly by polymorphic and parametric designs.
Chapter 18	*Design Patterns – Part II.* Armed with our knowledge of compositional design and its terminology I will review the design pattern concept. I will also look at how a good working knowledge of design patterns provides us with a roadmap that lessens the problem of overviewing large compositional designs.

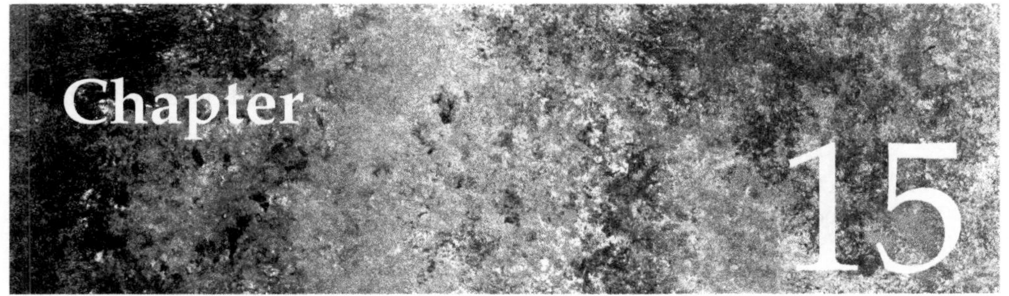

Roles and Responsibilities

Learning Objectives

Emphasis has primarily been put on the practical aspects of design patterns up until now. In this chapter, I will change to a more analytical and theoretical view. The learning objective of this chapter is to introduce three different perspectives on object-oriented programming, starting by asking the fundamental question: *What is an object?* Your answer to this question of course influences how you design object-oriented software in its most fundamental way. Knowing that there are indeed different perspectives and understanding the strengths of each will make you a better designer and software architect by extending the set of tools you have available to tackle design challenges.

One of the perspectives, the *role* perspective, is the central key to understand flexible software designs such as design patterns and frameworks so this chapter's focus is also on defining the central concepts within this perspective.

15.1 What are Objects?

Some time ago, I made a small study of how the concept "object" was defined and used in a number of object-oriented teaching books (Christensen 2005). It turned out that the definitions were broadly classified in three groups that I denote *language*, *model*, and *responsibility*-centric perspectives. The perspective taken has profound impact on the way systems are designed, the quality of the designs, and the type of problems that designs can successfully handle. One can see each perspective as a refinement of the preceding, so it is not a question of voting one as the champion, they all have their applicability. This said, the responsibility-centric perspective is the most advanced one, and it is important in order to deeply understand flexible and configurable designs. Over the next few sections, I will present and discuss each perspective.

15.2 The Language-Centric Perspective

The focus of the language-centric perspective is classes and objects as concrete building blocks for building software. A typical definition is:

> An object is a program construction that has data (that is, information) associated with it and that can perform certain actions. (Savitch 2001, p. 17)

The emphasis is thus on the program language structure: fields and methods. This is inherently a *compile-time* or *static* view—the definition speaks in terms of what we see in our editor. The classic example is the Account class that you can find in almost any introductory textbook on objects.

```
public class Account {
  int balance;
  public void withdraw(int amount) {
    balance -= amount;
  }
  public int balance() { return balance; }
  ...
}
```

The implicit consequence of this view is that an object is an entity in its own right—the definition is closed and any object can be understood in isolation—you simply enumerate the fields and methods and you are done. The advantage of this perspective is of course that it is very concrete, closely related to the programming language level, and therefore relatively easy to understand as a novice. Also, the perspective is fundamental: you cannot develop or design object-oriented software if you do not master this perspective.

The disadvantage is, however, that it remains relatively silent about how to structure the collaboration and interplay between objects, the dynamics, and this is typically where the hard challenges of design lie. As an example, an account has an owner who has a name. Taking the perspectives "class = fields + methods" literally the design below is fine:

```
public class Account {
  int balance;
  String ownerName; Date ownerBirthDate;
  public String getOwner() {
    return ownerName;
  }
  ...
  public void withdraw(int amount) {
    balance -= amount;
  }
  public int balance() { return balance; }
  ...
}
```

This design has several limitations, but the perspective itself offers little guidance in the process of designing any realistic system. It is the perspective that was most prominent in my survey of text books.

☞ Discuss the limitations of the design above.

15.3 The Model-Centric Perspective

The model-centric perspective perceives objects as parts in a wider context namely a *model*. A model is a simplified representation or simulation of a part of the world. The inspiration for the perspective was toy-models, simulations, and scientific models. For instance a remote-controlled model car has parts that are similar to a real car while others are abstracted away; a toy railway also displays many of the features of real-world railway systems while other features are missing.

A typical definition is:

> Java objects model objects from a problem domain. (Barnes and Kolling 2005, p. 3)

The model view has roots tracing back to the Simula tradition of simulation, Scandinavian object-orientation (Madsen et al. 1993), and the Alan Kay notion of *computation as simulation* (Kay 1977). Here the program execution is a simulation of some part of the world, and objects are perceived as the model's parts. A definition of object-orientation from the Scandinavian school is (Madsen et al. 1993, §18):

> Definition: **Object-orientation (Model)**
>
> A program execution is regarded as a physical model simulating the behavior of either a real or imaginary part of the world.

The key process for designing software, denoted "modeling", is the process of abstracting and simplifying (real-world) phenomena and concepts and representing them by objects and classes; and modeling (real-world) relations like association and aggregation by relations between objects.

Going back to the account case, this perspective would look at the world of banking and note the concepts "Account" and "Owner" as well as the relations "has-an-account" and "owned-by". As an account can have several owners, and a single person can have several accounts, this perspective would reject the design in the previous section. The modeling process would conclude that the real world concepts of account and owner should be reflected in the design leading to classes Account and Owner that are associated by a many-to-many relation, as shown in Figure 15.1.

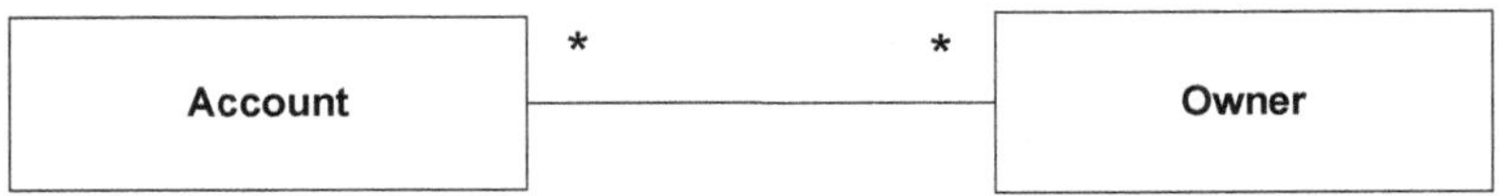

Figure 15.1: Modeling the Account Owner system.

This perspective stresses objects as entities in a larger context (they are parts of a model) as opposed to the self-contained language centric definition. This naturally leads to a strong focus on what the relations are between the elements of the model: association, generalization, composition.

Dynamics is an inherent part of the concept simulation and the explicit guideline for designing object interaction is to mimic real world interactions. Thus, the real-world scenario *the owner withdraws money from his account* tells the designer that the objects must have methods to mimic this behavior. The question is should the withdraw behavior belong to Account or Person? The encapsulation principle tells us to put it in the account class because it encapsulates the balance. However, this obvious decision that designers do all the time is actually not very faithful to the "real world": real accounts do not have behavior. Before computers did the hard work, bank accounts were simply inanimate records kept by the bank—a clerk did the paperwork to withdraw from the account, not the account itself. Thus, object-oriented objects are animistic mirrors of their real world role models, and a program execution resembles a cartoon full of otherwise inanimate objects springing to life, sending messages to each other.

> ☞ Find examples in programming books or your own programs of classes that model inanimate concepts but exhibit behavior.

This model has limitations as well, because it is relatively silent about those aspects of a systems that has no real world counterpart. Generally object-oriented design books like examples like the account system because the classes mirror real world concepts. But where do I get inspiration for designing a graphical user interface? For keeping multiple windows synchronized? For accessing a database?

15.4 The Responsibility-Centric Perspective

In the responsibility-centric perspective a program's *dynamics* is the primary focus and thus the object's behavior and its responsibilities are central.

One definition is the following:

> The best way to think about what an object is, is to think of it as something with responsibilities. (Shalloway and Trott 2004, p. 16)

This perspective can be traced back to the focus on responsibilities in Ward Cunningham's work on the CRC cards (Beck and Cunningham 1989) and the work by Wirfs-Brock on responsibility driven design (Wirfs-Brock and McKean 2003).

Both the language and model-centric perspective tend to focus on static aspects: objects, classes, and relationships. However, what makes a program interesting and relevant is the *behavior* that these parts have, individually and jointly. We can also state this more pragmatically: The customers of our software are quite indifferent about classes and relations; they care about the software's *functionality*—what does it do to make my work easier, more fun, more efficient? Thus, software behavior is the most important aspect, as it pays the bills! Wirfs-Brock and McKean express this:

> *Success lies in how clearly we invent a software reality that satisfies our application's requirements—and not in how closely it resembles the real world.*

Responsibility-centric thinking states that the two fundamental concepts, object and relation, have to be supplemented by a third equally fundamental concept: *role*. The role concept helps us to break the rigid ties between object and functionality. This leads to another definition of object-orientation and Budd (2002) has made the following:

> Definition: **Object-orientation (Responsibility)**
> An object-oriented program is structured as a community of interacting agents called objects. Each object has a role to play. Each object provides a service or performs an action that is used by other members of the community.

This statement emphasizes that the overall behavior and the functionality of a program is defined by lots of individual objects working together.

In this view, an executing program is perceived as a community. Human communities get work done by organizing a lot of individuals, defining roles and responsibilities for them and state the rules of collaboration between the different roles. The overall behavior of a community is the sum of many individual but concerted tasks being accomplished. One thing that Budd's definition is not very specific about, however, is that often a single actor performs multiple roles in a community depending on the specific context he or she is involved in. I will return to this point later.

Going back to the pay station case, the original design (see Chapter 4) was the result of a model perspective, looking at a real pay station that issues receipts. However, the analysis in the STRATEGY chapter ended up be deviating from the "real world model" perspective. Looking at the pay station down on the parking lot, I see the machine and the receipts, but no "rate calculator". The RateStrategy does not model anything real—it is purely a role with a single responsibility which I require *some* object to be able to play once the software starts executing.

15.5 Roles, Responsibility, and Behavior

I will elaborate the responsibility-centric perspective by looking at the central concepts that allow us to understand and design the functional and dynamic aspects of software systems. I start from the most basic level, behavior, and work my way up in abstraction level.

15.5.1 Behavior

Abstractly, behavior may be defined as:

> Definition: **Behavior**
> Acting in a particular and observable way.

That is, *doing something*. As an everyday example, I take the bag of garbage out from under the kitchen sink, tie a knot on the bag, and walk to the garbage can and throw it in. I acted in a particular and observable way.

In object-oriented languages behavior is defined by objects having methods that are executed at runtime. Methods are templates for behavior, algorithms, in the sense that parameters and the state of the object itself and associated objects influence the particular and observable acting.

Collective behavior arises when objects interact by invoking methods on each other (sometimes referred to as message passing). Message passing occurs when one object requests the behavior of one of its associated objects.

Method names and parameter lists, however, convey little information about the actual behavior. Often an object's behavior is the result of a concerted effort from a number of collaborating objects. For instance, when a flight reservation object is requested to print out, it will request the associated person object to return the person's name. UML sequence diagrams are well suited for describing object interaction.

Behavior is the "nuts-and-bolts" of a program execution in the sense that what actually gets done at runtime is the sum of the behavior defined by the methods that have been invoked. However, the concept of behavior is too low-level to be really useful when designing systems—we need a more abstract concept.

15.5.2 Responsibility

> Definition: **Responsibility**
>
> The state of being accountable and dependable to answer a request.

Responsibility is intimately related to behavior but it is at a more abstract level. Going back to the garbage example, I am *responsible* for getting the garbage from under the kitchen sink to the garbage can; but no particular behavior is dictated. I may decide to just throw the bag on the door step and wait to bring it to the can until next time I have to go there anyway—or more likely I yell at one of my sons that they must do it. How they do it is also not relevant—probably my youngest son will run to the can while fighting imaginary monsters. The point is that many different observable behaviors are allowed as long as the "contract" of the responsibility is kept: that the garbage ends in the can.

Responsibility is a more abstract way of organizing and describing object behavior and thus much better suited to the abstraction level needed for software design. It is a way to maintain the overview and avoid getting overwhelmed by algorithm details.

Responsibility is often best communicated in a design/implementation team in short and broad statements. For instance, in the PayStation interface header, the responsibilities are stated as:

```
Responsibilities:

1) Accept payment;
2) Calculate parking time based on payment;
3) Know earning, parking time bought;
4) Issue receipts;
5) Handle buy and cancel events.
```

Responsibilities should not be stated too programming specific (like "have an addPayment method taking an integer parameter amount") nor too broad and vague (like "behave like a pay station").

The technique of stating responsibilities was elaborated in the **CRC Card** technique, where classes are described at the design level using three properties: **C**lass name, **R**esponsibilities, and **C**ollaborators. A CRC card for the pay station would look like below: The **C**lass name is shown on top, the **R**esponsibilities in the left pane below and **C**ollaborating classes in the right pane.

PayStation	
Accept payment Calculate parking time based on payment Know earning, parking time bought Issue receipts Handle buy and cancel events	PayStationHardware Receipt

Behavior is defined by methods on objects at the programming language level—an object behaves in a certain way when a method is called upon it. What about responsibilities?

The language construct that comes closest is the interface. An interface is a description of a set of (related) method signatures but no method body (i.e. implementation) is allowed. The PayStation interface contains the method declarations that encode the responsibilities mentioned on the CRC card. Thus, an interface is much more specific than the above high level description, however an interface only specifies an *obligation* of implementing objects to exhibit behavior that conforms to the method signatures, not any specific algorithm to use. We say "conforms to the method signatures" but in practical programming an object that implements an particular method in an interface must also conform to the underlying contract—that "it does what it is supposed to do" according to the method documentation. The signature of method buy only tells me that a Receipt instance is returned, but the contract of course is that its value must match the parking time matching the entered amount.

The reason I argue that the language construct of interface is better than classes for expressing responsibility is that the developer is explicitly forced *not* to describe any algorithm—and thus keep focused on the contract instead of getting hooked on details too early. Objects are free to implement the methods in any way as long as the behavior adheres to the specification.

In the pay station, there are five responsibilities and four methods in the interface. Some responsibilities, like *know parking time bought* corresponds quite closely to a method, readDisplay, whereas others, like *calculate parking time*, have no associated method. This is common. The main point is that the interface exposes the proper set of methods for the responsibilities to be carried out in the context of the collaborating objects. For instance, the *calculate parking time* responsibility is served as the pay station hardware (or our JUnit testing code) invokes addPayment and next readDisplay.

15.5.3 Role

Responsibilities are only interesting in the context of collaboration: If no-one ever wants to insert coins in the pay station, there is no need for a "accept payment" responsibility. Thus, what makes the responsibility interesting and viable is its inherent obligation to someone else. In an executing program objects are collaborating, each object having its specific responsibilities. To collaborate properly they must agree upon their mutual responsibilities, the way to collaborate, and the order in which actions must be taken.

Just as responsibility is more abstract than behavior, we need a term for expressing mutual responsibilities and collaboration patterns.

> Definition: **Role (General)**
>
> A function or part performed especially in a particular operation or process.

This definition embodies the dual requirement: both "function performed" (responsibilities) as well as "in a particular process" (collaboration pattern/protocol). The role concept allows us to express a set of responsibilities and a specification of a collaboration pattern without tying it to a particular person or particular object.

The role concept is central for understanding any community or human society. Roles define how we interact and understand what is going on. At the university I play the role of **lecturer** a couple times a week, and around one hundred people play the role of **student**. We know the responsibilities of each other and therefore what to expect. It is my responsibility to talk and hopefully tell something interesting related to the course material; it is the responsibility of the students to stop talking when the lecture begins—and try hard not to fall asleep. Similarly, if I go to the hospital I will probably not know the individuals working there but I know the roles of **physician**, **nurse**, and **patient**, and thereby each individual knows and understands what to expect of each other. A community has severe problems functioning if people do not know the roles.

The relation between role on one hand and person on the other is a many-to-many relation. Taking myself I go in and out of roles many times a day: father, husband, teacher, supervisor, researcher, textbook author, etc. A single person can and usually does play many different roles although not at the same time. From the opposite perspective, a role can be played by many different persons. If I become sick, someone else will take on my teacher role. At the hospital, the person playing the ward nurse role changes at every shift. The same many-to-many relation exists between software design roles and objects. I will explore this in detail at the end of the chapter.

> **Key Point: The relation between role and object is a many-to-many relation**
>
> *A role can be played by many different types of objects. An object can perform many different roles within a system.*

Sometimes roles are invented to make an organization work better. As a simple example a pre-school kindergarten had the problem that the teachers were constantly interrupted in their activities with the children to answer the phone, deliver messages from parents, fetch meals, etc. They responded by defining a new role, the **flyer**, whose responsibility it was to answer all phone calls, bring all the meals, etc. Thus all other teachers were relieved of these tasks and allowed to pay attention to the children without interruptions. The teachers then made a schedule taking turns on having the role as flyer.

15.5.4 Protocol

Roles express mutual expectations. Students expect the lecturer to raise his voice and start presenting material. It will not work if he instead just sits down on a seat at the back row and keeps silent. Likewise the lecturer expects the students to keep silent while lecturing. A hospital will not work if all nurses jump into the hospital beds and start asking the patients for aspirin. Thus roles rely on more or less well-defined protocols.

Definition: **Protocol**

A convention detailing the sequence of interactions or actions expected by a set of roles.

Remember that an old interpretation of protocol is indeed "diplomatic etiquette", that is, the accepted way to do things. The student–lecturer protocol is clear though unspoken: "Lecturer starts talking, students fall asleep."

Software design roles depend even more heavily on understanding the protocols. Humans cope with minor defects in the protocol, but software is not that forgiving. The protocol between the pay station and the rate strategy dictates that the pay station is the active part and the rate strategy the reactive: the pay station requests a calculation and the rate strategy responds with an answer. At a more abstract level, this is the protocol of the STRATEGY pattern: **Context** initiates the execution of an algorithm, and a **ConcreteStrategy** reactively responds when requested. Of course, this is a very simple protocol, but some patterns in learning iteration 6, *A Design Pattern Catalogue*, have elaborate protocols that are the core of the pattern. For instance, OBSERVER's protocol requires objects to register before they can expect notifications using yet another protocol.

Protocols are extremely important to understand the dynamic, run-time, aspects of software. UML sequence diagrams are well suited to show protocols, both at the individual object level but more important also at the role level: instead of showing an object's timeline, you draw method invocations between roles. I will use sequence diagrams to show design pattern protocols for the complex patterns.

15.5.5 Roles at the Design Level

Another, more software oriented, definition of role is:

Definition: **Role (Software)**

A set of responsibilities and associated protocols.

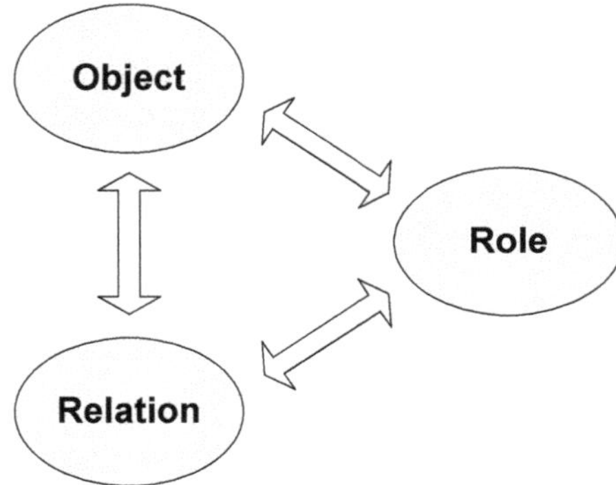

Figure 15.2: The three fundamental concepts in design.

Wirfs-Brock et al. simply defines role as "set of responsibilities" but I find the protocol aspect important as roles interact to fulfill complex responsibilities.

Roles do not have any direct counterpart in main-stream programming languages. The programming language construct that comes closest is again the "interface" that supports aspects of the concept of a role. However, main-stream languages have no way of forcing specific protocols, that is no way of enforcing that method A on object X is invoked before method B on object Y, etc. This is left for the developers to adhere to—and a constant source of software defects.

Throughout this book I have used **role description boxes** or just **role boxes** to define roles, like the pay station role:

PayStation

- Accept payment
- Calculate parking time
- Handle transactions (buy, cancel)
- Know time bought, earning
- Print receipt

The diagram is a simple adaptation of the CRC card: instead of class name at the top, I write the name of the role, and I have removed the collaborators pane. I find that the collaborators are more easily read from the UML class diagrams.

15.6 The Influence of Perspective on Design

Returning to the three perspectives, language, model, and responsibility-centric, these have strong impact upon our design. As indicated, the language-centric perspective is important at the technical programming level, but has little to say about design, so I will concentrate on the latter two.

In the model-centric perspective, the focus is modeling a part of the (real or imaginary) world which is then translated into the elements of our programming language: classes and objects. This leads naturally to a strong focus on structure first, and behavior next. That is, I first create a landscape of relevant abstractions and next assign responsibility and behavior to these abstractions. To paraphrase it, I first draw a UML diagram of my classes, and next try to find the most appropriate class to assign the responsibilities, the most appropriate place to put the methods in. Budd calls this the **who/what** cycle: first find *who*, next decide *what* they must do. In this perspective, you do not really need the role concept; objects and their relations are sufficient: the objects are already in place when you get to the point of assigning behavior.

The responsibility-centric perspective, in contrast, focuses on functionality but at the higher level of abstraction of responsibilities and roles. Here the design process first considers the tasks that have to be carried out and then tries to group these into natural and cohesive roles that collaborate using sensible protocols. Next, objects are assigned to play these roles. That is, the landscape of behavior and responsibilities is laid out first, and next objects are invented and assigned to fulfill the responsibilities. Budd calls this the **what/who** cycle: find out *what* to do, next decide *who* does it. There, the role concept is vital as the placeholder of responsibilities until it can be assigned.

Shalloway and Trott (2004) present a nice story to illustrate the different perceptions of these perspectives. They tell that they have an umbrella that shields them from the rain—very convenient as they live in Seattle that gets its fair share of rain. Actually it is a very comfortable umbrella, because it can play stereo music, and in case they want to go somewhere, it can drive them there—of course without getting wet. It is all quite mystical until the punch line is revealed: their "umbrella" is a car.

In the model perspective, this story is absurd. In this perspective, an umbrella is a set of stretchers and ribs covered by cloth. A car is not. Thus a car is *not* an umbrella. The Java declaration

```
public class Car extends Umbrella { ... }
```

does not make sense.

However, in the responsibility perspective, it *does* make sense, because it is not the object umbrella but the responsibility of an umbrella that is the focus. In this perspective, an umbrella is a canopy designed to protect against rain. The focus is on what it "does" not what it "is".

```
public class Car implements UmbrellaRole { ... }
```

Thus, a car does play the umbrella role when Mr. Shalloway or Mr. Trott drive around Seattle: it is responsible for protecting them from rain.

Sometimes, the two perspectives arrive at the same design. As an example, consider a temperature alarm system design to warn if the temperature of, say, a refrigerator comes above a threshold temperature. The system consists of a sensor in the refrigerator and a monitor station responsible for periodically measuring the temperature measured by the sensor and alarm if the threshold is reached. The model perspective *who/what* would identify two phenomena: the sensor and the monitor that are associated. Next the tasks are assigned: the monitor must periodically request temperature readings from the sensor; the sensor must measure and return temperature upon request. The UML class diagram ends up like in Figure 15.3.

In the *what/who* cycle, the designer would identify the responsibilities *to monitor temperature, to alarm if temperature threshold is exceeded* and *to measure temperatures*. "To measure" expresses an algorithm that depends upon the specific manufacturer of

Figure 15.3: Model perspective design.

the sensor, so it points to a STRATEGY pattern. As it has two roles it seems natural to group the first two responsibilities in a **monitor** role (**context** role in STRATEGY) and the last responsibility in a **temperature measure strategy** role (**strategy** role in STRATEGY). Thus the designs are almost identical except for the naming that focuses on either hardware objects or functionality.

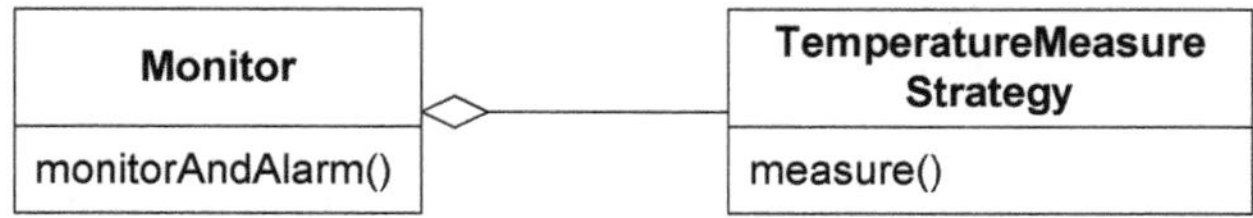

Figure 15.4: Role perspective design.

15.7 The Role–Object Relation

As argued above the introduction of roles as a fundamental design concept for object oriented design loosens the coupling between functionality and object. I will give some examples in this section.

15.7.1 One Role – Many Objects

The one-to-many relation between interface and objects manifests itself in that many different objects may implement a particular interface. This means that objects with otherwise rather different behavior may be used in a particular context as long as they adhere to the role this context expects.

A good example is from the Java library in which the only thing the sorting algorithm in the Collections class expects is that all objects in a given list implements the java.util.Comparable interface. Thus if we make a class representing apples then we can sort apple objects simply by implementing this interface:

```
public class Apple implements Comparable {
  private int size;
  [other Apple implementation]
  public int compareTo(Object o) {
    [apple comparison algorithm]
  }
}
```

Thus, in the context of the sorting algorithm it is irrelevant what the objects are (here apples), the only interesting aspect is that the objects can play the **Comparable** role. And the **Comparable** role simply specifies that objects must have the responsibility to tell whether it is greater than, equal to, or less than some given object; and the protocol is quite simple: it must return this value upon request.

In another application the sorting algorithm is reused as, say, Orange objects can also implement the Comparable interface.

15.7.2 Many Roles – One Object

The many-to-one relation between interface and object is possible in Java and C# as these languages support multiple interface inheritance. That is, a class may implement multiple interfaces. To rephrase this, we can assign several roles to a single object.

You may wonder if an object playing several roles may easily end as a *blob* class. It may be so, but it does not happen if you design your roles small and cohesive. This is best illustrated by an example. The example is from MiniDraw, the two dimensional graphics framework that I will present in learning iteration 7, *Frameworks*. A central role is the "drawing" that contains the set of figures to show: think of an UML class diagram editor in which you may add, move, and remove graphical objects like class rectangles, association lines, etc. The drawing also allows a set of figures to be selected and then, for instance, be moved as a group. Thus, the responsibilities of the drawing role[1] are

Drawing

- Be a collection of figures.
- Allow figures to be added and removed.
- Maintain a temporary, possibly empty, subset of all figures, called a *selection*.

If you look at the first two responsibilities it is basically the responsibilities of a collection. The last responsibility is basically the ability to handle a subset of figures, and as such independent of the two first responsibilities. Thus I can define yet another role.

SelectionHandler

- Maintain a selection of figures.
- Allow figures to be added or removed from the selection.
- Allow a figure to be toggled in/out of the selection.
- Clear a selection.

Thus the Drawing interface is actually defined as

```
public interface Drawing extends SelectionHandler {
  ...
}
```

[1]The actual role has a few more responsibilities but for the sake of the example they are not considered here.

A key point is that the SelectionHandler is a self-contained role and I can therefore make a default implementation in MiniDraw: StandardSelectionHandler. Thus the default Drawing implementation, StandardDrawing, simply creates a StandardSelectionHandler and delegates all selection handling to this object. It also means I can reuse the default selection handler in specialized drawing implementations for the projects later in the book.

> ☞ This is actually an example where the focus on roles leads to inventing objects, the standard selection handler, that would probably not have been identified by a model-perspective.

Another common usage is to integrate two frameworks. An example of this is again Minidraw, that needs to integrate with a concrete Java GUI framework. MiniDraw solves this problem by defining classes that simply play roles in both the MiniDraw framework as well as the Swing GUI framework. An example is the drawing window role that is defined by the DrawingView interface in MiniDraw. To integrate it with Swing, MiniDraw defines the StandardDrawingView class:

```
public class StandardDrawingView
  extends JPanel
  implements DrawingView,
             MouseListener,
             MouseMotionListener {
```

This way the concrete Swing drawing canvas JPanel and the object playing the MiniDraw canvas role, defined by the DrawingView interface, are directly coupled within the StandardDrawingView object. As it also plays the roles of mouse and mouse motion listener it can receive all types of mouse events.

15.7.3 Analysis

Both of the discussions above actually pull in the same direction: towards defining small and cohesive roles that can be expressed as interfaces. As a role is not one-to-one related to an object I still have the freedom to implement the roles in a number of different ways. And smaller roles increase the likelihood that objects implementing them can be reused.

> **Key Point: Define small and cohesive roles**
>
> *Roles should not cover too many responsibilities but stay small and cohesive. Complex roles may then be defined in terms of simpler ones.*

15.8 Summary of Key Concepts

Object-oriented design can be seen from different perspectives. In the *language-centric* perspective, objects are simply containers of data and methods. The *model-centric* perspective perceives objects as model elements, mirroring real world (or imaginary) phenomena. The *responsibility-centric* perspective views objects as interacting agents playing a role in an object community.

The responsibility-centric perspective puts emphasis on the behavior of software systems and the concepts used to do design are *behavior, responsibilities, roles, and protocol.* Behavior is the lowest, concrete, level of actual acting. Responsibility is an abstraction, being dependable to answer a request, but without committing to a specific set of behaviors. Role is a set of responsibilities with associated protocol. And protocol is the convention detailing the interaction expected by a set of roles.

The role concept is important because it allows designers to design system functionality in terms of responsibilities and roles and only later assign roles to objects. This *what/who* process is the opposite of the traditional modeling approach that focus on *who/what,* i.e. finding the objects first and next assigning behavior to these. The result is smaller and more cohesive objects but more complex protocols. It often also results in objects that have no real world concept counterpart.

The relation between role and object is a many-to-many relation. An object may implement several roles due to the multiple interface inheritance ability of Java and C#. And a role may be played by many different objects, as multiple concrete classes may implement the same interface. Therefore, it is advisable to define small and cohesive roles and express them as interfaces.

15.9 Review Questions

List the three different perspectives on what an object is, and outline the main ideas of each.

Define the concepts *behavior, responsibility, role,* and *protocol.* What do they mean? Provide examples of each.

Explain the difference between the *who/what* and *what/who* approach to design.

Give examples of a single role that is played by many types of objects. Give examples of a single object that plays several roles.

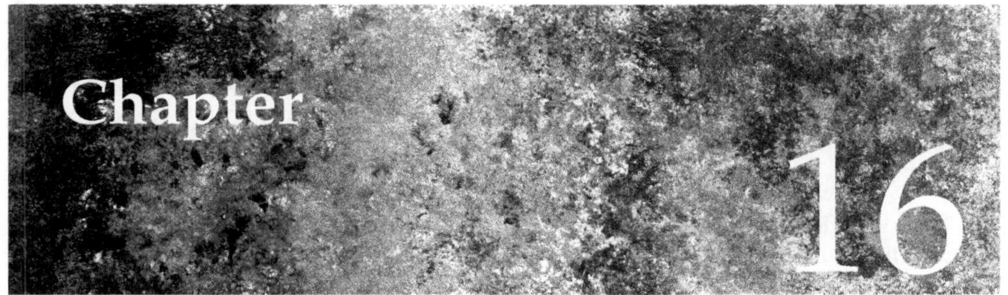

Compositional Design Principles

Learning Objectives

In this chapter, I will more formally introduce the three principles that form the ③-①-② process. The learning focus is understanding how these principles manifest themselves in our design and in our concrete implementation, and how they work in favor of increasing the maintainability and flexibility qualities in our software.

16.1 The Three Principles

The original design pattern book (Gamma et al. 1995) is organized as a catalogue of 23 design patterns. It provides, however, also an introduction that discusses various aspects of writing reusable and flexible software. In this introduction they state some principles for reusable object-oriented design.

> **Principles for Flexible Design:**
>
> ① *Program to an interface, not an implementation.*
>
> ② *Favor object composition over class inheritance.*
>
> ③ *Consider what should be variable in your design.*
> *(or: Encapsulate the behavior that varies.)*

The authors themselves state the first two directly as principles (p. 18 and 20) whereas the third principle is mentioned as part of the process of selecting a design pattern (p. 29) and thus not given the status of a principle. Shalloway and Trott (2004) later highlight the statement *Consider what should be variable* as a third principle. Grand (1998) restated the two first principles as *fundamental patterns,* named INTERFACE and DELEGATION.

These three principles work together nicely and form the mindset that defines the structure and responsibility distribution that is at the core of most design patterns. You have already seen these three principles in action many times. They are the ③-①-② process that I have been using over and over again in many of the preceding chapters.

③ I identified some behavior that was likely to change...	=	③ *Consider what should be variable in your design.*
① I stated a well-defined responsibility that covers this behavior and expressed it in an interface...	=	① *Program to an interface, not an implementation.*
② Instead of implementing the behavior ourselves I delegated to an object implementing the interface...	=	② *Favor object composition over class inheritance.*

16.2 First Principle

① *Program to an interface, not an implementation.*

Client → «interface» Service

A central idea in modern software design is *abstraction*. There are aspects that you want to consider and a lot of details that you do not wish to be bothered with: *details are abstracted away.* We humans have limited memory capabilities and we must thus carefully select just those aspects that are relevant and not overburden ourselves with those that are not.

In object-oriented languages, the *class* is a central building block that encapsulates a lot of irrelevant implementation details while only exposing a small set of public methods. The methods abstract away the implementation details like data structures and algorithms.

Encapsulation and abstraction lead to a powerful mindset for programming: that of a *contract* between a *user* of functionality and a *provider* of functionality. I will use the term *client* for the user class which is common for descriptions of design patterns—do not confuse it with the "client" term used in internet and distributed computing. The providing class I will term the *service*. Thus there exists a contract between the client (*"I agree to call your method with the proper parameters as you have specified..."*) and the server (*"if you agree to provide the behavior you have guaranteed"*).

The question is then whether the class construct is the best way to define a contract between a server and its client. In many cases, the answer is "no!" It is better to *program to an interface* for the following reasons:

Clients are free to use *any* service provider class. If I couple the client to concrete or abstract classes I have severely delimited the set of objects that can be used by the client: an object used by the client *has* to be a subclass! Thus the client has high coupling to a specific class hierarchy.

Consider the two situations a) and b) in Figure 16.1 that reflect a development over time. In situation a) the developers have applied the *program to an interface* principle

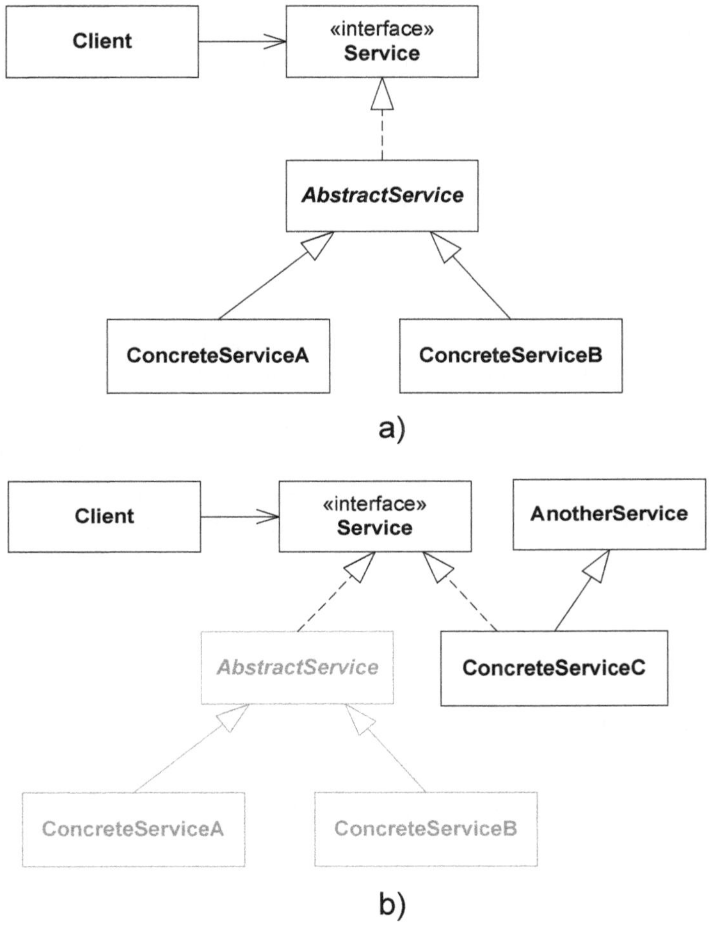

Figure 16.1: a) Original design b) Later design.

and provided a hierarchy of classes that the client uses. Later, however, it becomes beneficial to let the client collaborate with an instance of AnotherService. The interface decouples the client from the concrete implementation hierarchy.

> **Exercise 16.1:** Describe what would happen if in situation a) the client was directly coupled to the AbstractService and you had to make the ConcreteServiceC. How would you do that?

Interfaces allow more fine-grained behavioral abstractions. By nature, a class must address all aspects of the concept that it is intended to represent. Interfaces, however, are not coupled to concepts but only to behavioral aspects. Thus they can express much more fine-grained aspects. The classic example is the Comparable interface, that only expresses the ability of an object to compare itself to another. Another example is the SelectionHandler interface, explained in Section 15.7.2, that showed how introducing fine-grained abstractions can lead to reuse.

Interfaces better express roles. The above discussion can be rephrased in terms of the role concept. Better designs result when you think of the *role* a given server object will play for a client object. This mind set leads to making interfaces more focused and thus smaller.

Again, consider the Comparable interface in the java collection library. To the sorting algorithms, the only interesting aspect is that the objects can play the comparable role—just as a Hamlet play is only interested in a person's ability to play Hamlet. All other aspects are irrelevant.

Classes define implementation as well as interface. Imagine that the client does not program to an interface, but to a concrete service class. As a service class defines implementation, there is a risk that the client class will become coupled to its concrete behavior. The obvious example is accidentally accessing public instance variables which creates high coupling. A more subtle coupling may appear if the service implementation actually deviates from the intended contract as stated by class and method comments. Some examples are for methods to have undocumented side effects, or even have defects. In that case the client code may drift into assuming the side effects, or be coded to circumvent the defective behavior. Now the coupling has become tight between the two as another service implementation cannot be substituted.

16.3 Second Principle

> ② *Favor object composition over class inheritance.*

This statement deals with the two fundamental ways of reusing behavior in object-oriented software as outlined in Figure 16.2.

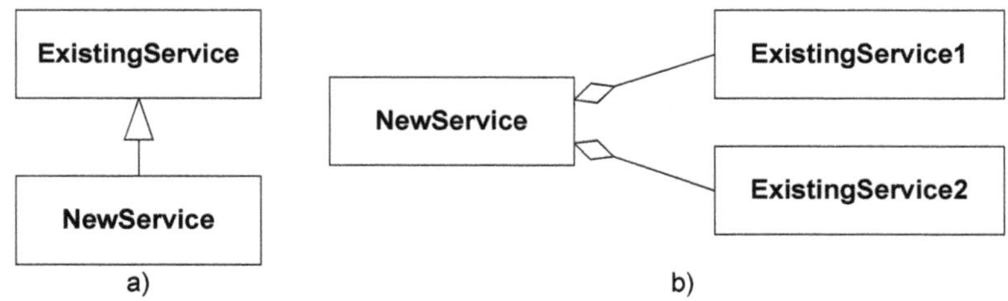

Figure 16.2: Class inheritance (a) and object composition (b).

Class inheritance is the mechanism whereby I can take an existing class that has some desirable behavior and subclass it to change and add behavior. That is, I get complex behavior by reusing the behavior of the superclass. *Object composition* is, in contrast, the mechanism whereby I achieve complex behavior by *composing* the behavior of a set of objects.

You saw these two techniques discussed in depth in Chapter 7, *Deriving Strategy Pattern,* and in many of the following chapters concerning design patterns. The polymorphic proposal suggested using class inheritance to introduce a new rate structure algorithm; the compositional proposal suggested using object compositions to do the same.

Class inheritance has a number of advantages. It is straightforward and supported directly by the programming language. The language support ensures that you write very little extra code in order to reuse the behavior of the superclass. Below, I will describe liabilities of class inheritance, followed by a few for object composition.

Encapsulation. It is a fact that "inheritance breaks encapsulation" (Snyder 1986). A subclass has access to instance variables, data structures, and methods in all classes up the superclass chain (unless declared `private`.) Thus superclass(es) expose implementation details to be exploited in the subclass: the coupling is high indeed. This has the consequence that implementation changes in a superclass are costly as all subclasses have to be inspected, potentially refactored, and tested to avoid defects.

Object composition, in contrast, depends upon objects interacting via their interfaces and encapsulation is ensured: objects collaborating via the interfaces do not depend on instance variables and implementation details. The coupling is lower and each abstraction may be modified without affecting the others (unless the contract/interface is changed of course).

You can only add responsibilities, not remove them. Inheriting from a superclass means *"you buy the full package."* You get *all* methods and *all* data structures when you subclass, even if they are unusable or directly in conflict with the responsibilities defined by the subclass. You may override a method to do nothing in order to remove its behavior, or indicate that it is no longer a valid method to invoke, usually by throwing an exception like UnsupportedOperationException. Subclasses can only *add,* never *remove* methods and data structures inherited. A classic example is *java.util.Stack.* A stack, by definition, only supports adding and removing elements by push() and pop. However, to reuse the element storage implementation, the developers have made Stack a subclass of Vector, which is a linear list collection. That is, an instance of stack also allows elements to be inserted at a specific position, `stack.add(7, item);`, which is forbidden by a stack's contract!

Composing behavior, in contrast, leads to more fine-grained abstractions. Each abstraction can be highly focused on a single task. Thus cohesion is high as there is a clear division of responsibilities.

Exercise 16.2: Apply the ② principle to the stack example above so clients cannot invoke methods that are not part of a stack's contract but the stack abstract still reuses the vector's implementation.

Compile-time versus run-time binding. Class inheritance defines a compile-time coupling between a subclass and its superclass. Once an object of this class has been instantiated its behavior is defined once and for all throughout its lifetime. In contrast, an object that provides behavior by delegating partial behavior to delegate objects *can* change behavior over its lifetime, simply by changing the set of delegate objects it uses. For instance, you can reconfigure a Alphatown pay station to become a Betatown pay station even at run-time simply by changing what rate strategy and what factory it uses.

> **Exercise 16.3:** Extend the pay station so it can be reconfigured at run-time by providing it with a new factory object. You will have to introduce a new method in the PayStation interface, for instance
>
> ```
> public void reconfigure(PayStationFactory factory);
> ```

Recurring modifications in the class hierarchy. A force I have often seen in practice is that classes in a hierarchy have a tendency to be modified often, as new subclasses are added. As an example, consider a service that fulfills its contract nicely using a simple ArrayList data structure, see a) in Figure 16.3. Later I need a better performing service implementation but if I simply subclass the original service class I have to override all methods to use a better performing data structure, and instantiated objects will contain both structures. The logical consequence is to modify the class hierarchy by adding a common, abstract, class, as shown in pane b) of the figure. While the modification is sensible, it does mean that three classes are now modified

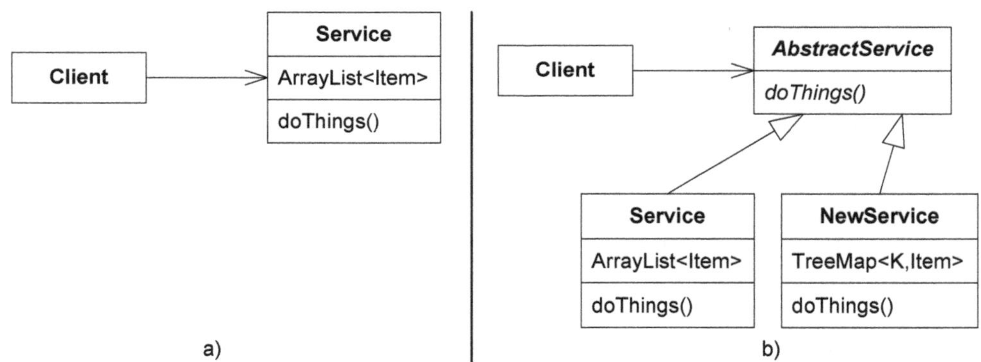

Figure 16.3: Modifications in hierarchy.

and have to be reviewed and tested to ensure the former reliability. Often, each new subclass added provides opportunities for reworking the class hierarchy and as a consequence the stability quality suffers. In Chapter 11, *Deriving State Pattern,* I discussed the tendency for subclass specific behavior "bubbling" up the hierarchy to end in the abstract superclass that becomes bigger and less cohesive over time.

In a compositional design, the array list based and tree map implementations would be separate implementations without overlap. However, this benefit may turn into a liability if the AbstractService can make concrete implementations of many of the methods. In that case, a compositional proposal would end up with duplicated code or be required to do further decomposition to avoid it. Thus, in this case one should carefully consider benefits and liabilities before committing to either solution. This particular case is explored in the exercise below.

Exercise 16.4: To make Figure 16.3 concrete, consider that the service is a list storing integers. A demonstration implementation may look like

Fragment: exercise/compositional-principles/InitialImplementation.java

```
class IntegerList {
  private int contents[]; int index;
  public IntegerList() { contents = new int[3]; index = 0;}
  public int size() { return index; }
  public boolean add(int e) {
    contents[index++] = e;
    return true;
  }
  public int get(int position) {return contents[position];}
  // following methods are data structure independent
  public boolean isEmpty() { return size() == 0; }
  public String contentsAsString() {
    String result = "[";
    for ( int i = 0; i < size()-1; i++ ) {
      result += get(i)+", ";
    }
    return result + get(size()-1)+"]";
  }
}
```

Note that the two last methods are implemented using only methods in the class' interface, thus they can be implemented once and for all in an abstract class.

Take the above source code and implement two variants of an integer list: one in which you subclass and one in which you compose behavior. Evaluate benefits and liabilities. How can you make a compositional approach that has no code duplication and does not use an abstract class?

Separate testing. Objects that handle a single task with a clearly defined responsibility may often be tested isolated from the more complex behavioral abstraction they are part of. This works in favor of higher reliability. Dependencies to *depended-on units* may be handled by test stubs. The separate testing of rate strategies, outlined in Section 8.1.5, is an example showing this.

Increased possibility of reuse. Small abstractions are easier to reuse as they (usually) have fewer dependencies and comes with less behavior that may not be suitable in a reusing context. The selection handler abstraction in MiniDraw, described in the previous chapter, is an example of this.

Increased number of objects, classes, and interfaces. Having two, three, or several objects doing complex behavior instead of a single object doing it all by itself naturally leads to an increase in the number of objects existing at run-time; and an increase in the number of classes and interfaces I as a developer have to overview at compile-time. If I cannot maintain this overview or I do not understand the interactions then defects will result. It is therefore vital that developers *do* have a roadmap to this web of objects and interfaces in order to overview and maintain the code. How to maintain this overview is the topic of Chapter 18.

Delegation requires more boilerplate code. A final liability is that delegation requires more "boilerplate" code. If I inherit a superclass, you only have to write Class B **extends** A and all methods are automatically available to any B object without further typing. In a compositional design, I have potentially a lot of typing to do: create an object reference to A, and type in all "reused" methods and write the delegation code:

```
void foo() { a.foo(); }
int bar() { return a.bar(); }
```

16.4 Third Principle

> ③ *Consider what should be variable in your design.*

This is the most vague of the three principles (perhaps the reason that Gamma et al. did not themselves state it as a principle). Instead of considering what might force a design change you must focus on the aspects that you want to vary—and then design your software in such a way that it can vary *without* changing the design. This is why it could be reformulated as *Encapsulate what varies in your design*: use the first two principles to express the variability as an interface, and then delegate to an object implementing it.

This principle is a recurring theme of many design patterns: some aspect is identified as the variable (like "business rule/algorithm" in STRATEGY) and the pattern provides a design that allows this aspect to vary without changes to the design but by changes in the configuration of objects collaborating.

16.5 The Principles in Action

The principles can be used by themselves but as I have pointed out throughout this book they often work nicely in concert: the ③-①-② process.

③–Consider what should be variable. I identify some behavior in an abstraction that must be variable, perhaps across product lines (Alphatown, Betatown, etc.), perhaps across computing environments (Oracle database, MySQL database, etc.), perhaps across development situations (with and without hardware sensors attached, under and outside testing control, etc.) as shown in Figure 16.4.

①–Program to an interface, not an implementation. I express that responsibility that must be variable in a new interface, see Figure 16.5.

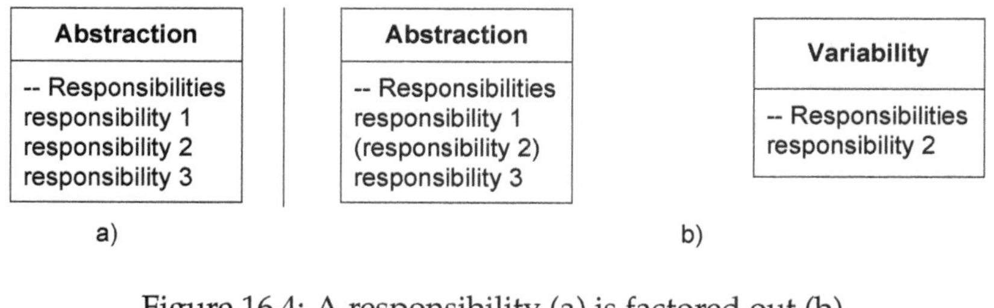

Figure 16.4: A responsibility (a) is factored out (b).

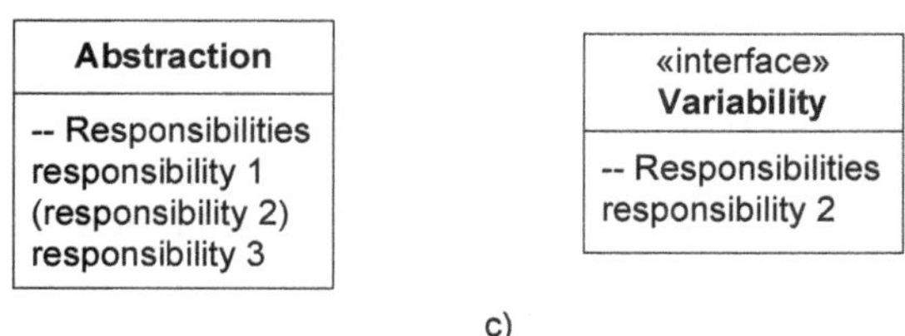

Figure 16.5: Expressing it as an interface (c).

②–Favor object composition over class inheritance. And I define the full, complex, behavior by letting the client delegate behavior to the subordinate object: *let someone else do the dirty job*, as seen in Figure 16.6.

Remember, however, that the ③-①-② is not a process to use mechanically. As was apparent in the discussion of the abstract factory you have to carefully evaluate your options to achieve a good design with low coupling and high cohesion. Note also that they are *principles*, not *laws*. Using these principles blindly on any problem you encounter may "over-engineer" your software. If you are not in a position where you can utilize the benefits then there is little point in applying the principles. Remember the TDD value: *Simplicity:* You should build or refactor for flexibility when need arises, not in anticipation of a need. Often when I have tried to build in flexibility in anticipation of a need, I have found myself guessing wrong and the code serving the flexibility actually gets in the way of a better solution.

16.6 Summary of Key Concepts

Three principles are central for designing compositional designs. These are:

Principles for Flexible Design:

① *Program to an interface, not an implementation.*

② *Favor object composition over class inheritance.*

③ *Consider what should be variable in your design.*
(or: Encapsulate the behavior that varies.)

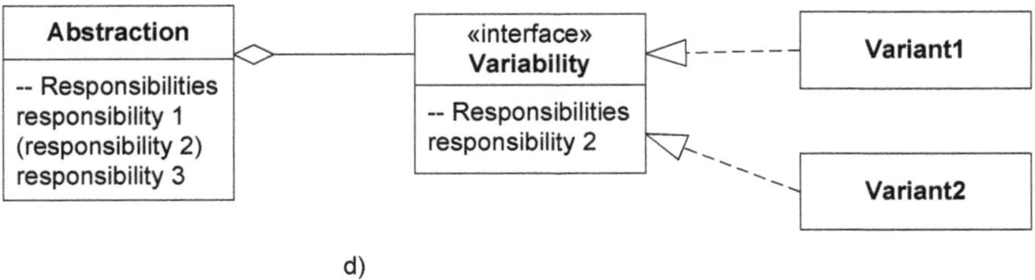

Figure 16.6: Composing full behavior by delegating (d).

Generally, applying these patterns makes your design more flexible and maintainable as abstractions are more loosely coupled (first principle), bindings are run-time (second principle), and abstractions tend to become smaller and more cohesive. The third principle is a keystone in many design patterns that strive to handle variability by encapsulation, using the first two principles.

16.7 Selected Solutions

Discussion of Exercise 16.1:

One possible way would be to create a subclass AbstractServiceD and let it create an instance of AbstractServiceC. All methods in AbstractServiceD (which are the ones the client invokes) are overridden to call appropriate methods in AbstractServiceC. However, the construction is odd, as AbstractServiceD of course inherits algorithms and data structures from AbstractService that are not used at all.

This proposal resembles the ADAPTER pattern, however adapter is fully compositional.

Discussion of Exercise 16.4:

You can find solutions to the exercise in folder *solution/compositional-principles*. Basically, you can do the same thing with a compositional design as with an abstract class: you factor out common code into a special role, CommonCollectionResponsibilities, implement it, and delegate from the implementations of the integer list. However, due to the delegation code and extra interfaces, the implementation becomes longer (100 lines of code versus 85) and more complex.

16.8 Review Questions

What are the three principles of flexible software design? How are they formulated? Describe and argue for their benefits and liabilities.

How do these principles relate to patterns like STRATEGY, ABSTRACT FACTORY and others that you have come across?

What are the alternative implementations that arise when these principles are not followed?

16.9 Further Exercises

Exercise 16.5:

Many introductory books on object-oriented programming demonstrate generalization/specialization hierarchies and inheritance by a classification hierarchy rooted in the concept *person* as shown in Figure 16.7. For instance a person can be a teacher or a student and by inheriting from the Person class all methods are inherited "for free": getName(), getAge(), etc.

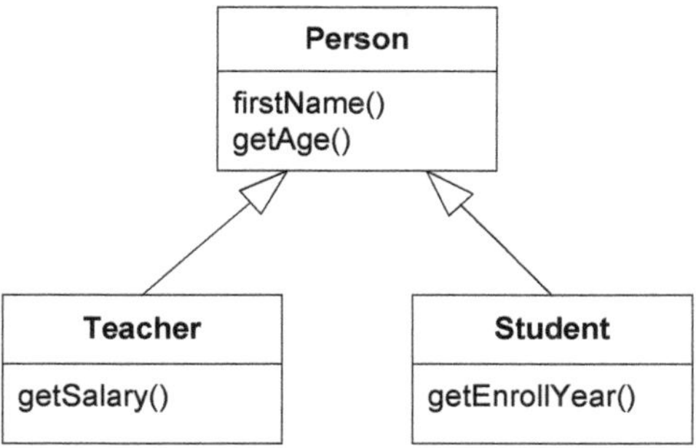

Figure 16.7: A polymorphic design for teachers and students.

This design may suffice for simple systems but there are several problems with this design that you should study in this exercise. You should analyze the problems stated in the context of an object-oriented university management system that handles all the university's associated persons (that is both teachers and students).

Life-cycle problem. Describe how to handle that a student graduates and gets employed as a teacher?

Context problem. Describe how the system must handle that a teacher enrolls as student on a course? How must the above class diagram be changed in order to fully model that a person can be both a student as well as a teacher?

Consistency problem. Describe how the system must handle a situation where a teacher changes his name while enrolled in a course.

Based on your understanding of roles and by applying the principles for flexible design propose a new design that better handles these problems. Note: It is not so much the ③-①-② process that should be used here as it is the individual principles in their own right.

As a concrete step, consider the following code fragment that describes the consistency problem above:

```
Teacher t = [get teacher ''Henrik Christensen'']
Student s = [get student ''Henrik Christensen'']

assertEquals(''Henrik'', t.firstName() );
assertEquals(''Henrik'', s.firstName() );
```

```
[Person Henrik renamed to Thomas]

assertEquals(''Thomas'', t.firstName() );
assertEquals(''Thomas'', s.firstName() );
```

The point is that the name change should be a single operation at the *person* level (as name changes conceptually has nothing to do with neither Henrik's teacher nor student association).

How would you make the person-teacher-student design so that this test case passes without making changes to multiple objects?

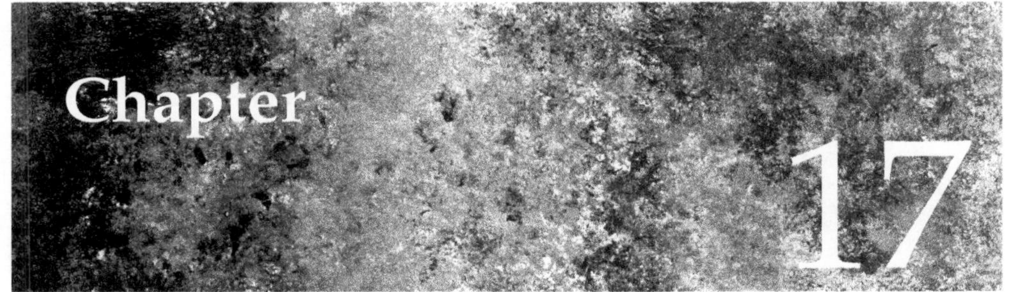

Multi-Dimensional Variance

Learning Objectives

So far in this learning iteration, I have focused on principles and concepts of compositional design. In this chapter I will return to the pay station case and the practical aspects. The learning focus is *variability along several dimensions*, i.e. when our production code must support combinations of variable aspects. Even in simple systems, you often see this kind of combined variability: a system must interface different types of hardware, run both in a production and test environment, use different types of persistent storage, handle different customer requirements, etc.

17.1 New Requirement

Alphatown is creative and comes up with a pretty reasonable new requirement. The value shown on the display is presently the number of minutes parking time that the entered amount entitles to. However, people prefer thinking in terms of the time when parking expires. Thus they want us to change the pay station so this value is shown on the display instead. As the hardware display can only display 4 digits, they want the time to be shown in the 24-hour clock format. That is, if I buy 10 minutes of parking time at 5:12 PM then instead of the display reading "0010" it should read "1722" to show that parking end time is 17:22 in the 24-hour clock. An example of the display output is shown in Figure 17.1.

17.2 Multi-Dimensional Variation

Analyzing the problem, it is apparent that I actually have a software system that is required to *vary along a set of distinct dimensions*. These dimensions are

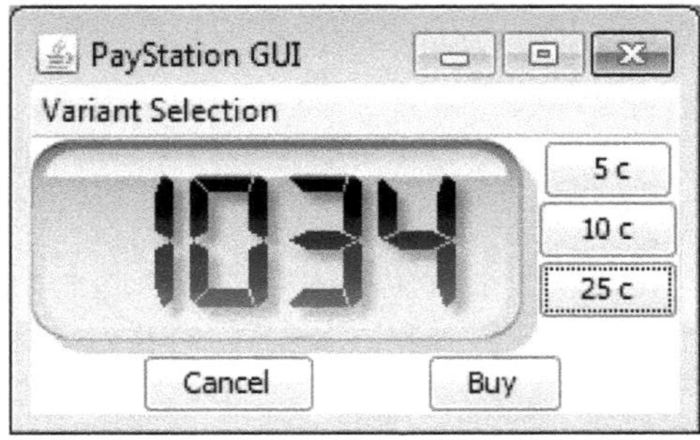

Figure 17.1: Displaying parking end time.

- *Rate calculation.* There are several different requirements to how the pay station must calculate rates: Linear, progressive, alternating, etc.
- *Receipt information.* There are at the moment two requirements regarding the information on the receipts: the "standard" and one with bar code.
- *Display output.* There are requirements of what output the pay station should give on the display: Either number of minutes parking time bought or the time when parking must end.
- *"Weekend" control.* Our team must be able to get control of whether the pay station believes it is the weekend or not in order to bring the Gammatown's alternating rate calculation under full testing control.

If I restrict myself to the non-testing related three dimensions, I can describe each product variant as the proper configuration of the three variability points in a **configuration table**:

	Variability points		
Product	**Rate**	**Receipt**	**Display**
Alphatown	Linear	Standard	End time
Betatown	Progressive	Barcode	Minutes
Gammatown	Alternating	Standard	Minutes

This way, a product variant becomes a *point* in this three dimensional variability space as shown in Figure 17.2. The figure plots the Alphatown variant at the (Linear rate, standard receipt, end time display) point in the coordinate system of the pay station's variability space. The variability space has three dimensions: Rate policy, receipt type, and display output type.

The interesting aspect is that these dimensions are *independent* of each other. There is no logical binding between them that dictates that if a customer wants, say, linear rates, then they are forced to use, say, end time display. It then follows that all combinations are valid, legal, and indeed possible. I will term this **multi-dimensional variability** which denotes variability of multiple, independent, aspects of the software product.

The number of possible variants of the current pay station design is already $3 \times 2 \times 2 = 12$ (3 different rate policies, 2 receipt variations, and 2 display policies). If I add, say, two new rate policy variants the equation yields 20 combinations—the number of combinations grows rapidly—I have a **combinatorial explosion** of variants.

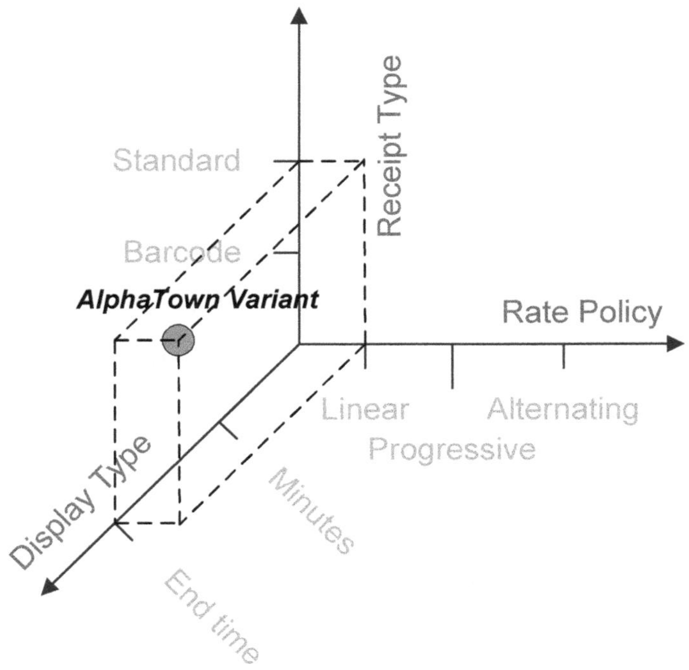

Figure 17.2: The Alphatown variant plotted in varibility space.

17.3 The Polymorphic Proposal

The polymorphic approach does not handle multi-dimensional variability well. In Figure 17.3 is shown the potential development of the class hierarchy for the three product variants. The classes containing the Alphatown, Betatown, and Gammatown variants are marked, and a potential fourth product for Deltatown that wants alternating rates, bar code receipts, and parking end time displayed is marked. The question for the Deltatown developers is which class is best to subclass (the question marks on the inheritance relation). No matter what the choice is, either the algorithms are code duplicated in the subclasses or they are moved into protected methods in the root class which therefore becomes a pile of methods that are only relevant for a few subclasses in the inheritance hierarchy (as discussed in Section 11.4). Cohesion suffers as does analyzability.

The problem is that inheritance is a one-dimensional mechanism (in Java and C#) and therefore it must handle multi-dimensional variability by "flattening" the variability space. This leads to odd names like PayStationAlternatingRateBarcodeReceiptEndTimeDisplay. In our case, as there are 12 potential product variations I would have to implement and maintain 12 different subclasses.

Note also that the reason that the immediate subclasses of PayStation are distinguished by the choice of rate policy is purely historical! If I had to make the polymorphic design with my present knowledge of the three products, I might just as well have chosen to make the first subclasses vary by choice of output on the display: minutes or end of parking time. The design would have been just as poor, but the point is that design is driven by the time a certain type of variation is introduced. This is in contrast to the compositional design that does not show a similar problem.

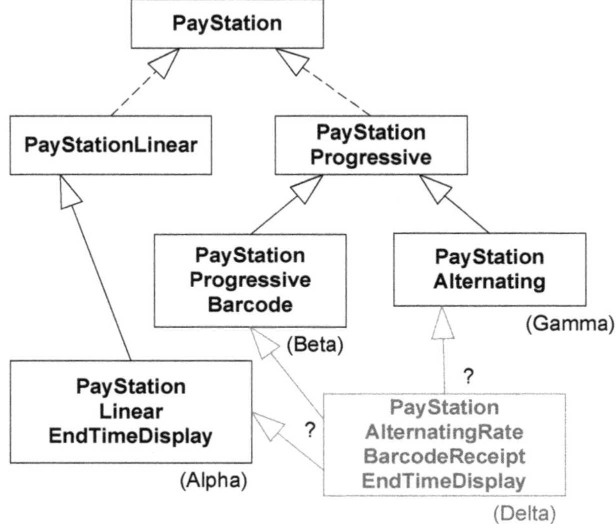

Figure 17.3: A combination of variability handled by inheritance.

Key Point: Do not use inheritance to handle multi-dimensional variation

As Java and C# only support single implementation inheritance and the inheritance mechanism therefore is one-dimensional, it cannot accommodate multi-dimensional variations without a combinatorial explosion of subclasses.

17.4 The Compositional Proposal

Taking the ③-①-② process the new requirement simply pinpoints a new behavior that may vary: the display output behavior. This insight is then the ③ step: *consider what is variable.*

The ① step, *program to an interface,* is to express the responsibility in an interface. As this is an algorithm to compute the output to display, it is the STRATEGY pattern.

Listing: chapter/compositional/iteration-1/src/paystation/domain/DisplayStrategy.java

```
package paystation.domain;
/** The strategy for calculating the output for the display.
*/

public interface DisplayStrategy {
  /** return the output to present at the pay station's
      display
      @param minutes the minutes parking time
      bought so far.
   */
```

```
  public int calculateOutput( int minutes );
}
```

The pay station must then be refactored to use objects realizing the DisplayStrategy interface instead of doing the job itself. This is the ② step: *favor object composition*. The refactoring and test-driven development process is well known by now and will not be repeated here. You can find the resulting source code on the web site. The variability point in the pay station is of course in the readDisplay method.

Fragment: chapter/compositional/iteration-2/src/paystation/domain/PayStationImpl.java

```
  public int readDisplay() {
    return displayStrategy.calculateOutput(timeBought);
  }
```

The compositional design does not suffer a combinatorial explosion of classes. You can make all 12 variants of the pay station by configuring the set of delegate objects that the PayStationImpl should use.

Exercise 17.1: What about the factory classes? Will I not get a combinatorial explosion of these as I have to define a factory object for each product variant I can imagine? Sketch one or two solutions to this problem.

17.5 Analysis

Compositional designs handle multi-dimensional variance elegantly, because each type of variable behavior is encapsulated in its own abstraction. In contrast, both the parametric and polymorphic designs have a single abstraction that must handle all responsibilities.

The compositional pay station design adheres to the definition of object orientation as *a community of interaction objects in which each object has a role to play.* One object plays the role of rate calculator, another receipt creator, and a third display output calculator, while the pay station object's primary function is to coordinate and structure the collaboration. The pay station fulfils its **Pay Station** role by defining a protocol of interaction with these different roles. The multi-dimensional variability then becomes a question of configuring the right set of objects to play each of the defined roles. The pay station system has become a framework or product line for building pay station systems. Frameworks are discussed in detail in Chapter 32.

17.6 Selected Solutions

Discussion of Exercise 17.1:

The problem is real: if I end up in a situation where all 12 variants of the pay station system are needed then I end up with 12 factory classes: AlphaTownFactory, ..., TwelfthTownFactory. This may seem just as bad as the 12 subclasses in the polymorphic case. However, on closer inspection the situation is less problematic. First, the amount of code that is duplicated in the factories is much smaller, as the factory's create methods should not contain much more than a single new statement. Second, in case all 12 variants are really needed one would most probably drop the idea of individual factory classes and instead write a single implementation class that reads a configuration file stating the particular configuration and then create the proper delegates. Java's ability to dynamically load classes at run-time allows such code to be become very compact and to contain no conditional statements.

17.7 Review Questions

Describe how the pay station's different variants can be classified according to variability dimensions and as points in a multi-dimensional variability space.

Define *multi-dimensional variance*. What does *combinatorial explosion of variants* mean?

Why is it problematic to handle variability along multiple dimensions using inheritance in single implementation inheritance languages like Java and C#?

17.8 Further Exercises

Exercise 17.2:

Sketch the Java code for the PayStation class that uses parametric variability to handle all pay station variants.

Exercise 17.3:

Sketch the Java code for the PayStation subclasses for the Gammatown and Deltatown variants in Figure 17.3.

Exercise 17.4. Source code directory:
`chapter/compositional/iteration-0`

Walk in my footsteps. Implement the pay station using the compositional approach so it can handle the new Alphatown requirement.

Exercise 17.5:

Refactor your pay station software so you can change delegate objects while running, that is, an Alphatown pay station should become, say, a Betatown pay station while executing. Be careful that the pay station keeps it state (the amount of payment entered so far) during reconfiguration.

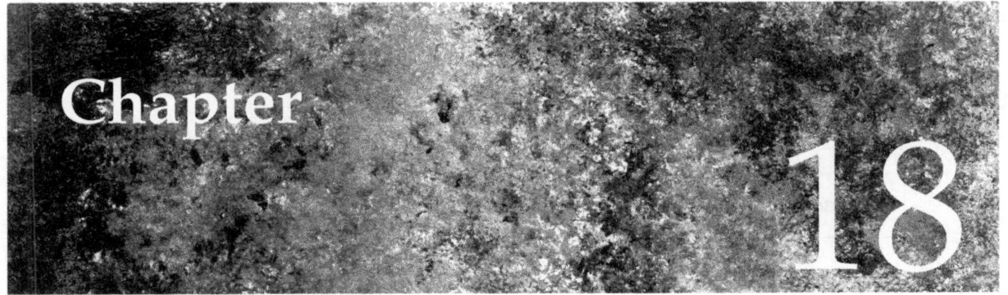

Design Patterns – Part II

Learning Objectives

In Chapter 9, *Design Patterns – Part I*, I presented two definitions of design patterns, one by Gamma et al. and one by Beck et al. The learning objective of this chapter is to present two additional definitions of design patterns in order to convey an even deeper understanding of the concept. The first definition recasts patterns in the responsibility-centric perspective, and the second looks at how patterns are key concepts for understanding and keeping overview of complex, compositional, designs.

18.1 Patterns as Roles

The structure of design patterns are usually documented using UML class diagrams. The diagrams for STRATEGY and STATE, reproduced in Figure 18.1 and Figure 18.2, consist of interface, classes, and relationships.

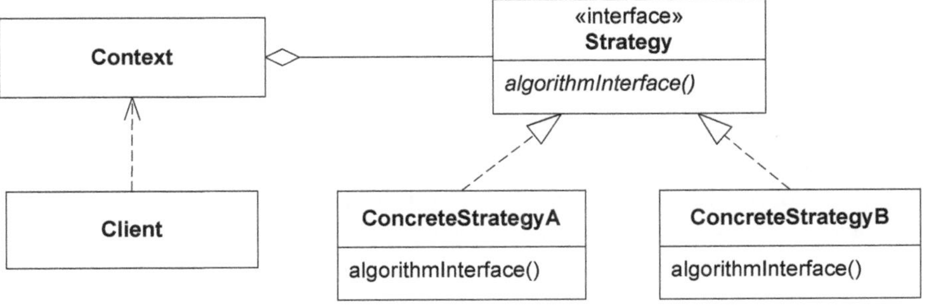

Figure 18.1: STRATEGY pattern structure in UML.

Now, take a moment to compare the design pattern structure diagrams with the design of the special Gammatown rate strategy, reproduced in Figure 18.3.

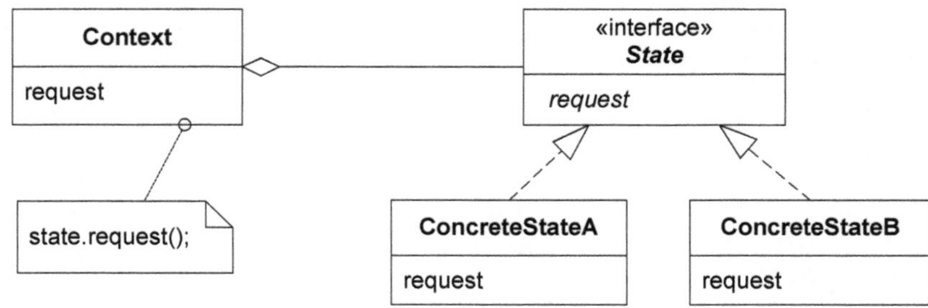

Figure 18.2: STATE pattern structure in UML.

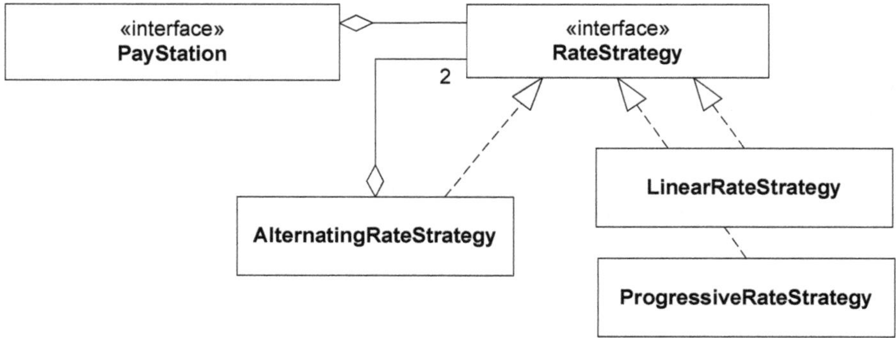

Figure 18.3: The combination of STRATEGY and STATE.

Do you see a problem? If I concentrate on the two patterns STRATEGY and STATE then the UML class diagrams for these patterns state that there is an interface called Strategy and an interface called State in the respective patterns. Looking at Figure 18.3 though, I can find the strategy interface (RateStrategy)—but where is the interface defining the **State** role that appears in the UML for the STATE pattern? Apparently—it is not there. The question is then: Are the pattern diagrams wrong? Or is it my pay station design that is wrong?

The answer lies in understanding that design patterns are *not* a fixed set of classes and interfaces. Interfaces and classes are the tools available in UML but what design patterns really express are roles.

Definition: **Design pattern (Role view)**

A design pattern is defined by a set of roles, each role having a specific set of responsibilities, and by a well-defined protocol between these roles.

The point is that when you see the Strategy interface in the STRATEGY pattern you must think of it as a *role*. In the pay station design the **Strategy** role is defined by the RateStrategy interface. And—the **State** role from the STATE pattern is also present—it is defined by the very same RateStrategy interface: it defines the common interface for all **ConcreteState** instances.

Thus I can annotate the abstractions for this part of the pay station design with the corresponding roles from the design patterns as done in Figure 18.4. I will call this type of diagram a role diagram.

Definition: Role diagram

A role diagram is a UML class diagram in which gray boxes either above or below each interface or class describe the abstraction's role in a particular pattern. The role is described by **pattern-name:role-name**.

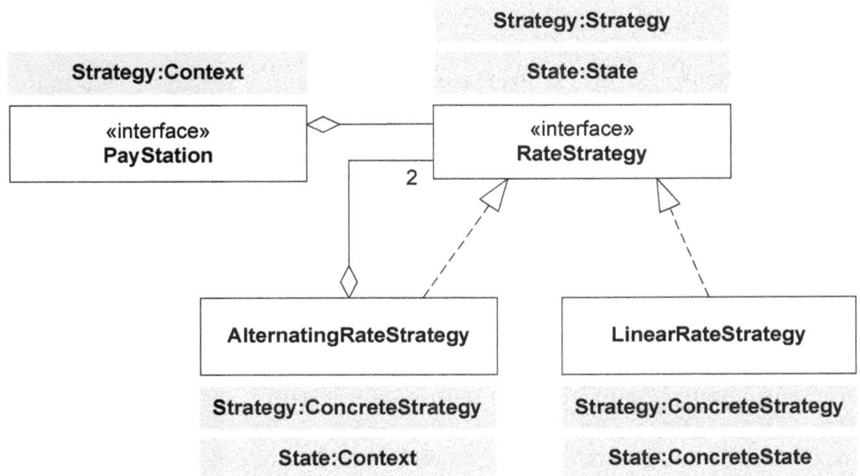

Figure 18.4: Partial pay station design annotated with roles.

Thus the RateStrategy interface serves both the strategy role in the Strategy pattern as well as the State role in the State pattern. It is even more evident at the object level where a concrete instance of LinearRateStrategy may play both the **Strategy:ConcreteStrategy** role as well as the **State:ConcreteState** role.

Exercise 18.1: Consider class AlternatingRateStrategy in role diagram 18.4. Explain why it can play the same role as LinearRateStrategy in STRATEGY but a different role in State? What consequences does it have on the coding? You may review the role section of respective design pattern boxes to answer this question.

Exercise 18.2: STRATEGY also defines a **Client** role. It is not shown on Figure 18.4. Which abstraction plays this role in the pay station system?

18.2 Maintaining Compositional Designs

I have argued in favor of compositional design, using design patterns, and stressed that my pay station production code has become flexible. The question is whether it is also *maintainable?* Remember that the definition of maintainability is:

Definition: Maintainability (ISO 9126)

The capability of the software product to be modified. Modifications may include corrections, improvements or adaptation of the software to changes in environment, and in requirements and functional specifications.

Maintainability is closely related to the architects' and developers' ability to read, understand, and reason about the system's behavior. If you consider the relatively small functional requirements of the pay station it may come as a surprise to see the full class diagram in Figure 18.5.

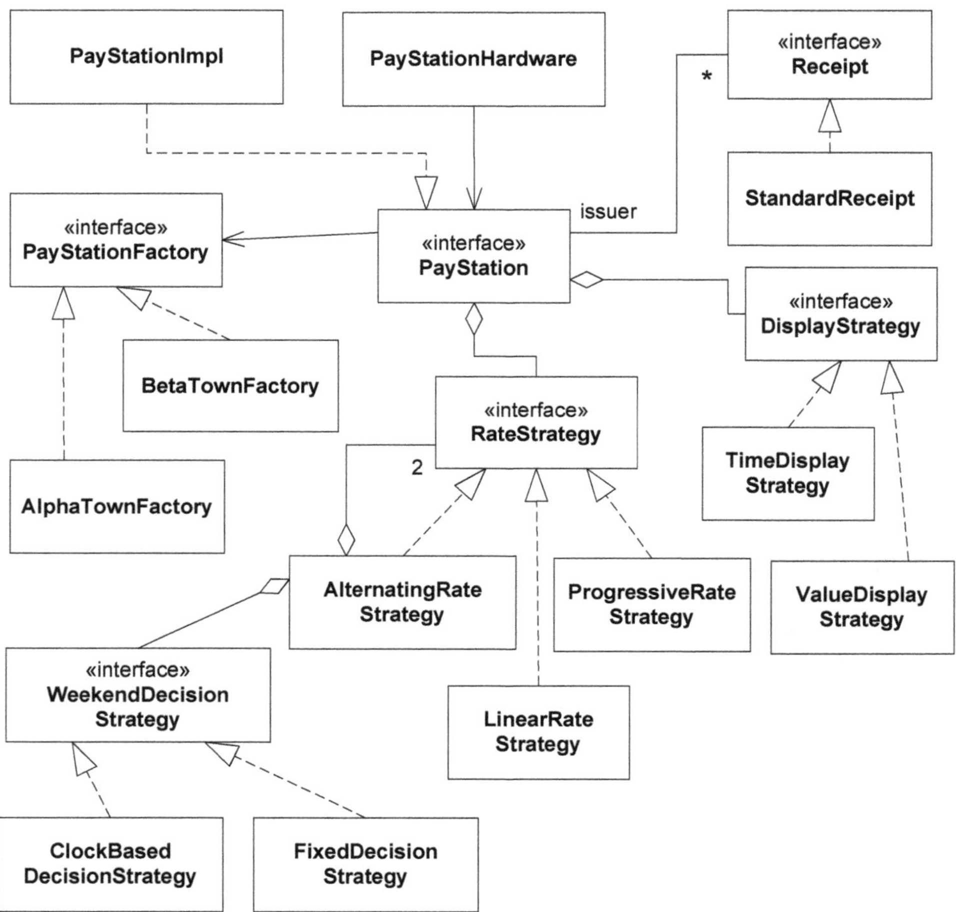

Figure 18.5: The pay station class diagram.

Exercise 18.3: Even though the class diagram is pretty large, it is actually a simplification compared to the real system. Identify some classes and relations that have been omitted in the diagram.

After all, the pay station is a behaviorally simple system, but apparently I have turned the class diagram into a big mess. OK, it is flexible and can exist in many different variants, but nonetheless the resulting design *is* complex. So, the really good question is: how do I overview and understand this big mess of classes? And even more challenging: communicate it with my fellow developers and architects? I could, as I have indeed done, write a several hundred pages long book about the design but this is of course absurd in real development where the business lies in the software produced, not in the teaching aspects nor the book produced.

This is indeed a major problem in compositional designs and frameworks that have a lot of delegation, lots of interfaces, and many aspects that may vary. The cure to the problem is to *know your patterns* and *document them in the design*. When I deeply understand the roles and protocols of the design patterns in my design, there are lots of details that I can either omit from my class diagrams or that I can read from the diagram without getting confused: all the jigsaw pieces form an understandable picture.

I have redrawn Figure 18.5 with emphasis on the central roles in the patterns used—and grayed those roles that are "merely" implementations of the roles, see Figure 18.6. For instance, once I understand that the RateStrategy interface in the diagram plays the **Strategy** role of the STRATEGY pattern I *know* that there must be several **ConcreteStrategy** objects in the diagram as well—and indeed there are: LinearRateStrategy and its siblings. They do not confuse, though. I know they have been there in order to provide concrete behavior to the strategy role.

Using the pattern's name directly in naming interfaces and classes provides strong clues to the patterns that are in play in a design, here ABSTRACT FACTORY and STRATEGY. It is not always possible as for instance when a given abstraction plays a part in several patterns. An example is AlternatingRateStrategy that plays both the **Strategy:Strategy** role as well as the **State:Context** role. However, the Strategy role is always in play whereas it is only for the Gammatown pay station that it acts as context for state. However, pointing towards the state pattern turned too odd in the naming. Maybe AlternatingRateStrategyStateContext but it becomes too long for my taste.

The documentation (JavaDoc or the like) of the interfaces and classes should describe the patterns they are part of as well as the roles. This is more important for the central roles and less so for the concrete implementations.

In the diagram, note also that there are quite a lot of relations that I have not drawn at all. I have omitted the relations between the ABSTRACT FACTORY and the strategies they instantiate. The reason is that the diagram would become cluttered with association lines. This would make it harder to read even though it would be more correct. I consider class diagrams to be *roadmaps* that should emphasize overview more than correctness. As I know my ABSTRACT FACTORY pattern well I know that each factory has relations to a set of **ConcreteProduct** roles. If I am interested in finding the true configuration for, say AlphaTownFactory, then I must go to the production code (or a table in the documentation, perhaps) to extract this information. The class diagram provides the roadmap while the production code provides the "truth" about the details of the road.

Thus, it is possible to provide yet another classification of what design patterns are:

Definition: **Design pattern (Roadmap view)**

Design patterns structure, document, and provide overview of the roles and protocols in complex, compositional, designs. A design pattern serves as a roadmap of a part of the design.

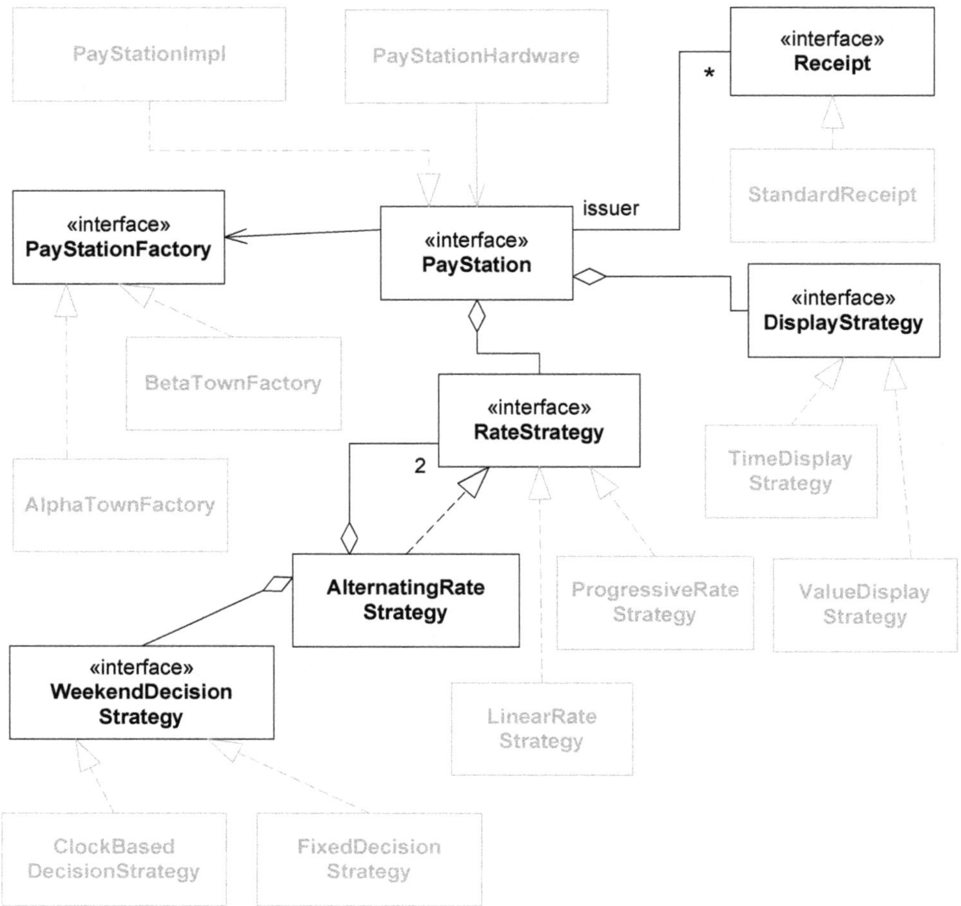

Figure 18.6: The central roles in the class diagram.

The argumentation above can also be reversed. What happens if a developer that has never received any training in design patterns and compositional design processes is requested to make modifications or implement new requirements in the design? The answer is that he *will* just see one big mess of interfaces and classes that interact in, to him, overly complex ways. I once participated in a research project where this happened (Christensen and Røn 2000) and the conclusion was that "The newcomers were unable to produce code that followed the intent of the patterns and much code therefore had to be rewritten."

Key Point: Maintaining compositional designs requires appropriate training

Compositional designs are complex in terms of the protocols and number of roles and objects involved. Software designers and developers must therefore have a deep understanding of compositional design principles and design patterns in order to successfully maintain such designs.

Exercise 18.4: You now have four different definitions of design patterns, two from Chapter 9 and two from this chapter. Argue why it is possible to have different definitions without them being in conflict.

18.3 Summary of Key Concepts

The structure of design patterns are normally documented by UML class diagrams, but patterns are not a fixed set of interfaces and classes. Instead *patterns are a set of roles and their protocols* which can be mapped to concrete interfaces and classes in many different ways. A *role diagram* annotate each class or interface in a class diagram with the respective roles they play in a set of patterns.

Compositional designs are complex because of the large number of interfaces and classes that interact in complex ways. Therefore, they present a challenge to software architects and developers maintaining these systems because they need to overview the structure, reason about its behavior, and avoid introducing code that breaks the conventions. A deep knowledge of the principles of flexible design and design patterns is vital in order to cope with this complexity. Design patterns define the central roles that each object will ultimately play and the protocols that govern how it will interact. Thus, one can define *design patterns as a roadmap of a design* that allows developers to maintain overview.

18.4 Selected Solutions

Discussion of Exercise 18.1:

Class AlternatingRateStrategy as well as LinearRateStrategy serve the **ConcreteStrategy** role that is described in design pattern side bar 7.1 as *defines concrete behavior fulfilling the algorithmic responsibility*. As both classes do the same thing, namely perform the rate policy calculation, they obviously serve this role.

In the STATE pattern, however, the **Context** *object delegate to its current state object* while the **ConcreteState** *objects define the specific behavior associated with each specific state*. And here the difference appears also at the coding level. The AlternatingRateStrategy contains the state object decision code as well as the delegation and therefore conforms to the **Context** role. The LinearRateStrategy only contains algorithmic code, that is, the state specific behavior.

Discussion of Exercise 18.2:

The **Strategy:Client** role is played by the pay station hardware (or the GUI or the JUnit integration test cases).

Discussion of Exercise 18.3:

First of all, the GammaTownFactory class is missing (as is the "helper" class IllegalCoinException which it purposely has been on all diagrams). Also the special test rate strategy One2OneRateStrategy is not shown. And a final point, all the relations between the factories to the concrete products are missing. If they had been included, the diagram would have been heavily cluttered with association lines that would have made it difficult to read.

Discussion of Exercise 18.4:

The definitions are not in conflict. The reason that it makes sense to have several different definitions of the same concept is that the concept is deep and has many facets. The four different definitions represent different perspectives or views upon the same concept and as such they complement and extend each other.

18.5 Review Questions

What is the definition of design patterns from the role view? Argue why design patterns are not a fixed set of interfaces and classes but must be understood as a set of roles and protocols.

What does a role diagram show?

What is the definition of design patterns from the roadmap view? How can design patterns provide overview and understanding in complex designs made by a compositional design approach?

What are the rules for naming interfaces and classes in complex designs using design patterns? What is the justification for these rules?

18.6 Further Exercises

Exercise 18.5:

Draw one or several role diagrams that outline all roles for all interfaces/classes in the pay station design.

Iteration 6

A Design Pattern Catalogue

The learning objective of this iteration is to extend your design toolbox with more design patterns. The format of the chapters in this part will deviate from that of the rest of the book as this part of the book is by nature a reference section. The chapter overview column below first names the pattern, next states the pattern's intent.

Chapter	Pattern and Intent
Chapter 19	*Facade.* Provide a unified interface to a set of interfaces in a subsystem. Facade defines a higher-level interface that makes the subsystem easier to use.
Chapter 20	*Decorator.* Attach additional responsibilities to an object dynamically. Decorators provide a flexible alternative to subclassing for extending functionality.
Chapter 21	*Adapter.* Convert the interface of a class into another interface clients expect. Adapter lets classes work together that couldn't otherwise because of incompatible interfaces.
Chapter 22	*Builder.* Separate the construction of a complex object from its representation so that the same construction process can create different representations.
Chapter 23	*Command.* Encapsulate a request as an object, thereby letting you parameterize clients with different requests, queue or log requests, and support undoable operations.
Chapter 24	*Iterator.* Provide a way to access the elements of an aggregate object sequentially without exposing its underlying representation.
Chapter 25	*Proxy.* Provide a surrogate or placeholder for another object to control access to it.
Chapter 26	*Composite.* Compose objects into tree structures to represent part-whole hierarchies. Composite lets clients treat individual objects and compositions of objects uniformly.
Chapter 27	*Null Object.* Define a no-operation object to represent null.
Chapter 28	*Observer.* Define a one-to-many dependency between objects so that when one object changes state, all its dependents are notified and updated automatically.
Chapter 29	*Model-View-Controller.* Define a loosely coupled design to form the architecture of graphical user interfaces having multiple windows and handling user input from mouse, keyboard, or other input sources.

Please note that the patterns FACADE, COMPOSITE, NULL OBJECT, OBSERVER, and MODEL-VIEW-CONTROLLER, are all important in order to understand the MiniDraw framework presented in the next learning iteration.

Patterns DECORATOR, FACADE, and ADAPTER continue the pay station case study.

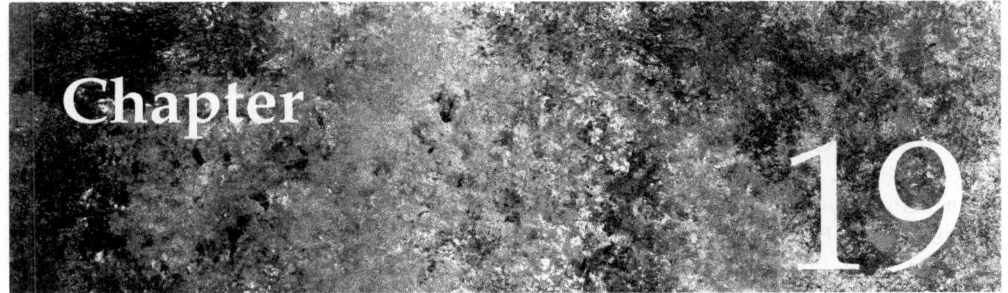

Facade

19.1 The Problem

Throughout the pay station story, I have only relied on my test cases for verifying my code's behavior. In practice it is also important to test the software in its proper context using the real hardware where users can enter coins, push buttons, and inspect receipts. This system testing level often also finds some defects, defects that are best reproduced as automatic test cases and next corrected.

In our case, however, setting up the hardware is tedious so a second best approach is to equip the pay station with a graphical user interface that mimics a real pay station. I have developed a user interface as shown in Figure 19.1[1]. Buttons, marked with coin values, replace inserting coins, and receipts appear as separate windows with the proper text. You can find the source code on the website in folder *chapter/facade*.

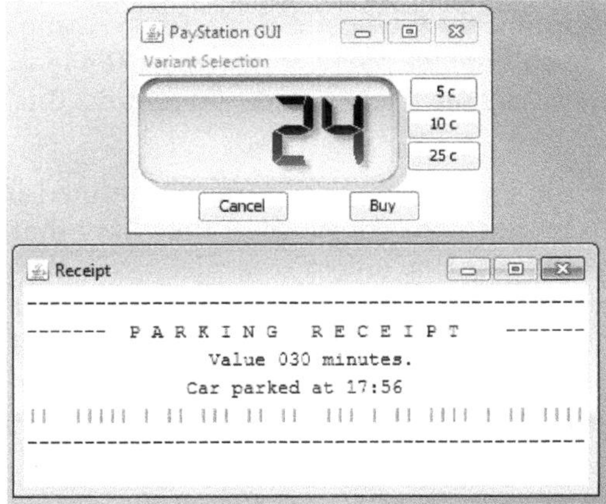

Figure 19.1: A graphical user interface for the pay station.

[1]The digital number display used by permission by SoftCollection.

Originally, I defined the protocol between the hardware and the pay station code in a sequence diagram, Figure 4.4 on page 48. The question is whether the graphical user interface (GUI) forces me to make changes in the PayStation interface or in its complex design? The answer is fortunately *no*. Looking over the sequence diagram I see that the GUI needs no further methods to add coins, read the display, nor receive receipts. All interaction is via the methods defined in the original PayStation interface. Thus all the complexity of rate strategies, receipts, factories, etc., is nicely encapsulated behind this interface. If you inspect the folder structure of the production code, you will see that I have added another package, *paystation.view*, that contains the Swing based GUI. If you inspect the class implementing the GUI you will furthermore discover that it is only coupled with the two interfaces of the paystation, PayStation and Receipt, as outlined in Figure 19.2.

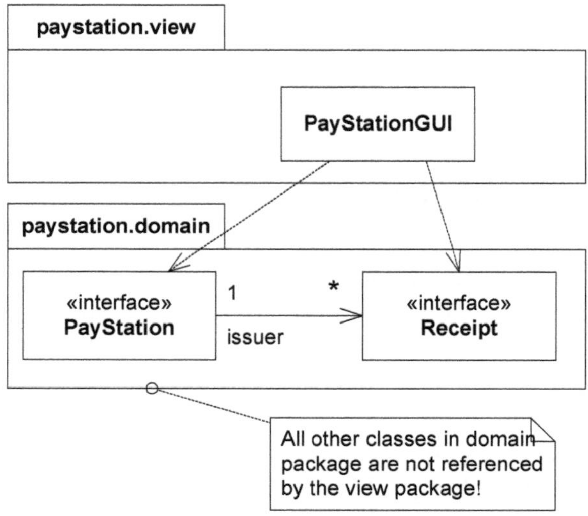

Figure 19.2: PayStation and Receipt acting as a FACADE.

Exercise 19.1: Actually, the GUI code also refers to some concrete classes from the *paystation.domain* package as well. Review the production code and find these classes. How could you remove this coupling?

This is an example of the FACADE design pattern, outlined in pattern box 19.1 on page 282. The pattern defines two central roles: the **client** that interacts with a complex subsystem, and the **facade** that shields the client from the subsystem's complexity by defining a simple interface. A good example of a FACADE pattern is a compiler. A compiler is a vastly complex piece of software with a lot of substructure, yet the interface is basically very simple: you invoke it with the name of the source file you want to be compiled; or press a single key in your integrated development environment.

My pay station design has thus embodied a facade pattern from the very beginning. Was this accidental? No. I did not spend much time discussing my original design proposal in Chapter 4. At that time it was postulated as a premise for our continued process. However, this design was also created based on the ③-①-② process.

③ *I identified some behavior that varied.* The hardware may have to drive different kinds of pay station domain implementations: I envisioned that Alphatown would not be the only customer.

① *I stated the pay station domain responsibility in an interface.* The PayStation interface encapsulates all behavior related to what pay stations must be able to do.

② *I composed the full behavior by letting the hardware delegating concrete pay station behavior to a subordinate object.* Instead of integrating the pay station domain behavior like calculating rates, keeping a sum of entered amount, etc., directly in the hardware near code (or in the user interface code) I delegated all these aspects to the object that implements the PayStation interface.

Exercise 19.2: Actually the PayStation interface also acts as facade for client code beside the hardware and the GUI. Which client code is that?

☞ Study the source code provided in folder *chapter/facade* on the web site.

19.2 The Facade Pattern

The key aspect of the FACADE (design pattern box 19.1, page 282) pattern is encapsulation behind an interface (thus the ① part of the ③-①-② process). Its intent is

> *Provide a unified interface to a set of interfaces in a subsystem. Facade defines a higher-level interface that makes the subsystem easier to use.*

Facades shield clients from a subsystem's complexity and as subsystems tend to get more complex as they age and evolve, this is important. Most patterns result in more and smaller classes which makes the subsystem more reusable and easier to customize, but it also becomes harder to use for clients that don't need to customize it.

The decoupling goes both ways. The subsystem is also shielded from change in the clients. In the pay station case, the pay station domain code is decoupled from the concrete kind of client: GUI or hardware. Thus, facade supports a many-to-many relation between clients and subsystems.

In the presentation of FACADE in the design pattern box, the client only interacts with a single interface. In reality, the subsystem designer has to consider how data and objects are exported out to the clients over the facade interface. Several options exist.

- *Make the facade opaque.* Clients only communicate in simple data types over the facade—no object references to objects created within the subsystem must be returned to clients. Alternatively, you may define "dumb" data objects (objects containing public instance variables but no methods) that are passed to clients. The facade must then typically convert internal objects into data objects by extracting their information and copy it into the data objects before returning these objects to the client.

- *Make the facade export read-only objects.* This way the facade in reality consists of multiple interfaces and is allowed to export references to objects created within the subsystem. However, exported objects must only be known to the client by a read-only interface, i.e. an interface that contains accessor methods but no mutator methods. Obviously if the exported object had mutator methods, the client would be able to change state in the subsystem by these and thus bypass the facade. The exported objects appear immutable to the client, but can of course be mutable by subsystem objects behind the facade that knows their concrete class.

Exercise 19.3: Classify the pay station facade. Which of the two types of facade is it?

FACADE does not require *all* clients to use it. For instance a complex subsystem could provide a facade to provide easily understandable access to the most common uses of the subsystem but not access to all functionality. If a client is required to access all functionality it can bypass the facade but developers must then be more careful and understand the subsystem in considerably more detail.

19.3 Selected Solutions

Discussion of Exercise 19.1:

The GUI class also refers to PayStationImpl and one of the ABSTRACT FACTORY classes. This is because I have made the GUI class responsible for creating and configuring the concrete variant of pay station to use: in the constructor and in the menu handling code. However, all other methods in the GUI are independent of concrete classes from the pay station domain package. It is thus a relatively simple exercise to split the present code into a *configuration* part (that couples to concrete classes) and a *graphical user interface* part (that only refers to interfaces).

Discussion of Exercise 19.2:

The JUnit integration test cases act as a third type of client as they only interact with the pay station through the facade.

Discussion of Exercise 19.3:

The pay station exports receipt objects which are a direct reference to an object created by the subsystem—it is thus of the latter, non-opaque, type. The Receipt interface only contains accessor methods, so the client cannot change it.

19.4 Review Questions

Describe the FACADE pattern. What problem does it solve? What is its structure and what is the protocol? What roles and responsibilities are defined? What are the benefits and liabilities?

19.5 Further Exercises

Exercise 19.4:

It seems that FACADE is very much like the *interface* language construct found in Java and C#. So—what is it that makes facade more than just stating that you should *program to an interface?* As an example, the Receipt interface also encapsulates the receipt behavior. But, why is this not a facade pattern?

Exercise 19.5. Source code directory:
`exercise/tdd/breakthrough`

The Breakthrough interface can be viewed as a FACADE to a Breakthrough game. Argue in favor of this interpretation.

Exercise 19.6:

Consider a software based media player system that can play CDs, DVDs, MP3 files, and other media. Consider that the system is divided into a domain part and a graphical user interface part. Sketch a FACADE for the domain part.

[19.1] Design Pattern: Facade

Intent Provide a unified interface to a set of interfaces in a subsystem. Facade defines a higher-level interface that makes the subsystem easier to use.

Problem The complexity of a subsystem should not be exposed to clients.

Solution Define an interface (the facade) that provides simple access to a complex subsystem. Clients that use the facade do not have to access the subsystem objects directly.

Structure:

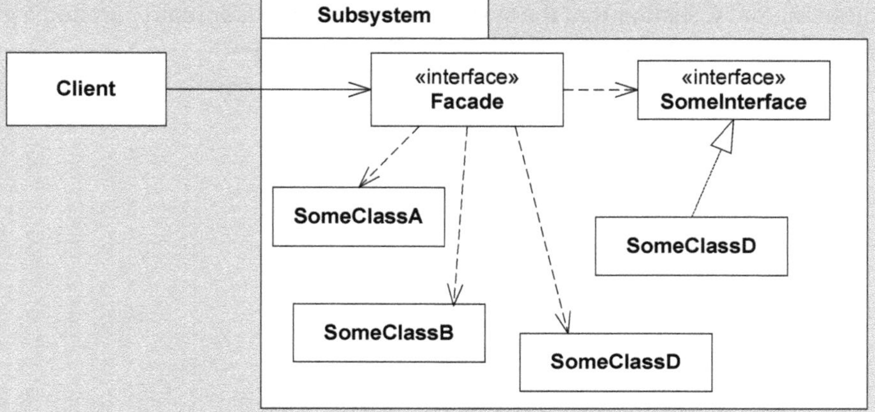

Roles **Facade** defines the simple interface to a subsystem. **Clients** only access the subsystem via the **Facade**.

Cost - Benefit The benefits are that it *shields clients from subsystem objects*. It *promotes weak coupling* between the client and the subsystem objects and thus lets you change these more easily without affecting the clients. A liability is that a **Facade** can bloat with a large set of methods in order for clients to access all aspects of the subsystem.

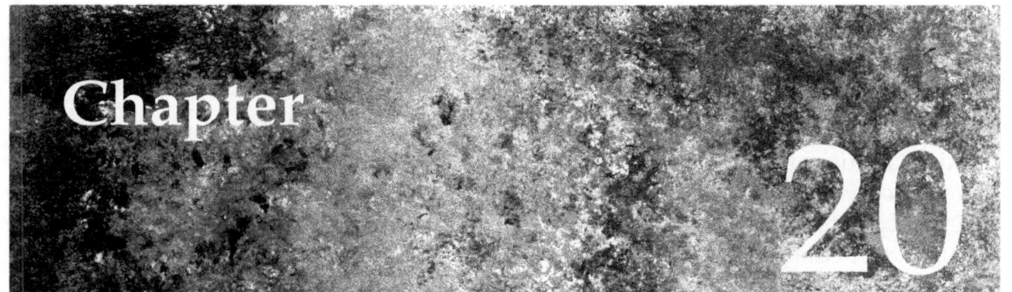

Decorator

20.1 The Problem

Alphatown contacts us with a new requirement. They have a single pay station that often overflows with 5 cent coins and would like to find out if there is any pattern in this odd phenomenon. Thus, they would like the pay station to maintain a log file of all coins entered into each pay station, recording coin type and a time stamp. The log file of the pay station could then be examined to detect a pattern.

One entry of the log file could look like:

```
5 cents  : 08:35
10 cents : 08:35
25 cents : 08:47
...
```

20.2 Composing a Solution

I first identify the behavior that must vary. This is clearly associated with the coin entry and thus the responsibility *Accept payment*. Thus one plausible path is to factor out payment acceptance using the strategy pattern and then provide two different concrete payment accept strategies: the standard one and one that in addition makes entries in the log file.

There is a twist here, though. We are actually not required to *vary* the behavior rather we are required to provide *additional* behavior over and above the standard one. This allows me to proceed by another path.

Figuratively speaking I could get my job done by hiring a person to stand in front of the pay station. This person would mediate all handling of the pay station for the customer. He would accept each coin from the customer, note coin type and time in his log book, and then of course put the coin into the pay station. He would push the buy button when requested, take the receipt and hand it over to the customer. This way we would get the intended log file without changing the pay station software at all. Thus, the hired person essentially has the same interface as the pay station but adds functionality to one of the actions, namely inserting coins.

Talking about software, I can *compose* the required behavior by putting *an intermediate object with the same interface* in front of the pay station object. All requests are ultimately passed on to the pay station object, but additional processing can be made in the intermediary. The client does not know that an intermediate object is used because it responds to exactly the same interface and protocol. A sequence diagram for the add payment scenario will then look like in Figure 20.1.

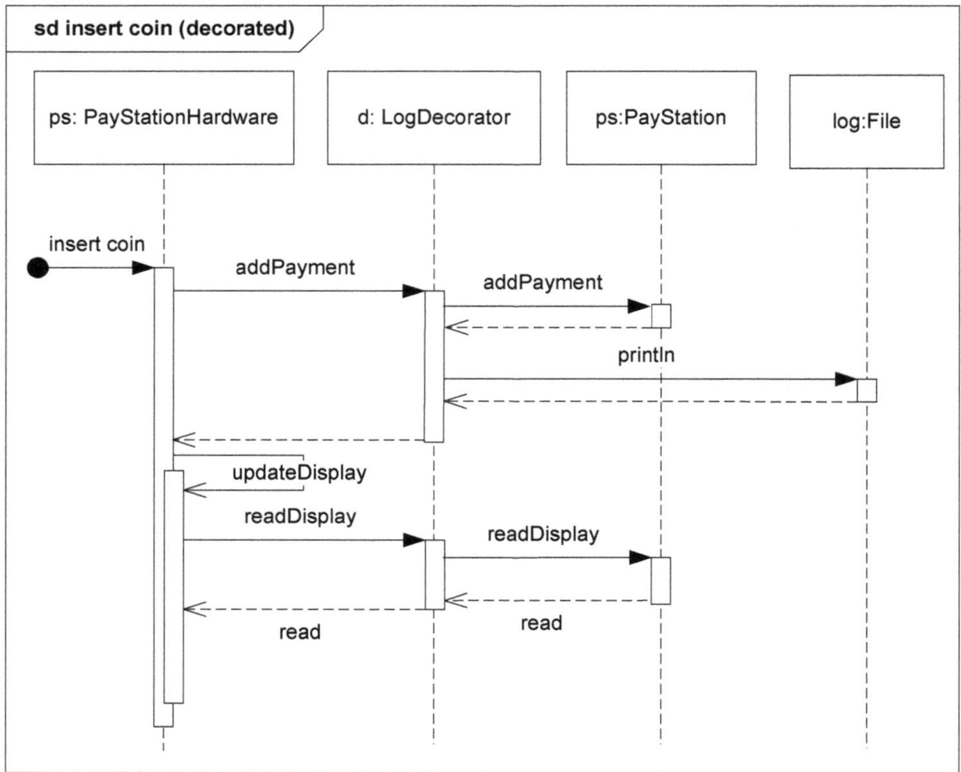

Figure 20.1: Decorating with logging payments.

This is the essence of the DECORATOR pattern: I have *decorated* the pay station's behavior with additional behavior, the logging of coins. The graphical user interface (or hardware) object cannot tell that it does not operate a "normal" pay station as the decorator has exactly the same interface. The decorator itself delegates any request to the decorated object. A fine example of the ① *program to an interface* and ② *favor object composition* principles at work. The decorator code itself is simple, basically just delegation code.

Listing: chapter/decorator/src/paystation/domain/LogDecorator.java

```
package paystation.domain;
import java.util.Date;
```

```
/** A  PayStation  decorator  that  logs  coin  entries.
*/
public class LogDecorator implements PayStation {
  private PayStation paystation;
  public LogDecorator( PayStation ps ) {
    paystation = ps;
  }
  public void addPayment( int coinValue )
         throws IllegalCoinException {
    System.out.println( ""+coinValue+" cents: "+new Date() );
    paystation.addPayment( coinValue );
  }
  public int readDisplay() { return paystation.readDisplay(); }
  public Receipt buy() { return paystation.buy(); }
  public void cancel() { paystation.cancel(); }
}
```

Exercise 20.1: Draw the UML class diagram for the structure of the logging decorator for the pay station.

Exercise 20.2: Discuss whether I could have used a polymorphic technique by subclassing instead of using a decorator.

☞ Study the source code provided in folder *chapter/decorator* on the web site.

20.3 The Decorator Pattern

The key aspect of DECORATOR (design pattern box 20.1, page 289) is composition, the ② *favor object composition* principle. Its intent is

> *Attach additional responsibilities to an object dynamically. Decorators provide a flexible alternative to subclassing for extending functionality.*

Rephrasing this, decorator allows you to dynamically add responsibilities to a role. The underlying object is unaffected and in this way a decorator can help keeping the number of responsibilities of a role low—I can always decorate them later. For instance, I would definitely not feel comfortable about adding a "Log time of coin entry" to the pay station role, it is not a responsibility that belongs naturally there. The decorator helps me out of this dilemma. In addition, decorators enjoy several benefits and a few liabilities as outlined below.

First, any object implementing the interface may be decorated. Alternative implementations of the PayStation interface may just as easily be decorated with the LogDecorator. Contrast this to the inheritance based solution: if I had subclassed the Alphatown class to add coin logging then it had become specific for the Alphatown variant. The decorator solution is general.

Second, decorators can easily be **chained** so one decorator decorates another decorator and so forth until the final, base, object. For instance, I could define other pay station decorators that reject 10 cent coins, or counts the number of cancel operations called. I could then combine all behaviors with a declaration like

```
Paystation ps =
  new Reject10CentDecorator(
   new LogDecorator(
    new CountCancelDecorator(
     new PayStation(
      new BetaTownFactory()
  ))));
```

Third, the coupling between the decorator and the decorated component is dynamic which means that you can "rewire" it at run-time. As an example, you can add and remove the logging behavior dynamically to a pay station instance by code like this (both payStation and decoratee are of type PayStation):

```
if (payStation == decoratee) {
  // enable the logging by decorating the component
  decoratee = payStation; // but remember the component
  payStation = new LogDecorator(payStation);
} else {
  // remove logging by making payStation point to
  // the component object once again
  payStation = decoratee;
}
```

Note that the decorated object keeps its state; it knows the amount entered in the current transaction and what to display; and is unaffected by any decorators. Again, this is not possible in an inheritance based design.

> ☞ Argue why state cannot be kept when adding/removing behavior if an inheritance based design was adopted.

The strength of the decorator: the dynamic and compositional nature; is also its liability. In a system relying heavily on decorators, the behavior of objects is assembled at run-time and this assembly process may be distributed in the code. Each fraction of the resulting behavior is defined in separate, small, classes where most methods are simply delegations. Thus *analyzability* suffers because there is no localized place in the code where "the algorithm is written". The result is that the system is hard to debug and learn.

In the pay station case above I simply made all the delegations directly in the LogDecorator class. Of course this will lead to a lot of redundant code if several different pay station decorators are needed. In that case, it is better to define an (abstract) class that defines all the delegation and only provide additional behavior in its subclasses, as shown in the description in pattern box 20.1.

One example of a decorator is the JScrollPane class from the `javax.swing` package. A JScrollPane is a subclass of Component, the basic graphical user interface unit in the Java graphical user interface library. When you construct a scroll pane it takes a Component instance as parameter. Thus the component is decorated with scroll bars to allow panning of the underlying component. The Java Collection Framework also contains *wrapper implementations* of the common types of collections which are decorators.

20.4 Selected Solutions

Discussion of Exercise 20.1:

The class diagram for the pay station logging decorator looks like this.

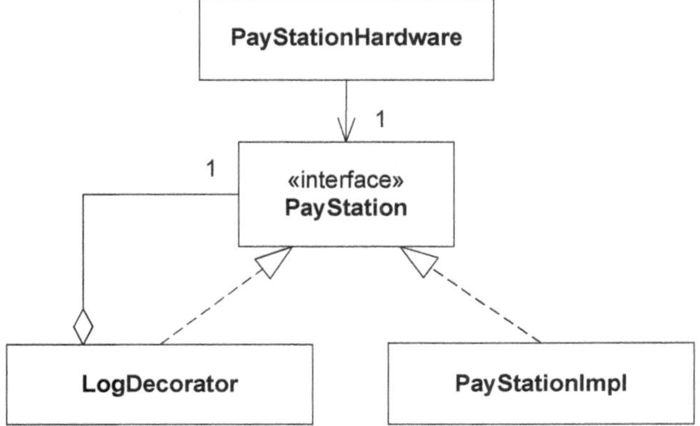

Discussion of Exercise 20.2:

You could subclass the implementation class for Alphatown's pay station and override the addAmount method. In this method you could add the coin logging behavior.

20.5 Review Questions

Describe the DECORATOR pattern. What problem does it solve? What is its structure and what is the protocol? What roles and responsibilities are defined? What are the benefits and liabilities?

Explain how decorators can be *chained*. How and why does this work on the code level? What are the consequences?

Explain why and how you can add and remove logging behavior at run-time while still retaining the pay station object's state (like amount earned, payment entered in this buy session, etc.).

20.6 Further Exercises

Exercise 20.3:

Walk in my footsteps. Introduce the DECORATOR that can wrap a pay station and log all coins entered into the machine.

Exercise 20.4:

Make a decorator that adds behavior to the pay station such that it refuses to accept more than 10 coins of value 5 cents since the last buy operation. Combine it with the previous decorator to make a decorator chain.

Exercise 20.5:

The Alphatown municipality decides that in the time interval between 08:00 PM in the evening and 07:00 AM in the morning parking is free. Thus during this time coins are simply returned (that is, acts as if cancel was pressed).

Sketch a design that handles this requirement using a decorator.

Exercise 20.6:

Describe the roles for the design resulting from exercise 20.3 and/or 20.4 by a role diagram (as done in Figure 18.4).

[20.1] Design Pattern: Decorator

Intent Attach additional responsibilities to an object dynamically. Decorators provide a flexible alternative to subclassing for extending functionality.

Problem You want to add responsibilities and behavior to individual objects without modifying its class.

Solution You create a decorator class that responds to the same interface. The decorator forwards all requests to the decorated object but may provide additional behavior to certain requests.

Structure:

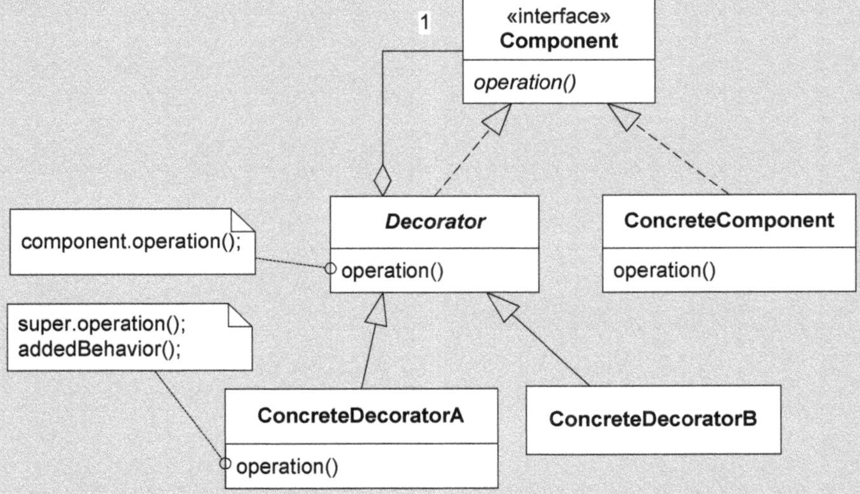

Roles **Component** defines the interface of some abstraction while **ConcreteComponents** are implementations of it. **Decorator** defines the basic delegation code while **ConcreteDecorators** add behavior.

Cost - Benefit Decorators allow *adding or removing responsibilities at run-time* to objects. They also allow *incrementally adding responsibilities* in your development process and thus help to keep the *number of responsibilities of decorated components low*. Decorators can provide *complex behavior by chaining* decorators after one another. A liability is that you end up with *lots of little objects* that all look alike, this can make understanding decorator chains difficult. The delegation code for each method in the decorator is a bit *tedious to write*.

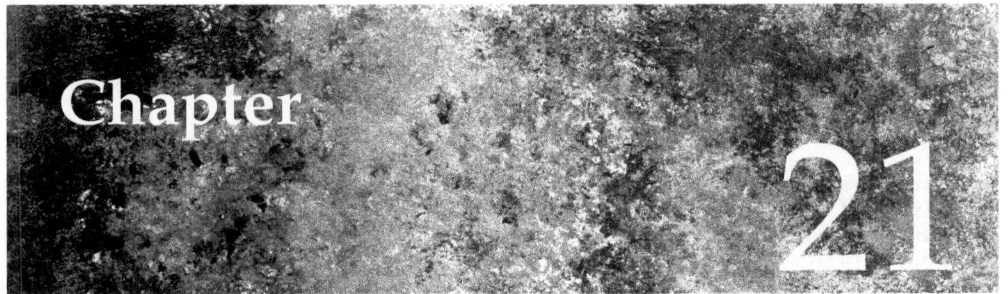

Adapter

21.1 The Problem

Our pay station company has been contacted by Lunatown that wants to buy our pay stations but they have a very peculiar requirement: the rate should be correlated to the phases of the moon. At full moon the rates should equal that of Alphatown while at new moon they should be doubled. In the period in between, the rate should proportionally vary between these extremes. Lunatown has provided us with a Java class for doing the calculation—the problem is that the interface of the class does not follow the conventions used in our own production code:

Fragment: chapter/adapter/src/paystation/thirdparty/LunaRateCalculator.java
```
public int calculateRateForAmount( double dollaramount ) {
```

The parameter, amount, is a double and in dollars, not cents, and the method has a different name. Moreover, the class is not open source, and the municipality will not give us access to the source code as it belongs to a third-party company. However, it is very tempting to use the package instead of trying to figure out the astronomical calculations ourselves.

21.2 Composing a Solution

The pay station design is already well prepared for configuring a product for Lunatown as the rate strategy has already been factored out in our design. However, I cannot simply configure the pay station with an instance of the LunaRateCalculator as it does not implement the RateStrategy interface (it would be pretty odd if it did: it is developed by another company!) nor use the same parameters. What I need to do is to *favor object composition* one step deeper. I put an intermediate object in between to handle the translation process back and forth between the pay station and the luna rate calculator. The concrete adaptation code is pretty simple.

Listing: chapter/adapter/src/paystation/domain/LunaAdapter.java

```
package paystation.domain;
import paystation.thirdparty.*;

/** An adapter for adapting the Lunatown rate calculator
*/
public class LunaAdapter implements RateStrategy {
  private LunaRateCalculator calculator;
  public LunaAdapter() {
    calculator = new LunaRateCalculator();
  }

  public int calculateTime( int amount ) {
    double dollar = amount / 100.0;
    return calculator.calculateRateForAmount( dollar );
  }
}
```

This intermediate object is the **adapter** which is the central role in the ADAPTER pattern.

> **Exercise 21.1:** Draw the UML class diagram and the sequence diagram for the Lunatown adaptation.

21.3 The Adapter Pattern

Adapters are well known for anyone who has struggled with the power plugs around the globe—even in Europe there are many different types of outlets that require special plugs. The software world is much less standardized so in practical software development, adapters play an important role to "glue" software units from different vendors, open source contributors, or even different teams within the same organization, together.

The ADAPTER pattern (design pattern box 21.1, page 295) is a classic example of the *favor object composition* principle. Its intent is

> *Convert the interface of a class into another interface clients expect. Adapter lets classes work together that couldn't otherwise because of incompatible interfaces.*

The adapter contains a reference to the third party object, the **adaptee**, and performs parameter, protocol, and return value translations. The amount of translation made range from simple, such as simple interface conversion (changed method names, different parameters), to complex (different protocols). To give an example of the latter, consider a client that interfaces a sensor, and expects a protocol in which the sensor will deliver measured values every 10 seconds (for instance using an OBSERVER pattern). That is, the client expects active sensor software. If a sensor comes with a software unit that is passive, ie. expects the client to request the measurements, then the adapter becomes much more complex, involving a thread to make the passive adaptee appear active to the client.

A given adapter can usually adapt all subclasses of the adaptee, and is thus reusable. Of course, it cannot be reused for other adaptee classes.

For the sake of completeness, the ADAPTER pattern presented here is what is called an *object adapter* by Gamma et al. They also discuss a *class adapter* that relies on multiple inheritance but this is of course not possible in Java nor C#.

21.4 Selected Solutions

Discussion of Exercise 21.1:

The class diagram is shown in Figure 21.1.

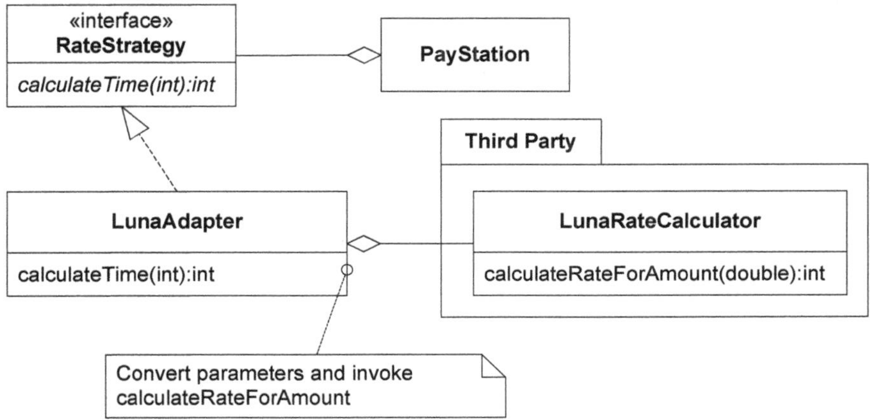

Figure 21.1: Adapting the Lunatown rate calculator.

21.5 Review Questions

Describe the ADAPTER pattern. What problem does it solve? What is its structure and what is the protocol? What roles and responsibilities are defined? What are the benefits and liabilities?

Give some examples on the type of translation that an adapter can make between the client and the adaptee.

21.6 Further Exercises

Exercise 21.2:

Consider a cooling system for a refrigerating store. The system monitors the temperature using sensors in the storage room and turns cooling on and off. The cooling algorithm reads the temperature via a TemperatureSensor interface that has a single method

```
/** read temperature in Celsius */
public double readTemperature();
```

Now, an existing refrigerating store wants to use our system but their existing temperature sensors have another interface:

```
/** return present temperature
 * @return the temperature in Fahrenheit; the returned reading
 * is the actual measured value times ten. Example: 212.34
 * Fahrenheit is returned as integer value 2123
 */
public int getValue();
```

Construct an ADAPTER that will allow our software to use the existing sensors.

[21.1] Design Pattern: Adapter

Intent Convert the interface of a class into another interface clients expect. Adapter lets classes work together that couldn't otherwise because of incompatible interfaces.

Problem You have a class with desirable functionality but its interface and/or protocol does not match that of the client needing it.

Solution You put an intermediate object, the adapter, between the client and the class with the desired functionality. The adapter conforms to the interface used by the client and delegate actual computation to the adaptee class, potentially performing parameter, protocol, and return value translations in the process.

Structure:

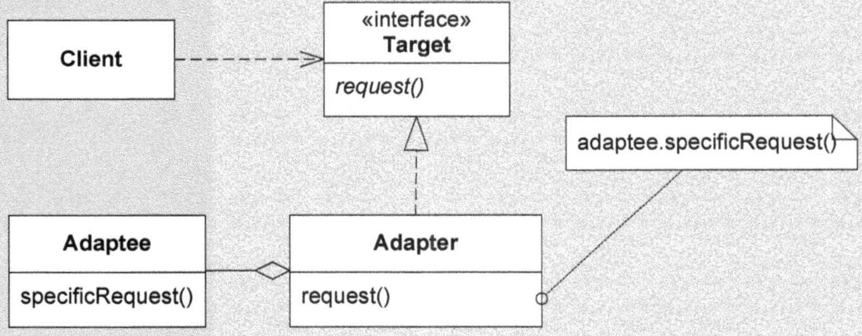

Roles **Target** encapsulates behavior used by the **Client**. The **Adapter** implements the Target role and delegate actual processing to the **Adaptee** performing parameter and protocol translations in the process.

Cost - Benefit Adapter *lets objects collaborate that otherwise are incompatible.* A single adapter can work with many adaptees—that is, all the adaptee's subclasses.

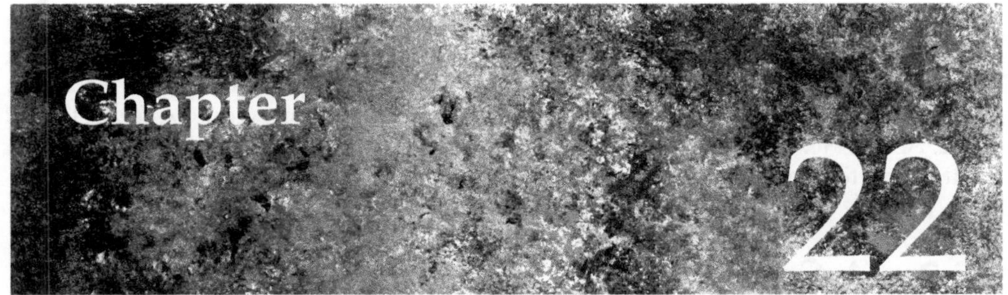

Builder

22.1 The Problem

Consider a word processor program that allows us to write documents with a standard set of typographical options: sections and subsections, emphasize, quotes, lists, etc. Our program maintains an internal data structure that stores both the text as well as the typography, the markup, of the text. When it comes to saving the data structure I would like to be able to save in different formats so it is possible to export my document to other word processing programs or save it as a web page.

For example, I would like it to be able to save in XML, like:

```
<document name=''The Pattern Book''>
  <section name=''Builder''>
    <paragraph>
      This is my section on builder.
    </paragraph>
    <subsection name= ``Analysis''>
      <paragraph>
        Here is my analysis of builder.
      </paragraph>
    </subsection>
  </section>
</document>
```

And the same document could be output in HTML in which the section would instead be encoded as:

```
<H1>Builder</H1>
```

while the section in ASCII would perhaps look like:

```
Builder
=======
```

The problem is that if I write software to build each representation then much of it would be the same code in all variants, namely the code that iterates through the data structure and determine the type of typographical node, like "document", "section", etc. Only the parts that build the actual output representation would differ: HTML, XML, ASCII, etc. Thus I once again face a multiple maintenance problem if I program each formatter from scratch.

22.2 A Solution

Thus it is a classic variability problem and when I apply the three principles and the ③-①-② process the analysis goes like this:

- ③ All outputs consist of the same set of "parts" (section, subsection, paragraphs, etc.) but how the parts are built varies. That is, concrete construction of the individual node is variable.
- ① I encapsulate the "construction of parts" in a **builder** interface. A builder interface must have methods to build each unique part: in our case methods like buildSection, buildQuote, etc. Instances realizing this interface must be able to construct concrete parts to be used in the data structure.
- ② I write the data structure iterator algorithm once, the **director**, and let it request a delegate builder to make the concrete parts as it encounters them.

Figure 22.1 illustrates how the word processor can save in, say, HTML format. The word processor first creates a HTML builder object (denoted b in the diagram), and next ask its associated director object to start constructing. The director contains the common iteration over the data structure containing the document, and request the builder to build the specific parts. Once the construction process is finished, the word processor requests the built output from the concrete builder.

> ☞ Study the source code provided in folder *chapter/builder* on the web site.

22.3 The Builder Pattern

This is the BUILDER design pattern (design pattern box 22.1, page 301). Its intent is

> *Separate the construction of a complex object from its representation so that the same construction process can create different representations.*

The two main roles are the **Director** that contains the construct() method responsible for iterating the data structure, and the **Builder** that contains the methods to build each particular part of the product. **ConcreteBuilder**s implement the particular representation of the **Product**, that is the output of the construction phase. Note that it is the responsibility of the concrete builders to create the product and ultimately give the client access to it when it is finished: only concrete builders have getResult methods. Finally the **Client** is responsible for creating the concrete builder, ask the director to construct and finally to retrieve the product from the builder.

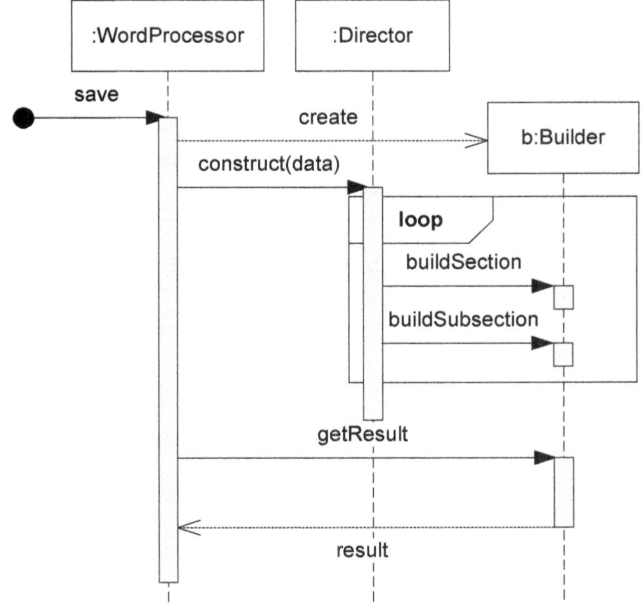

Figure 22.1: Saving a document using a builder pattern.

Exercise 22.1: Argue why it is not possible to put the getResult method in the Builder interface itself.

Separating the construction process and the concrete part building opens up for using builders for other purposes than pure construction. For instance you can easily do statistics with builders, like in the document case above where a CountingBuilder may count the number of sections, subsections, and paragraphs. Another benefit of the separation is a well-known consequence of the ② *favor object composition* principle, namely that each of the two roles becomes more focused and thus more cohesive leading to better maintainability and overview of the code.

BUILDER is a creational pattern, ie. its purpose is to create objects. ABSTRACT FACTORY is also a creational pattern. Compared to abstract factory, builder provides much more fine-grained control over the individual elements of the product. Thus, builders are typically used for creating complex data structures while abstract factory is typically for simple objects.

A liability of BUILDER is the relative complexity of setting up the construction process involving several different objects.

22.4 Selected Solutions

Discussion of Exercise 22.1:

The getResult method cannot be defined in the Builder interface because the concrete data structure to store the **Product** is not known. One concrete builder may want to build a string representation, another a binary tree, and a third a bit image. This is also the reason that there must be a **Client** role whose responsibility it is to know the concrete type of builder whereas the **Director** does not.

22.5 Review Questions

Describe the BUILDER pattern. What problem does it solve? What is its structure and what is the protocol? What roles and responsibilities are defined? What are the benefits and liabilities?

22.6 Further Exercises

Exercise 22.2. Source code directory:
`chapter/builder`

Extend the builder example.

1. Make an XML builder that builds a XML representation of the document, e.g. uses tags like

   ```
   <HEADER>The Builder Pattern</HEADER>
   ```

   etc.

2. Make a builder that counts the total number of words in the document.

[22.1] Design Pattern: Builder

Intent Separate the construction of a complex object from its representation so that the same construction process can create different representations.

Problem You have a single defined construction process but the output format varies.

Solution Delegate the construction of each part in the process to a builder object; define a builder object for each output format.

Structure:

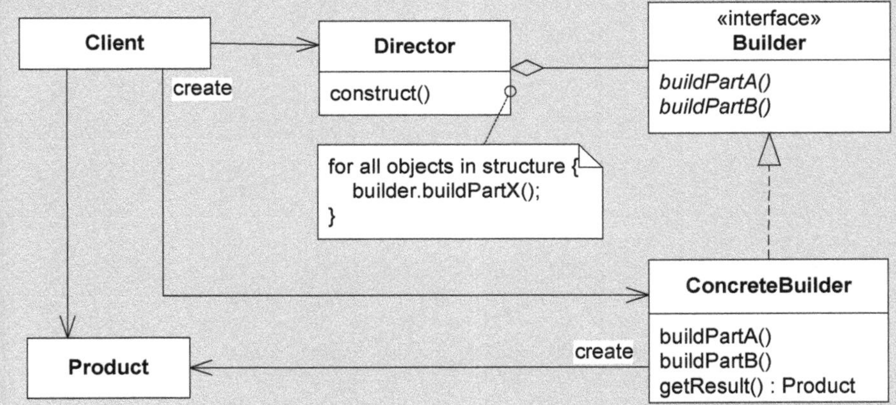

Roles **Director** defines a building process but constructing the particular parts is delegated to a **Builder**. A set of **ConcreteBuilder**s is responsible to building concrete **Product**s.

Cost - Benefit It is *easy to define new products* as you can simply define a new builder. The *code for construction and representation is isolated*, and thus multiple directors can use builders and vice versa. Compared to other creational patterns (like ABSTRACT FACTORY) products are not produced in "one shot" but stepwise meaning you have *finer control over the construction process*.

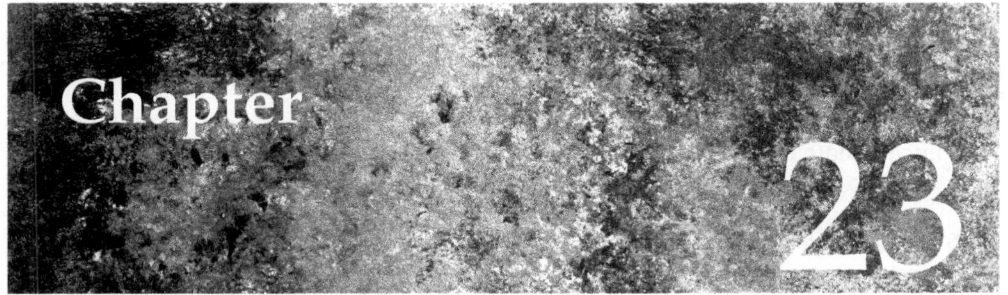

Command

23.1 The Problem

Consider a graphical user interface that lets the user parameterize the meaning of short-cut keys and action buttons in the interface. For instance one user assigns the "open document" functionality to the "F1" button while another user assigns "save" to this button. That is, the same event, pressing the F1 key, should invoke different methods on potentially different objects. Consider another situation where a user finds himself repeating the same set of operations over and over again. He would like to be able to record the operations in a "macro" and then assign this macro to a short-cut key. A third scenario: a user has regretted the last three operations on the document, and wants to undo them.

All these requests are actually pretty difficult to handle because behavior is defined by object methods, and methods are not objects that can be stored or passed as parameters. Consider a method that is called whenever the user presses F1. How can I code this method in such a way that it is the user who decides if its contents is

```
public void F1Press() {
  editor.showFileDialogAndOpen();
or
  editor.save();
or
  some other behavior?
}
```

I may come up with a parametric solution with a (very) long list of potential assignments of the F1 button. Still the list is hardcoded into the code and the user cannot assign any operation outside the list defined by the developer.

☞ Consider how to handle the macro and undo scenarios.

23.2 A Solution

The basic solution to the problem of methods not being objects—is to make objects that encapsulate the methods. The ③-①-② process applies:

③ *Encapsulate what varies.* I need to handle behavior as objects that can be assigned to keys or buttons, that can be put into macro lists, etc. The obvious responsibility of such a "request object" is to be executable. The next logical step is to require that it can "un-execute" itself in order to support undo.

① *Program to an interface.* The request objects must have a common interface to allow them to be exchanged across those user interface elements that must enact them. This interface is the **Command** role that encapsulate the responsibility "execute" (and potentially "undo").

② *Object composition.* Instead of buttons, menu items, key strokes hard coding behavior, they delegate to their assigned command objects.

Thus the method call to save a document

```
editor.save();
```

becomes something like

```
Command saveCommand = new SaveCommand(editor);
saveCommand.execute();
```

Note that creating the "method" and execution of it is now two distinct steps, thus you can create the object in one place, and defer execution to another part of the code, say when a short-cut key is pressed.

☞ Study the source code provided in folder *chapter/command* on the web site.

Exercise 23.1: In the associated source code, the user assigns a new command to the F2 key:

Fragment: chapter/command/CommandDemo.java

```
Command write4 = new WriteCommand(doc,"A wrong line");
F2.assign(write4);
F2.press();
```

Draw a UML sequence diagram showing the interaction between the roles in the COMMAND pattern when the last statement executes.

23.3 The Command Pattern

This is the COMMAND pattern (design pattern box 23.1, page 308): objects that take on the single responsibility to represent a method. Its intent is

> *Encapsulate a request as an object, thereby letting you parameterize clients with different requests, queue or log requests, and support undoable operations.*

The central roles are the **Command** that defines the interface for execution which is then called by the **Invoker**. **ConcreteCommand** implements the Command interface and defines the concrete behavior. The concrete command objects must know the **Receiver**, that is the object to invoke the method on. A standard object-oriented method invocation has a receiver and a set of parameters

```
object.method(a,b,c);
```

Here object is the receiver, and therefore a command object must have the exact same set of parameters in order to be executable. Typically these parameters are set in the constructor:

```
Command method = new MethodCommand(object,a,b,c);
```

This creation of the command object and binding it to the **receiver** is the responsibility of the **Client** role. The client can then configure the invoker with the command object, and the invoker can later perform the method call:

```
  method.execute();
```

As a developer can always create new classes implementing the Command interface the set of commands is not limited to the imagination of the original developers: it is *change by addition, not by modification.* And as the invoker only expects the Command role, all new commands can be handled exactly as the old ones.

While it is not mandatory, it is possible to add undo when using command objects. It of course requires that the command *can* be undone and that the receiver supports reversing the state changes from a given method call:

```
public class MethodCommand {
  ...
  public void execute() {
    object.method(a,b,c);
  }
  public void undo() {
    object.undoTheMethod(a,b,c);
  }
}
```

As requests are now objects, they can be manipulated in all the usual ways. For instance if all commands support undo, then all the executed commands in a session can be stored on a stack to support unlimited undo: just pop the next command object from the stack and invoke its undo method. You can store a list of commands on disk and recover from a crash by executing them in sequence. You can define a macro command as a COMPOSITE of COMMAND objects.

The major liability of COMMAND is the large overhead in writing and executing commands: compare the simple object.method(a,b,c); call with all the extra typing to make command interfaces, concrete classes, and setting up the command object. Thus, COMMAND is a heavy weight approach that only should be used when the required flexibility makes the effort worthwhile.

23.4 Selected Solutions

Discussion of Exercise 23.1:

As shown in Figure 23.1 the sequence is rather simple, however the construction of the write command object is not drawn.

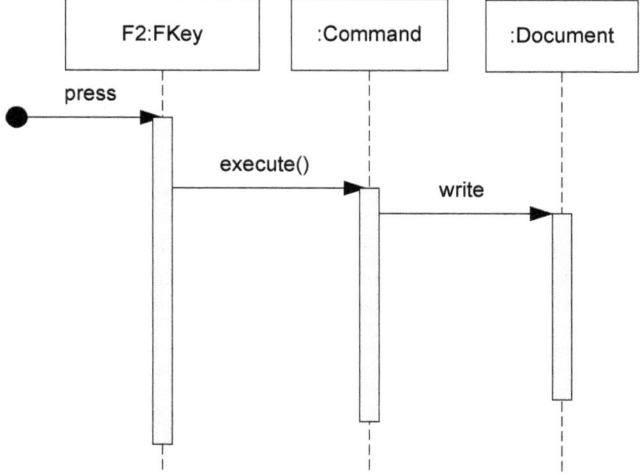

Figure 23.1: Executing a write command assigned to F2.

23.5 Review Questions

Describe the COMMAND pattern. What problem does it solve? What is its structure and what is the protocol? What roles and responsibilities are defined? What are the benefits and liabilities?

23.6 Further Exercises

Exercise 23.2. Source code directory:
`chapter/command`

The example code used in this chapter should be extended with a MacroCommand class whose responsibilities are

MacroCommand

- To record a set of commands (add commands to a list)
- To execute all commands in the list as a unit

[23.1] Design Pattern: Command

Intent Encapsulate a request as an object, thereby letting you parameterize clients with different requests, queue or log requests, and support undoable operations.

Problem You want to configure objects with behavior/actions at run-time and/or support undo.

Solution Instead of defining operations in terms of methods, define them in terms of objects implementing an interface with an execute method. This way requests can be associated to objects dynamically, stored and replayed, etc.

Structure:

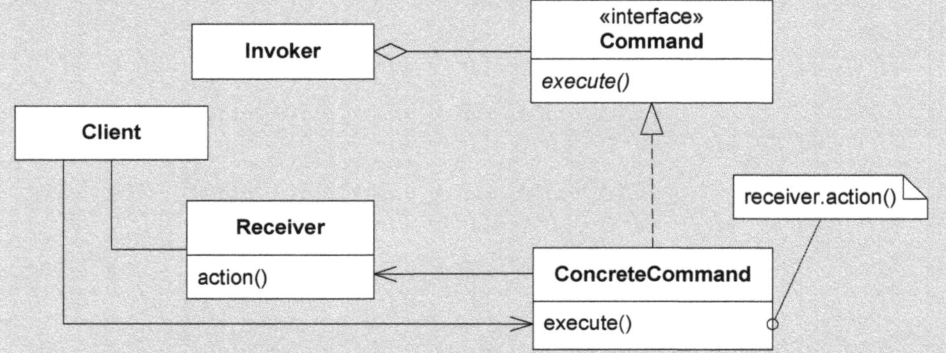

Roles **Invoker** is an object, typically user interface related, that may execute a **Command**, that defines the responsibility of being an executable operation. **ConcreteCommand** defines the concrete operations that involves the object, **Receiver**, that the operation is intended to manipulate. The **Client** creates concrete commands and sets their receivers.

Cost - Benefit Objects that invoke operations are decoupled from those that know how to perform it. *Commands are first-class objects*, and can be manipulated like all other objects. You can assemble commands into *composite commands* (macros). It is *easy to add new commands*.

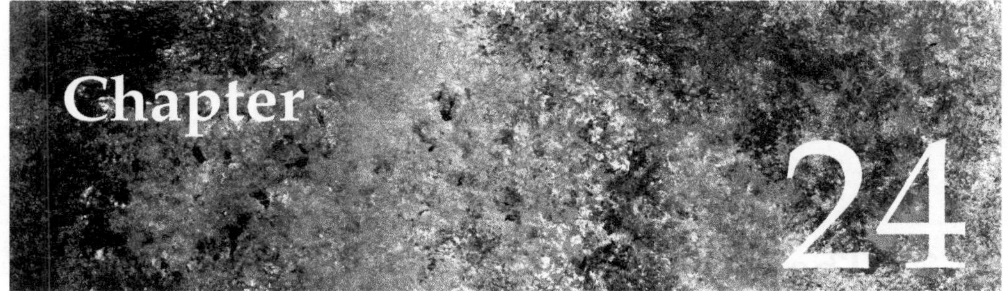

Iterator

24.1 The Problem

The Java Collection Library contains a long list of different collections each with benefits and liabilities in terms of flexibility, performance versus memory trade-offs, etc. However, we normally want to decouple our client code as much as possible from the implementation details of the data structures. One particular aspect is iteration. Iterating over the elements in a linked list (following the next reference) is radically different from iterating in an array (indexing). This creates a strong coupling between client code and the choice of data structure: if you change your mind and want to use a linked list instead of an array, you have to modify all the iterations.

24.2 A Solution

Again, this problem can be rephrased as a variability problem that can be addressed by the ③-①-② process.

③ *Encapsulate what varies.* Iteration is variable depending on the data structure wanted. Thus iteration itself is the variable behavior to encapsulate.

① *Program to an interface.* Create an interface that contains the central responsibilities of iteration: get the next element; and test if there are any more elements left to iterate.

② *Object composition.* Instead of the client doing the iteration itself, it delegates this to the iterator object.

The protocol between the client and the collection is for the client to request an iterator object. Given this, the client may iterate over all elements. This type of Java code pervades all collection oriented programming.

```
Collection<Item> c = ...;
Item current;
for ( Iterator<Item> i = c.iterator(); i.hasNext(); ) {
  current = i.next();
  [process current]
}
```

24.3 The Iterator Pattern

This is the ITERATOR pattern (design pattern box 24.1, page 312). Its intent is

> *Provide a way to access the elements of an aggregate object sequentially without exposing its underlying representation.*

The central roles in the iterator is the **Collection** and **Iterator**. Collection is responsible for storing elements while iterator is responsible for the iteration: keep track of how far the iterator has moved, and retrieving the next element, etc.

Iterator is a central design pattern in the Java Collection Framework. It is even supported by the language by the *for-each loop*; if a class implements Iterable (as does all collections) you may write the iteration in the previous section as:

```
for (Item current : c) {
  [process current]
}
```

> ☞ Review the Java Collection Framework in the *java.util* package for its use of iterators.

Developers use iterators without much thought but you may define many interesting iterators that do more interesting things than just enumerating elements from start to end. You may define an iterator that returns elements in random order instead of shuffling the deck of cards. Trees may be iterated breadth-first or depth-first. Return the elements in a collection in reverse order or only every second element.

Many board games are played on a matrix, for instance chess or checkers. Here iterators may list all possible moves that, say, a knight may make from a given square on the board.

```
for ( Iterator<Square> moves =
        board.getKnightPositionIterator(position);
      moves.hasNext(); ) {
  Square s = moves.next();
  [evaluate benefit of moving here]
}
```

Iterators are often implemented as inner classes in Java. The inner class allows the iterator to access the detailed data structure of the collection implementation without exposing it.

The iterator provides several benefits. The compositional design means the collection role and iterator role are smaller and more cohesive abstractions. You can, as argued above, define many different types of traversals but the traversal algorithm, the for loop, always looks the same. Finally, you may have several different iterations pending on the same collection at the same time, as the iteration state is stored in the iterator itself.

One issue to consider if whether the iterator is **robust** or not. The issue arises when a collection is modified while an iterator is traversing it. Non-robust iterators may give incorrect results like returning the same element twice or not at all during the traversal. Robust iterators, however, guaranty to make a proper traversal—like for instance by making a copy of the collection before starting the iteration. Making robust iterators is a complex topic that I will not discuss further.

Iterator's liabilities should be obvious. In contrast to the simple integer index into Java's array construct, iterator is complex with additional interfaces, classes, and complex protocol. The introduction of the for-each loop has lessened this complexity in Java, and similar constructs exist in C#.

24.4 Review Questions

Describe the ITERATOR pattern. What problem does it solve? What is its structure and what is the protocol? What roles and responsibilities are defined? What are the benefits and liabilities?

Describe some non-standard iterations that are easily made by custom iterators.

24.5 Further Exercises

Exercise 24.1. Source code directory:
`exercise/iterator/chess`

Consider a chess game that is played on a 8×8 board on which each square is identified by a Position class encapsulating row and column (or rank and files). Lower, left corner is (1,1), black queen is at (8,4), etc.

To get all the squares that a knight at a given position (r,c) can attack, you can define an iterator that returns all valid positions, like:

Fragment: exercise/iterator/chess/Position.java

```
public static Iterator<Position>
        getKnightPositionIterator(Position p) {
```

1. Implement the knight positions iterator.
2. Implement an iterator that will return all valid positions that a rook may move to (on an empty board).
3. Implement an iterator that will return all valid positions that a bishop may move to (on an empty board).
4. Implement an iterator that will return all valid positions that a queen may move to (on an empty board).

[24.1] Design Pattern: Iterator

Intent Provide a way to access the elements of an aggregate object sequentially without exposing its underlying representation.

Problem You want to iterate a collection without worrying about the implementation details of it.

Solution Encapsulate iteration itself into an object whose responsibility it is to allow access to each element in the collection.

Structure:

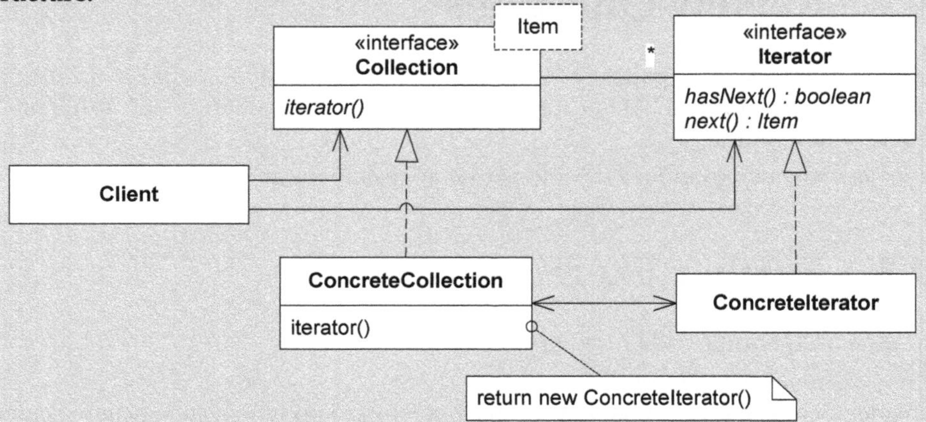

Roles **Collection** is some data structure that can be iterated. The **Iterator** defines the iteration responsibility, and the collection can upon request return an **ConcreteIterator** that knows how to iterate the specific **ConcreteCollection**.

Cost - Benefit It *decouples iteration from the collection* making client code more resilient to changes to the actual collection used. It *supports variations in the iteration* as the collection can provide a variety of iterators. The *collection interface is slimmer* as it does not itself need to provide iteration methods. You can have *several iterators working on the same collection at the same time* as each iterator holds its own state information. A liability is the *added complexity in protocol* in contrast to traditional iteration.

Proxy

25.1 The Problem

Consider a large document with a lot of images in it. Images are expensive objects in terms of memory size and thus time to load and decode. This means the document will be slow to load as it takes a long time to read from disk. The result is that the user will perceive the word processor as slow and perhaps buy another product. So, the challenge is to make the system load the document fast even if it contains a large number of objects that are slow to load.

25.2 A Solution

The key insight to solve the problem is to realize that most of the images will not be visible once the document has been loaded. Usually a word processor starts by showing page one. If the document contains 50 images but only one appears on page one, it suffices to load the text and the single image on the first page and defer loading the other images until they become visible. If the user only looks at the first couple of pages before closing the document, the system has even avoided the cost of loading most of the images all together. So, I need a mechanism to delay loading images until they need to be shown. In design language, I can state this as defer loading until the show() method is called on image objects. A classic variability challenge that calls for the ③-①-② process.

③ *Encapsulate what varies.* Seen from the client (the word processor) I want the image objects to have variable behavior; those that become visible will fetch image data and show themselves whereas those that have not yet been visible simply do not spend time loading the image data.

① *Program to an interface.* By insisting that images are only accessed from the client via an interface I can provide it with an intermediate object that will defer the loading until the show() method is called but in all other respects acts just like a real image object.

② *Object composition.* Just like DECORATOR I can compose the real image behavior by putting an "object-in-front", the proxy, that will only fetch the real image data once it needs to be shown.

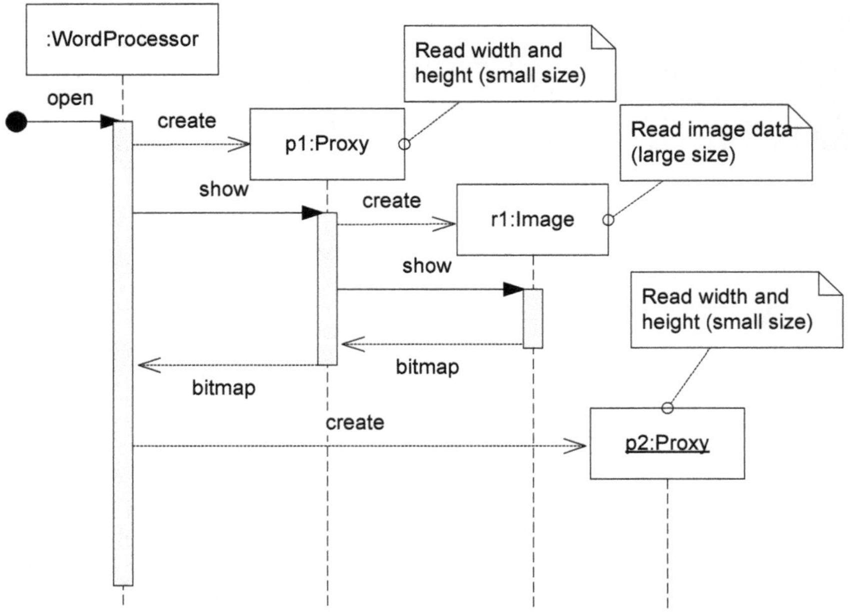

Figure 25.1: Proxy defers the loading of image data.

Figure 25.1 shows a sequence diagram of a potential load of a document with two images, one that is shown and one that is not. Typically, the proxies read essential but small sized data, like the width and height of the image, thus its getWidth() and getHeight() methods return proper values so the word processor can layout pages correctly. When the bulky data is required for the show() method, the proxy creates the real image object which then goes on to load the raster image. Note that to the client the first invocation of show() is much slower than subsequent invocations.

☞ Review and execute the demonstration of the Proxy pattern. The source code is in folder *chapter/proxy* at the web site. Try to let WordProcessor declare JPGImage directly and see the difference in behavior.

25.3 The Proxy Pattern

This is the PROXY pattern (design pattern box 25.1, page 317). Its intent is

Provide a surrogate or placeholder for another object to control access to it.

The central roles are the **Subject** that defines the interface for the objects that can be proxied, **RealSubject** is the real implementation of the object, while **Proxy** is the intermediate object that represents the real subject.

If the developer has adhered to the ① *program to an interface* principle it is easy to introduce PROXY at a later stage in the development as both **proxy** and **real subject** roles have the same protocol and interface.

Proxies are very versatile in their use. Typical uses are:

- *Protection proxies / Access control.* Protection proxies may check that the caller has the correct permissions to interact with the real subject. If not, requests are not granted. You may also use it to handle concurrent access to it by locking.
- *Virtual proxies / Performance control.* Proxies that cache information or results that are expensive in terms of computation time or memory consumption. The image proxy above is an example of a virtual proxy.
- *Remote proxies / Remote access.* Proxies that act as local representatives of objects that are really located on a remote computer. Remote proxies primary responsibility is to encode method calls and parameters into a binary string that can be sent over the network to the real object on the remote computer, accept the return result, decode it and return it to the caller.

The proxy must of course maintain a reference to the real subject to delegate requests to it. However, this reference may take various forms depending on the type of proxy. In the case of remote proxies, the reference is indirect, such as host address and local address at host. For virtual proxies, the reference will first be resolved when it is needed: for instance in case of the image proxy the real subject is not created until `show()` is called and until then it is probably an image file name or an offset into the document's data on disk.

Proxy has the benefit that it strengthens reuse potential. As "housekeeping" tasks (like access control, caching, etc.) are the responsibility of the proxy I avoid putting them in the real subject implementations increasing the likelihood they can be reused somewhere else. This is the classic benefit of compositional designs: abstractions tend to be smaller and with a few clear responsibilities leading to higher cohesion and easier code to read. The liabilities are the extra level of indirection inherent to compositional designs; and if legacy code has not been *programmed to an interface* then there will be an overhead in introducing it.

> **Exercise 25.1:** If you look at the structure of PROXY and DECORATOR they are very similar. Outline their similarities. Explain the differences between the two, and argue why proxy is not just a decorator.

If a proxy needs to create or delete real subjects the coupling between them becomes tight. Thus if you have several different implementations of the real subject you will have to have multiple proxy implementations as well. If not you may use a single proxy implementation for all types of real subjects.

Typically, it is the client that must create instances of the subject interface which creates a hard coupling between the client and the proxy class, as you saw in Figure 25.1. You may use ABSTRACT FACTORY to reduce coupling.

The proxy pattern is the key pattern used in Java Remote Method Invocation (RMI) and C# Remoting that allows distributed object programming. These techniques mask distribution by providing a pseudo object model for interacting with objects located on remote machines in a network. The client interacts with a proxy of the remote object; the proxy then forwards methods calls to the remote object, waits for the response, and translates it back to a normal method return value. Standard or special compilers can generate the proxies classes based upon the interfaces that define remotely accessible objects.

☞ Study the Java RMI system. You can find several good resources on the internet. The online "Java Tutorial" provides small examples of RMI programs and guidelines for compiling and executing them.

25.4 Selected Solutions

Discussion of Exercise 25.1:

Indeed they are very similar in that both the decorator and the proxy contain references to their decorated/proxied object. However, their intents are different: decorators add responsibilities to an object whereas proxies control access to it. Also at the implementation level there are differences. Proxies are typically tightly bound to the object type they control; for instance virtual proxies are responsible for creating the real objects. Decorators are loosely coupled to their decorated object as they only know them by interface, and they are not responsible for configuration as it is the client that sets up the chain of decorated objects.

25.5 Review Questions

Describe the PROXY pattern. What problem does it solve? What is its structure and what is the protocol? What roles and responsibilities are defined? What are the benefits and liabilities?

25.6 Further Exercises

Exercise 25.2. Source code directory:
`chapter/proxy`

Consider that some images in a document are allowed to be viewed by persons with a special security clearance. In order to view images in the document they have to type a password the first time they are about to view a protected image. Once the password has been typed, all images in the document can be viewed.

1. Enhance the ProxyDemo with such an image protection proxy.
2. Add an access proxy that counts the number of times each image has been viewed.

[25.1] Design Pattern: Proxy

Intent Provide a surrogate or placeholder for another object to control access to it.

Problem An object is highly resource demanding and will negatively affect the client's resource requirements even if the object is not used at all; or we need different types of housekeeping when clients access the object, like logging, access control, or pay-by-access.

Solution Define a placeholder object, the Proxy, that acts on behalf of the real object. The proxy can defer loading the real object, control access to it, or in other ways lower resource demands or implement housekeeping tasks.

Structure:

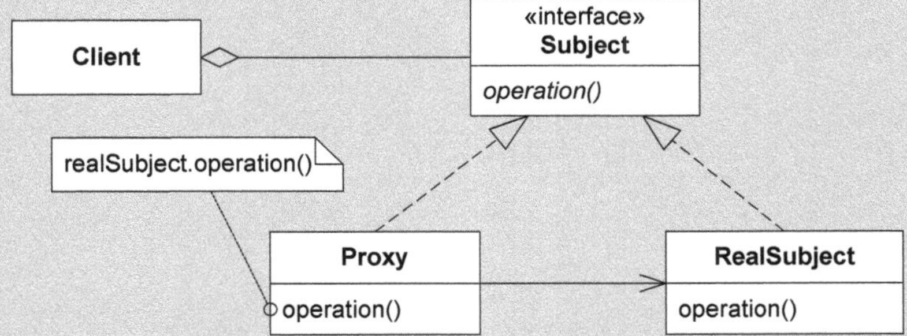

Roles A **Client** only interacts via a **Subject** interface. The **RealSubject** is the true object implementing resource-demanding operations (bandwidth, computation, memory usage, etc.) or operations that need access control (security, pay-by-access, logging, etc.). A **Proxy** implements the **Subject** interface and provides the relevant access control by holding a reference to the real subject and delegating operations to it.

Cost - Benefit It *strengthens reuse* as the housekeeping tasks are separated from the real subject operations. Thus the subject does not need to implement the housekeeping itself; and the proxy can act as proxy for several different types of real subjects.

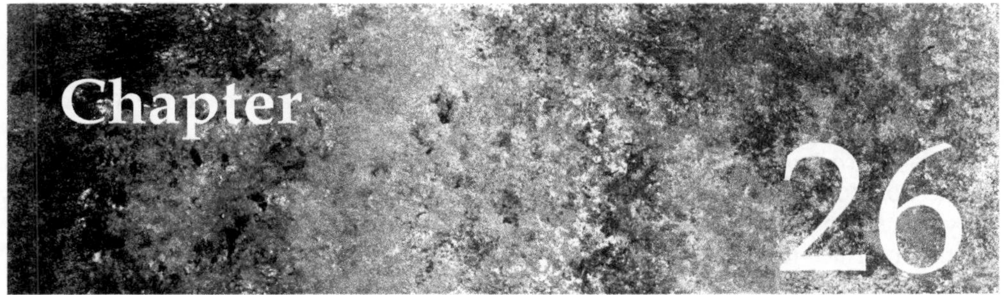

Composite

26.1 The Problem

Many problems require our software to handle *part-whole* objects, that is, objects that are defined by a hierarchical structure. As an example, consider folders on a file system. Folders contain files but they often also contain other folders that again may contain files and folders. Another example is a graphics editor in which several graphical objects may be grouped into a single object and moved, resized, and manipulated as a single entity. As such a group of figures may in itself be part of a larger group, it has the same hierarchical, part-whole, structure.

By nature, the part objects (files, individual graphical objects) are different from the whole objects (folders, groups), and designers are inclined to let them be defined by different classes. For instance, the design may contain a Folder class having methods like addFile, addFolder, removeFile, etc., and another class File having methods like delete, size, etc. However, many operations are actually the same irrespective if it is a folder or a file: both may be moved around in the folder structure, may be deleted, have a size, may be made read-only, etc. This similarity has the unfortunate consequence that the code must contain a lot of conditional statements just to pacify the type system. To see this, consider a user that invokes the size operation on some item in the folder hierarchy:

```
private static void displaySize(Object item) {
  if (item instanceof File) {
    File file = (File) item;
    System.out.println( "File size is "+file.size() );
  } else if (item instanceof Folder) {
    Folder folder = (Folder) item;
    System.out.println( "Folder size is "+folder.size() );
  }
}
```

These if-statements and casts will be present for every operation that is shared by folders and files. The stability and changeability problems associated with large amounts of similar looking code leads to the solution proposed by the COMPOSITE pattern.

26.2 A Solution

A solution is to apply the ① principle *program to an interface,* and define a common interface for both the *part* entity as well as the *whole* entity. Both part and whole entities are *components* which are defined by a Component interface. The methods of the Component interface defines all the methods that both part and whole objects may have, like addComponent, toogleReadOnly and size for a folder structure. As a partial interface for a folder hierarchy (implementing only the responsibility to add folders/files and calculate size to keep the demonstration code small), it may look like this:

Fragment: chapter/composite/CompositeDemo.java

```
/** Define the Component interface
 * (partial for a folder hierarchy) */
interface Component {
  public void addComponent(Component child);
  public int size();
}
```

The Component interface is implemented by two classes, the File class that defines the *part* objects, and the Folder class that defines the *whole* objects. To handle many of the methods in the Folder class, the ② principle is used to *recursively compose the behavior.* As an example, consider the size() method: for a file it is just the size in bytes of the file on the hard disk, but for a folder, the size is calculated by summing the individual sizes of each entry in the folder:

Fragment: chapter/composite/CompositeDemo.java

```
/** Define a (partial) folder abstraction */
class Folder implements Component {
  private List<Component> components = new ArrayList<Component>();
  public void addComponent(Component child) {
    components.add(child);
  }
  public int size() {
    int size = 0;
    for ( Component c: components ) {
      size += c.size();
    }
    return size;
  }
}
```

Note how the simple implementation of method size() is actually a depth first recursive traversal in the folder structure.

26.3 The Composite Pattern

This is the COMPOSITE pattern (design pattern box 26.1, page 322). Its intent is

> *Compose objects into tree structures to represent part-whole hierarchies. Composite lets clients treat individual objects and compositions of objects uniformly.*

The central roles are the **Composite**, defining the common interface for both part and whole objects, the **Leaf** that defines the primitive, atomic, part component, and finally the **Composite** that aggregates components.

The main advantage of the COMPOSITE pattern is the identical interface, shared between leaf and composite entities in the hierarchical data structure. This makes the use of the individual entities look similar. To some extent it often also allows an abstract AbstractComponent class to define some operations that are implemented identically in both the leaf and the composite class.

It does, however, also open for a concern, namely the methods to handle the list of components in the composite object. The add and remove methods can add and remove components to a component, but these operations are of course meaningless for a leaf object as it has no substructure.

> ☞ Restate this reflection in terms of the cohesion property discussed in Chapter 10.

One solution is to remove the add and remove methods from the Component interface, and only define them in Composite. The problem, however, is that we are then back in the switch and cast problem that Composite sets out to solve. Thus this pattern trades lower cohesion of the leaf abstraction in order to get a uniform interface for all abstractions in the part-whole structure.

26.4 Review Questions

Describe the COMPOSITE pattern. What problem does it solve? What is its structure? What roles and responsibilities are defined? What are the benefits and liabilities?

26.5 Further Exercises

Exercise 26.1. Source code directory:
`chapter/composite`

Review the CompositeDemo code and extend it.

1. Add a method print to print the hierarchical structure of any item. The substructure should be shown by indentation and file marked with an a star character, like

```
root
  programs
    emacs.exe *
    vi.exe *
  src
    editor.java *
    utilities
      search.java *
```

2. Add a method delete that deletes any item.

[26.1] Design Pattern: Composite

Intent Compose objects into tree structures to represent part-whole hierarchies. Composite lets clients treat individual objects and compositions of objects uniformly.

Problem Handling of tree data structures.

Solution Define a common interface for composite and atomic components alike. Define composites in terms of a set of children, each either a composite or atomic component. Define composite behavior in terms of aggregating or composing behavior of each child.

Structure:

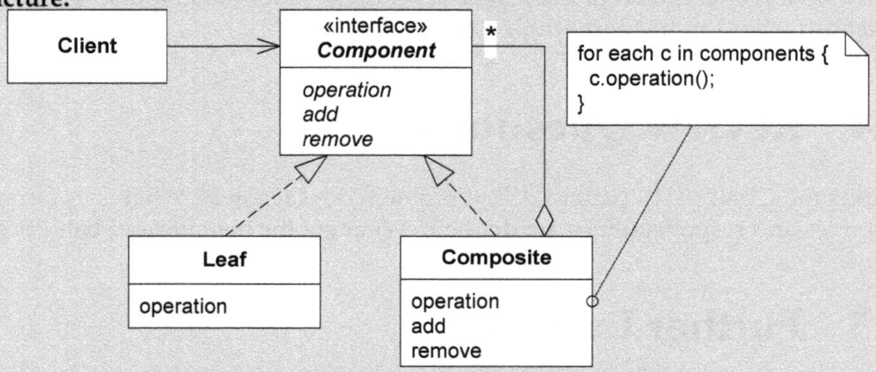

Roles **Component** defines a common interface. **Composite** defines a component by means of aggregating other components. **Leaf** defines a primitive, atomic, component i.e. one that has no substructure.

Cost - Benefit It defines a *hierarchy of primitive and composite objects*. It makes the *client interface uniform* as it does not need to know if it is a simple or composite component. It is *easy to add new kinds of components* as they will automatically work with the existing components. A liability is that the *design can become overly general* as it is difficult to constrain the types of leafs a composite may contain. The *interfaces may method bloat* with methods that are irrelevant; for instance an add method in a leaf.

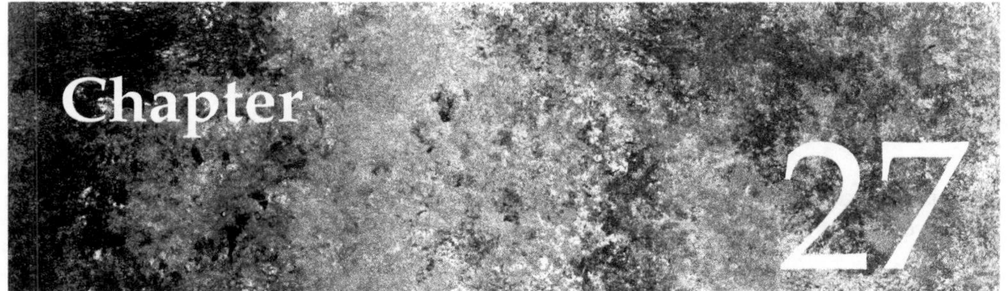

Null Object

27.1 The Problem

Consider a class that contains one or several methods whose execution takes a long time, say 1–15 minutes, and whose execution is commonly made while a user is expected to wait for it to complete. One example could be a software installation procedure, or a compilation. To assure the user that the system is not hanging or broken it is common to show progress. I could code a progress indicator by inserting reporting checkpoints in my code, something like

```
public void lengthyExecution() {
  ...
  progress.report(10);
  ..
  progress.report(50);
  ...
  progress.report(100);
  progress.end();
}
```

Here the parameter is a percentage of completion. The object progress can be implemented as a visual indicator, as we are used to in modern installation procedures.

Now, consider the situation where I want to do automated testing of the above method. It makes no sense to bring up dialogs while executing test suites. The traditional programmer's way of saying "I do not need this behavior" is to set the object reference to null. After all, null means absence of an object and therefore absence of behavior. However, the cost of this is a lot of tests in the code, as invoking a method on null leads to a null pointer exception.

```
public void lengthyExecution() {
  ...
  if (progress != null )
    progress.report(10);
  ..
  if (progress != null )
    progress.report(50);
```

```
    ...
    if (progress != null ) {
      progress.report(100);
      progress.end();
    }
  }
```

This is tedious. Even worse, it is quite easy to forget one of the checks, especially if in some code that is only rarely executed.

27.2 A Solution

Looking over the problem it is not really "absence of object" that is required in the case above. It is "absence of behavior". So, instead of representing behavioral absence by a null reference, I can represent it with absence of behavior in a special object, the **null object**, whose methods all simply do nothing. When I do not want any progress reporting behavior, it set the progress object reference to this null object, after which all calls of report simply do nothing. This way I do not need to guard all my method invocations by checks for null.

27.3 The Null Object Pattern

This is the NULL OBJECT pattern (design pattern box 27.1, page 325). Its intent is

Define a no-operation object to represent null.

The central roles are **Service** that defines the interface for some abstraction, **ConcreteService** that implements the service, and finally the **Null Object** that contains empty implementations of all methods in the service interface.

This pattern generally aids in increasing both reliability and maintainability. As absence of behavior is represented by the null object, the object reference is always assigned to a valid object and the use of null avoided. Thereby the **if** (obj != **null**) checks are not needed and the risk of having forgotten it in a single or few places is eliminated. The result is less risk of null pointer exceptions. If there is a lot of such checks that are not needed it also makes the production code easier to read (compare the two code fragments in the first section), increasing analyzability and thus maintainability.

The only liability is if the design was made without much attention to the ① *program to an interface* principle and the **Client** is directly coupled to **ConcreteService**. Then there is an overhead in introducing the **Service** interface in order to allow replacing the concrete service with a null object.

The NULL OBJECT pattern was first described by Wolf (1997).

27.4 Review Questions

Describe the NULL OBJECT pattern. What problem does it solve? What is its structure and what is the protocol? What roles and responsibilities are defined? What are the benefits and liabilities?

[27.1] Design Pattern: Null Object

Intent Define a no-operation object to represent null.

Problem The absence of an object, or the absence of behavior, is often represented by a reference being null but it leads to numerous checks to ensure that no method is invoked on null. It is easy to forget such checks.

Solution You create a Null Object class whose methods have no behavior, and use an instance of this class instead of using the null type. Thereby there is no need for null checking before invoking methods.

Structure:

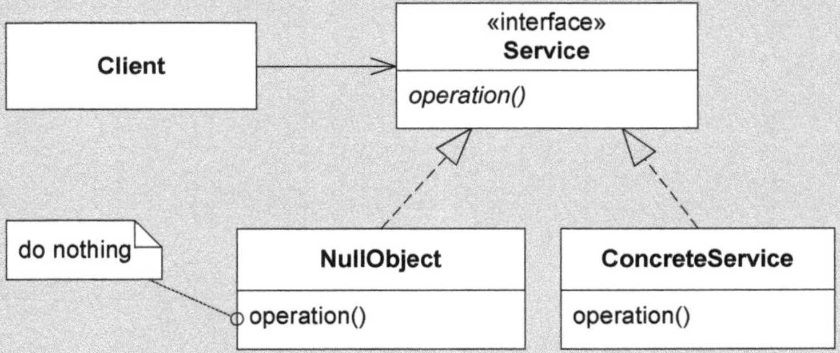

Roles **Service** defines the interface of some abstraction while **ConcreteService** is an implementation of it. **NullObject** is an implementation whose methods do nothing.

Cost - Benefit It reduces code size and increases reliability because a lot of *testing for null is avoided.* If an interface is not already used it *requires additional refactoring to use.*

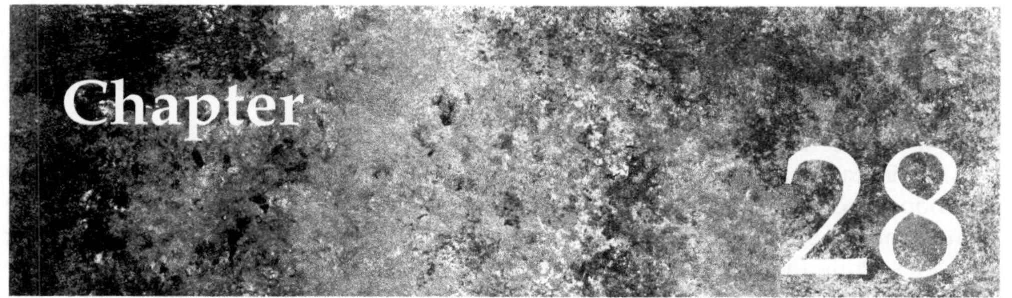

Observer

28.1 The Problem

Often systems have objects that are dependent on some underlying core information: if this information changes then the objects must react accordingly. One such classic example is a spreadsheet where the data in the sheet may be simultaneously displayed as bar charts and pie charts in their own windows. Of course I want these windows to be synchronized i.e. if I change a value in a cell in the spreadsheet then the pie chart and bar chart should immediately redraw to reflect the change. Many other examples exist as for instance

- A central computer to monitor a parking lot may receive information about bought parking time from the lot's set of parking pay stations in order to calculate the number of free parking spaces and display it at the entrance.
- A calendar application shows current time both as text in a status field and as a highlight of entries in the day view. As time passes both need to be updated. It must also pop up reminders for important meetings at the correct time.
- In a UML diagram editor, the object representing an association line between two classes must monitor any movement of either of the connected classes in order to reposition and redraw.

Common to all these examples is that one or several objects can only behave properly if they are constantly notified of any state changes in the monitored object.

☞ Review the set of computer applications that you normally use. Find examples in which some objects need to be synchronized with others for the application to work correctly.

28.2 A Solution

I can use the compositional design principles and the concepts of *roles and responsibilities,* to find a solution to this challenge. I first note two distinct roles in the problem: the monitored object (e.g. the spreadsheet cell) and the dependent objects (e.g. the pie chart window, the bar chart window, and potentially lots of other windows showing the cell's value in some way). These roles are traditionally termed the **subject** role and the **observer** role. Observers are the dependent objects while the subject contains the state information that they monitor.

Looking for variability, the ③ *consider what should be variable in your design* principle, I conclude that I cannot in advance know the type of processing to make when the subject's state changes; the only thing I know is that the observers will have to make *some kind* of processing. For example, the spreadsheet cell should not know about drawing pie charts or bar charts as this would lead to tight coupling. But it should allow the observers, like the pie chart window and the bar chart window, to discover that it has indeed changed its value. So, the variable behavior is the actual *processing* which must take place whenever the cell changes value—I do not know in advance the kind of diagrams that must be redrawn or the type of recalculations that must be made based on the change. The common behavior is the *notification*—I do know that dependent objects have to be told that the cell's value has changed.

I can now use principle ① *program to an interface* to define an interface that encapsulates the processing responsibility. Traditionally, this interface is called Observer and contains a single method responsible for the processing named update.

Listing: chapter/observer/Observer.java

```
/** Observer role in the Observer pattern
*/

public interface Observer {
  /** Perform processing appropriate for the changed state.
   * Subject invokes this method every time its state changes.
   */
  public void update();
}
```

Thus, e.g. the pie chart window must implement Observer and put its redrawing behavior in the update method.

Finally, I ② *favor object composition* by letting the subject maintain a set of observers, and every time the subject changes state, it is responsible for invoking the update method of all observers, as shown in Figure 28.1. Traditionally, this is handled by a method called notify. The subject must of course also have methods to allow *registering* observers, that is, adding observers to and removing observers from the set (not shown in the figure).

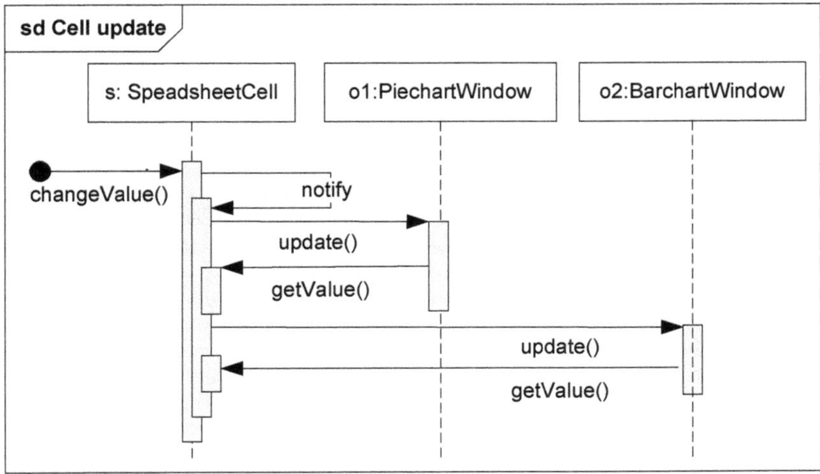

Figure 28.1: Spreadsheet updating based on cell change.

28.3 Example

As a bare bone example, consider the following code fragment.

Fragment: chapter/observer/DemoObserver.java

```
public class DemoObserver {
  public static void main(String[] args) {
    SpreadsheetCell a1 = new SpreadsheetCell();
    Observer
      observer1 = new PieChartWindow(a1),
      observer2 = new BarChartWindow(a1);
    a1.addObserver(observer1);
    a1.addObserver(observer2);

    a1.changeValue(32);
    a1.changeValue(42);

    a1.removeObserver(observer1);
    a1.changeValue(12);
  }
}
class PieChartWindow implements Observer {
  SpreadsheetCell myCell;
  public PieChartWindow(SpreadsheetCell c){
    myCell = c;
  }
  public void update() {
    System.out.println( "Pie chart notified: value: "+
                        myCell.getValue() );
  }
}
class BarChartWindow implements Observer {
  SpreadsheetCell myCell;
  public BarChartWindow(SpreadsheetCell c){
    myCell = c;
  }
```

```
  public void update() {
    System.out.println( "Value "+ myCell.getValue()+
                        " in Bar chart" );
  }
}
```

The SpreadsheetCell is the subject and in the main method I create two observers (of different types) and register them at the subject using addObserver. Next, the value of the cell is changed a couple of times, leading to notifications to its observers. When you run the application, the output is

```
Pie chart notified: value: 32
Value 32 in Bar chart
Pie chart notified: value: 42
Value 42 in Bar chart
Value 12 in Bar chart
```

☞ Review the other interfaces and classes for the example in folder *chapter/observer*.

28.4 The Observer Pattern

This is the OBSERVER pattern (design pattern box 28.1, page 335). Its intent is

> *Define a one-to-many dependency between objects so that when one object changes state, all its dependents are notified and updated automatically.*

The OBSERVER pattern is a pattern in which the protocol aspect is very important. Remember the definition of protocol in Chapter 15 as *a convention detailing the sequence of interactions expected by a set of roles.* In order for an observer to get notified, it must first register itself in the subject so the subject knows who to notify. This is the *registration protocol,* the first frame in the sequence diagram shown in Figure 28.2.

The loop frame represents the second protocol, the *notification protocol,* that is, the typical interaction that takes place while the application is running. Here the subject's state is changed in some way (shown by the setState() call) and the subject then notifies all registered observers by invoking their update() method in turn. To rephrase the loop frame in "protocol talk", the observer protocol dictates that any state change in the subject role must result in an update invocation in all registered observers.

There are some comments on this protocol. First, the sequence diagram shows that it is an observer that force the subject's state change. This is a typical situation when the observer pattern is used to handle multiple graphical views (as in the MODEL-VIEW-CONTROLLER pattern, discussed in the next chapter). But generally, the state change can come from any source, not just observers. Still, any state change starts the notification protocol. Second, any observer is free to do anything it wishes. In Figure 28.2 they both retrieve the subject's state but an observer may decide to ignore a state change.

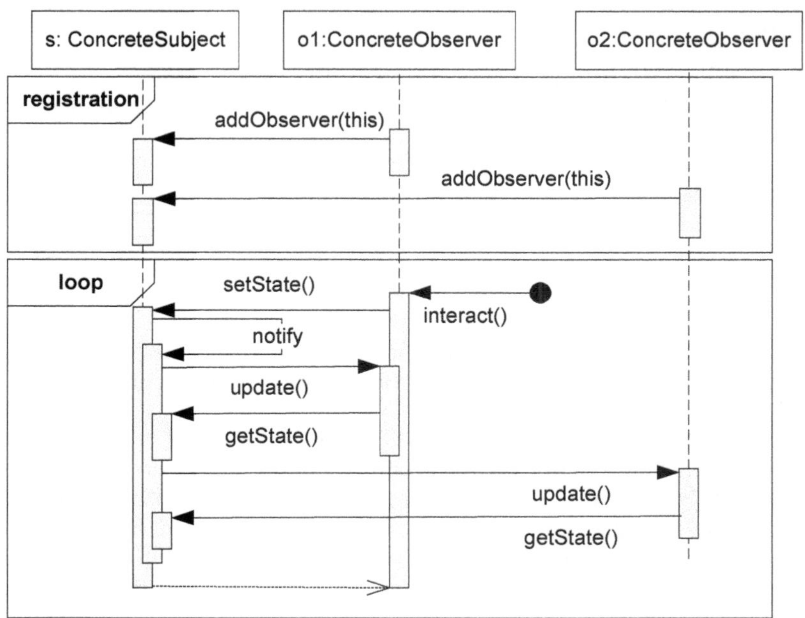

Figure 28.2: Observer pattern protocol.

An interface for the subject role typically looks like:

Listing: chapter/observer/Subject.java

```
/** Subject role in the Observer pattern
*/

public interface Subject {
  /** add an observer to the set of observers receiving notifications
   * from this subject.
   * @param newObserver the observer to add to this subject's set */
  public void addObserver(Observer newObserver);
  /**  Remove the observer from the set of observers receiving
   * notifications from this subject.
   * @param observer the observer to remove from the set.*/
  public void removeObserver(Observer observer);
  /** notify all observers in case this subject has changed state. */
  public void notifyObservers();
}
```

However, it is not in general possible to make a single interface that describes all types of subjects. The reason is that the subject must have methods to manipulate its state and these are specific for the particular domain, for instance, the methods for changing state in a spread sheet cell are different from those that change state in a pay station. However, we can list the responsibilities that the two roles must have.

Subject

- Must handle storage, access, and manipulation of state
- Must maintain a set of observers and allow adding and removing observers to this set
- Must notify every observer in the set of any state change by invoking each observer's update method

Observer

- Must register itself in the subject
- Must react and process subject state changes every time a notification arrives from the subject, that is, the update method is invoked

The discussion above is the classic description of OBSERVER as it appeared in the book by Gamma et al. (1995), but the pattern comes in variants. The description above is the **pull variant**. In the pull variant the update method call is simply a notification of a state change, but no information is provided on the nature of the state change: the observer must itself retrieve the state from the subject by calling get-methods. An alternative is the **push variant** protocol. Here there may be several update methods, and the update methods include parameters. The parameters and set of update methods provide detailed information about the actual state change in the subject. This variant eliminates the need for getState() calls in the sequence diagram above. If the subject keeps a lot of distinct state information this variant is better as the observers do not have to waste time figuring out what actually changed.

A good example of the push variant observer protocol is the AWT and Swing graphical user interface library. For instance, the MouseListener interface is the **Observer** role while a graphical canvas/panel is the **Subject**. The listener interface declares several update methods, for instance mousePressed(MouseEvent e) and mouseReleased(MouseEvent e). Therefore an observer immediately knows if the mouse was pressed or released, and furthermore the MouseEvent object holds the X and Y coordinates of the mouse position.

In learning iteration 7, you will see several applications of the OBSERVER pattern in the MiniDraw framework.

28.5 Analysis

The OBSERVER pattern's intent states that it defines a one-to-many relation: one subject may have many observers. Actually, it is a many-to-many relation, as a single observer can of course register itself at many different subjects at the same time.

Exercise 28.1: In Section 28.1 I gave a few examples of systems that may be implemented using the OBSERVER pattern. Analyze them and explain those where a single observer may register itself at several subjects.

The observer pattern's main benefit is the *loose coupling between subject and observer role*. All the subject needs to know is the observer interface: it is then able to notify any type of observer now and in the future. Furthermore, the pattern defines a *broadcast communication protocol* as a subject can handle any number of observers.

A liability is the *inability to distinguish types of state changes*. This is most easily demonstrated by an example: consider a subject that holds a coordinate (x,y) as two integer instance variables each with a set method: setX and setY. As both methods change the subject's state, both will trigger a full notification protocol. This means that a change to both coordinates at the same time, which conceptually is a single state change, will nevertheless generate *two* update invocations in all observers. In a graphical application, for instance, this may introduce "screen flicker" where the graphics are redrawn multiple times and therefore flickering. One possible solution is to add methods to the subject role that are similar to a database commit, like for instance beginUpdate and endUpdate. The first method simply disables the notification protocol, while the latter enforce a notification. This way several state changing calls can be made to the subject before the notification is made. While it solves the problem at the technical level, it suffers that programmers have to remember to encapsulate state changes in the transaction methods. If they are not paired correctly it leads to defects that can be difficult to identify.

A final thing to consider is cyclic dependencies: A observes on B that observes on C that observes A (note that A serves both the **Observer** and **Subject** roles here). Any state change will then lead to an infinite loop of update calls. Standard circular dependence detection code must then be added to break the loop. For instance the notify method in A may include an internal flag:

```
private boolean inNotify = false;
public void notifyObservers() {
  if (inNotify) { return; }
  inNotify = true;
  [notify all observers]
  inNotify = false;
}
```

The use of OBSERVER is pervasive in modern software and there are other terms for the roles. Subject is often called *observable* while observer is called *listener* in the Java Swing libraries. The Java library *java.util* contains an Observer interface (push variant) and a default Observable class that may come in handy.

If you look at the **Subject** role it actually has two rather distinct responsibilities: handling state changes and handling observer notifications. The former is domain specific while the latter is similar for all subjects. It therefore sometimes makes sense to encapsulate the latter code in a separate object and then let the subject delegate this handling. I will show how this can be done in the discussion of MiniDraw.

28.6 Selected Solutions

Discussion of Exercise 28.1:

As an example of an observer that registers itself at multiple subjects, consider a UML diagram editor. The association line object (observer) will register itself in both class box objects (subjects) and receive events whenever either of them are moved so it can redraw itself correctly to keep the class boxes connected.

Also, the parking lot monitor that displays the number of free parking spaces needs to monitor several pay stations that each have the subject role.

28.7 Review Questions

What is the intent of the OBSERVER pattern? Describe some typical problems in systems that it addresses.

Describe the OBSERVER pattern solution: What roles are involved, what are their responsibilities, what is the protocol?

Describe how the OBSERVER pattern solution can be viewed as an example of compositional design.

28.8 Further Exercises

Exercise 28.2:

Design a pay station monitoring system. It should be responsible for monitoring a set of pay stations on a parking lot and keep track of each buy transaction in each pay station. Based on the amount of parking time bought in each transaction and knowledge of the total number of parking spaces it should be able to calculate the number of free parking spaces. Take your starting point in the design for the pay station, and focus your work on the event notification mechanism.

Exercise 28.3:

Develop the production and test code based on exercise 28.2. You may disregard the algorithm to calculate free parking space and replace it with *Fake It* code.

[28.1] Design Pattern: Observer

Intent Define a one-to-many dependency between objects so that when one object changes state, all its dependents are notified and updated automatically.

Problem A set of objects needs to be notified in case a common object changes state to ensure system wide consensus and consistency. You want to ensure this consistency in a loosely coupled way.

Solution All objects that must be notified (**Observers**) implements an interface containing an update method. The common object (**Subject**) maintains a list of all observers and when it changes state, it invokes the update method on each object in the list. Thereby all observing objects are notified of state changes.

Structure:

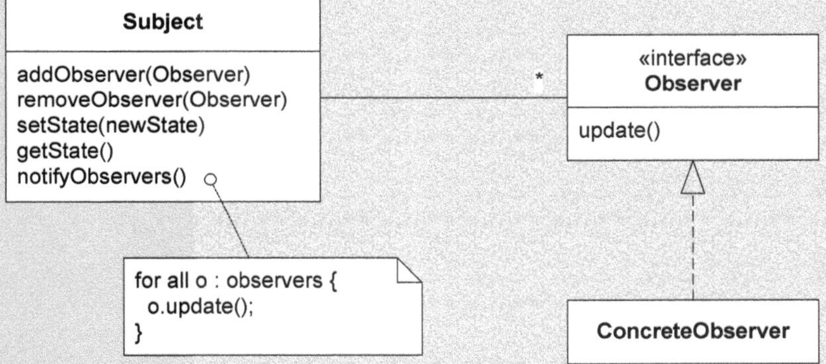

Roles **Observer** specifies the responsibility and interface for being able to be notified. **Subject** is responsible for holding state information, for maintaining a list of all observers, and for invoking the update method on all observers in its list. **ConcreteObserver** defines concrete behavior for how to react when the subject experiences a state change.

Cost - Benefit The benefits are: *Loose coupling between Subject and Observer* thus it is easy to add new observers to the system. *Support broadcast communication* as it is basically publishing information in a one-to-many relation. The liabilities are: *Unexpected/multiple updates:* as the coupling is low it is difficult for observers to infer the nature of subject state changes which may lead to the observers updating too often or spuriously.

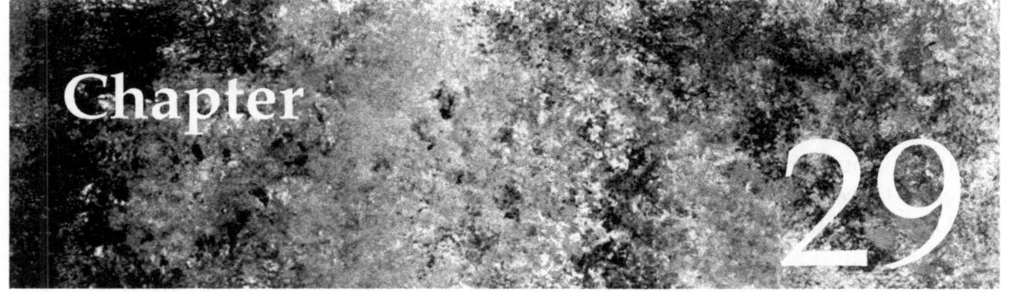

Model-View-Controller

29.1 The Problem

Most computer programs running on personal computers have a *graphical user interface*, involving several windows and input from both the keyboard as well as the mouse. A complex example of such an application is a *vector graphics editor* (see Figure 29.1) like for instance Adobe Illustrator, XFig, Inkscape, or Microsoft Visio. UML diagram editors can also be considered vector graphics editors. These present a palette of figures: rectangles, lines, ovals, etc., that the user can add to a drawing and next manipulate using the mouse. Several windows can be opened on the same drawing showing different parts and in different scales. In such a system the underlying drawing needs to be rendered in multiple windows at the same time while the drawing also needs to process input events from multiple windows. The challenge is to structure graphical applications such that coupling between the application's domain objects and the graphical views is low. Sidebar 29.1 is a war story of how early GUI builders often led developers to make a high coupling.

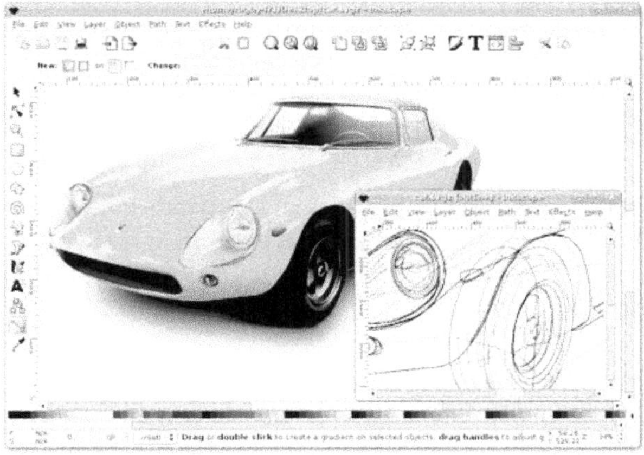

Figure 29.1: The Inkscape vector graphics editor.

Sidebar 29.1: Early GUI Builders

I had the opportunity to use some early programs that allowed graphical user interfaces to be developed using a graphical editor. This was of course a big improvement to the former practice of writing GUI code by hand. I have wasted my fair share of hours making dialogs appear tidy by trial and error: *I try width 100 and height 20 pixels, (compile and run), oops, that was too much, let me try width 90, (compile and run), oops that was too little, ...*

However, all those builders that I have tried lured me into tight coupling between the view and the model code. Typically if I positioned a button on the dialog using my GUI builder I could click on the events associated with the button, like `mouseClick()`. If I selected that, an editor would pop up and I could enter source code directly to be executed when the button was clicked. The result was of course that model manipulation code was scattered all over the place in my GUI code. It made it difficult to overview and next to impossible to reuse if the same model operation was required by some other event, like a menu selection.

29.2 Model-View-Controller Pattern

The challenge facing a design to handle graphical user interfaces is actually twofold: first the need to keep multiple windows consistent and second to handle and interpret multiple input sources: keyboard, mouse, and maybe others. A well-established solution to this challenge is the MODEL-VIEW-CONTROLLER pattern, or just MVC pattern for short.

The first challenge is solved by the OBSERVER pattern. OBSERVER states that the underlying information, like the drawing's list of figures, must be stored in a **Subject** object that can notify its **Observers**, i.e. the windows rendering the drawing. In MVC these roles are called **Model** (containing state and notifying upon state changes) and **View** (rendering the graphics) respectively.

The second challenge is receiving and interpreting events from the user. To see why this is a problem consider what it means that a user clicks in a window. If the mouse hovers above a button it means that the button's command should be executed, if it hovers above a figure it means that the figure should become selected, if it hovers over some text in a text editor it means that the cursor position should be changed, etc. Thus, the same user event, a mouse click, has to be interpreted based upon the particular type of application and type of object.

> ☞ Consider some of the applications you use regularly (or start them) and think about the resulting behavior it exhibits when you click and drag with the mouse. Do you see different behaviors even in the same application depending upon its state?

The STATE pattern provides a compositional solution to this problem. Remember the intent of STATE. *Allow an object to alter its behavior when its internal state changes.*

Here it is obviously the window (**View** role) that receives input events but the resulting behavior depends upon the internal state: the type of application and the application's state. The **Context** role of STATE is the **View** role in MVC while the **State** role is denoted **Controller**. However, the controller is more specific in that it has the responsibility to modify the model appropriately. The resulting structure contains the three parts: model, view and controller, as outlined in Figure 29.2, with the following responsibilities.

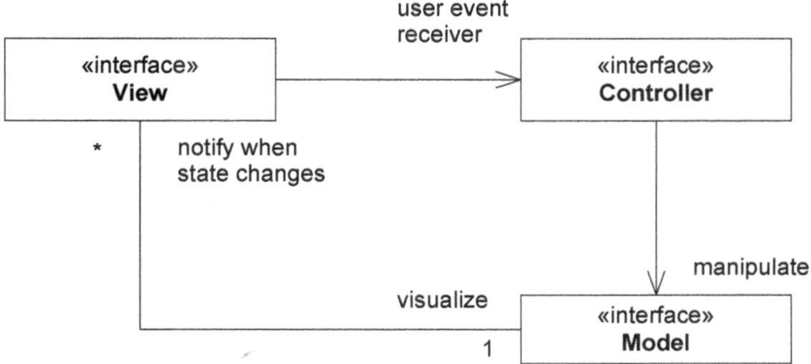

Figure 29.2: MVC role structure.

Model

- Store application state.
- Maintain the set of Views associated.
- Notify all views in case of state changes.

View

- Visualize model state graphically.
- Accept user input events, delegate them to the associated Controller.
- Manage a set of controllers and allow the user to set which controller is active.

Controller

- Interpret user input events and translate them into state changes in the Model.

☞ As the controller usually translates simple input events into the relevant method call on the model (for example mouse drag events into move() calls on a figure) the controller actually acts as an ADAPTER for the model.

The protocol of MVC is shown in Figure 29.3. Only the notification protocol is shown. Of course views must also register in the model to receive update events, and the view must be associated with the proper controllers.

The MVC pattern is the fundamental pattern in the MiniDraw framework, described in learning iteration 7.

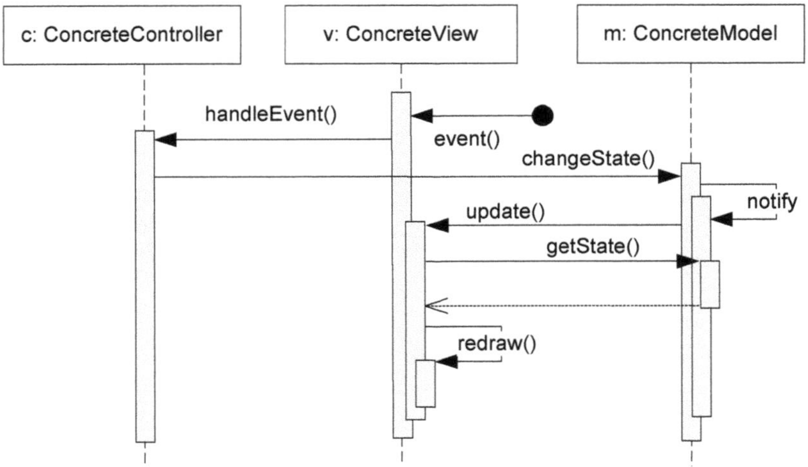

Figure 29.3: MVC protocol.

29.3 Analysis

The MVC patterns of course inherits the benefits and liabilities of OBSERVER and STATE. First, the broadcast mechanism of OBSERVER ensures that the user can open as many windows as he or she likes and they are all ensured to be consistent and to show the same model—any change in the model are reflected in all windows. The coupling is loose so any window may choose to render the model as it sees fit, as exemplified in Figure 29.1 where one window shows a wireframe image of the car model while the other shows a fully rendered car image. The user event delegation to the **Controller** objects ensures that model changes are not tightly coupled to the particular window object and that they can be changed at run-time. Consider the palette in a graphics editor: choosing the rectangle tool over the oval tool changes what is drawn with the mouse. This simply maps to changing the controller associated with the window which demonstrates how easy it is to change behavior at run-time.

The liabilities of the pattern are the classic ones. The structure and protocol is a bit complex and care must be exercised during programming to get it right. The problems of multiple updates and circular update sequences are inherited from the OBSERVER pattern and have to be considered.

MVC is an **architectural pattern**. Design patterns are not tied to any particular domain but can find usage in more or less all types of applications. Architectural patterns are more coarse grained and focus on a particular architectural problem and a particular domain. MVC presents a qualified solution to the problem of structuring graphical user interfaces and of course if your application does not have such it is of no interest. MVC is also not the only possible solution—others exist such as the PRESENTATION-ABSTRACTION-CONTROL pattern (Buschmann et al. 1996).

In the presentation so far, the **Model** is shown as a single object. In practice, a model is often complex and consists of a lot of objects with different interfaces. It is up to the concrete design decision whether the controller should access individual objects in the model or if it is beneficial indeed to have a single interface for manipulating all aspects of the model. In the latter case, the model interface becomes a FACADE.

The MVC pattern is treated in detail by Buschmann et al. (1996). The pattern was first described by Reenskaug (1978).

29.4 Review Questions

Describe the type of applications that MVC outlines a plausible architecture for.

Name the three basic roles of the pattern and describe the responsibilities of each. How are the three roles related (type of relation and multiplicity)? What is the protocol once an application using the pattern is running?

Describe benefits and liabilities of the pattern.

Describe why MVC is an architectural pattern rather than a design pattern.

29.5 Further Exercises

Exercise 29.1. Source code directory:
`chapter/facade`

Review the GUI for the pay station from Chapter 19, *Facade*. Analyze the production code and evaluate whether the MVC pattern has been used to structure the GUI.

[29.1] Design Pattern: Model-View-Controller

Intent Define a loosely coupled design to form the architecture of graphical user interfaces having multiple windows and handling user input from mouse, keyboard, or other input sources.

Problem A graphical user interface must support multiple windows rendering different visual representations of an underlying set of state-full objects in a consistent way. The user must be able to manipulate the objects' state using mouse and keyboard.

Solution A **Model** contains the application's state and notifies all **Views** when state changes happen. The **Views** are responsible for rendering the model when notified. User input events are received by a **View** but forwarded to its associated **Controller**. The **Controller** interprets events and makes the appropriate calls to the **Model**.

Structure:

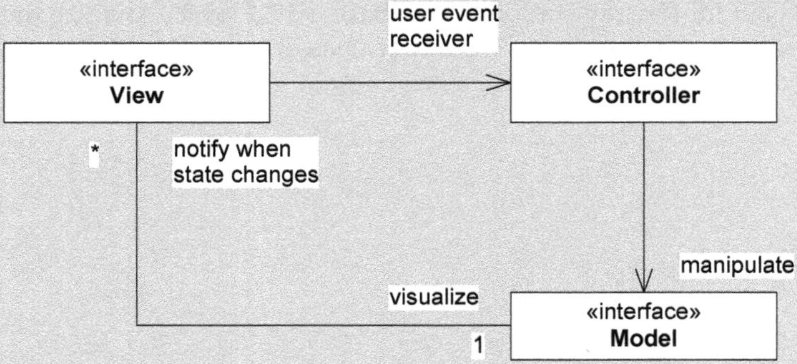

Roles **Model** maintains application state and updates all associated **Views**. **View** renders the model graphically and delegates user events to the **Controller** that in turn is responsible for modifying the model.

Cost - Benefit The benefits are: *loose coupling between all three roles* meaning you can add new graphical renderings or user event processing. *Multiple views/windows* are supported. It is possible to *change event processing at run-time*. The liabilities are: *unexpected/multiple updates:* as the coupling is low it is difficult for views to infer the nature of model state changes which may lead to graphical flickering. *Design complexity* is another concern if the development team is untrained.

Iteration 7

Frameworks

As the title of this learning iteration suggests, the focus is *frameworks*: the concepts and terminology used in frameworks as well as the set of techniques available when designing, programming, and using frameworks. Actually, you can rest easily as you have already learned the techniques: as the mission of frameworks is to provide a reliable, flexible, and reusable software platform for building systems, the compositional design approach is used throughout. Thus the example framework, MiniDraw, also serves to show how design patterns play well together.

Chapter	Learning Objective
Chapter 30	*Introducing MiniDraw.* This chapter has two learning objectives: first, it demonstrates a small framework, MiniDraw, to show how frameworks are typically customized to make applications. Second, MiniDraw is compositionally designed and have a high density of patterns to enable its flexibility, and thus serve to show the principles applied on a larger example.
Chapter 31	*Template Method.* This pattern is described in this learning iteration as it is at the heart of a framework. If you deeply understand TEMPLATE METHOD you understand frameworks. The intent of the pattern is: *Define the skeleton of an algorithm in an operation, deferring some steps to subclasses or delegates. Template Method lets the behavior of certain steps of an algorithm be varied without changing the algorithm's structure.*
Chapter 32	*Framework Theory.* The learning objective here is to introduce the theoretical basis: the terminology, the concepts, and the techniques; for frameworks.

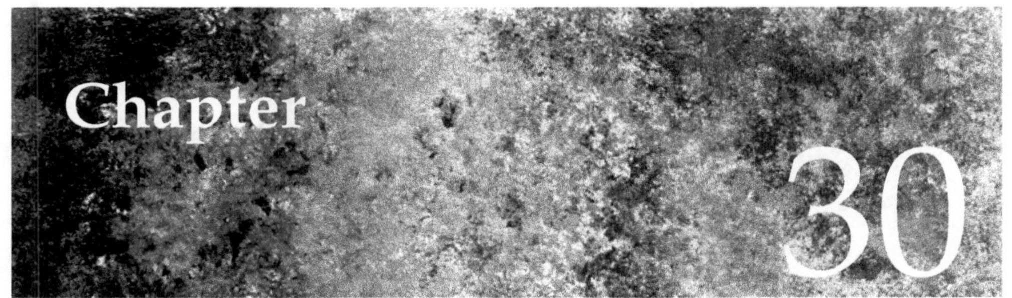

Introducing MiniDraw

Learning Objectives

The learning objective of this chapter is two-fold. The first one is to give an example of a *framework* which is the central topic of this learning iteration. A framework provides many variability points that let a developer customize the framework. Therefore, I will present a set of applications that are all based upon MiniDraw and demonstrate some of the aspects that can be tailored. Second, MiniDraw is an example of a design that has a high density of design patterns and is almost exclusively designed by a compositional approach. By going over the design you will therefore see the principles applied on a larger system than the pay station.

30.1 A Jigsaw Puzzle Application

MiniDraw is a small and simple framework that defines basic support for *direct manipulation* of two dimensional image-based graphics. Direct manipulation simply means that the user interacts with graphical objects on the screen "directly" using the mouse: movement, selection, resizing, etc. A simple MiniDraw application is shown in Figure 30.1. It shows a background image of the seal of Aarhus University in wrong colors and on top of that, there are nine puzzle pieces, the seal in the proper blue-white colors, that the user can move into their proper position with the mouse. This is not terribly exciting but it illustrates some of the basic functionality that MiniDraw provides: user interaction with graphical images.

MiniDraw does not by itself know anything about jigsaw puzzles but it knows about GIF images and defines behavior to draw and manipulate them. Thus we must *customize* MiniDraw to become a jigsaw puzzle application. The customization code is shown below.

Listing: chapter/minidraw-demo/test/puzzle/LogoPuzzle.java

```
package puzzle;
import minidraw.standard.*;
import minidraw.framework.*;
```

Figure 30.1: A simple jigsaw puzzle application based on MiniDraw.

```
import java.awt.*;
import javax.swing.*;

/** A (very small) jigsaw puzzle on the Aarhus University seal.
   A demonstration of a "minimal" MiniDraw application.
 */
public class LogoPuzzle {

  public static void main(String[] args) {
    DrawingEditor editor =
      new MiniDrawApplication( "Put the pieces into place",
                               new PuzzleFactory() );
    editor.open();
    editor.setTool( new SelectionTool(editor) );

    Drawing drawing = editor.drawing();
    drawing.add( new ImageFigure( "11", new Point(5, 5)) );
    drawing.add( new ImageFigure( "12", new Point(10, 10)) );
    drawing.add( new ImageFigure( "13", new Point(15, 15)) );
    drawing.add( new ImageFigure( "21", new Point(20, 20)) );
    drawing.add( new ImageFigure( "22", new Point(25, 25)) );
    drawing.add( new ImageFigure( "23", new Point(30, 30)) );
    drawing.add( new ImageFigure( "31", new Point(35, 35)) );
    drawing.add( new ImageFigure( "32", new Point(40, 40)) );
    drawing.add( new ImageFigure( "33", new Point(45, 45)) );
  }
}

class PuzzleFactory implements Factory {

  public DrawingView createDrawingView( DrawingEditor editor ) {
    DrawingView view =
      new StdViewWithBackground(editor, "au-seal-large");
    return view;
  }
```

```
  public Drawing createDrawing( DrawingEditor editor ) {
    return new StandardDrawing();
  }

  public JTextField createStatusField( DrawingEditor editor ) {
    return null;
  }
}
```

30.1.1 Code Outline

In the main method I instantiate a **DrawingEditor**. The editor is both the main window application (a JFrame in Java Swing) as well as a "central storage" of references to the central objects in MiniDraw. MiniDraw comes with a concrete implementation of the **DrawingEditor** role that I can use directly: MiniDrawApplication. Its constructor takes two parameters: a window title, and an instance of an ABSTRACT FACTORY. Thus MiniDraw uses the same abstract factory technique for configuring as did the pay station. As I will explain in a minute it is the factory that defines the background image: the University of Aarhus' seal in wrong colors.

Next, the editor is opened (open), a tool is selected (setTool), and nine **Figure**s are added to the editors Drawing. Starting backwards, Figures are MiniDraw's abstraction for some graphical element that is shown in the window. Figures may be added, removed, moved, and in other ways manipulated by the user or under program control. Again, MiniDraw comes with a standard implementation, ImageFigure, that is a figures whose graphical appearance is defined by a GIF image file. MiniDraw automatically loads the bit maps of the GIF files during startup if a few rules are obeyed (the details are explained in sidebar 30.1). The parameters of the ImageFigure constructor define the name of the GIF image (I have named them "11", "12", etc. You provide the GIF image file name without the ".gif" extension) as well as the (x,y) position of the figure. As each image figure is created, it is immediately added to the editor's drawing (add). The Drawing is the collection of all figures—creating a figure is not enough, you have to add it to the drawing. Once added to the drawing, it will show in the window.

Two things remain to be explained: the factory and the tool.

The idea of a **Tool** to manipulate figures in a 2-D drawing application is well established nowadays. Most paint programs have a toolbox where the user can select various tools that manipulate the drawing area in various ways: add a rectangle, draw a line, move or resize figures, etc. MiniDraw uses the same idea and defines a **Tool** role that developers may implement to provide just the kind of manipulation they want. In the puzzle application I simply tell the editor to use a SelectionTool. This tool is defined by MiniDraw itself and provides move and selection behavior: if you click on a figure (a puzzle piece) you can move it to another position; if you hold down the shift key you can click and select multiple figures; and if you click outside a figure you can select multiple figures by rubber-band selecting them. If several figures are selected, they are highlighted with a red line and they all move as a unit.

The factory must define the concrete implementations that MiniDraw uses to maintain the set of figures, the **Drawing**, as well as display them, the **DrawingView**, and an optional status text field. In our simple case, I do not want a status field so I just return null, and I want to use the standard implementation of the **Drawing** role, StandardDrawing, that is part of the MiniDraw distribution. For the **DrawingView** role, I choose an implementation that draws a background image, the StdViewWithBackground. Just as for the ImageFigure, I can simply provide the StdViewWithBackground with the GIF image file name as parameter. Just as for the images of the puzzle pieces, the "au-logo" GIF file is loaded automatically by MiniDraw.

Thus, by defining new images for figures, new tools, etc., I am able to reuse the MiniDraw behavior to quickly make two dimensional graphics, direct-manipulation, graphical user interfaces. MiniDraw is small and provides only a small set of roles that can be defined by its developers restricting its applicability to a subset of all possible graphical user interfaces: you will not use MiniDraw to make dialogs nor three dimensional games, but it is feasible to use for instance for board and card game user interfaces.

☞ Find the puzzle application in folder *chapter/minidraw-demo* and try it out. Try to select two puzzle pieces and move them as a group.

30.2 A Rectangle Drawing Application

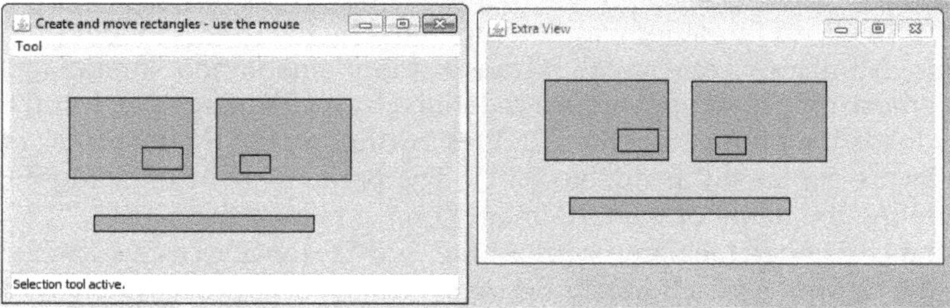

Figure 30.2: MiniDraw "Rect" application.

This application is somewhat more complex and utilizes more variability points in MiniDraw. You can see a screen shot in Figure 30.2, where I have drawn a set of rectangles. In the Rect application, you may alter between using two tools (available in the menu), one that creates green rectangles, and the SelectionTool that allows moving the rectangles. Below you will see the code of the main method to configure and instantiate MiniDraw for this application.

Fragment: chapter/minidraw-demo/test/rect/ShowRectangle.java

```
public static void main(String[] args) {
  Factory f = new EmptyCanvasFactory();
  DrawingEditor editor =
    new MiniDrawApplication( "Create and move rectangles "+
                             "- use the mouse", f );
  Tool
    rectangleDrawTool = new RectangleTool(editor),
    selectionTool = new SelectionTool(editor);
  addToolSelectMenusToWindow( editor,
                              rectangleDrawTool,
```

```
11                                     selectionTool );
12     editor.open();
13
14     editor.setTool( rectangleDrawTool );
15     editor.showStatus( "MiniDraw version: "+DrawingEditor.VERSION );
16
17     // create second view
18     JFrame newWindow = new JFrame("Extra View");
19     newWindow.setLocation( 620, 20 );
20     newWindow.setDefaultCloseOperation(JFrame.EXIT_ON_CLOSE);
21
22     DrawingView extraView = f.createDrawingView(editor);
23     JPanel panel = (JPanel) extraView;
24     newWindow.getContentPane().add(panel);
25     newWindow.pack();
26     newWindow.setVisible(true);
```

As you see, the template for configuring MiniDraw is the same: instantiate the drawing editor with an appropriate factory, open it, and set the tool. This application, however, demonstrates three new features. First, it defines a new class, RectangleFigure, that plays the **Figure** role (not shown in the listing). Instances of these are the visible, green, rectangles on the drawing. Second, it defines a new tool, RectangleTool, where mouse events are interpreted as defining a new rectangle for the user to draw (a tool of this type is declared in line 7, and the editor configured to use it in line 14). Finally, a second JFrame is created and the factory requested for another instance of a **DrawingView** which is then inserted in the JFrame (lines 17–25); thereby you get two views of the **Drawing** that are kept synchronized—you may even draw rectangles in either of them.

☞ Review the entire source code for the rectangle application to see how the RectangleFigure and RectangleTool are defined.

30.3 A Marker Application

The final example of an application shows a white figure with the Aarhus University seal and two "marker" figures, a blue and an orange arrow, see Figure 30.3. When you move the seal figure with the mouse, the two markers move along the horizontal and vertical axes respectively, and ensure that they always point to the middle of the seal figure.

The marker figures utilize the FigureChangeListener behavior of MiniDraw's figures. That is, any object may register as an observer of change events from a figure, and these are broadcast every time a figure changes state, typically when it is moved.

☞ Review the marker application code to see how the observer protocol is implemented.

Exercise 30.1: There is no special figure class that implements an arrow that moves along when the seal is moved. Instead it is implemented by a DECORATOR pattern. Argue what benefits it has.

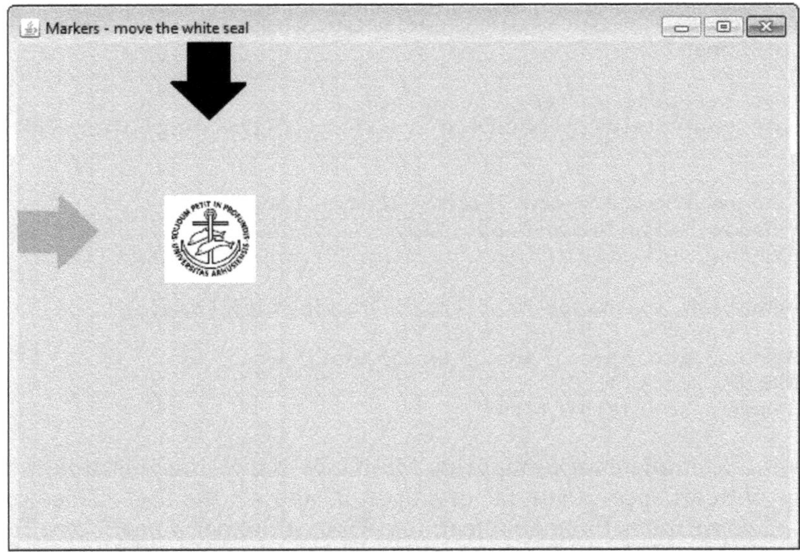

Figure 30.3: MiniDraw Marker application.

30.4 MiniDraw History

MiniDraw is largely a scaled down version of the JHotDraw framework that was developed in the 1990s by Thomas Eggenschwiler and Erich Gamma. JHotDraw again is inspired by HotDraw and ET++. HotDraw is a drawing framework for Smalltalk. It was originally developed by Kent Beck and Ward Cunningham. ET++ is a comprehensive and portable application framework and class library for C++. ET++ was developed by Andre Weinand and Erich Gamma.

☞ Find resources on the internet on JHotDraw and HotDraw.

JHotDraw is called a 2-D semantic graphics editor and has been used to make simple UML class diagram editors and similar diagram editors. It is, however, not that good at handling image graphics. MiniDraw has removed a great deal of the behavior that is not essential to board game user interfaces, and added behavior for aspects more relevant for board games. The basic rendering pipeline based upon the observer pattern has been maintained.

☞ MiniDraw is constantly being improved and extended so check the book's web site for the latest changes, documentation, and examples.

30.5 MiniDraw Design

MiniDraw is (like HotDraw and JHotDraw) based on the MVC architectural pattern that has been described in Chapter 29. Figure 30.4 shows an overview of the main

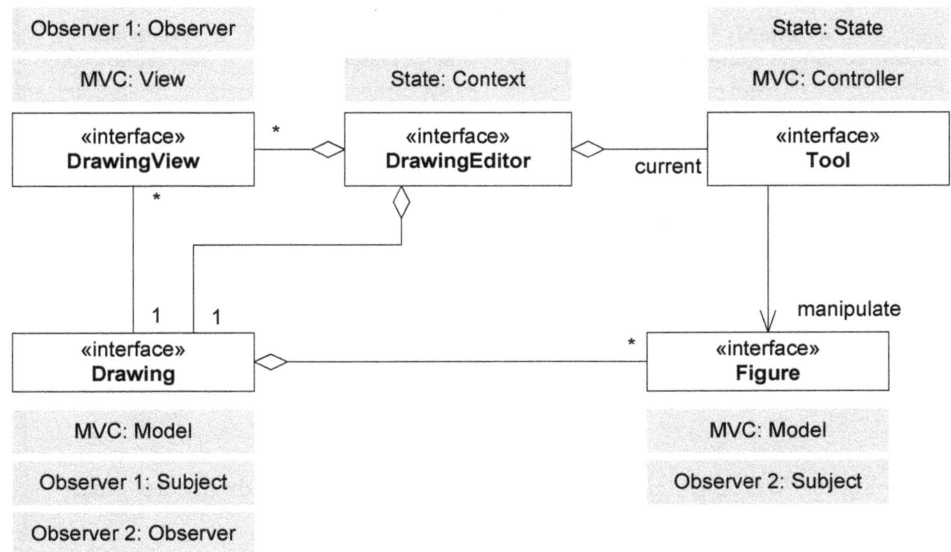

Figure 30.4: UML class diagram showing central Minidraw roles.

abstractions in the MiniDraw architecture in a role diagram. The use of MVC is not surprising as MiniDraw is a graphical user interface application. As is apparent from the figure, MiniDraw's architecture has a high density of design patterns. This is common for frameworks as a framework has to achieve a high degree of flexibility to allow customization. In the next sections, I will treat each of the four main parts of MiniDraw: the Drawing, the View, the Tool, and the Editor.

☞ You will find the complete source code for MiniDraw in folder *library/MiniDraw*.

30.5.1 Drawing (MVC: Model)

Looking a bit more in detail in the model part, it contains roles as outlined in Figure 30.5. The responsibilities of the **Drawing** are those of **Model** from MVC but with some additions to handle modifications of the set of figures and the selection:

Drawing

- Be a collection of figures.
- Allow figures to be added and removed.
- Maintain a temporary, possibly empty, subset of all figures, called a *selection*.
- Broadcast DrawingChangeEvents to all registered DrawingChangeListeners when any modification of the drawing happens.

Note that MiniDraw follows the tradition in Java Swing to use the term "listener" for the **observer** role. It also uses the *push-variant* protocol in that it passes an event

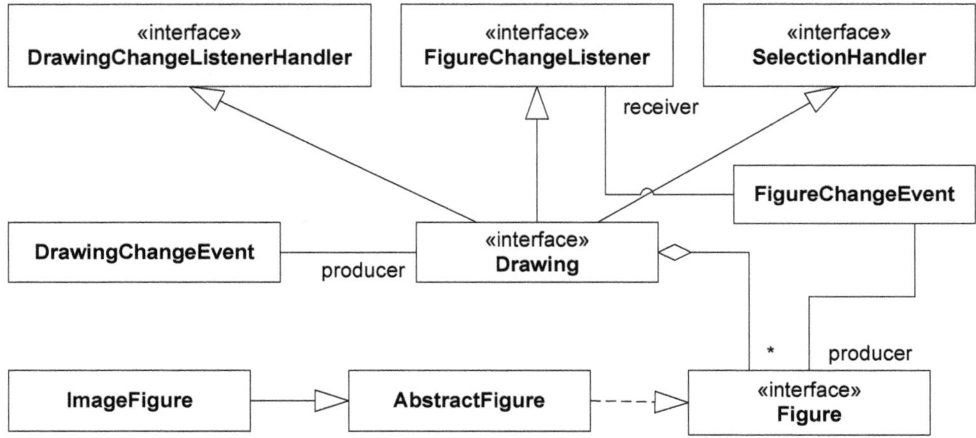

Figure 30.5: UML class diagram showing the roles in the model part.

object containing information about the model's state change as a parameter to the update method.

Some of these responsibilities are expressed in smaller and more fine-grained interfaces: the DrawingChangeListenersHandler defines the management of listeners (**Observers**) while the SelectionHandler defines the selection handling responsibility. There are implementations of these roles in the `minidraw.standard` package that any Drawing implementation can make good (re)use of. For instance, the default implementation, StandardDrawing, heavily uses the ② *favor object composition* principle as much of its behavior is simply delegated to small default implementations of the selection and observer handling, like the code fragments below show:

Fragment: library/MiniDraw/src/minidraw/standard/StandardDrawing.java

```
/**
 * Adds a listener for this drawing.
 */
public void addDrawingChangeListener(DrawingChangeListener
                                     listener) {
  listenerHandler.addDrawingChangeListener(listener);
}
[...]
/**
 * Get a list of all selected figures
 */
public List<Figure> selection() {
  return selectionHandler.selection();
}
```

The figure is responsible for:

Figure

- Knowing how to draw itself.
- Knowing its display box.
- Can be moved.
- Broadcast FigureChangeEvents to all registered FigureChangeListeners when any modification of the figure happens.

The *display box* is the smallest rectangle that completely covers the figure. It is used internally by MiniDraw's drawing system to make repainting efficient.

Note that a figure plays the **Subject** role in the OBSERVER pattern: when it is changed, it invokes the method figureChanged method on all FigureChangeListener instances that have registered themselves on the figure, as required by the OBSERVER pattern protocol.

As MiniDraw supports board games in particular where there are often graphical images used to represent checkers, dice, cards, and other game elements, there is an implementation, ImageFigure, that takes a GIF image name as constructor parameter. This was used in the puzzle application shown in the beginning of the chapter.

FigureChangeListener

- React appropriately when a figure is invalidated or changed.

MiniDraw has inherited JHotDraw's distinction between a figure being invalidated or being changed. Invalidation events are events for the graphics redrawing system (identify the parts of the raster image that need to be redrawn) whereas change events are events that mark some domain change of the figure (new size, new position, etc.).

FigureChangeEvent

- Know the source of the change: the figure that has changed.
- Know the rectangle that has been invalidated.

A simple way for a drawing to know that something has changed is thus to register itself as a FigureChangeListener on all the figures that it contains. Therefore Drawing is required to play the **FigureChangeListener** role.

The same observer protocol is used for the drawing:

DrawingChangeListener

- React appropriately when a drawing has changed.

The DrawingChangeListener contains two methods: drawingInvalidated and drawingRequestUpdate. It is only the latter that triggers a repaint operation.

DrawingChangeEvent

- Know the source of the change: the drawing that has changed.
- Know the rectangle that has been invalidated.

This means that Drawing plays **both** the **Subject** role and **Observer** role in the observer pattern at the same time. This emphasizes the point made earlier: design patterns define roles for objects to play, and one object may easily play several roles at the same time, here even from the same pattern.

Thus a typical movement of a figure will result in a number of interactions that resemble that shown in the sequence diagram shown in Figure 30.6. The sequence diagram only shows the first invalidation event being broadcast. For each figure modification two invalidate events (before and after the change) and one change event (after the change) are sent.

The change events can be used to connect figures in the sense that moving one will affect another, as was done in the marker application.

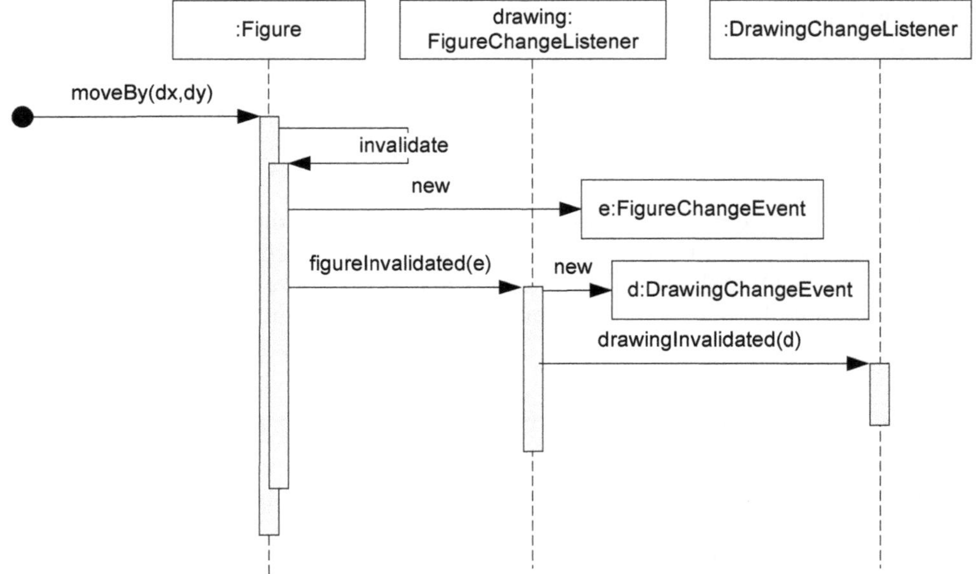

Figure 30.6: Sequence diagram over a figure's first invalidation event.

Exercise 30.2: If you look into the MiniDraw source code you will also find a CompositeFigure. Identify the roles, relations, and patterns involved between Figure and CompositeFigure.

30.5.2 View

The view part of the MVC pattern is rather simple, as shown in Figure 30.7. The central role is the **DrawingView**.

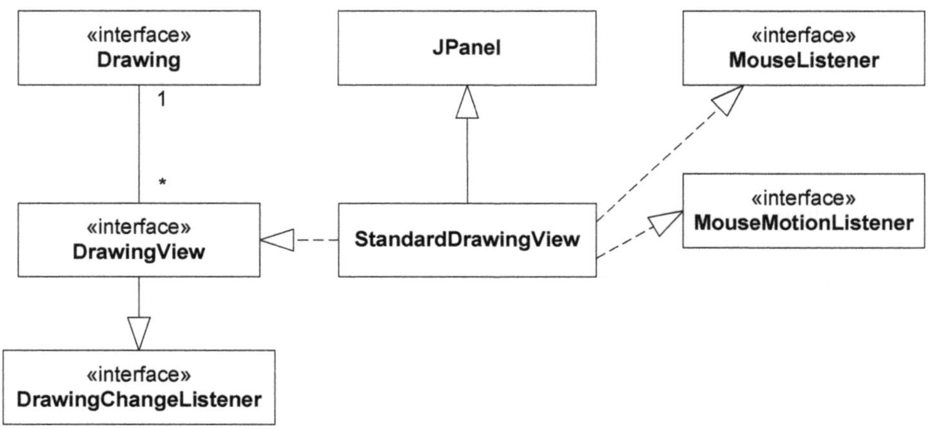

Figure 30.7: The View part of MiniDraw.

DrawingView

- Define four layers of graphics, drawn in order: background, drawing contents, selection highlights, overlay.
- Respond to change events from its associated Drawing and ensure redrawing.
- Forward all mouse and key events to the editor's associated tool.

DrawingView defines four layers of graphics: first the *background* graphics is drawn (like the university seal in the puzzle application), next the drawing's set of figures (the nine jigsaw pieces), next graphics that show selected figures (try to select several jigsaw pieces in the puzzle application, and a fine red line will be shown around the selected images), and finally static graphics overlay. The latter is not used in any of the demonstration applications.

The DrawingView acts as an observer of DrawingChangeEvent coming from its associated Drawing and must respond by redrawing the graphics appropriately.

The standard implementation, StandardDrawingView, is an example of a class that implements multiple roles to combine the MiniDraw and the Java Swing GUI toolkit frameworks. It does so by subclassing a JPanel and therefore has all the characteristics of a Java panel: it draws graphics and receives mouse and keyboard events. At the same time it plays the **DrawingView** role and thus forward user events to the tool and draws the content of the drawing.

StandardDrawingView defines a light gray background while the subclass StdViewWithBackground uses an image for the background layer whose name you specify in the constructor, as demonstrated by the jigsaw puzzle application.

30.5.3 Tool

The **Tool** is the **Controller** role of the MVC, see Figure 30.8. As mentioned above all mouse and key events from the view is forwarded to the tool that is presently active in the editor. The Tool is an example of the STATE pattern: the state of the MiniDraw editor is determined by the selected tool.

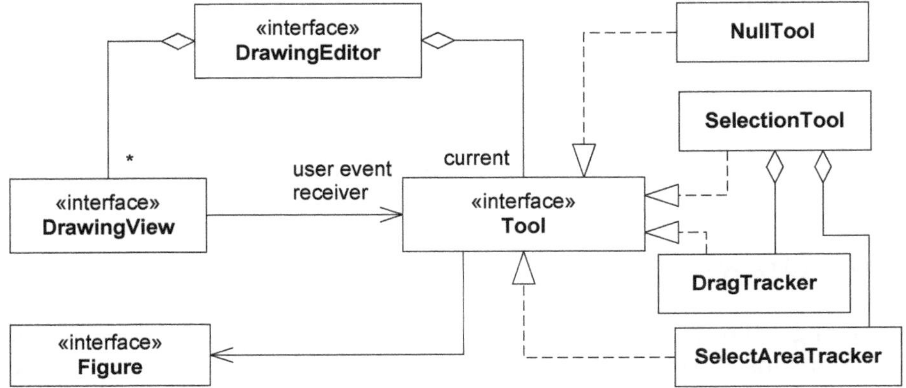

Figure 30.8: The Tool part of MiniDraw.

Tool

- Receive mouse events (mouse down, up, drag, etc.) and key events.
- Define some kind of manipulation of the contents of the Drawing or other changes relevant for the application.

MiniDraw's standard editor defaults to the NullTool that simply does nothing (a NULL OBJECT). The SelectionTool provides behavior similar to what is known from many drawing applications: you can drag a figure or a selection of figures, or you can select figures by drawing a rubber-band spanning them. SelectionTool is compositionally implemented so the "drag-a-figure" behavior is itself a tool, DragTracker, and the rubber-banding is a tool, SelectAreaTracker.

As an example Figure 30.9 shows how a figure is moved: the mouse down event of the DragTracker finds the figure to be moved and mouse drag events invoke the figure's moveBy method. The actual sequence is a bit more complex, as selection tool and drag tracker tool collaborate to find the figure. The general idea, however, is correct.

> **Exercise 30.3:** Review the MiniDraw SelectionTool code to see the complete interaction when a figure is selected and moved.

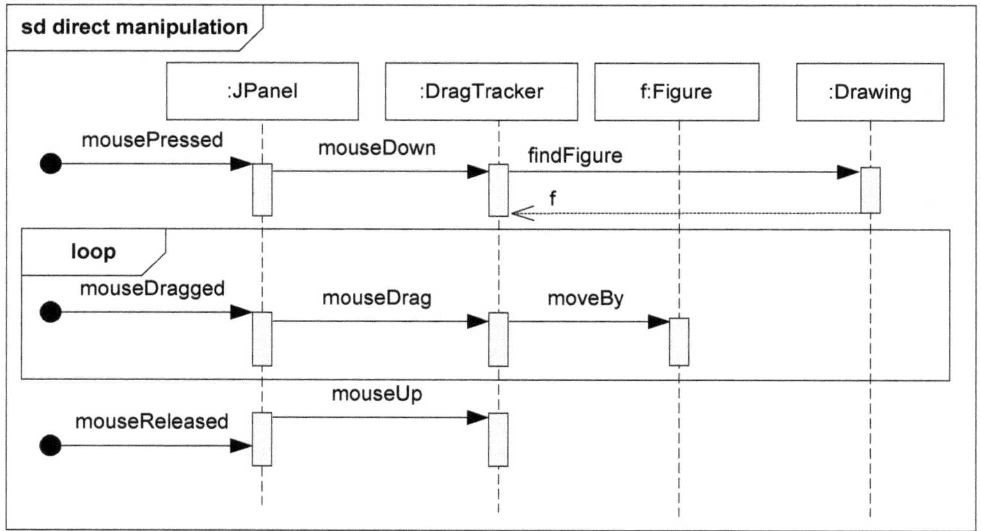

Figure 30.9: Moving a figure

30.5.4 DrawingEditor

The drawing editor is the "main" class of a minidraw application and is thus responsible for instantiating all relevant parts of a minidraw application as well as open a visible window to allow users to interact with it. As shown in Figure 30.10, the standard implementation MiniDrawApplication uses an instance of an ABSTRACT FACTORY for instantiating these parts. It subclasses JFrame to provide the standard

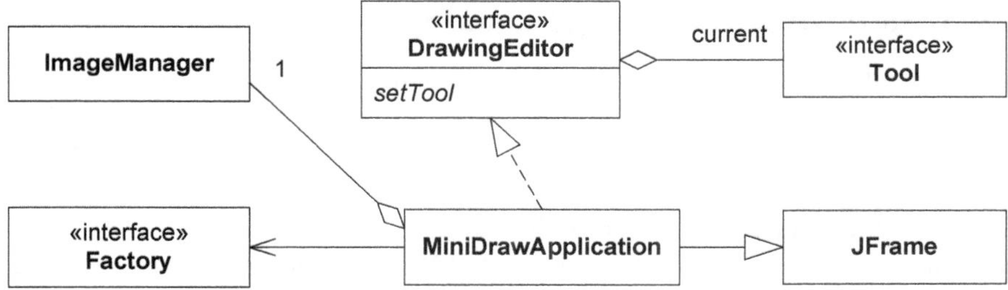

Figure 30.10: The Editor part of MiniDraw.

Swing context of a graphical application. Finally, it creates an ImageManager that acts as a "database" of GIF images; the image manager automatically loads a set of images as outline in sidebar 30.1.

DrawingEditor

- Main class of a minidraw application, that is the editor must instantiate all parts of the application.
- Opens a window to make a visible application.
- Acts as central access point for the various parts of MiniDraw.
- Allows changing the active tool.
- Allows displaying a message in the status bar.

The drawing editor acts as the central *"octopus"* in the middle, coordinating the collaboration between the different roles: drawing, view, and (active) tool. Thus, the **View** does not cache the object reference to the active tool; instead it requests the active tool from the editor every time it needs it. This ensures that it always gets the active tool as defined by the editor, as shown in line 5 below.

Fragment: library/MiniDraw/src/minidraw/standard/StandardDrawingView.java

```
1   public void mousePressed(MouseEvent e) {
2     requestFocus();
3     Point p = constrainPoint(new Point(e.getX(), e.getY()));
4     fLastClick = new Point(e.getX(), e.getY());
5     editor.tool().mouseDown(e, p.x, p.y);
6     checkDamage();
7   }
```

30.6 MiniDraw Variability Points

The main variability points of MiniDraw are:

- Images. As described in sidebar 30.1 MiniDraw automatically loads images from a special folder. By storing image files in this folder a MiniDraw application can easily render backgrounds and use images as figures. In the projects in part 9, there are special graphics to make the graphical user interface for a backgammon board game and a strategy game.

Sidebar 30.1: MiniDraw Image Loading

Minidraw automatically loads GIF files that are stored in a folder named *resource* in the root folder of your MiniDraw application. A special Ant target, `copy-resource`, in the build description ensures that the relevant files are copied into the proper position in the build tree.

When MiniDraw starts, all GIF files in the directory are automatically read into a "database" object in MiniDraw, the ImageManager. So, when you construct an ImageFigure you can retrieve these preloaded bit maps from the image manager simply by providing the name of the file (without the ".gif" extension) as parameter to the constructor, as this line of code from the marker application demonstrates.

```
Figure logo = new ImageFigure( "au-seal-small",
                               new Point(200, 200));
```

- Tools. By telling the editor which tool to use, MiniDraw can be customized to handle figures in different ways or do other operations.
- Figures. You may define your own figures that do their own graphical rendering.
- Views. You may reconfigure MiniDraw to use your own type of **DrawingView** that can provide special rendering. One specialization is provided, namely one that uses an image as the background for showing the figures. Naturally this is useful for board games where the image can represent the game board, like a chess board or the like.
- Drawing. You may reconfigure MiniDraw with your own collection implementation to store and remove figures. This is useful to ensure that the set of figures accurately mimics some domain abstraction. For instance that the set of chess piece images always match that of the underlying chess game implementation: if a piece is taken and removed from the game, then the corresponding figure image must also be removed from the drawing.
- Observer on Figure state changes. You can make figures (or other objects) listen to state changes in figures. The original JHotDraw denoted this *semantic constraints* between figures, like shown in the marker application where the marker figures are constrained to follow the seal.

30.7 Summary of Key Concepts

MiniDraw illustrates two things. First, it is an example of a *framework* which is a highly flexible software system customizable in a number of different ways. MiniDraw is especially suited to support the graphical aspects of board games and the like that let users manipulate two dimensional graphical objects. Second, its design is an example of compositional design with a high density of patterns.

The underlying architectural pattern is MVC. MiniDraw illustrates that MVC does not usually simply define three classes: here each are actually small subsystems with their own internal structure. Each subsystem by itself is programmed with focus on the principles of flexible design: ① program to an interface and ② favor object composition, and makes use of several design patterns.

MiniDraw has variability points that allow it to be customized with regards to the figures to show, the set of images to load, the tools that affect the figures, the type of view and drawing to use, and the ability to make objects observe figure state changes.

30.8 Selected Solutions

Discussion of Exercise 30.1:

The advantage of using a DECORATOR is that any figure can become a marker figure that tracks another figure. Thus we have not made a tight coupling to the specific kind of figure that may act as a marker.

30.9 Review Questions

What kind of applications can you make with the MiniDraw framework? What is the central architectural pattern in the MiniDraw design? Describe some of the central abstractions in each subsystem. Mention some of the variability points of MiniDraw and explain the mechanisms used to customize them.

30.10 Further Exercises

Exercise 30.4:

The marker application in Section 30.3 demonstrates how one figure can listen to change events from another figure and update its own position accordingly. An application where this behavior is desirable is an UML class diagram editor in which association and generalization lines and arrows must always connect the associated class boxes. In this exercise you are asked to implement similar behavior.

1. Sketch a design for a MiniDraw application that displays two images (for instance the seal from the marker application) that are always connected by a line figure. No matter how the images are moved, the connecting line must update itself to keep the images connected. Use a sequence diagram to outline the line update and redraw protocol.
2. Implement your design in MiniDraw.

Exercise 30.5:

Make a MiniDraw drawing application.

1. Implement figures to represent ovals, straight lines, and triangles.

2. Implement tools to create the above figures.
3. Implement a resize tool: when active any figure is resized if it is clicked and the mouse moved while holding down the shift key.

Exercise 30.6:

The puzzle application does not work quite as people expect it because the puzzle pieces can be put anywhere and it is thus very difficult to make each piece match correctly with its neighbors.

1. Develop a "puzzle piece" tool that allows moving the puzzle pieces but when dropped the are moved so they align correctly with the spaces of the 3×3 grid.

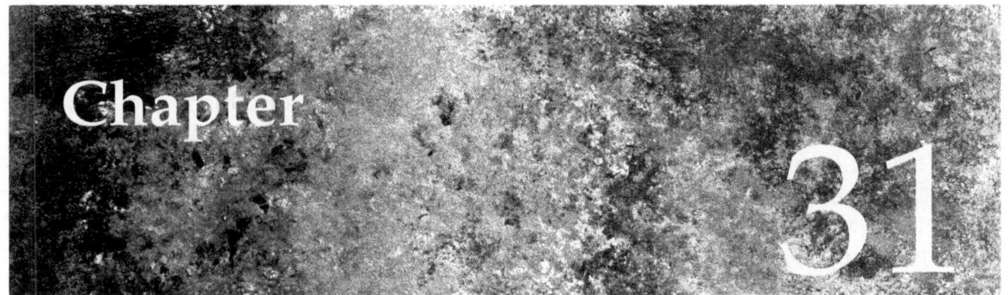

Template Method

Learning Objectives

The learning objective is the TEMPLATE METHOD. This pattern is in this learning iteration of the book because it is really the heart of object-oriented frameworks. TEMPLATE METHOD should pose no surprises as you have already seen and hopefully implemented dozens of template methods already. The primary focus is thus to define the terminology of the pattern: the roles and the structure; as well as introduce the terms used for the polymorphic and compositional variants of the pattern.

31.1 The Problem

An algorithm is a series of steps of computations with the aim of producing a result. For instance in the pay station I have the (very simple) algorithm defined to receive payment. In pseudo-code, this algorithm is

```
validate it is a proper coin
add coin value to sum of payment
calculate minutes of parking this sum entitles to
```

Needless to say, I do have to validate the coin *before* I add it to the sum, and I *do* have to calculate the sum before it makes sense to calculate the parking time. This is a general aspect of most algorithms so obvious that we seldom think about it: it defines a strict sequence of steps that cannot be altered as it would make the algorithm incorrect.

Sometimes, however, we would like to tweak the behavior of the individual steps while retaining the overall structure of the algorithm. Looking back at the STRATEGY chapter, this was actually what the whole chapter was about. The first two steps of the payment algorithm was fixed but the *calculate minutes* behavior I wanted in two different variants.

31.2 The Template Method Pattern

The STRATEGY chapter did a very thorough analysis of this problem and I will not repeat it here. It turns out that the polymorphic solution analyzed in that chapter is the classic formulation of the TEMPLATE METHOD design pattern (design pattern box 31.1, page 366) as described by Gamma et al. The intent is stated:

> *Define the skeleton of an algorithm in an operation, deferring some steps to subclasses. Template Method lets subclasses redefine certain steps of an algorithm without changing the algorithm's structure.*

That is, it is explicitly defined to be a class-subclass structure that is used to tweak behavior of a step. At the code level, it looks something like

```
abstract class AbstractClass {
  public void templateMethod() {
    [fixed code part 1]
    step1();
    [fixed code part 2]
    step2();
    [fixed code part 3]
  }
  protected abstract void step1();
  protected abstract void step2();
}
class ConcreteClass extends AbstractClass() {
  protected void step1() {
    [step 1 specific behavior]
  }
  protected void step2() {
    [step 2 specific behavior]
  }
}
```

Thus the *template method* defines the invariant parts of the algorithm while abstract methods in subclasses define the specific behavior for the steps. These "step methods" are often called the *hook methods*.

Needless to say, the inheritance based approach for handling variability points has some severe limitations. As analyzed in Chapter 17, *Multi-Dimensional Variance*, the polymorphic solution leads to a combinatorial explosion of subclasses if the steps may vary independently of each other. That is, if I want to have three variants of step1() and three of step2() and all combinations are feasible, I end up with nine subclasses of the template method class.

It is therefore natural to restate template method as a compositional design. The implementation should be obvious at this point.

```
class Class {
  private HookInterface1 delegate1; private HookInterface2 delegate2;
  public void setHook( HookInterface1 del1, HookInterface2 del2) {
    delegate1 = del1; delegate2 = del2;
  }
  public void templateMethod() {
    [fixed code part 1]
    delegate1.step1();
```

```
    [fixed code part 2]
    delegate2.step2();
    [fixed code part 3]
  }
}
interface HookInterface1 {
  public void step1();
}
interface HookInterface2 {
  public void step2();
}
class ConcreteHook1 implements HookInterface1() {
  public void step1() {
    [step 1 specific behavior]
  }
class ConcreteHook2 implements HookInterface2() {
  public void step2() {
    [step 2 specific behavior]
  }
}
```

They are both the TEMPLATE METHOD pattern but to distinguish between the two implementations, they must be classified as either *unification* or *separation*. These terms are defined by Pree (1999).

Definition: Unification

Both template and hook methods reside in the same class. The template method is concrete and invokes abstract hook methods that can be overridden in subclasses.

Definition: Separation

The template method is defined in one class and the hook methods are defined by one or several interfaces. The template method is concrete and delegates to implementations of the hook interface(s).

Having two different implementation strategies also means the intent must be redefined:

> *Define the skeleton of an algorithm in an operation, deferring some steps to subclasses or delegates. Template Method lets the behavior of certain steps of an algorithm be varied without changing the algorithm's structure.*

In TEMPLATE METHOD, the important roles are not really the classes nor interfaces, but the method abstractions. The **template method** is the method that implements the structure of the algorithms, defines the fixed steps, and calls the **hook methods** that encapsulate the behavior that may vary.

31.3 Review Questions

Describe the TEMPLATE METHOD pattern. What problem does it solve? What is its structure and what is the protocol? What roles and responsibilities are defined? What are the benefits and liabilities?

[31.1] Design Pattern: Template Method

Intent Define the skeleton of an algorithm in an operation, deferring some steps to subclasses or delegates. Template Method lets the behavior of certain steps of an algorithm be varied without changing the algorithm's structure.

Problem There is a need to have different behaviors of some steps of an algorithm but the algorithm's structure is otherwise fixed.

Solution Define the algorithm's structure and invariant behavior in a template method and let it call hook methods that encapsulate the steps with variable behavior. Hook methods may either be abstract methods in the same class as the template method, or they may be called on delegate object(s) implementing one or several interfaces defining the hook methods. The former variant is the *unification* variant, the latter the *separation* variant.

Structure:

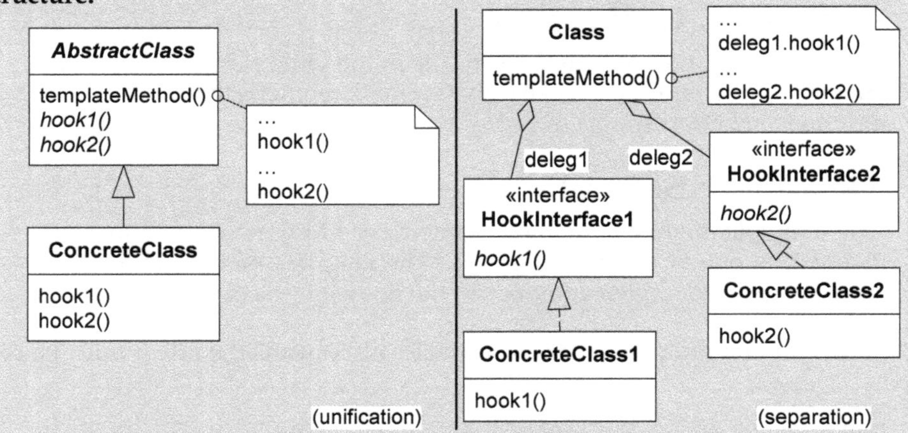

Roles The roles are method abstractions: the **template method** defines the algorithm structure and invariant behavior. **Hook methods** encapsulate variable behavior. The **HookInterface** interfaces define the method signatures of the hook methods.

Cost - Benefit The benefits are that the *algorithm template is reused* and thus avoids multiple maintenance; that the *behavior of individual steps, the hooks, may be changed*; and that *groups of hook methods may be varied independently* (separation variant only). The liability is *added complexity of the algorithm* as steps have to be encapsulated.

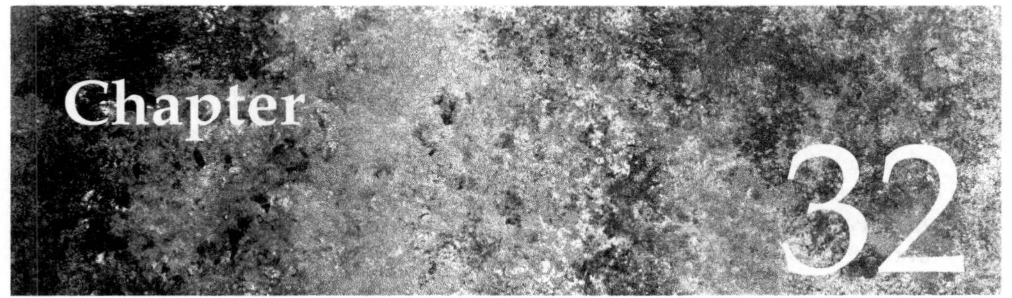

Framework Theory

Learning Objectives

The learning objective of this chapter is primarily to define the terminology associated with the concept of object-oriented *frameworks*, as the implementation techniques have already been accounted for. Thus, the discussion will take a more theoretical standpoint.

32.1 Framework Definitions

If you look up the term "framework" in a dictionary you will find definitions like *a basic conceptual structure* or *a skeletal or structural frame.* If we look to the software engineering community, a number of authors have presented definitions of their own.

- A framework is: a) a reusable design of an application or subsystem b) represented by a set of abstract classes and the way objects in these classes collaborate (Fraser et al. 1997).
- A framework is a set of classes that embodies an abstract design for solutions to a family of related problems (Johnson and Foote 1988).
- A framework is a set of cooperating classes that make up a reusable design for a specific class of software (Gamma et al. 1995, p. 26).
- A framework is the skeleton of an application that can be customized by an application developer (Fayad et al. 1999a, p. 3).
- A framework defines a high-level language with which applications within a domain are created through specialization (Pree 1999, p. 379).
- A framework is an architectural pattern that provides an extensible template for applications within a domain (Booch et al. 1999, p. 383).

32.2 Framework Characteristics

If we look closer at these definitions they use different terminology and they have different perspectives. For instance, they use various terms, like "skeleton", "architectural pattern", "design", "high-level language", for basically the same underlying concept. Regarding perspective, Gamma et al. define frameworks in terms of what it *is* whereas Fayad et al. and Pree define it in terms of what is can be *used for*. However, they all try to express the characteristics that identify a piece of software as a framework as opposed to an application, a subsystem, an algorithm, or a library. These characteristics are:

- *Skeleton / design / high-level language / template*: that is, the framework delivers application behavior at a high level of abstraction. This is much in line with the general definition of a framework as *a basic conceptual structure.*
- *Application / class of software / within a domain*: that is, a framework provides behavior in a well-defined domain.
- *Cooperating / collaborating classes*: that is, a framework defines the protocol between a set of well-defined components/objects. To use the framework you have to understand these interaction patterns and must program in accordance with them.
- *Customize / abstract classes / reusable / specialize*: that is, a framework is flexible so that you can tailor it to a concrete context, as long as this context lies within the domain of the framework.
- *Classes / implementation / skeleton*: that is, a framework is reuse of working code as well as reuse of design.

Given these characteristics of a framework I can now state that what started as a pay station *application* for a single customer, Alphatown, has evolved into a configurable pay station *framework*. The pay station system fulfills all the characteristics mentioned above: it is a *skeleton* within a particular *domain*, namely pay stations, and consists of *collaborating classes*, some of which are *customized* for a particular product variant. And it comes with *implementation* and thus embodies both design as well as code reuse.

Exercise 32.1: Given these characteristics, determine whether Java Swing is a framework.

32.3 Types of Users and Developers

In normal software development, we classify stake holders as *developers* and *users*. Developers they, well, develop the software, hopefully listening to the opinion of the users which are the people that in the end will use the software to get their work done efficiently.

With regards to framework development, there are actually three types of stakeholders: *framework developers*, *application developers*, and *users*. The framework developers are the people that design and code the framework while the application developers are the programmers that customizes the framework to the particular needs of the users. Thus one can say that the application developers are actually the "users" of the framework. The application developers are the customers that framework developers must listen to in order to produce a good framework that will make them work efficiently.

Application developers on the other hand have to decide whether to use a framework or not. The things to consider are:

- the framework's domain must be sufficiently close to the domain/problem that the application developers are trying to address.
- the framework must be sufficiently flexible so the application developers can adopt it to the specific context. If the framework is lacking ways to customize it in places where the application developer needs to adjust the provided functionality then the framework is of course less suited or inappropriate for the problem at hand.
- the framework must deliver a design, functionality, and domain knowledge that otherwise is very expensive to acquire. This speaks in favor of frameworks of some complexity and size.
- the framework implementation must be reliable. Reusing a framework that is full of defects is definitely only "reused" once.

However if these properties are met, then a major development investment is saved: a good framework provides a quality design and reliable implementation of complex functionality. Thus there is a saving both in immediate development time due to the reuse as well as a saving in the following maintenance period as the framework code is thoroughly tested and less defects are expected to appear.

If the application developers have adopted a certain framework then a contract must be followed. Successful use relies on that the application developers:

- understand the protocols between the framework and the customization code they have to provide.
- understand the aspects that can (and cannot) be customized as well as the concrete techniques used for the customization.

If the framework's interaction patterns are not understood then the application developers are in big trouble, and the result is that developers "fight" the framework rather than follow its guidelines. This leads to bulky, error prone, and unstable code. In the early days of event-driven programming for window and mouse based applications, many programmers that were used to programming console-based applications had great difficulties in understanding the new guidelines leading to unreliable and slow applications.

Thus, a framework requires a substantial initial investment in training that should not be overlooked. Consider, for example, the number of books published about Swing, Enterprise JavaBeans, and other big frameworks.

32.4 Frozen and Hot Spots

A framework consists of *frozen spots* and *hot spots*, a terminology introduced by Pree (1994). The frozen and hot spots are the parts of the framework code that is fixed or variable.

> Definition: **Frozen spot**
>
> A part of framework code that cannot be altered and defines the basic design and the object protocols in the final application.

> Definition: **Hot spot**
>
> A clearly defined part of the framework in which specialization code can alter or add behavior to the final application.

Thus, the challenge for the framework designers is both to identify the overall architecture, the frozen parts, as well as define which parts that are allowed to be customizable, the hot parts. The latter of course involves defining the concrete programming techniques to allow application developers to insert their code to add or alter behavior.

The frozen term is good because it points to an important property of frameworks:

Key Point: Frameworks are not customized by code modification

A framework is a closed, blackbox, software component in which the source code must not be altered even if it is accessible. Customization must only take place through providing behavior in the hot spots by those mechanisms laid out by the framework developers.

Usually, frameworks are delivered as sealed components, for instance in the form of a binary library. As an example, MiniDraw is a Java jar file and customization is only done by defining new tools, putting image files in the right folder, and/or configuring the factory with proper implementations of MiniDraw's roles. Even though you can find the MiniDraw source code on the website and thus alter it, this is not the proper way to use it: remember *change by addition, not by modification.*

The term "hotspot" is not a very precise term. Other terms you may see is **hook method** or simply hooks, or **variability point**. The hook metaphor is a good one—think of the framework as "software with some hooks", you can then attach your own code to the hooks to alter the behavior of the framework. Many frameworks come with standard implementations for most or all of the hooks, so you only need to fill out a few to get something going. However, as I have used the term *variability point* during most of the book I will generally stick to it.

I will use the term **framework code** to identify the code that defines the framework whereas I use the term **application code** for the code that defines the specialization of the variability points and the "boilerplate" code for initializing the framework. Often the application code also contains code that is not related to the framework: as an example consider using MiniDraw to make a small UML class diagram editor that could generate Java classes from the class diagrams. The application code would have to define both MiniDraw customizations such as UML class box figures etc., as well as the code to generate Java classes.

32.5 Defining Variability Points

Given that framework code cannot be altered and an application developer has to customize it, he has to have mechanisms to "glue" his code into the frameworks variability points. The underlying techniques for object-oriented software have already been thoroughly treated in this book: the relation between frozen and hot spots and the TEMPLATE METHOD should be obvious. The template method defines the algorithm's structure as well as the fixed behavior, that is the frozen part, while hook methods are called that may add or alter behavior, the hot parts. Thus the most common way of defining variability points are either by subclassing or by delegation.

The next issue is how to tell the framework which concrete instances to use? One thing is to implement a HookInterface, the next thing is to give the framework the object reference to an instance of the implementing class. The answer is basically the *dependency injection* principle: let the client objects (those in the application) establish the dependencies between framework objects and objects implementing the variability points.

Key Point: Frameworks must use dependency injection

Framework objects cannot themselves instantiate objects that define variability points, these have to be instantiated by the application code and injected into the framework.

A more hands-on rule is that framework code must never contain a new statement on classes that have hot spot methods defined.

Exercise 32.2: List the techniques that the MiniDraw example applications used to inject dependencies to the application specific objects. Discuss them in light of the key point above.

Frameworks present a range of possibilities for defining the hot spot objects.

- *Existing concrete classes.* The framework comes along with a (large) number of predefined classes and your job is to compose these into something sensible. AWT and Swing are examples where you compose new graphical user interfaces from predefined components.
- *Subclassing an abstract class:* the framework contains abstract classes so most of a high quality implementation is already given, leaving you with the task of filling out the last details.
- *Implementing an interface:* the framework contains an interface, giving the application developer the opportunity to exercise full control over the hot spots.

The list above is of course also a spectrum of ease and speed versus control. It is easy and fast to configure a framework purely by injecting dependencies to the proper components but you have only a limited set of options. In the opposite end of the spectrum you can develop all the details in an object that simply implements a framework interface but this is of course much slower and there is a larger potential of defects. The latter also require you to have an intimate understanding of the framework protocol: in which order are which methods called and what are the pre and post conditions that must be satisfied?

This spectrum also describes a best strategy for defining variability point classes in a framework.

> **Key Point: Frameworks should support the spectrum from no implementation (interface) over partial (abstract) to full (concrete) implementation for variability points**
>
> *A framework provides the optimal range of possibilities for the application developer if all variability points are declared in interfaces, if these interfaces are partially implemented by abstract classes providing "common case" behavior, and if a set of concrete classes for common usages is provided.*

In this way the application developer has the full range of possibilities at his disposal.

> **Exercise 32.3:** Review the MiniDraw framework code and find examples of MiniDraw following the above guideline.

> **Exercise 32.4:** Analyze to what degree Swing graphical component classes obey the key point above.

It should be mentioned that of course *parameterization* can also be used to change framework behavior. Simple parameterization is for instance to set some parameters in a framework call. Advanced parameters can be given in property files or XML files whose format the framework defines.

Frameworks is not purely an object-oriented construct. At the machine language level, polymorphic method invocation is simply jumps via a jump table, so you can define frameworks in assembler or procedural languages using function pointers.

32.6 Inversion of Control

A prominent feature of frameworks is that they define the flow of control in the resulting application. This is also covered by some of the framework definitions mentioned that speak of "collaborating classes". The instances in the running framework call each other in predefined ways and occasionally "sneak out" into your code when they invoke a hotspot method. This is called the principle of **inversion of control**: the framework defines the flow of control, not you. A more colorful rephrasing is "the Hollywood principle," that is, "Don't call us, we'll call you." As an example, once you call `open()` on the MiniDraw editor, it does all the processing of mouse events and calls your tool and draws your images at the appropriate times.

> **Exercise 32.5:** Relate the inversion of control property to the use of TEMPLATE METHOD in frameworks.

Thus, frameworks are reusable pieces of code that are very different from traditional libraries. This is shown in Figure 32.1. A traditional library is shown on the left and an application reusing code from the library maintains the overall control during execution; occasionally calling a method in the class library. An example of a library in Java is *java.lang.Math*: it contains a lot of code to calculate cosine, logarithms, etc., but it does not dictate the flow of control in your application. In a framework, shown on the right, the overall control during execution remains in the framework that occasionally calls a method in some application specific code via a hotspot.

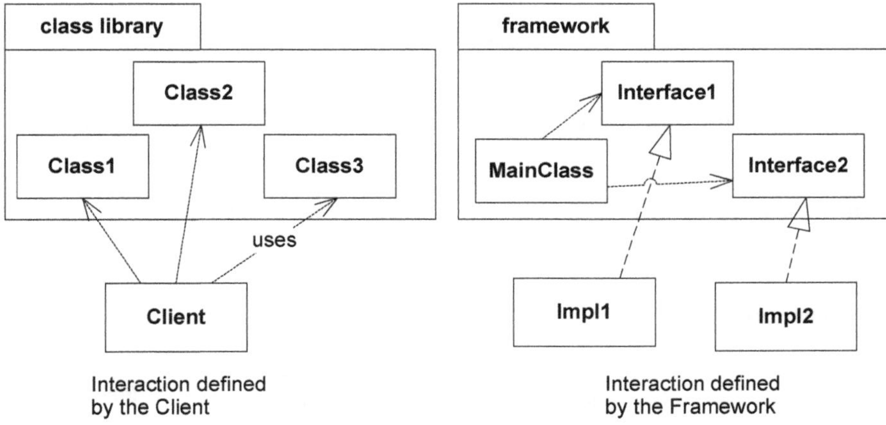

Figure 32.1: Inversion of control in frameworks.

32.7 Framework Composition

Frameworks are a way of reusing software and thus speed up development and save a lot of money at the same time. In many large scale applications it is therefore interesting to use two or more frameworks as many types of domains may be covered in a single system. For instance it may be obvious to reuse a graphical framework, a framework for distributed objects, a framework to handle transactions, etc.

If the frameworks are based upon subclassing of abstract classes then application developers will run into a **framework composition problem**. This is illustrated in Figure 32.2. We are faced with the problem that in the same class we must redefine hotspots from *two* different classes, one from each framework, but both frameworks define the classes as abstract. In Java we have no way of multiple inheriting from two abstract classes. In this situation we are quite stuck and have to either forget about using both frameworks or come up with some very clumsy adaptation code.

The situation could have been avoided if the framework developers had followed the ① *program to an interface* principles as shown in Figure 32.3. Here interfaces have been used and we have no problem in Java as we can inherit all the contracts defined by the interfaces. The figure also shows that the customization class can itself inherit from an application specific class, a thing that was also ruled out in the previous figure. This technique is employed to compose MiniDraw with Swing as explained in Section 30.5.2. Note that the concrete class can still reuse functionality provided by

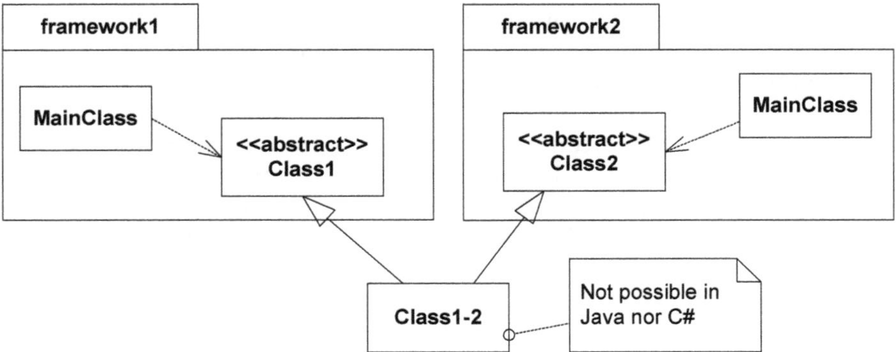

Figure 32.2: Composition problems in inheritance based frameworks.

the frameworks by delegating to instances defined therein, as is shown by Class1-2 delegating requests to Class1 from framework 1.

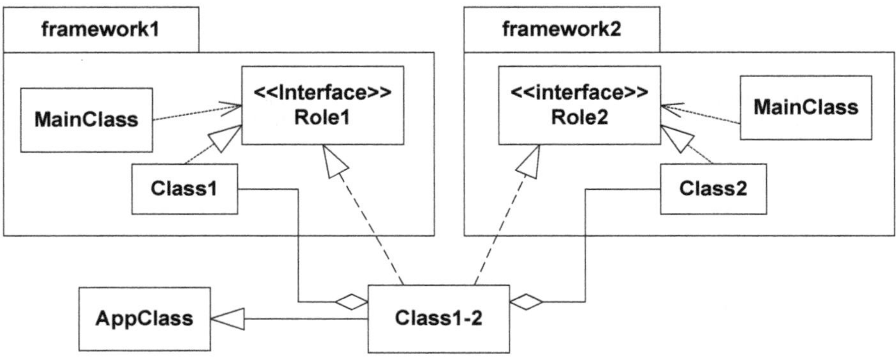

Figure 32.3: Avoiding the composition problem in delegation based frameworks.

Some frameworks pose additional problem of composition. Some frameworks insist on having the user event processing loop: Java Swing is an obvious example. If two frameworks both insist on having the event processing loop then combining them becomes highly problematic. Similar problems may occur if one framework is multi-threaded by design and the other inherently single-threaded. These problems can be very tricky to tackle and lead to the glue code being very difficult to overview and understand.

32.8 Software Reuse

The reason that frameworks are interesting is that it is one way of *reusing* software. Software reuse is the appealing idea of using existing software instead of writing it from scratch. This idea is of course attractive but the seemingly obvious potential has turned out to be rather complex to realize in practice.

Sidebar 32.1: MiniDraw Reuse Numbers

MiniDraw is approximately 1,600 lines of code (LOC) including comments, and the jar file about 30KB. The numbers for the three demonstration applications are: puzzle 55 LOC, rect 200 LOC, and marker 125 LOC. Thus if I calculate the percentage of lines of code that is reused in the final applications I get:

Puzzle: 97 %   Rect: 89 %   Marker: 93 %

Object-oriented frameworks have, however, gained quite some success in delivering the promise of software reuse. You can find some numbers on MiniDraw in sidebar 32.1. High reuse is primarily possible because A) a framework limits its functionality to a certain domain and B) it dictates the way it should be tailored. This allows the developers of the framework to cope with the problems that traditionally hinder software reuse, namely that the reusable software component does not fit the context of the software that it is going to be reused in. For frameworks, this problem is solved simply by the framework developers defining the context a priori.

Reuse can appear at many different levels in a software development project, for instance one may reuse code (by copy and paste, by using libraries of code made earlier), or one may reuse design (reusing a good solution for a known problem, like algorithms or design patterns). Frameworks are quite unique in this respect.

Key Point: Framework reuse is reuse of both design and code

A framework is a tangible unit of software, thus it is code reuse. However, due to the inversion of control property, it also defines the flow of control, object protocols, and clearly defines the variability points, and thus bundles a quality design as well.

A framework dictates how you must design your program—and if you do not follow these guidelines you are in a big mess. That is, the framework is reuse of a design—a way to structure a particular type of application or system. For instance Java AWT and Swing define a rigid way of structuring a graphical application: you must create a Frame instance, register listeners for window close events, add graphical components, etc. Thus you cannot structure a Swing application the same way as a console based one.

But a framework also comes with working code that you can use right away. For instance Swing comes with a large set of predefined graphical components that you can use and most standard graphical applications can be made just by reusing the provided components without modification.

32.9 Software Product Lines

The process that has been going on with the pay station—new customers with new requirements and my ambition to address these requirements in a way that keeps cohesion high, coupling low, and the production code under testing control to ensure reliability—has gradually transformed the production code to a framework. Frameworks are an important aspect of the larger context known as software product lines.

Definition: Software product line

A *software product line* is a set of software intensive systems sharing a common, managed set of features that satisfy the specific needs of a particular market segment or mission and that are developed from a common set of core assets in a prescribed way. (Bass et al. 2003, p. 353)

A software product line is similar to product lines in more traditional manufacturing like car production where a given product usually comes in different variants: standard model, deluxe, convertible, etc. It is the same basic software system but with a managed set of features, that is, variants.

However, a framework is just the technical, software development, aspect. A software product line must also consider the managerial, economic, strategic, and market aspects. These aspects each pose their own and complex sets of problems, but is beyond the scope of this book. Just to mention a few aspects, it does not help a company to develop a framework if the sales people are not trained so they know which features that are easy to make (i.e. have a well-defined variability point in the framework) or difficult to make (i.e. is not addressed by the framework): odds are they will not negotiate to neither the customer's nor the company's advantage. Another aspect is the organizational aspects like "lost empires": if product line reuse will lead to a 50% cut in testing compared to building applications from scratch, the testing department may fight this idea vigorously.

32.10 Summary of Key Concepts

A framework is a reusable design together with implementation for a specific class of applications. The users of frameworks are application developers that tailor the framework so it fits the needs of the end users. The advantage of using a framework instead of building the application from scratch is that you get a reliable implementation with few defects, development time is cut due to the code you get from the framework, and you learn a high quality design for building applications within the domain. The disadvantage is the time and effort invested in learning the framework.

At the code level, a framework is considered to consist of *frozen spots* and *hot spots*. The frozen spots cannot be altered whereas the hot spots define the parts of the code where the application developer may alter or add behavior. Frameworks are customized by *dependency injection*, that is, the objects defining the exact behavior of the variability points are injected into the framework. A special characteristic of frameworks is the *inversion of control* which means the framework decides flow of control and invokes the application developer specified variability points at well-defined spots. A framework is a special case of software reuse, and is unique in that it combines reusing design as well as concrete implementation. *Software product lines* are frameworks combined with an organization that considers the managerial, economic, strategic, and market aspects of delivering highly flexible software systems.

32.11 Selected Solutions

Discussion of Exercise 32.1:

Given the characteristics, Java Swing is a framework: it is a *skeleton within a domain*, graphical user interfaces, and consists of a large number of *collaborating classes*. You generally *customize* it by composition, that is you create a dialog by composing the right set of buttons, list boxes, panels, etc. And of course, Swing comes with an immense amount of code.

Discussion of Exercise 32.2:

Concrete objects that were all injected into MiniDraw by the example applications are:

- ImageFigure instances with specific images of e.g. the nine puzzle pieces were injected through following the convention detailed by MiniDraw of how to automatically load GIF images.
- A factory was injected that itself injected the type of drawing, drawing view, and status field to use.
- New tools were defined and injected by a simple setTool method call on the editor.
- New figure types were injected simply by adding them to the drawing's collection of figures.

Discussion of Exercise 32.3:

The MiniDraw **Figure** role has the full spectrum. As seen in Figure 30.5 there is the Figure interface, an AbstractFigure (which is reused to create the RectangleFigure in the "Rect" application), as well as the concrete ImageFigure defined by MiniDraw.

The **Tool** role also has interface, abstract class, as well as default concrete classes.

Discussion of Exercise 32.4:

Generally, the visible components of both the AWT and Swing are concrete classes that are rooted in an abstract class: *java.awt.Component* or *javax.swing.JComponent* respectively. This makes it impossible to make a dialog where a JLabel is replaced by a third party graphical label without modifying the dialog code: you cannot inject another type of label .

Discussion of Exercise 32.5:

They are two sides of the same coin. It is the template method that defines the flow of control through its definition of algorithm structure and only call out into the application developer's code when hook methods are called. Of course a framework is not a single template method but a large set of ordinary and template methods that execute in the framework thereby calling a lot of different hook methods defined by many different hook interfaces or abstract methods in the framework.

32.12 Review Questions

What is a framework? Mention some of the characteristics of frameworks and relate them to for instance the pay station system, MiniDraw, Java Swing, or other frameworks.

Mention some of the considerations an application developer must consider when deciding to use a framework or not.

Define and explain the concept: Frozen spot, hot spot, variability point, and inversion of control.

Relate the TEMPLATE METHOD design pattern to the inversion of control property.

Describe implementation techniques to define variability points and discuss each technique's benefits and liabilities.

Describe the problems that may arise when several different frameworks must be combined in a single application.

Explain why A) copy a piece of code from the last project and paste it into my new project; B) enter an algorithm I have read in a magazine; C) call methods in the *java.lang.Math* package; are not considered framework reuse.

Iteration 8

Outlook

In this learning iteration, the focus is software engineering practices that are highly relevant for producing reliable software.

Chapter	Learning Objective
Chapter 33	*Configuration Management.* This chapter introduces version control terminology, practices, and tools. A primary advantage of having your projects under version control is smooth collaboration between developers as it supports merging parallel development efforts.
Chapter 34	*Systematic Testing.* Test-driven development relies on testing to improve production code reliability but says little about what constitutes a *good test case.* Systematic testing techniques come with a solid foundation for finding the minimal set of test cases that have the highest probability of detecting defects in the code. This chapter presents two important black-box testing techniques: equivalence class partitioning and boundary value analysis.

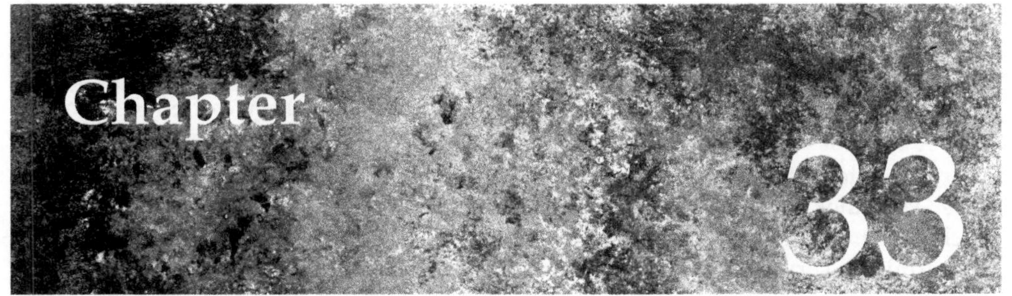

Configuration Management

Learning Objectives

In this chapter, the learning objective is the terminology and theory of software configuration management (SCM). You will also become briefly introduced to a few concrete tools for doing configuration management.

33.1 Motivation

The pay station system that has formed the central case study in this book is a small system that can be developed by a single person and as such not typical of modern software development: software today is a team effort. When working in teams, policies have to be defined for how people collaborate on the concrete entities that defines a software system: the production code, test code, graphics, sound, documentation, etc. If you are not careful, all sorts of really nasty things may happen—I have outlined a few of my own painful experiences in sidebar 33.1.

A classic problem facing development when several developers need to work on the same set of source code files is either A) how to ensure that all individual modifications are properly integrated in the source code or B) how to avoid overwriting the modifications of the other developers. If you work on personal copies of the source code files then you face problem A) while if you store your source code files in a shared file folder you face B).

Another classic problem is to identify the exact contents of a release. Consider that you have made a first release of a software system to a customer. Now you work hard for several months on introducing additional features for the next release. These features, however, are not fully tested nor fully working. Now, if the customer discovers a major defect that renders the system unusable, you need to fix it in the original source code that went into the release, not in the half finished new release. If you do not have a copy of the original source code files you are of course in deep trouble and unable to fix just that one defect in the released system.

Sidebar 33.1: Configuration Management in SAWOS

I worked on the SAWOS system at a time when SCM tools were not widely available or known. And as I worked very close with two colleagues and we often were forced to add and modify in the same C++ files we quickly ran into trouble.

Our first attempt was each to have a copy of the several thousands of source code files. We quickly abandoned this as keeping our individual copies consistent with each other took an awful lot of time. Our next attempt was to store all files on a central file server so there was only one copy of each source code file but then we ran into an "inverted race problem": the person to save a source code file *last* won the race. To see the problem consider that I and my colleague edit the same source code file: at that time integrated development environments (IDE) copied source code into memory and compiled them there. Thus I could add a feature, compile, edit, and test it in the IDE without saving the file. Thus when the feature was working, I saved the source file. The problem appeared when my colleague finished his feature later than I, as the copy in his IDE of course did not have the code implementing my feature: and upon saving he would simply overwrite it. All that work had gone forever! Once I did a demo for my project manager only to find that the feature I had made had gone—not the best starting point for discussing a salary raise.

Our final solution was to make a copy of the server files each morning, and just before leaving in the afternoon, we ran a tool that located all files changed on that particular day. These two lists we compared to find any files we had both edited. If so, we manually merged these. Tedious! This is basically what a software configuration management tool does automatically.

One of my other colleagues adopted another policy. He had a notice-board with a list of all source code files in the project. He then had colored pins stuck into the list, one for each file. If you needed to edit a file, you would have to go to the list and take the pin—and put it back into place once you were finished with the editing. If the pin was missing, then editing that file was not allowed. The idea was good but never worked in practice: developers of course forgot all about fetching pins once they started editing.

These problems are intrinsic in any large software development process and of course people have invested time and effort into solving it. The result is software configuration management systems.

33.2 Terminology

The development of a large software system is a process that produces a lot of interrelated products, like source code, graphics, sound files, documents, etc., that are all necessary for the final delivery to the customer. Usually these products are the result of many people working together. And finally, these products emerge over time and usually change quite a lot during the time-span of a development project. Tichy (1988) defines software configuration management as:

Definition: Software configuration management

Software configuration management (SCM) is the process of controlling the evolution of a software system.

Below, I will first define what it is that a SCM system needs to control, the entities, and next how the evolution of them are tracked.

33.2.1 Naming the Entities

SCM systems view software as a hierarchical structure of some atomic items.

Definition: Configuration item

A configuration item is the atomic building block in a SCM system. That is, the SCM system views a configuration item as a whole without any further substructure. A configuration item is identified by a name.

Definition: Configuration

A configuration is a named hierarchical structure that aggregates configuration items and configurations.

The definition of configuration is a recursive one, as a configuration may aggregate other configurations. It is essentially the COMPOSITE design pattern (Chapter 26). Thus, a SCM system is really very similar to a file system. A file system views a file as an atomic entity whose substructure it ignores. For instance an XML file contains hierarchical structured contents, however, from the viewpoint of the file system this is completely irrelevant. A file system contains folders, and folders may contain both files as well as other folders. Thus you can think of configuration items as files and configurations as folders as an analogy. Indeed most commercial and open source SCM tools use files and folders as their structuring mechanism. Some research SCM tools, however, have used individual characters in text as their configuration items, thus being able to track changes at a very fine-grained level. The CVS and Subversion tool, discussed later, both use the file as a configuration item.

33.2.2 Versions

A file system does not have any sense of evolution of time. The contents of it just reflect the result of an evolution, not the evolution itself. In a given folder you may have added files, deleted files, and rewritten a given file any number of times; however the file system just reflects what the world looks like right now. The purpose of SCM is to track the evolution itself—i.e. it must be able to tell what the world looked like at some earlier time. Thus time is an essential aspect to get hold of, and SCM systems therefore define the concept of a *version* as means to capture the state of an entity at a given instance in time.

Definition: **Version**

A version, v_i, represents the immutable state of a configuration item or configuration at time t_i.

You could envision a SCM system that would save the state of every item every second, thus t_i would represent a specific second in time. However, no SCM system does that because the granularity would be way too fine for normal work. Instead, the time t_i is defined by the developer who makes a deliberate choice when to save the state of an item. Note that I have deliberately not stated whether a version represents a version of a configuration item or a configuration. Though it is a general principle to be able to identity versions of both, many older SCM systems handle versions of configuration items and versions of configurations radically different.

Definition: **Version identity**

A version is identified by a version identity, v_i, that must be unique in the SCM system.

The standard way of identifying v_i is by enumerating the versions using increasing numbers thus version 1 is before version 2 etc. Different numbering schemes are in use, from a single number (used by Subversion) to version numbers consisting of numbered parts: for instance my Firefox is version 3.0.10 and my Outlook is version 12.0.6316.5000. For these composite version numbers, the first number is incremented only for major changes (new features) and the rest for minor changes like bugfix releases down to day to day development. Once a "major" number is incremented then the "minor" numbers are reset: like going from 2.3.132 to 3.0.0. The simplest form of just two numbers, 12.323, is denoted **dewey** numbers.

Versions defines a progression in the development of an entity. That is version 1.56 was the result of modifying a copy of version 1.55. We denote this the **ancestor-relation** i.e. version 1.55 is the ancestor of version 1.56. Versions of an entity and the ancestor-relations are often shown as a *version graph* for the entity.

Definition: **Version graph**

A version graph is an oriented graph that shows the ancestor-relation between versions of an entity.

Figure 33.1 shows a simple version graph for a Java source file "Receipt.java", numbered using dewey notation. The arrow can be read as "is modified to become."

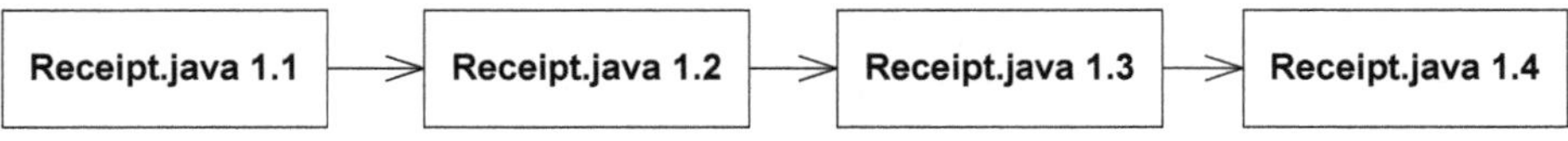

Figure 33.1: A simple version graph.

33.2.3 Operations

Versions of entities are created by the SCM system when the developer requests it. Every SCM system unfortunately seems to take great pride in inventing their own names for this operation. However I will use:

Definition: Commit

A commit is an operation that

1. generates a new, unique, version identity for the given entity.
2. stores a copy/snapshot of the entity under this identity.

Thus a programmer may commit a file "Receipt.java" which will make a snapshot of the file in the exact state it has in this moment in time, and return a version identity, for instance "1.45", for identifying this exact snapshot. Commit is sometimes termed "check-in". An important feature of SCM systems is that they strive to minimize the amount of data stored. Thus all SCM systems adhere to a certain scheme for making version identities:

> *If an entity has not been changed between two successive commit's then no snapshot is stored and the version identity is maintained.*

Thus, if a programmer commits "Receipt.java" a second time but has not made any changes, then the second commit operation will not perform any operation at all. This of course saves an enormous amount of space if, say, 1000 files are committed but only 5 files have been changed.

The reason for storing identifiable states of an entity is that we may need to inspect them at a later point in time. For instance, inspect the source files for a product that we have released to a customer a couple of months ago. SCM systems of course must provide an operation to retrieve the individually stored states of an entity.

Definition: Check-out

A check-out is an operation that, given a unique version identity, is able to retrieve an exact copy of an entity as it looked when the given version identity was formed during a commit.

Check-out is also termed "update" or "get." Thus commit and check-out defines a way to copy entities between a database and your file system. These two "places" have their own names in SCM terminology.

Definition: Repository

The repository is a central database, maintained and controlled by the SCM system that stores all versions of all controlled entities.

Note that the repository stores *immutable objects*. You cannot alter objects in the repository, only add new objects. Thus, changing objects (i.e. editing source files) is not performed in the repository, but in another place:

> **Definition: Workspace**
>
> A workspace is a local file system in which individual versions of entities can be modified and altered. Only one version of a given entity is allowed at the same time in the workspace.

Now we can reformulate commit as the operation of moving a copy of a software entity from the workspace to the repository; and check-out as the operation of moving a copy of an entity from the repository to the workspace.

There is a one-to-many relation between repository and workspace. A given repository may have an unlimited number of workspaces associated. Thus to compare, say, version 1.45 with version 1.46 of Receipt.java, a developer could create two workspaces, check-out 1.45 in one and 1.46 in the other, to make the comparison. (Most SCM systems offer to do that in a single operation by creating a temporary workspace for you.) Note that the repository contains all versions of a given entity, whereas a workspace can only contain a single version of a given entity. Schematically we can show the relations as outlined in Figure 33.2:

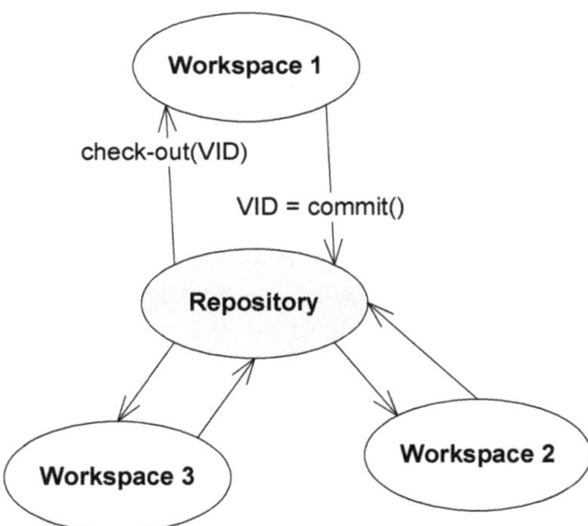

Figure 33.2: Repository and workspaces. VID is a version identity.

33.2.4 Versioning Items and Configurations

Two of the principal responsibilities of a SCM system are to

1. Ensure a unique, automatic, identification of versions. That is, it is the SCM system that assigns version identities to snapshots upon commit.

2. Organize versions with respect to each other. That is, the SCM system imposes and handles a rigid structure that defines the relations between versions. This structure is organized using the ancestor relation which means that if A is ancestor to B, then B is a result of modifying a copy of A. Usually the version organization is shown graphically by the version graph.

We need to version both individual configuration items (like a single Java source file) as well as configurations (like a Java package containing subpackages and many Java source files). As an example of the latter we are used to identifying versions of configurations by names or numbers like "Java version 6" or "Windows Vista". Both are large configurations containing a lot of substructure and individual configuration items, yet we are able to identify the exact snapshot by a single version identity. Thus we can speak of version 6 of both a single file (a configuration item) and of a large hierarchical structure (a configuration).

Probably due to historical reasons, however, many SCM systems handle versioning of configuration items and versioning of configurations very differently. In systems like CVS, versions of configuration items are created and identified by the SCM system. Thus commit of a modified copy of version 1.4 of a file will return a new version identity 1.5 of the file. Thus, the SCM system handles the generation of version identity as well as keeps track of the ancestor relation: that version 1.5 is a modification of a copy of version 1.4. However, when it comes to versions of configurations many tools support neither automatic identity generation nor keeping track of ancestor relations. Instead you have to manage it yourself which carries a rather high probability of going wrong. As an example, in CVS you can commit a folder but the commit of this configuration does not produce any version identity for the configuration itself, only for the individual configuration items it contains. As an example, consider a folder "project" containing files "main.java" and "gui.java". A commit of "project" will generate new version identities for the two files, but not for folder "project" itself. Folders are not versioned in CVS. Instead CVS provides another mechanism called "labels" or "tags". A label is simply a string value of your own choice. If you need to provide a version identity for a configuration (like a release of a product: version 6 of Java SDK), you can ask CVS to assign a tag, like "release_6" to all configuration items in some configuration. Thus, if you want to re-establish version 6 of your configuration then you ask CVS to check-out all configuration items in the versions that bear the tag "release_6".

Several problems exist with this technique.

- Version identification is not automatic. Thus if you forget to tag a given configuration—well you are just unlucky. You cannot reestablish it. Thus—remember to tag when you release a system.

- No tracking of the ancestor relation is made for you. Essentially you have to manually keep track of all tags used and how they relate to each other. For instance nothing hinders you from assigning tag "release_3" to a later version than "release_6". To CVS it is simply string values.

- If you tag a configuration with a tag you have already used, then the old one simply disappears. Thus a project must globally ensure that no person ever uses a tag that has been used before. This is tricky and prone to errors especially in projects with a large number of developers.

- If you remove or add directories or files between tagged configuration versions, CVS simply gives up; it cannot cope consistently with these situations. For instance if a file does not have any version with a given tag, then what does it mean? Has it been added after the tag was assigned or has the user just forgotten to tag it?

Newer tools, like Subversion, has fortunately adopted a unified approach to versioning both configurations and configuration items and simply assigns version numbers to everything upon each commit: configurations as well as configuration items. For instance, I use Subversion for version controlling the about 450 text and graphics files in about 35 folders that makes up the main text of this book. The preprint of the book I made for my last class was given version identity 1485 by Subversion. This means that if I check-out the book's root folder in version 1485 I will get not only the root folder but all subfolders and files as they appeared when the preprint was produced.

33.2.5 Collaboration

With several workspaces accessing and adding versions to the repository, a SCM system must define a schema for handling concurrency issues—i.e. the way it handles the possibility for two or more users modifying the same version of the same entity at the same time. The schema chosen has major implications on how collaboration between developers is done. Basically there are two schemas that are denoted *pessimistic* and *optimistic* concurrency respectively. But, before we define these, let us define a term that is essential to understand why these schemas have been made.

> Definition: **Conflict**
>
> A conflict is a situation where the same piece of code has been changed at the same time in two or more different workspaces.

That is, it is a conflict if developer A changes the first line of a text file version 1.1. to "A is great" while developer B also changes the same version 1.1. of the text file to "B is even greater". Which change is the one that should go into the final version of the file? The schemas take two different views on conflicts: either avoid it or handle it when it occurs.

> Definition: **Pessimistic concurrency**
>
> Ensure strict sequential modifications by *locking* configuration items during modification.

In this schema, the developer has to explicitly state to the SCM system: "I want to change this file". Doing so, he/she puts a "lock" on the file making it read-only when all other developers check it out. If a second developer makes the same request for modification, it is simply denied. Once a modified version of the file has been committed the lock is again removed from the file, making is available for modification by other developers. This is very much like the semaphore idea known from concurrent programming.

This schema has the benefit that no conflicts are ever going to happen. (In practice, this is not quite true because all SCM systems have operations to "break a lock"—consider a situation where one developer forgets to check in a locked file before going off for holidays for three weeks.)

Definition: Optimistic concurrency

Allow for parallel modification and handle conflicts by merging.

In this schema, no locks are put onto the entities. Thus, both developer A and B may change the same file or modify the contents of the same folder. The first developer, say A, is allowed to commit as normal. However, when B attempts the same, he/she is notified that commit is not possible until B has incorporated A's changes. The SCM system will assist in this by adding A's changes into the entity B has in his workspace. If both A and B have changed the same piece of code then B is notified that there is a conflict. B must then manually sort out the conflict. Now B can commit the file because it contains A's changes and thus the new version will respect the ancestor relation: B's version has A's version as ancestor that has the original file as ancestor.

Please note that the definition of conflict is rather narrow-minded. It is purely syntactic conflicts that SCM systems can detect. Let us take an example. A and B both checkout a Java source file. Now B introduces a new method that accesses an instance variable X of type `int`. Meanwhile A changes the definition of X to be a `String` instead, and makes changes in the source file so the class behaves correctly with the new definition of X—and checks in. Now A has obviously not made the changes to B's new method as he is first to commit and thus has no knowledge of the work B is making. When B merges A's changes into his source file in his workspace then no conflicts are detected because B has not made any changes in the same code as A. Thus B can commit. But the code will not compile! The conflict is semantic, not syntactic.

Exercise 33.1: Tools like CVS and Subversion default to optimistic locking because experience has shown that conflicts appear rather seldom in practice. However, for some types of entities a conflict is almost impossible to resolve and a pessimistic policy is preferable. Which types of entities are best handled by pessimistic concurrency?

Exercise 33.2: Sidebar 33.1 outlined two approaches for handling concurrent modifications: A) copy server files in the morning and use a tool to find concurrent modifications in the afternoon and B) retrieve a pin from a notice-board when editing a file. Classify these two approaches as either pessimistic or optimistic concurrency.

33.2.6 Merge

Definition: Merge

A merge is a operation where the sum of changes since the last common ancestor in the version graph is included in a configuration item or configuration.

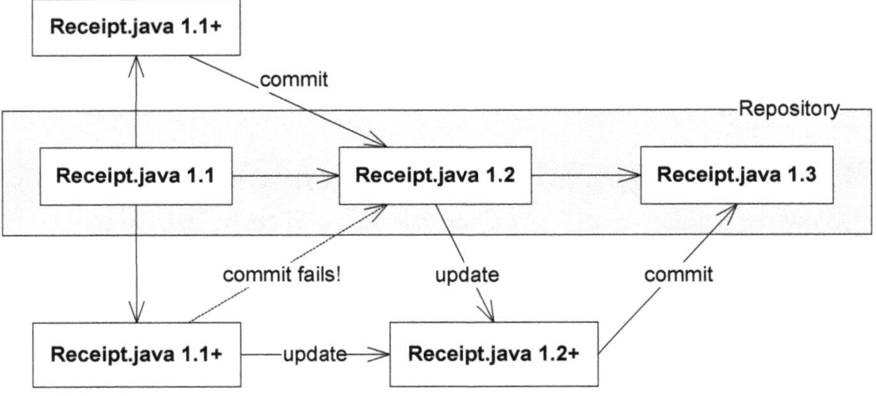

Figure 33.3: Merging in CVS and Subversion.

Figure 33.3 illustrates this. The middle part shows the view in the repository and the upper and lower parts show two workspaces. In the beginning, two developers check out version 1.1 and begin modifying it (indicated by the +). The upper developer commits generating version 1.2. The lower developer attempts commit but is informed that a merge is required. She then makes a merge to make a version 1.2+ in her workspace (version 1.2 plus her own changes). Then the commit is possible to generate version 1.3.

During a merge two situations can occur: Either there is a syntactic conflict or there is not. If there is a conflict then the SCM system will report it for a developer to sort things out. CVS for instance, will show the conflicting changes in the file using "<" and ">" as brackets. If no conflicts are reported then the configuration item in the workspace will contain all changes.

33.2.7 SCM system

We are now in a position to define what a SCM system is:

Definition: SCM system

A SCM system is a tool set that defines

1. A central repository that stores versions of entities.
2. A schema for how to setup multiple, individual, workspaces.
3. A commit and a check-out operation that transfer copies of versions between the repository and a workspace.
4. A schema for handling/defining version identities for configuration items and configurations.
5. A schema for collaboration/concurrent access to versions.

33.3 Example Systems

In this section we will look at three example systems and describe them using the definition from the previous section.

33.3.1 RCS

RCS (Tichy 1985) is one of the earliest SCM systems with restricted functionality geared towards versioning. The research challenge of the time of RCS was to minimize disk space usage for the repository and RCS implemented some novel storage schemes to minimize the size of the repository as well as increase performance of check-out. With respect to the definition RCS can be classified as:

1. The repository is simply a folder named RCS. This repository contains one version file per file in the workspace (versions of file 'a.x' is stored in a file 'a.x,v' in the repository). This file contains the complete version history and can reproduce all versions of the file.
2. A workspace is simply a single folder in which developers commit and check-out files to and from the repository.
3. Commit is handled by a stand-alone tool `ci` (check-in) and check-out with a stand-alone tool `co` (check-out). Upon commit every file is assigned a dewey number version identity.
4. RCS only version control files, folders are not supported. Thus a configuration is restricted to all the files in a single folder. This configuration could be versioned by tagging all the file versions.
5. RCS uses the pessimistic concurrency model, ie. locking files.

33.3.2 CVS

CVS (Berliner 1990) was created to solve two issues with RCS: the lack of handling hierarchical folders and the pessimistic concurrency scheme. CVS can be classified as:

1. The repository is a hierarchical folder structure identical to the structure of the workspace. The repository is rooted in a folder pointed out by the value of an environment variable `CVSROOT` (or `CVSHOME`)—or it can be specified directly. This latter option is important as CVS can communicate with a remote repository using a secure network connection. The contents of the repository is simply RCS coded files for the version history of the configuration item.
2. A workspace is a folder structure.
3. All cvs commands are handled by the `cvs` tool. The second parameter of cvs is the operation to perform. Commit is denoted `commit` while check-out is denoted `update`. Both operate on configurations, namely rooted in the folder the command is issued in and working on all files in the subfolder structure.

4. CVS normally works on configurations, but you can also commit/update a single file if you wish. While CVS depends on RCS functionality for the handling of individual configuration items, the dewey numbers are seldom used for anything except reporting, as most operations work on the folder level. Instead, just as RCS, tags are used to define version identities for configurations.

5. CVS uses the optimistic concurrency model.

33.3.3 Subversion

Subversion (Collins-Sussman et al. 2004) defines itself as "a better CVS." CVS has been the default free software tool for configuration management for many years. While the CVS tool over the years have been updated to become a real client-server architecture its implementation is still historically rooted in RCS and file manipulations; and as stated above it inherited the tagging scheme for configurations. Subversion solves this in a much cleaner way. Still quite a lot of effort has been invested by Subversion to make it appear as CVS-like as possible. If you are used to the CVS command line syntax you can make Subversion do more or less exactly the same just by substituting 'cvs' with 'svn': "cvs commit" becomes "svn commit" etc. Using our scheme we can classify Subversion:

1. The repository is a real database system with a database server. Several protocols can be used to communicate with the server: HTTP, HTTPS, SVN, and file. The first two are supported by the WebDAV protocol on Apache servers; the SVN is a special protocol supported by a supplied server application, and finally the 'file' protocol allows the clients to use a local folder as repository. The repository is a true database where versions are stored in binary format. Subversion also handles binary files more elegantly and efficiently than CVS.

2. A workspace is a standard folder structure.

3. All svn commands are handled by the `svn` tool (or a file browser plug-in). The second parameter of `svn` is the operation to perform and follows more or less the CVS syntax.

4. Subversion can operate both on configurations as well as on individual configuration items; but conceptually it simply copies the complete configuration and assigns a new version identity. See below.

5. Subversion by default uses an optimistic concurrency model, but can also use a locking based model.

Subversion uses a unified approach to configurations and configuration items. This means that Subversion simply maintains a single version number for all items within a repository (even if it contains many unrelated projects). Thus it does not matter if you checking 50,000 files or just a single one: the global version number will be incremented and assigned to all modified items: folders and files.

A good way to understand this is that for every commit, Subversion simply makes a full and deep copy of all files and all folders, and assigns the new version number to it. Think of it like making a new zip file for every commit, where the zips are numbered 1, 2, 3, ... Thus when you checkout a version you simply get all the files that went into that particular zip file. It has the funny consequence that version numbers "crosstalk" between projects. Thus if you have an old project and left it in version 1623 then when you modify something half a year later the next version of it may be 2393 because there have been numerous commits in other projects. Thus Subversion deals elegantly with changes even in the folder structure, like moving, adding, and deleting folders and files. CVS was not very good at handling this.

33.4 Branching

A software system seldom follows a purely linear development history. An often occurring situation is that a product is released but developers keep working on it, making new versions of it. However, if a bug is found that needs immediate attention, you often cannot simply fix the bug in the present version as it contains features the customer has not yet paid for.

In this situation, the development history of the product splits as the old release version must be checked out, the modification made, and a new version containing the bug fix must be made. Thus the product release version now is ancestor for *two* versions. This is called a branch:

Definition: Branch

A branch is a point in the version graph where a version is ancestor to two or more descendant versions.

The original development line is often called the **main** or **trunk** line. Subversion uses trunk and the metaphor of a tree with a central trunk and branches is natural.

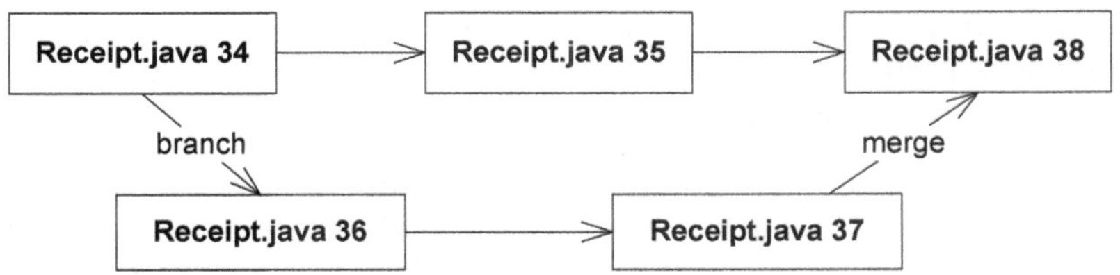

Figure 33.4: A version graph with a branch and later merge.

An example is shown in Figure 33.4 using Subversion sequential numbers and for a single configuration item only. The situation can be viewed as a 'release' of Receipt in version 34. Development continues in version 35, adding more features, but then a defect is discovered in the released version that needs immediate fixing. Thus the item is branched to version 36 and the defect is fixed in version 37 and shipped to the customer. Naturally the defect must be fixed also on the main development line so the changes applied in the branch are finally merged into the trunk to produce version 38. Note that when a merge is made of a branch, then all changes made in all versions in the branch are applied to the resulting merged version.

Branches work fine in the simple cases but it can become difficult to overview what is happening in a complex version graph with many branches and merges. Take care...

33.5 Variant Management by SCM

While versions represent the evolution of items, branches represent alternatives or *variants*. And as SCM systems can handle branches many considered SCM tools the solution to handling variants of software products, like the Alphatown and Betatown variants of the pay station case study. Thus the discussion of handling the two variants that I analyzed in Chapter 7 could be augmented with a fifth possibility, namely using branches in the version graph. Upon close analysis, however, a branch is simply a "copy with modifications" and thus branching is simply a tool supported source code copy proposal for variant handling. Thus the analysis of benefits and liabilities is identical: it is generally a bad idea to handle variants by branching, primarily due to the multiple maintenance problem.

33.6 Summary of Key Concepts

Software configuration management (SCM) is the process of controlling the evolution of the entities that make up a software system, typically source code files, documentation, resources like graphics and sounds, etc. The central concept is that of a *version* of an entity which is a copy of that entity at a certain point in time. A SCM tool maintains a database, the *repository*, in which all versions of all controlled entities are stored as immutable objects. Copies of entities are transferred into the repository using a *commit* operation while a *check-out* operation creates copies of entities in a local *workspace* where the developer can alter, add, and delete. Entities are either *configuration items* which are atomic units (files) or *configurations* that are composite objects (folders) consisting of other configurations and configuration items. During commit, the SCM system associates a new *version identity* with each modified entity. Older SCM systems only versioned configuration items, i.e. by assigning new version numbers, but left the versioning of configurations to the developer, i.e. by manually assigning labels to all configuration items in a configuration. Newer SCM systems assign new version numbers to all committed entities, that is, also to configurations.

A SCM system provides good support for collaboration between many developers on a software system. Two schemes to handle *conflicts*, i.e. concurrent changes in the same code fragment, are the *pessimistic* and *optimistic* policies. In the pessimistic policy, concurrent changes are prohibited, whereas the process of combining the two individual changes are supported by the tool in the optimistic case. The combination of two or several concurrent changes into a single new version is called *merging*. Merging combines changes, the opposite action where a version is split into two parallel variants is called *branching*.

33.7 Selected Solutions

Discussion of Exercise 33.1:

SCM tools are good at merging *text* but it is more or less impossible to merge *binary* files. Consider two developers that each modify the same JPEG image or the same

WAV sample. In this case, it may be better to use a pessimistic locking scheme to avoid resolving merge conflicts.

Discussion of Exercise 33.2:

The *copy server files and later identify concurrent modifications* technique was a manual way of implementing optimistic concurrency. During our work day we could each modify any source code file and thus it allowed concurrent modifications. At the end of the day we (manually) identified and merged those source code files that two or several had made modifications to.

The *take the pin for the file to edit* approach is basically a way to ensure sequential updates to each source code file and thus a manual implementation of the pessimistic concurrency scheme.

33.8 Review Questions

What is a software configuration management system? How is configuration and configuration item defined? Explain and relate the concepts *version, version identity,* and *version graph.*

Explain the concepts *repository* and *workspace* and describe the operations that move objects between the two. Describe two different approaches for versioning configurations.

Describe the problems that may occur when several people work on the same configuration items in a system—and describe the various techniques for solving them.

Explain what *merging* and *branching* are.

33.9 Further Exercises

Exercise 33.3. Source code directory:
`exercise/tdd/breakthrough`

Put the development environment for the breakthrough production and test code (exercise 5.4 or 6.6) under software configuration management with a tool of your choice.

Exercise 33.4:

Take a small project under SCM control and check-out the most recent version into two workspaces. Make two different changes in each workspace, in the same file but different portions of the file.

1. Explain how your tool supports combining the two changes. Does it warn of a potential conflict?
2. Repeat the experiment but now make different changes in the same portion of the file. How does the tool warn and tackle the merging?

Exercise 33.5:

Take a small project under SCM control and make one or two branches of it at some earlier versions, to simulate fixing defects in previously released versions. Make changes in the branches, and next describe and explain how these changes are merged back into the main development line.

Exercise 33.6:

If you are using CVS or Subversion, experiment with these tool's support for pessimistic locking.

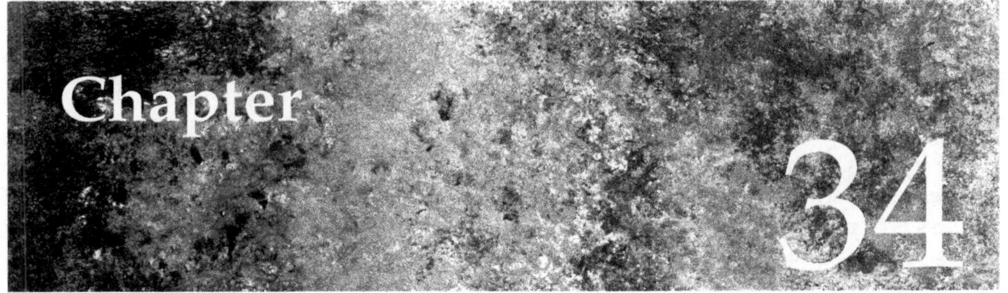

Systematic Testing

Learning Objectives

The test-driven development approach puts much emphasis on automated tests and several TDD principles emphasize the importance of quality test cases, such as *Evident Tests* and *Evident Data*. However, tests can only demonstrate the presence of defects, not that no defects remain in the production code. The learning objective of this chapter is to present a few systematic testing techniques that increase the chance of finding defects while keeping the number of test cases low. Thus systematic testing is not an alternative to TDD but rather a different aspect of testing: TDD is focused on the process of building reliable software fast while systematic testing is focused on increasing the ability of test cases to expose defects. As such they complement each other.

34.1 Terminology

As defined in Chapter 2 a failure is the situation in which the system's behavior deviates from the expected, and is caused by a defect in the production code. Thus, if I can reduce the number of defects in my software, it will exhibit fewer failures and thus increase the software's reliability.

> **Exercise 34.1:** Actually, this statement is not always true. Find situations where A) a removed defect in the code does not alter the resulting system's reliability, and B) removing defect 1 gives a high increase in reliability while removing defect 2 gives a low increase in reliability.

It should therefore be obvious that techniques that increase the likelihood of finding a defect are important and interesting in software engineering. These techniques are called *systematic testing* techniques.

Definition: Systematic testing

Systematic testing is a planned and systematic process with the explicit goal of finding defects in some well-defined part of the system.

Note by this definition testing is a *destructive* process in contrast to almost all other processes in software development which are *constructive*. In testing, *your criteria of success is to prove that the system does not work*! This is perhaps one of the reasons why it is so hard—developers are naturally reluctant to prove they have done a poor job!

Research and practice have evolved a large number of techniques over the years. Generally, these techniques are classified into two major classes.

Definition: Black-box testing

The *unit under test* (UUT) is treated as a black box. The only knowledge we have to guide our testing effort is the specification of the UUT and a general knowledge of common programming techniques, algorithmic constructs, and common mistakes made by programmers.

Definition: White-box testing

The full implementation of the unit under test is known, so the actual code can be inspected in order to generate test cases.

I will only discuss black-box testing techniques in this book. You will find some references to books that have a comprehensive overview of techniques in the summary section at the end of the chapter.

Generally, the systematic techniques are quite demanding and thus costly in terms of effort you have to invest. You should always balance the invested effort with the expected increase of reliability. As an example, consider a modern web browser. A web browser has numerous options you can set, however, the vast majority of users never change these options from their default setting. From a return-on-investment point of view it therefore makes sense to test the browser with the default options set much more thoroughly than when the options are set to specialized values.

The complexity of the unit under test is also important to consider when picking your testing strategy. I find the following classification of testing approaches appropriate based upon the complexity of the UUT.

- *No testing*. Many methods are so small that they are not worth testing. Examples are accessor methods that can be assumed simply to return the value of some instance variable. The testing code for such a method will become longer than the production code and thus increase the probability of tests failing due to defects in the test code rather than the production code.

- *Explorative testing*. Explorative tests are tests you make based on experience and "gut feeling" but you do not follow any rigid method. The explorative tests are well suited for medium complex methods and are characterized by their low cost. They are quite efficient as you gain experience as a tester and TDD developer. The test-driven development process basically uses an explorative test strategy as a fast development cycle is considered very important.

- *Systematic testing*. Here you follow a rigid method for generating test cases in order to increase the probability of finding defects. Systematic testing is costly as quite a lot of effort is invested in careful analysis of the problem. Thus this technique is best used for highly complex methods where the investment is worthwhile; or systems where reliability is of upmost importance such as machinery that may pose a safety risk for humans or the environment if they fail.

☞ Review the chapter on test-driven development using the classification above to see if you can find examples of no testing, explorative testing, and systematic testing.

Below, I will present two central black box testing techniques: *equivalence class partitioning* and *boundary value analysis*.

34.2 Equivalence Class Partitioning

The equivalence class partitioning technique relies on the fact that many input values are treated alike by our programs. To motivate this, let us consider a very simple example, the method int Math.abs(int x) in the Java system libraries. This simple method calculates the absolute value of an integer: *If the argument is not negative, the argument is returned. If the argument is negative, the negation of the argument is returned.* One test case table for this function could look like this:

Unit under test: Math.abs	
Input	Expected output
x = 37	37
x = 38	38
x = 39	39
x = 40	40
x = 41	41

The question is if I can be sure that the function is reliably implemented based upon these five test cases and if these particular five test cases are the best test cases to pick. The answer to both questions is *no*. The specification of Math.abs states that *If the argument is not negative, the argument is returned* and thus all the input values above are treated alike. Any competent programmer will write an implementation in which all the above input values are handled by the same code fragment. Thus if the x=37 test case passes then so will x=38 etc. I do not find more defects by adding more test cases for positive x values.

On the other hand, the test case table above has no test cases for negative x. Thus the code fragment to handle negative arguments is simply not exercised and the test cases above will not catch a faulty implementation like

```
public static int abs(int x) { return x; }
```

This insight is the core of the equivalence partitioning technique: find a single input value that represents a large set of values. If the test case x=37 exposes a defect in the implementation then x=41 will probably expose the same defect. You say that 37 is a **representative** for the class of all positive integers when testing Math.abs. Likewise I can choose x=-42 to represent all negative values. Thus the input space becomes partitioned into *equivalence classes*.

> Definition: **Equivalence class (EC)**
>
> A subset of all possible inputs to the UUT that has the property that if one element in the subset demonstrates a defect during testing, then we assume that all other elements in the subset will demonstrate the *same* defect.

Thus I have reduced the vast input space of abs into just two ECs and just two test cases are needed. These two test cases have a high probability of finding defects as they represent all aspects of the absolute value specification.

In the Math.abs examples, all possible input values are valid but often this is not the case. As an example, consider Math.sqrt(double x) (square root of a number) that is undefined for negative x. Therefore a distinction is made between **valid equivalence classes** whose elements will be processed normally, and **invalid equivalence classes** whose elements define special processing, like throwing an exception, returning an undefined value, or otherwise result in abnormal processing. I find that the terms "valid" and "invalid" are a bit unfortunate as it is sometimes a good idea to classify ECs as invalid even though they strictly speaking are valid to the method. My rule of thumb is that if elements from the EC will typically be processed early in the algorithm by simple switches and lead to the method *bailing out* then I classify it as invalid. You will see examples of this rule of thumb applied in examples later, as well as see why it is important.

When partitioning the input space into ECs, two properties must be fulfilled in order for the partitioning to be sound:

- **Coverage:** Every possible input element belongs to at least one of the equivalence classes.
- **Representation:** If a defect is demonstrated on a particular member of an equivalence class, the same defect is assumed to be demonstrated by any other member of the class.

☞ Argue that the two properties are fulfilled for the Math.abs example.

A good and handy way to document a set of ECs is by an **equivalence class table**. I will use the format below, here shown on the abs example.

Condition	Invalid ECs	Valid ECs
absolute value of x	–	$x > 0[1]$ $x \leq 0[2]$

The first column describes the condition that has led to partitioning, as outlined in the next section, and the next two columns describe the invalid and valid ECs. I generally prefer inserting the specification of the EC directly into the table, using a semi-mathematical set notation, and label each EC by a number, like [1] and [2] above, so they are easy to refer to later. A proper mathematical formulation of EC [1] would be $\{x \in \mathbb{Z} | x > 0\}$ but to conserve space I will usually write it as "$x > 0$" or even just "> 0". You can also choose to write out the EC in natural language in a separate list and just use the labels as cross references, like:

Condition	Invalid ECs	Valid ECs
absolute value of x	–	[1] [2]

where

[1] *are positive integers*

[2] *are negative integers.*

34.2.1 Finding the Equivalence Classes

Unfortunately finding a good set of ECs is often a difficult process that requires skills and experience. Below I will present a set of guidelines and heuristics, adapted from Myers (1979), that are helpful but remember that there are no hard and fast rules. The best way forward is an iterative process where you refine the ECs and test cases as you gain insight into the problem: *take small steps* is a valuable principle in systematic testing as well.

A good source for partitioning is to look for *conditions* in the specifications of the unit under test. These conditions are often associated with the input values to the unit (as was the case for the absolute value method) but sometimes also on its output (the formatting method in Section 34.2.6 is an example). Given a condition, you can derive a first set of ECs following the guidelines below:

- **Range:** *If a condition is specified as a range of values,* select one valid EC that covers the allowed range, and two invalid ECs, one above and one below the end of the range.
- **Set:** *If a condition is specified as a set of values* then define an EC for each value in the set and one EC containing all elements outside the set.
- **Boolean:** *If a condition is specified as a "must be" condition* then define one EC for the condition being true and one EC for the condition being false.

As an example of the set guideline, consider the pay station whose specification states that it must accept 5, 10, and 25 cent coins. This is the set of valid values and thus four ECs emerge:

Condition	Invalid ECs	Valid ECs
Allowed coins	$\notin \{5, 10, 25\}$[1]	$\{5\}$[2]; $\{10\}$[3]; $\{25\}$[4]

Remember that ECs are mathematical sets and thus set notation often comes in handy. I, however, often write the ECs rather informally but readable (as is the case with the invalid EC above) as ECs are means to generate test cases more than an end in themselves.

An example of the boolean guideline, consider a method to recognize a properly formatted programming language identifier that is required to start with a letter. This is clearly a "must be" condition leading to two ECs.

Condition	Invalid ECs	Valid ECs
Initial character of identifier	non-letter [1]	letter [2]

Finally, for the range guideline, consider a method to test if a position on a standard chess board numbering columns a–h and rows 1–8 is valid. It is of course not valid to specify positions outside the board, leading to these six ECs:

Condition	Invalid ECs	Valid ECs
Column	< 'a' [1]; > 'h' [2]	'a'–'h' [3]
Row	< 1 [4]; > 8 [5]	1–8 [6]

The examples later in the chapter will demonstrate further uses of the guidelines.

These guidelines are rooted in how programmers would normally handle the three types of conditions. Ranges are typically coded by conditional statements guarding the ends of the range

```
if ( row < 1 || row > 8 ) { ... }
```

Sets are often handled by membership testing, like

```
if ( coin == 5 || coin == 10 || coin == 25 ) { ... }
// alternative
switch ( coin ) { case 5: case 10: case 25: { ... }}
```

or by putting elements into a data structure and then testing for membership. In any case there are specific and potentially defective code fragments handling each member of the set: either the case or conditionals, or the code that insert members into the data structure. Note that if a set contains a large number of members it may be infeasible to make ECs for each member. However, be sure to include at least elements inside and outside the set.

34.2.2 Generating the Test Cases

Once the ECs have been established I can generate test cases by picking elements from each EC. For primitive units where the ECs are disjoint this is trivial, consider the absolute value example:

ECs covered	Test case	Expected output
[1]	$x = 42$	$+42$
[2]	$x = -37$	$+37$

I have documented the generated test case by an **extended test case table** in which I write the number(s) of the EC(s) that the test case input belongs to in the first column.

More often, however, the ECs are generated from a set of conditions and they therefore overlap. In this case, you have to make test cases by combining the ECs. A simple example is the chess position validation method above in which you cannot only supply e.g. the row parameter to the method without also providing a column parameter. Thus any test case for this unit draws upon elements from two ECs. The test cases could be:

ECs covered	Test case	Expected output
[1], [4]	(' ',0)	illegal
[2], [4]	('i',-2)	illegal
[3], [4]	('e',0)	illegal
[1], [5]	(' ',9)	illegal
[2], [5]	('j',9)	illegal
[3], [5]	('f',12)	illegal
[1], [6]	(' ',4)	illegal
[2], [6]	('i',5)	illegal
[3], [6]	('b',6)	legal

As you imagine, the set of test cases can become very large if there are many ECs for many independent conditions. Essentially you get a combinatorial explosion as each EC must be combined with all ECs developed for all independent conditions. You see it in the above where the column EC [1] has to be combined with all row ECs [4], [5], [6] to cover all combinations. To limit the number of test cases, Myers (1979) suggested the following heuristics:

1. Until all valid ECs have been covered, define a test case that covers as many uncovered valid ECs as possible.
2. Until all invalid ECs have been covered, define a test case whose element only lies in a single invalid ECs.

These guidelines allow me to reduce the number of test cases for the above example somewhat. The first rule concerning valid ECs does not change anything because there is only one valid test case for the [3], [6] combination. However, for the invalid test cases there is a change, as most of the test cases in the above table combine invalid EC for both column and row. If only one is allowed to be invalid at the time I get:

ECs covered	Test case	Expected output
[1], [6]	(' ',5)	illegal
[2], [6]	('j',3)	illegal
[3], [4]	('b',0)	illegal
[3], [5]	('c',9)	illegal
[3], [6]	('b',6)	legal

I have thus reduced the number of test cases from the original nine to now only five. If you have more conditions and more partitions for each condition the reduction in number of test cases is even greater.

There is a strong argumentation for these guidelines. Taking the guideline for letting only one condition be invalid at a time first, it is actually a way to avoid test cases that pass for the wrong reason due to **masking**. To see masking in action, consider an (incomplete) implementation of the chess board position method that checks its parameters one by one:

Listing: chapter/blackbox-test/ChessBoard.java

```
/** Demonstration of masking of defects.
*/
public class ChessBoard {
  public boolean valid(char column, int row) {
    if ( column < 'a' ) { return false; }
    if ( row < 0 ) { return false; }
    return true;
  }
}
```

Note that the column check is correct with respect to the low boundary but the row check is not—it should have read "row < 1". However, the test case (' ', 0) derived from ECs [1], [4] correctly pass as the method indeed returns false to indicate an illegal position. This is an example of masking that leads to the tester making the wrong conclusion: The production is deemed correct as the test passes but it is indeed wrong. The correct column checking line *masks* for the defect in the row checking line. By *only* making *one* condition invalid at a time you avoid the masking problem. The test case table generated based on Myers' heuristics will catch the erroneous row checking line.

The rule to cover as many valid ECs as possible is also driven from facts about the production code. As we must assume that any provided valid input values to a unit under test is used in its algorithms at some point there is no masking problem for valid values.

34.2.3 The Process

The process of equivalence partitioning is roughly the same every time:

1. Review the requirements for the UUT and identify *conditions* and use the heuristics to find ECs for each condition. ECs are best written down in an *equivalence class table.*

2. Review the produced ECs and consider carefully the representation property of elements in each EC. If you question if particular elements are really representative then repartition the EC.

3. Review to verify that the coverage property is fulfilled.

4. Generate test cases from the ECs. You can often use Myers heuristics for combination to generate a minimal set of test cases. Test cases are best documented using a *test case table.*

Applying the process and using the heuristics require some practice. In the remainder of this section I will present some examples of applying both process and heuristics.

34.2.4 Example: Weekday

Consider the following (somewhat contrived) method:

```
public interface weekday {
  /** calculate the weekday of the 1st day of the given month.
      @param year the year as integer. 2000 means year 2000 etc. Only
      years in the range 1900-3000 are valid. The output is undefined
      for years outside this range.
      @param month the month as integer. 1 means January, 12 means
      December. Values outside the range 1-12 are illegal.
      @return the weekday of the 1st day of the month. 0 means Sunday
      1 means Monday etc. up til 6 meaning Saturday.
  */
  public int weekday(int year, int month)
     throws IllegalArgumentException;
}
```

Step 1: The conditions are easy to spot. As they are all about ranges, I can apply the range heuristics to get the following equivalence class table.

Condition	Invalid ECs	Valid ECs
year	< 1900 [1]; > 3000 [2]	$1900 - 3000$ [3]
month	< 1 [4]; > 12 [5]	$1 - 12$ [6]

Using my compact semi-mathematical set notation, you can read the first line like: *The requirement for "year" has conditions that lead to an invalid EC, numbered* 1, *having all elements year* $<$ 1900*; an invalid EC, numbered* 2, *having elements year* $>$ 3000*; and a valid EC, numbered* 3, *having elements in the valid range year* $\in \{1900..3000\}$.

Step 2: What about leap years? I conclude that EC 3 needs to be repartitioned as e.g. leap year 1976 may not be a good representative for non leap years. So I repartition according to the leap year definition (the table below omits repeating EC 1, 2, 4, 5, and 6):

Condition	Invalid ECs	Valid ECs
year (y)		$\{y \mid y \in [1900; 3000] \land y\%400 = 0\}$ [3a]
		$\{y \mid y \in [1900; 3000] \land y\%100 = 0 \land y \notin [3a]\}$ [3b]
		$\{y \mid y \in [1900; 3000] \land y\%4 = 0 \land \notin [3a] \cup [3b]\}$ [3c]
		$\{y \mid y \in [1900; 3000] \land y\%4 \neq 0\}$ [3d]

One may also argue that weekday calculation is influenced by leap years with respect to months that are before and after the leap day in February. Thus we may question the representation property of partition [6]. A further division seems worth the effort.

Condition	Invalid ECs	Valid ECs
month		$1 - 2$ [6a]; $3 - 12$ [6b]

Step 3: The coverage is OK, all possible values of the vector (year, month) belongs to one or another EC.

Step 4: For the test case generation, I can apply Myers heuristics for finding test cases. First cover as many valid partitions as possible; next define one for each invalid one. Thus we end up with the following test cases (I've been a bit lazy about the 'expected' values as this would require consulting the calendars; and I've shortened year to y and month to m).

ECs covered	Test case	Expected output
$[3a], [6a]$	$y = 2000; m = 2$	-
$[3b], [6b]$	$y = 1900; m = 5$	-
$[3c], [6b]$	$y = 2004; m = 10$	5
$[3d], [6a]$	$y = 1985; m = 1$	-
$[1]$	$y = 1844; m = 4$	[exception]
$[2]$	$y = 4231; m = 8$	[exception]
$[4]$	$y = 2004; m = 0$	[exception]
$[5]$	$y = 2004; m = 13$	[exception]

Note how one test case covers all valid partitions while we define one test case for each illegal partition. Also note the very important property that only one parameter is illegal at a time to ensure that no masking occurs. Even though we defined quite a few more partitions than in the original proposal (without leap year) it has led to only three extra test cases.

34.2.5 Example: Sum

It is important that you focus on the *requirements* and the conditions associated with them instead of just looking at parameters to a method. Consider the following requirement:

```
public class PrettyStupid {
  private int T;

  /** return true iff x+y < T */
  public boolean isMoreThanSumOf(int x, int y)
}
```

If I just write the EC table based upon the input parameters then I will end in a situation that leads nowhere:

Condition	Invalid ECs	Valid ECs
x		?
y		?

This is because the ECs are not associated with the input parameters in themselves but on the condition in the specification: $x + y < T$. It is therefore this condition (a boolean condition) that defines the ECs:

Condition	Invalid ECs	Valid ECs
x+y	-	$< T$ [1]; $\geq T$ [2]

The result is the following tests.

ECs covered	Test case	Expected output
[1]	$x = 12; y = 23; T = 100$	true
[2]	$x = -23; y = 15; T = -10$	false

34.2.6 Example: Formatting

Conditions on the output are just as important as conditions on the input. Consider the following formatting method:

```
/** format a string representing of a double. The string is always
    6 characters wide and in the form ###.##, that is the double is
    rounded to 2 digit precision. Numbers smaller than 100 have '0'
    prefix. Example: 123 -> '123.00'; 2,3476 -> '002.35' etc. If the
    number is larger or equal to 999.995 then '***.**' is output to
    signal overflow. All negative values are signaled with '---.--'
*/
public String format(double x);
```

Here, there are a few partitions on the input x, but there are also several conditions on the output side that define interesting input to present to the method.

Condition	Invalid ECs	Valid ECs
overflow / underflow	$\geq$ 1000.0 [1]; $<$ 0.0 [2]	
2 digit rounding		(,00x round up) [3]; (,00x round down) [4]
prefix		no '0' prefix [5] exact '0' prefix [6] exact '00' prefix [7] exact '000' prefix [8]
output suffix		'.yx' suffix ($x \neq 0$)[9] '.x0' suffix ($x \neq 0$)[10] exact '.00' suffix [11]

Note that I here apply my rule of thumb for overflow and negative values. Arguably, these inputs are not invalid, but they will most likely be treated as the first thing in the method and the method will "bail out" once it detects it—and then return without further processing:

```
if (x < 0.0) return "---.--"
[...]
```

The next ECs concern that the rounding works correctly and that the '0' are prefixed ('001.03' and not '1.03') and suffixed ('123.30' and not '123.3') correctly on the output. The test cases could thus look like:

ECs covered	Test case	Expected output
[1]	1234.456	'***.**'
[2]	-0.1	'—.–'
[3][5][9]	212.738	'212.74'
[4][6][10]	32.503	'032.50'
[3][7][11]	7.995	'008.00'
[4][8][9]	0.933	'000.93'

Note that the first conditions (6 characters wide and a "." in the 4th position) are covered though not mentioned in the EC table.

34.2.7 Example: Chess King

Consider a method to validate if a move from position (c1,r1) to position (c2,r2) on a chess board is valid for a chess king.

```
// Precondition: column, row are within the board
// Precondition: player in turn is not considered
public boolean kingMoveIsValid(char c1, int r1, char c2, int r2);
```

The first thing I do is to look at the conditions (the type of condition given in parentheses):

1. the distance between the "from" and "to" square ((c1,r1),(c2,r2)) is exactly one: vertically, horizontally, or diagonally (Range).
2. the king is not in check at the "to" square (Boolean).
3. additionally a king can make a castling move, if
   (a) the king and the rook in question have never been moved (Boolean).
   (b) there are no pieces on the row section between the rook and the king (Boolean).
   (c) the king is not in check (Boolean).
   (d) the king does not move through a square that is attacked by a piece of the opponent (Boolean).
4. there are no friendly pieces at the "to" square (Boolean).

All conditions are formulated such that if they are true then the move is valid. Note also that the preconditions mean I do not have to consider moving off the board nor moving the opponent's king. The validation method, as seen from a testing viewpoint, has more input parameters than appears in the parameter list: the state of the board is of course an essential "input" to the method.

Based on the single range and multiple boolean conditions, my first sketch of an EC table looks like (again classifying input leading to "bail out" processing as invalid ECs):

Condition	Invalid ECs	Valid ECs
1. distance (d)	$d = 0$ [1]; $d > 1$ [2];	$d = 1$ [3]
2. not in check at "to"	false [4]	true [5]
3.(a)	false [6]	true [7]
3.(b)	false [8]	true [9]
3.(c)	false [10]	true [11]
3.(d)	false [12]	true [13]
4. no friendly at 'to'	false [14]	true [15]

Upon reviewing EC [3] I discover that this partitioning will lead to only one test case for the proper distance $d = 1$, for instance a move one square vertically up like ('f',5)–('f',6). However, is this single test case really representative for all $d = 1$ moves? No, I think it is not. Consider a programmer pressed for the delivery deadline and thus in a terrible rush—he may just be subtracting the column and row values without considering taking absolute value like e.g.

```
...
if ( r2 - r1 == 1 ) return true;
```

Note that this implementation passes the ('f',5)-('f',6) test case. So I repartition [3] to ensure that moves are tested both vertically and horizontally in both directions:

Condition	Invalid ECs	Valid ECs
row distance		-1 [3a]; 0 [3b]; +1 [3c]
column distance		-1 [3d]; 0 [3e]; +1 [3f]

This ensures I generate valid test cases in which the king moves in all directions and both vertically and horizontally. Note that the combination [3b] [3e] is of course not possible as the distance is zero.

The start of a test case table for the valid ECs may look like

ECs covered	Test case	Expected output
[3a][3e][15]	('f',5) to ('f',4)	valid
[3b][3f][15]	('f',5) to ('g',5)	valid
[3c][3d][15]	('f',5) to ('e',6)	valid
...		

I now have three test cases for legal moves instead for only one, and these three test cases are guaranteed to test absolute value in the distance calculations in both vertical and horizontal directions. Note that the test cases are formulated terse but there are several underlying assumptions: there is no blocking friendly piece on the 'to' square, and there is indeed a king located on ('f',5).

A further repartitioning concern is "does capture work correctly?" Perhaps a programmer just rejects the move as invalid if any piece is located on the 'to' square, not just a friendly piece? I can repartition the *no friendly at "to" square* condition into a set condition: *contents of "to" square* and update the EC table:

Condition	Invalid ECs	Valid ECs
4. 'to' square contents	friendly [14]	empty [15a]; opponent [15b]

Exercise 34.2: Review the table for more potential repartitioning. Complete the EC and test case tables.

34.3 Boundary Analysis

Experience shows that test cases focusing on *boundary conditions* have a high payoff. Boundaries are usually expressed by conditional statements in the code, and these conditionals are often wrong (the notorious "off by one" error) or plainly missing. Well known examples are for instance iteration over a C array that runs just over the maximal size or calling methods on an object reference that may become null.

> Definition: **Boundary value**
> A boundary value is an element that lies right on or next to the edge of an equivalence class.

As an example, consider the chess board position example. As the conditions on row and column are of the range type, the boundaries are explicit: 'a', 'h', 1 and 8, and testing on and just next to these boundaries are very important as conditions can easily be coded incorrectly:

```
if ( row <= 1 ) return false; // should have been row < 1
```

The set and boolean condition guidelines generate ECs that have the boundaries embodied in the ECs themselves: for instance, *true* and *false* are the only valid elements for the boolean condition.

Another example is the case of the formatting method in which there is an abrupt change of behavior at the boundary value of negative values. Thus 0.0 is an interesting value because an error in the condition may return '—.–' for this value. The same argument goes for the overflow boundary making 999.94 and 999.95 obviously interesting.

Boundary value analysis is an important tool to detect some of the most difficult defects; but you should always be aware what the underlying implementation actually does. Some algorithms define a "continuum of computation" where an *off by one* error at a boundary will not show up at all. As an example, consider an algorithm to add interest to a bank account: if the balance is above $0 then a 2% interest rate is added, otherwise an 8% interest rate is deducted. An obvious boundary is of course 0. But—the problem is that we cannot detect any difference in the output no matter what the interest rate calculation is for an account with balance 0. Thus boundary values are less interesting here.

34.4 Discussion

Equivalence partitioning and boundary value analysis are important techniques for finding high quality test cases. Here "high quality" means test cases that have a high probability of finding defects. Still, remember that they are both means to an end, not the end itself. This perhaps obvious fact is however easy to miss once you get absorbed in partitioning, describing ECs using set notation, and combining ECs to produce test cases. Here are some of the pitfalls I often see people fall into.

Key Point: Observe unit preconditions

Do not generate ECs and test cases for conditions that a unit specifically cannot or should not handle.

I often see a tendency to generate lots of test cases for invalid ECs and rather few test cases for valid ECs. However, once people start to convert the invalid test cases into automated tests in for instance JUnit they experience that they either cannot express the test case in code or the unit under test is not designed to cope with the input values after all. If a method states that it is a precondition that some input parameter is within a certain range then it does not make sense to generate a test case with a value outside this range. For instance an algorithm to calculate some value based upon a wind direction in degrees may state the precondition that it is within the 0–359 degree range. This is plausible as the hardware simply cannot produce any value outside this range. It is thus a waste of effort to define ECs and test cases above 359 and below 0 degrees. Another example is graphical user interfaces that often do partial range checks before calling domain units. For instance, a method move(from, to) of any board game domain implementation can have as precondition that there is indeed a piece located on the "from" location, because a user cannot grab a non-existing piece using the mouse on a graphical playing board.

Key Point: Systematic testing assumes competent programmers

Equivalence partitioning and other testing techniques rely on honest and competent programmers that are using standard techniques.

Consider a programmer that implements Math.abs using an incredible long switch statement:

```
public int abs(int x) {
  switch(x) {
   case 1: return 1;
   case 2: return 2;
   case 3: return 3;
   case 7123: return 8222;
   case -1: return -1;
   ...
}
```

A black box testing technique only considers the specification and this incredibly stupid implementation is hidden from the tester. In this case, of course, the element 7123 from the EC = $\{x|x > 0\}$ is not representative of the other elements, but a tester has no chance of knowing that. Also, black box techniques cannot discover "easter eggs" or real malicious code fragments that are triggered by special input values, combinations of them or special sequences.

Key Point: Do not use Myers combination heuristics blindly

Myers heuristics for generating test cases from valid and invalid ECs can lead to omitting important test cases.

Many algorithms simply return the result of a complex calculation but with very few special cases and thus the specification contains few or no "conditions". Focusing on conditions in the EC finding process is good at treating the special cases but the combination rule that merge as many valid ECs as possible sometimes leads to a situation where just zero or a single test case are defined for the complex computation! Of course, test cases must also be defined for the ordinary computations.

34.5 Summary of Key Concepts

Systematic testing is a systematic process for finding defects in some unit under test. Testing techniques are generally considered either *black-box* or *white-box*. In black-box techniques you only consider the specification and common knowledge of programming while in white-box testing you in addition inspect the source code. Many systematic testing techniques require a substantial effort and is thus best used on complex and/or essential software units.

The *equivalence class partitioning* technique is based on partitioning the input space into *equivalence classes* which are subsets of the input space. Elements in an equivalence class (EC) must all have the *representation* property, that is, if one element in the EC exposes a defect during testing, then all other elements in the EC must expose the same defect. The set of all ECs must *cover* the full input set for the set of ECs to be considered sound. Finding ECs is an iterative and heuristic process: a good starting point is *conditions* in the specification of the unit. Guidelines for *ranges*, *sets*, and *boolean conditions* allow a first partitioning to be found. These partitions should be closely reviewed to ensure the representation property, if in doubt, then ECs should be further repartitioned. Next, test cases are generated by combining ECs. One approach is to make every combination of ECs. This, however, often leads to a very high number of test cases. Another approach is that of Myers in which as many valid ECs are covered as possible until the valid ECs are exhausted; and next invalid ECs are covered in which only one element is taken from an invalid EC at the time. The latter rule is important to avoid *masking*: the ability for the error checking code for one parameter to mask a defect in the error checking code for another parameter.

Finally, *boundary analysis* complements EC testing as it identifies the values right on or next to edges of ECs as particularly important to test as experience has shown that programmers often have "off by one" errors in their conditions. Boundary analysis is important for range conditions but is often not applicable for other types of conditions.

The treatment in this chapter is inspired by heuristics first outlined by Myers (1979) and later restated by Burnstein (2003). Binder (2000) is a comprehensive book on testing object-oriented software.

34.6 Selected Solutions

Discussion of Exercise 34.1:

A) Removing a defect in *dead* code (i.e. code that can never be executed) does not change the software's reliability.

B) As an example, if there is a single defect in an application's "save" feature it may make the application useless; contrast this to a defect in some obscure, seldom used, function of the software.

34.7 Review Questions

Define the concepts *systematic testing*, *black-box* and *white-box testing*.

Define what an *equivalence class* is and name the properties that must be fulfilled for the set of ECs to be sound. Why is partitioning the input space into ECs interesting?

Describe the process of finding test cases using the EC technique: what steps are involved? What guidelines are used to find ECs? What guidelines are used to construct test cases based on the ECs. Why is ECs often repartitioned further?

Define *boundary value analysis* and explain what it is.

34.8 Further Exercises

Exercise 34.3:

Generate test cases using the equivalence class partitioning technique for the method to validate moves in Breakthrough, defined in exercise 5.4.

1. Outline the EC table. Describe the analysis in terms of the guidelines applied and argue for *coverage* and *representation*.
2. Outline the test case table, and argue how the test cases have been generated.

Exercise 34.4:

Add test cases to your test case table for Breakthrough move validation from the previous exercise based on a boundary value analysis.

Exercise 34.5:

The MET REPORT encodes local airport weather information in an internationally accepted format. The MET REPORT is broadcasted locally in the airport to flight leaders and forwarded to incoming aircrafts. To a pilot the characteristics of the wind on the landing strip is important and a MET REPORT contains a 5 character field denoted `dddff` that provides wind data. For instance, if the field contains "09012" then a 12 knot wind blows in direction east and "00005" is a 5 knot wind blowing north. The first three digits (ddd) code the *wind direction* in degrees [0;359] where 0 is north, 90 is east, etc. The last two digits (ff) code the *wind speed* in knots. Both `ddd` and `ff` are calculated based upon the *two minute mean wind*, that is, the wind direction and speed is sampled every 10 seconds and a floating mean is calculated over the samples from the last two minutes. A 2 minute mean measurement contains also the upper and lower extremes for the wind direction. For example the mean wind direction may be 90, the low extreme 60 and the high extreme 200; this would show that the prevailing wind has been east but there seems to have been a sudden, short, change towards south.

You can consider that the method to calculate the string representing `dddff` is defined by a method:

```
public String dddff( TwoMinuteMeanWind w )
```

that takes an object, w, representing the two minute mean wind coded as a simple data object:

```
public class TwoMinuteMeanWind {
  /** true iff sensor readings are valid */
  public boolean valid;
  /** two minute mean wind direction; the value
      is between 0 and 359 degrees. */
  public int direction;
  /** two minute mean wind speed in knots; the
      value is between 0.0 and 99.9 */
  public double speed;
  /** low extreme wind direction in the
      two minute time span; range [0;359] degrees.
      PostCondition: low < high always. */
  public int low;
  /** high extreme wind direction in the
      two minute time span; range [0;359] degrees.
      PostCondition: low < high always. */
  public int high;
}
```

Note that 'low' is always the numerical lowest value, that is it is always true that 'low' < 'high'. This data object is guaranteed to be correct by the wind measuring hardware and obey all post conditions and specifications.

The output string of dddff is defined as follows:

1. The output `dddff` string is always a full 5 character string. If a direction or speed is not three digits or two digits respectively, then '0's are prefixed. That is, direction 7 degrees and speed 2 knots is coded "00702".

2. However, if the sensor is broken ('w.valid'==false), no samples are provided and `dddff` is coded as "**** " indicating 'not known'. (Note the space character at the end.)

3. If the wind speed is below 0.5 knots, then the `dddff` output string is "CALM " no matter what the wind direction is. (Again, note the space at the end.)

4. If the difference between the lower and upper extremes of wind direction is more than 180 degrees then the `ddd` is coded as "VRB" meaning *variable wind*. Note that you cannot simply subtract 'high' – 'low' to find if it is a VRB condition; you have to take the wind direction into account. (Example: low = 80 and high = 280 is not a VRB condition if ddd=10; but it *is* a VRB condition if ddd=180.)

5. CALM takes precedence over VRB (the wind sensor simply does not move in CALM conditions thus the lower and upper extremes are simply non-sense.)

Generate test cases using the equivalence class partitioning technique for the method `dddff`.

1. Outline the EC table. Describe the analysis in terms of the guidelines applied and argue for *coverage* and *representation*.

2. Outline the test case table, and argue how the test cases have been generated.

Exercise 34.6:

Add test cases to your test case table for `dddff` from the previous exercise based on a boundary value analysis.

Part 9

Projects

This part of the book is not a learning iteration but instead outlines two projects. These projects are defined in terms of a sequence of exercises and some template production and test code to get you started. By working on the exercises for either of the projects you will cover the learning objectives of most of the techniques and topics presented in the book. Both projects are divided into six *learning releases*: each learning release's objective is practical and theoretical training in the topics from the corresponding learning iteration in the book, starting from learning iteration 2: *The Programming Process*. Each learning release is also a *small release* in the XP sense as new features are added to the code developed so far and thus the system grows from a simple application to a complex and configurable framework.

Chapter	Project Domain
Chapter 35	*The HotGammon Project.* The HotGammon project is a project where the product goal is to build a framework for variants of the backgammon game, a classic board game for two players.
Chapter 36	*The HotCiv Project.* HotCiv is a project whose product goal is a framework for designing strategic "conquer the world" computer games, inspired by the *Civilization* line of games.

The HotCiv project is somewhat more complex than the HotGammon project. Note also that most of the exercises in the framework learning iteration of the projects are based upon MiniDraw that has a rather steep learning curve.

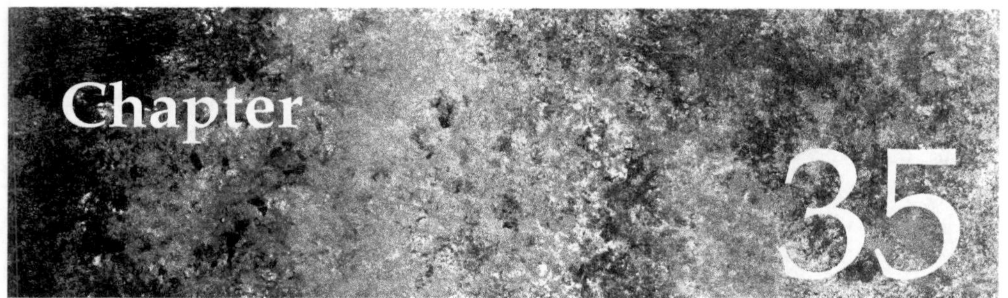

The HotGammon Project

Learning Objectives

This project is a progression of assignments that gives you hands-on experience with central techniques covered in the book. Each section in this chapter defines exercises that roughly correlate to a learning iteration in the book. Each section is also a *small release* in that you are supposed to deliver a partial implementation that nevertheless implements relevant features. Taken together the exercises lead to a framework for playing **backgammon** and variants of the game using a graphical user interface as shown in Figure 35.1.

The set of exercises and releases are organized in an agile fashion so in keeping with the agile spirit of "keep it simple" I advise not to read far ahead and design in anticipation of future assignments. Instead, *keep focus* on the assignments included in the next small release. In future assignments, you may then refactor your design to better suit whatever set of assignments is defined as part of the next small release.

☞ Search the internet for resources on backgammon and variations of the game. You will also be able to find playable implementations.

35.1 HotGammon

In this section, the general aspects of backgammon are described for reference, but remember that you are not supposed to implement all the complex details from the start: *take small steps* and *keep focus* on one particular aspect at a time.

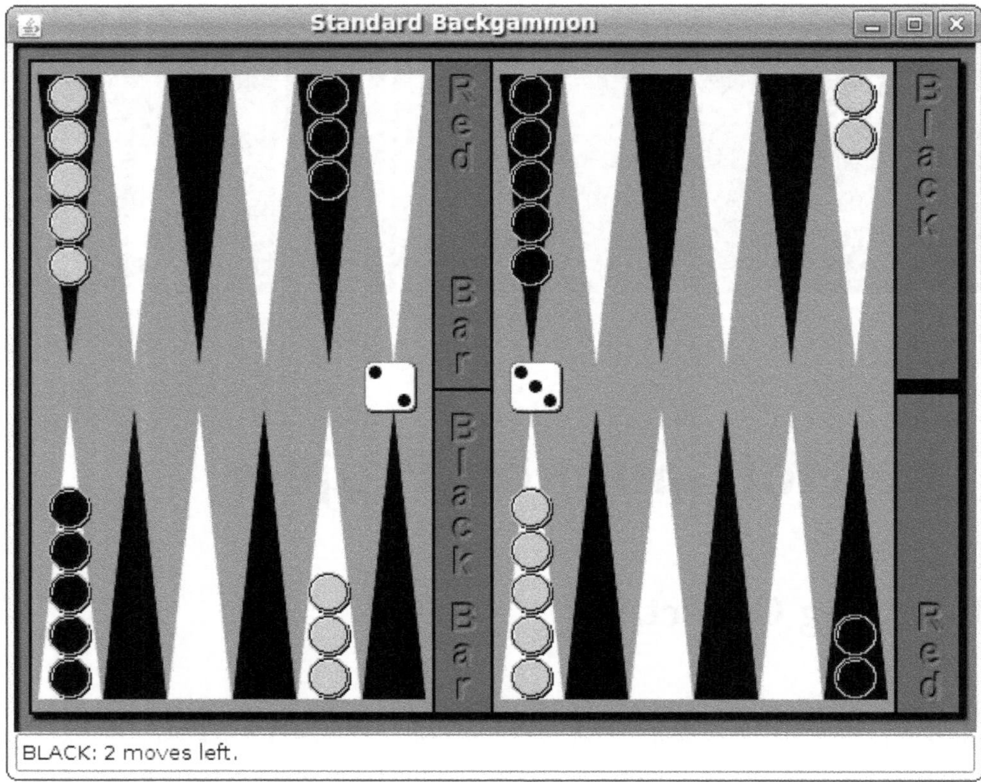

Figure 35.1: A screen shot of the MiniDraw based graphical user interface for the HotGammon framework, configured for standard backgammon.

35.1.1 Object of the Game

Backgammon is a board game for two players, here called *red* and *black* in which checkers are moved according to the roll of a pair of dice. Normally, the winner is the first to remove all of his or her own pieces from the board. However, particular variants of the game may state other objectives.

The board is shown in Figure 35.2. The triangles where checkers are located are called *points* or *locations*. The figure shows the notation used for the locations: those at black's side are named B1 to B12 and those at red's side are named R1 to R12. B1–B6 is called black's inner table while B7–B12 is black's outer table. Similarly, R1–R6 is red's inner table and R7–R12 is red's outer table.

Each player has 15 checkers that are moved according to the roll of the dice and according to the rules of the particular variant of backgammon that you are playing. Both players move their checkers towards their own inner table, that is, in the direction shown on the figure.

In standard backgammon the checkers are initially positioned as shown in Figure 35.1. Checkers may rest on four other locations besides the triangular locations you see: on the red or black *bar* (in the middle of the board) and on the *bear off* (right side of the board). The bar is the middle line between the outer and inner tables and is the

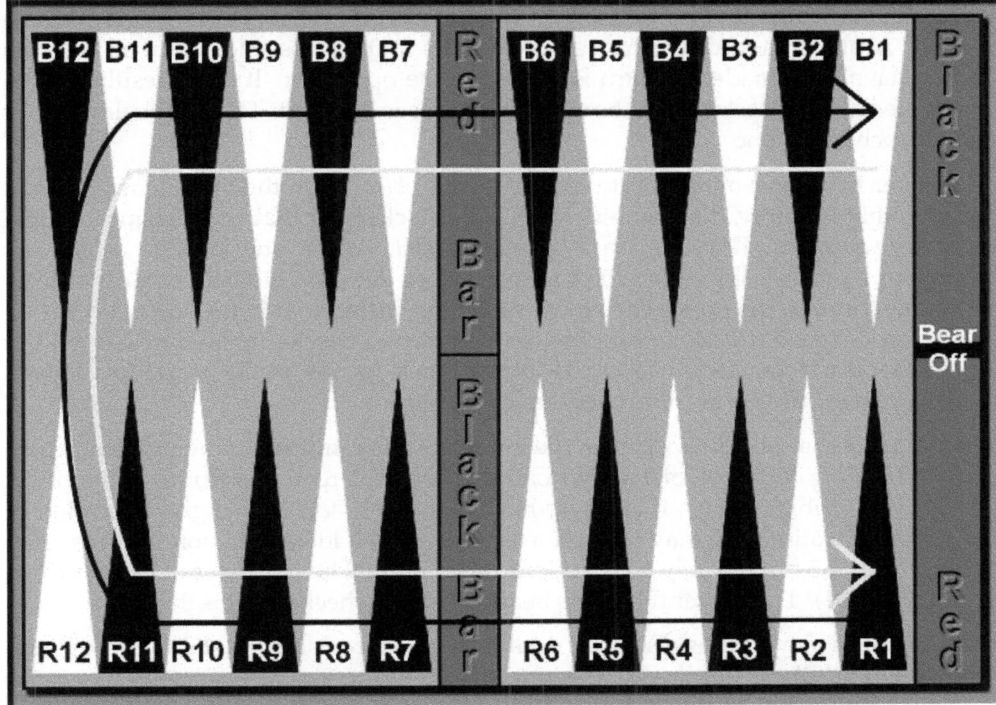

Figure 35.2: Backgammon notation for its locations and movement direction.

place where checkers that have been hit by opponent checkers are placed. (In normal backgammon you do not distinguish between red's and black's bar but in a computer version this becomes handy.) The bear off is the place where checkers that are removed from the board are stored.

35.1.2 Backgammon Rules

Checkers are moved on the board according to the roll of two dice subject to the particular rules of each variant. In this project, the rules will start out very simple and incrementally increase in complexity to handle standard backgammon. Here a brief summary of backgammon rules are given. Consult text books or online resources for a more in-depth treatment.

Initially, each player rolls one die. The player with the higher number moves first, using the values of the thrown dice. After that, players alternate turns, throwing the dice at the beginning of each turn. I will use the notation 3-4 to indicate that one die shows 3 and the other 4 after rolling them. The first die value is considered red's die, so the 3-4 roll will mean black is first to move when the game starts.

Each die value forces the player to move a checker the distance indicated by the number. Thus rolling 3-4 require a player to move one checker three locations forward and one checker four locations forward. The same checker may be moved twice as long as the two moves are distinct. This is important because a checker cannot land on a location occupied by two or more of the opponent's checkers: such a location is *blocked*. A player is forced to move his checkers if at all possible. Once all possible moves have been made, the turn is passed to the opponent. If a roll results in two equal die values, like 4-4, then the count of moves is doubled. That is 4-4 allows four moves each of distance 4.

A checker may land on all locations that are not *blocked* by the opponent, that is, a location that is empty, that contains your own checkers, or that contains just a single opponent checker. The latter case is called a *blot*. When you land on a blot, the opponent checker is moved to the bar. A checker put onto the bar can only reenter the game through the opponent's inner table. For instance, if black has a checker on the bar, rolling 2-3 will allow him to move his barred checker to either R2 or R3 but of course only if they are not blocked. No ordinary moves on the board are allowed while a player has one or more checkers in the bar.

Once a player has all his checkers in the inner table he can start removing them which is called *bearing off*. A roll of 2 allows one checker to be removed from location 2 (R2 for red, B2 for black), etc. If a player has no checkers left on the given location or any higher locations, he may bear off a checker from a lower location. For instance, if black rolls 4-5 but his only has checkers on B1 and B2 he may bear of two checkers from B2 (or B1). The player that firsts bears off all his checkers wins the game.

Backgammon players may also use a doubling cube for raising the stakes during play. The doubling cube is not used in this project.

35.2 Test-Driven Development of AlphaMon

The learning objective of this iteration is practical experience with, and reflection over, test-driven development. The product goal is to develop *AlphaMon* that is an extremely simple (and from a gamer's perspective: rather boring) HotGammon variant. While being a simple game, it nevertheless represents a functionally complete game serving as a small release, and a stepping stone towards a full backgammon game.

AlphaMon is played on a standard Backgammon board and its rule set is identical *except* for the following rather drastic changes :

- The dice rolls are not random but produce a fixed sequence of values. The first roll gives die values 1-2, the next 3-4, next 5-6, and then it starts all over again. Note that this sequence will never result in a doubling of number of moves—a player always moves two checkers per turn. Note also that it means black starts the game.
- The game ends after 6 rolls of the dice. The winner is always Red. Note the consequence is that you may disregard rules of how to get checkers off the board.
- A player may move any of his/her checkers to any location on the board *except* to a location that has one or more of the opponents checkers (thus there are no blots, and no coupling to the values of the dice). Note that the consequence is that the rules for moving checkers in and out of the bar can be disregarded.

- It is still only legal to move checkers for the player in turn and only when there are still moves left to make.

35.2.1 Provided Code

As a starting point an interface for a backgammon implementation, Game, is provided as is two enumeration types, Color and Location. The source code files are located in *project/hotgammon/alphamon* and responsibilities outlined below.

Location

- Represents a specific location, B1..B12, R1..R12, bars, etc., on the backgammon board.
- Can calculate the signed distance between two locations; a positive distance is towards black's inner table.
- Can calculate target location given a start location, player color, and a distance

Color

- Represents a color: Red, Black, or None; of a player, a checker, or the color of checkers on a specific location on the board.

The Game interface expresses all the responsibilities of a backgammon domain implementation and therefore has a fair number of responsibilities as well as methods.

Game

- Knows the game's state: player in turn, moves left in turn, dice thrown.
- Knows the state of the board: number of checkers and their color on a given location.
- Knows the values of the dice rolled.
- Knows if the game has been won and by who.
- Allows moving a checker or reject move if it is illegal.
- Allows rolling the dice.
- Allows starting a new game.

An implementation of this interface will allow a user interface both to access all relevant game state in order to draw the board and dice as well as change the game's state based upon interaction with one or two users. As an example the following code fragment may draw the game's board.

```
for( Location l : Location.values() ) {
  int numberOfCheckers = game.getCount(l);
  Color checkerColor = game.getColor(l);
  [draw the checkers on the location]
}
```

☞ You may modify these interfaces and classes but remember that the graphical user interface depends on these abstractions.

The provided code represents a set of design decisions I have made and these are discussed below.

Representation of Checkers. Why are checkers not represented by objects, instances of a Checker class? The point is that checkers do not expose any interesting behavior in themselves—they simply exist. As the interesting aspect of checkers is their number and color on a given location, I prefer to query the game directly, like this code that asserts that B1 contains two red checkers:

```
assertEquals( 2, game.getCount(Location.B1) );
assertEquals( Color.RED, game.getColor(Location.B1) );
```

Representation of Locations. Once that I have decided that checkers are not represented directly as objects, locations do not need to store checker objects and thus are in no need of behavior. I have therefore decided to represent them as a Java enumeration type: *Location.B1, Location.B2*, etc. *Location.B1* of course corresponds to the B1 point on Figure 35.2.

The advantage of an enumeration instead of using, say, string values to represent locations in method calls to the board instance is that I get higher reliability and I need to write less parameter checking code:

```
// This is NOT the way the interface is!!!
assertEquals( 2, game.getCount(''B1'') );
```

In the method call above I could by mistake have written

```
// This is NOT the way the interface is!!!
assertEquals( 2, game.getCount(''Bq'') );
```

This defect must be caught by our testing code whereas it is impossible to write an unknown location using the enumeration as the compiler will catch the mistake.

The Location enumeration contains methods that makes it easy to calculate distances and target locations on the board. For instance to assert that the distance between B1 and B2 is 1 you write the following:

```
assertEquals( 1, Location.distance( Location.B2, Location.B1 ) );
assertEquals( -1, Location.distance( Location.B1, Location.B2 ) );
```

Note that distance is signed: moving towards black's inner table is a positive distance. Similarly you can easily find the target location to move a checker given a player and a distance, like Red player wanting to move distance 4 from B2:

```
assertEquals( Location.B6,
              Location.findLocation( Color.RED, Location.B2, 4) );
```

Dual Bar and Bear Off Locations. The special locations for bear off and the bar are split into those for red and those for black. This way, black and red checkers are not mixed at any time on any location . Note that for these locations the prefix defines the only checker color that can stay on them: *Location.B_BAR* is where black checkers are in the bar and *Location.B_BEAR_OFF* is the bear off location of black checkers.

The reason for having bear off locations (instead of removing checkers from the board) is that it enables easy testing if a game is won (15 checkers at the bear off location) and it allows stating a class invariant that the game board always contain 30 checkers.

Preconditions on Game methods. A few methods in the Game interface have rather strict preconditions. For instance, consider the nextTurn() method that has the following precondition:

```
* PRECONDITION: The player in turn has indeed exhausted
* his/her ability to make moves.
```

Thus, it is up to the client software unit (the object using the game instance, typically a graphical user interface), to ensure these preconditions. It of course also means you should not make tests that break the preconditions.

No Board abstraction? The provided code does not contain a Board interface encapsulating the responsibilities of the board. This does not mean it is not a good idea to introduce it. Remember though the agile principle of *simplicity*: introduce it when your TDD process tells you that the production code will become more maintainable by having it.

35.2.2 JUnit Tests

Skeleton code for the JUnit test suite is defined in TestAlphamon. Also tests are defined for the Location enumeration in the TestLocation test class.

35.2.3 Exercises

Exercise 35.1. Source code directory:
`project/hotgammon/alphamon`

> *Based upon the skeleton code, develop the AlphaMon variant using the test-driven development process.*

In this exercise, the learning objective is practicing the TDD process: the rhythm, the principles, and the values of *taking small steps, keep focus, speed.* Do not design ahead in anticipation of future requirements (in the later learning iterations), but remember *simplicity.* Please consult sidebar 35.1 on page 430 on ideas on how to organize your team work.

To get you going, here is a potential first few items for your test list:

* After nextTurn() is invoked the first time, Black is in turn.
* There are two black checkers on R1.
* Moving a checker from R1 to R2 at the start of a game is valid according to the AlphaMon rules. After the move there is one black checker on R1 and one black on R2. After the move there is only one move left for Black to make.
* Moving a checker from R1 to B1 is invalid as there is an opponent (red) checker there.
* After moving the two black checkers, the number of moves left is 0.
* Red player is in turn after nextTurn() is invoked the second time; and the die values are 3-4
* ...

Sidebar 35.1: Organizing Teams for TDD

I advise teams to **pair program** and record the learning process as part of the programming process: take turns of about half an hour where one of you is the *driver/programmer*: has the keyboard and writes the test and production code; one is the *navigator/test list maintainer*: maintains the test list, invents new items for the test list, and reviews the written testing and production code to spot defects and opportunities for refactoring; and one has the role of *recorder* that writes down the iteration focus, the actions taken in each step of the rhythm, formulates and discusses the TDD principles used, and interrupts the process if the programmer or the test list maintainer stop using the TDD process, start taking large steps, lose focus, or there is a need for redoing an iteration. (This way, the recorder is developing the report for the exercise.) If you are only two in the team, then the person without the keyboard must do both the test list maintainer and the recorder role.

I clearly advise the teams to work together at the *same time*, and in the *same location*. If that is completely impossible, I advise each member individually to do several iterations in completion by themselves and take on all three roles (as I do in the TDD chapter in the book). Later, the teams should discuss each member's experiences and summarize them.

1. Develop production and test code for AlphaMon using TDD.
2. Write a report that includes
   (a) The final test list.
   (b) An outline of two or three *interesting* TDD iterations in detail, outlining the steps of the rhythm, testing principles used, and refactorings made.
   (c) A reflection of observed benefits and liabilities of the TDD approach.

Exercise 35.2:

Try to swap your team's developed test cases with another team and execute them on your production code.

1. Classify the reasons for test cases failing. Potential classes are 1) changed interface(s), 2) defects in the production code that your own test cases did not find, 3) defects in the test code, 4) vague specification of AlphaMon that has led to different interpretations in the teams, etc.
2. Consider/count the number of test cases and number of asserts. Do more test cases (asserts) find more defects?

Exercise 35.3:

Refactor the development environment for your developed AlphaMon to use the Ant build management tool.

Introduce the build management environment using *the rhythm* and *taking small steps*.

1. Develop Ant targets to compile production and test code and execute your developed tests.
2. Refactor your targets to split the source and build tree, and further split the source tree into a production code and test code tree.
3. Use Ant to create JavaDoc for the production tree code.
4. Write a report that includes
   (a) A short outline of iterations made.
   (b) A reflection of observed benefits and liabilities of using the rhythm and small steps in refactoring the build environment.

Exercise 35.4:
Make a short oral presentation of key concepts and techniques in *test-driven development* for your team members/class, acting as opponents. The opponents should give constructive critique on correctness and presentation technique.

35.3 Strategy, Refactoring, and Integration

The learning focus of this small release is to get experience with the STRATEGY pattern and compositional design, as well as refactoring and integration testing.

The product oriented perspective is to develop new variants, BetaMon and others, of the game. Each variant adds more backgammon-like behavior to the program. Below the variants are presented first, followed by a set of exercises related to the variants.

35.3.1 BetaMon

BetaMon is identical to AlphaMon except the rules for checking that a move is valid are the real backgammon rules. Specifically:

- A checker may only move in the direction of the player's own inner table.
- The distance travelled must equal the value of a rolled die, and a die value must only be "used" once. That is, roll 2-3 allows one checker to move 2 and one checker (possibly the same) to move 3: it should not be allowed to move a checker, say 3 and then 3 again.
- A player moving a checker to a location where the opponent has exactly one checker will lead to the checker moving to the bar. Example: Red has a single checker at R8 and black moves a checker there. After this move, there must be one black checker at R8 and one (more) red checker at R_BAR.

- A location with two or more opponent checkers is a *blocked point* and you are not allowed to move there.
- A checker in the bar must move to the opponent's inner table. For instance if Black has a checker in the bar and rolls 1-4 then he must see if he can move a checker to either R1 or R4. Moves on the board are not allowed when a player has checkers left in his/her bar.
- Checkers are borne off according to the standard rules: You can only bear off once all your checkers are in your inner table. You are allowed to bear off checkers if the die value is higher than the distance if there are no checkers with a distance higher or equal to the die value. For example a die value of 5 may be used to bear off a checker on R4 if the red player has no checkers on R5 nor R6.

All other aspects of BetaMon are like AlphaMon: the dice are predictable, red wins after six turns, etc.

35.3.2 GammaMon

GammaMon is identical to AlphaMon (note: **not BetaMon**) except the way the winner is determined. The GammaMon game continues until one player has borne off all his/her checkers. The player who bears off first wins the game. All other aspects of GammaMon are like AlphaMon: the dice are predictable, the rules of movement are simple, etc.

35.3.3 DeltaMon

DeltaMon is identical to AlphaMon (note: **not BetaMon nor GammaMon**) except the way the turns change between players. Inspired by a backgammon variant called "Acey-Deucey" a player is allowed an extra turn if he throws the die roll 1-2 (or 2-1). That is, if the red player throws 1-2 then he makes two moves of checkers as usual, but is then allowed to throw the dice once more and move again according to the roll. If the second roll is also 1-2 he/she is granted yet another turn, etc.

35.3.4 Exercises

Exercise 35.5:

Develop the BetaMon variant using TDD by refactoring the AlphaMon production code. All HotGammon variants must be maintained.

1. Sketch a compositional design for the HotGammon system that supports the variants.
2. Refactor the AlphaMon production code to implement your design. Ensure your AlphaMon passes all test cases before starting to implement BetaMon. I advise to put common code into a package, like *hotgammon.common*, and variant code in some other package, like *hotgammon.variants*.

3. Implement the BetaMon variant using TDD.

Note: Some of the BetaMon rules, like bearing off, cannot be properly tested in the context of the full BetaMon system as it will end after only six turns. You may choose to implement only those aspects that can be TDD developed within the six turns. You will return to implement the full set of rules in exercise 35.15 in the next learning iteration.

Exercise 35.6:

Compare your design of the BetaMon compositional solution from the previous exercise with the STRATEGY pattern as outlined in the pattern box on page 130. Explain and argue which abstractions match the different roles of the pattern.

Exercise 35.7:

Develop the GammaMon variant using TDD by refactoring the developed HotGammon production code. All HotGammon variants must be maintained.

1. Sketch a compositional design for the HotGammon system that supports the GammaMon variant.
2. Refactor the existing HotGammon production code to support the new design while all existing variants pass their test suites.
3. Implement the GammaMon variant using TDD.

Exercise 35.8:

Develop the DeltaMon variant using TDD by refactoring the developed HotGammon production code. All HotGammon variants must be maintained.

1. Sketch a compositional design for the HotGammon system that supports the DeltaMon variant.
2. Refactor the existing HotGammon production code to support the new design while all existing variants pass their test suites.
3. Implement the variant using TDD.

Exercise 35.9:

Analyze and describe your testing code and highlight which parts are unit tests of the variants and which parts are integration tests.

Exercise 35.10:

The BetaMon, GammaMon, and DeltaMon variants could of course be implemented using other variability techniques. Sketch designs and/or code fragments that represent:

1. A source code copy proposal.
2. A parametric proposal.
3. A polymorphic proposal.

Exercise 35.11:

Analyze the compositional solution for the variants with respect to coupling and cohesion. Argue why coupling is low or high. Argue why cohesion is low or high.

Exercise 35.12:

Make a short oral presentation of the STRATEGY pattern and different implementation techniques for handling variable behavior.

35.4 Test Stubs and Variability

This small release focuses on learning test stubs and the STATE and ABSTRACT FACTORY design patterns. The product objectives are more variants of the HotGammon system.

35.4.1 EpsilonMon

EpsilonMon is identical to AlphaMon except that the die rolls are random. All other aspects of the game are identical to AlphaMon.

35.4.2 ZetaMon

ZetaMon is identical to AlphaMon except that the starting position is inspired by the Hypergammon variant: Each player only has three checkers positioned on the first, second, and third location in the opponent's inner table. That is, black player has his checkers on R1, R2 and R3.

35.4.3 Exercises

Exercise 35.13:

Develop the EpsilonMon variant using a compositional approach by refactoring the HotGammon production code. As much production code as possible must be under automated testing control.

1. Sketch a design for EpsilonMon and discuss it using the terminology of test stubs.
2. Implement the variant using TDD by refactoring the existing HotGammon system.

Exercise 35.14:

Develop the ZetaMon variant using a compositional approach by refactoring the HotGammon production code.

1. Sketch a design for ZetaMon and implement the variant by refactoring the existing HotGammon system.
2. Implement the variant using TDD by refactoring the existing HotGammon system.

Exercise 35.15:

Developing the code for all the rules of BetaMon was impossible using a strict TDD process as the game ends after only six turns. Having six turns is too short to get all checkers into the inner table, which is required to test the production code to validate bear off moves. However, the ZetaMon variant and its solution are a strong hint on how to make automated tests even for the bear off moves.

1. Using the terminology of test stubs, discuss and analyze how the design for ZetaMon allows writing automated tests for the bear off validation in BetaMon.
2. Implement the remaining aspects of the BetaMon requirements using TDD.

Exercise 35.16:

A programmer wants to make a variant that allows *handicap*, that is, the two players play by different rules. Specifically, the game should use the rules of AlphaMon when black moves while it should use the rules of BetaMon while red moves.

1. Sketch a STATE pattern based design for this variant.
2. Implement the design using TDD.

Exercise 35.17:

> *Introduce* ABSTRACT FACTORY *for configuring all your supported HotGammon variants.*

That is, there should be a factory for each variant, AlphaMon, BetaMon, etc., that is responsible for creating the proper strategies, delegate objects, etc., for configuring the common HotGammon production code for the variant in question.

1. Sketch the design using class and sequence diagrams.
2. Refactor your present code to implement the design.

Exercise 35.18:

Your HotGammon system will contain test stubs at present.

1. Analyze and describe coupling and cohesion of your test stubs with respect to naming and position within the package and folder structure.
2. Refactor your production and test code so test stubs are properly named and cohesive classes, and located into packages and folders that express their testing purpose nature.

Exercise 35.19:

Make a short oral presentation of key concepts and techniques associated with test stubs for your team members/class, acting as opponents.

Exercise 35.20:

Make a short oral presentation of STATE and ABSTRACT FACTORY for your team members/class, acting as opponents.

35.5 Compositional Design

The learning objective of this iteration is exploring the compositional design approach and its ability to handle multiple dimensions of variability. The product objective is to configure the HotGammon system for an almost complete backgammon configuration: *SemiMon*.

35.5.1 SemiMon

SemiMon is a HotGammon variant that combines advanced aspects of the previous variants. Specifically, SemiMon

- uses the advanced rules for movement as defined by BetaMon.
- uses the strategy to determine a winner as defined by GammaMon.
- uses a random strategy for rolling a die as defined by EpsilonMon.

35.5.2 Exercises

Exercise 35.21:

Develop the SemiMon variant.

1. Produce a configuration table (see Section 17.2) outlining all variants and their variability points.
2. Analyze the amount of modifications in the HotGammon production code that are necessary to configure the SemiMon variant. Analyze if any design changes are necessary.
3. Implement the SemiMon variant.

Exercise 35.22:

Consider a purely parametric design of the AlphaMon, BetaMon, ..., ZetaMon variants. That is, all variable behaviors are controlled by if's and switches in a single large implementation of Game containing code for all the requirements.

1. Analyze this solution with respect to the amount and type of parameters to control variability.
2. Sketch the code of a few Game methods with emphasis on the variant handling code.

Exercise 35.23:

Consider a polymorphic design proposal for the AlphaMon, BetaMon, GammaMon, and EpsilonMon suite of variants, as outlined in Figure 35.3. Thus, for instance, the EpsilonMon would override the nextTurn() method in AlphaMon to roll random dice instead of advancing through the fixed sequence, while GammaMon would override the winner() to calculate the winner according to GammaMon rules, etc.

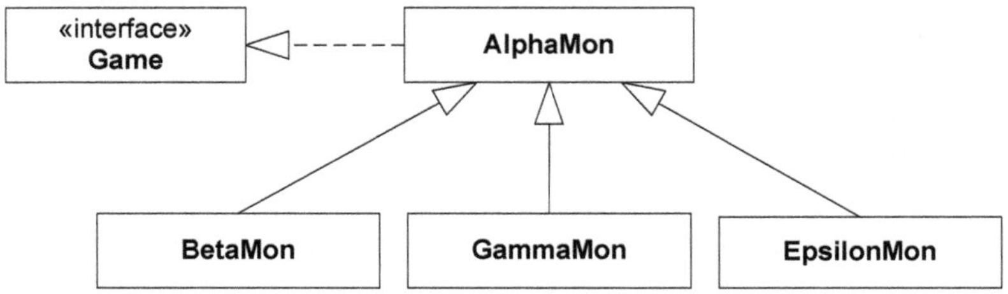

Figure 35.3: A polymorphic design for the Alpha, Beta, etc., suite.

1. Sketch one or two plausible ways of implementing SemiMon based on the polymorphic design outlined above, for instance by showing class diagrams, sequence diagrams, and/or code fragments.
2. Discuss benefits and liabilities of the polymorphic design in comparison with the compositional design .

Exercise 35.24:

Implement a full backgammon game variant.

Exercise 35.25:

In the EpsilonMon exercise (exercise 35.13) you factored out the ability to throw either fixed sequence or random dice rolls. Consider these two design statements:

A *The die is a real world phenomenon and I identify a class, named* Die, *to represent instances of a die concept.*

B *The game needs someone that is responsible for calculating a random die value between 1 and 6, and I encapsulate this algorithm in a* DieRollStrategy.

1. Discuss and classify the two design statements according to the classification of perspectives on object-oriented design and the various definitions of object-orientation.
2. Which perspective have you used in your own design?

Exercise 35.26:

Relate your design to the concepts of behavior, responsibility, role, *and* protocol.

Find examples of abstractions, objects, and interactions in your HotGammon system that are covered by each of the concepts above.

Exercise 35.27:

Relate your design to the three compositional design principles.

Find examples in your design where you have used the first, the second, and the third principle. Describe aspects of your design that fit the ③-①-② process.

Exercise 35.28:

Draw a *role diagram* (see Chapter 18) for your SemiMon showing the design patterns involved in your design.

Exercise 35.29:

Refactor HotGammon to allow run-time reconfiguration of which variant is used.

1. Analyze your present design and consider the changes required to allow reconfiguring one variant to another at run-time, for instance reconfigure a SemiMon game to become a BetaMon game while playing the game.
2. Refactor your code to support this requirement.

Exercise 35.30:

Make a short oral presentation of key concepts and techniques in compositional design, including definitions of role, responsibility, and protocol, and discuss the challenges of multi-dimensional variance. Your team members/class act as opponents.

35.6 Design Patterns

The learning focus of this iteration is to sharpen your ability to pick a proper design pattern for a problem at hand.

Note: The assignments in this iteration is not a prerequisite for the next framework iteration. Also note that some design patterns are treated in detail in the framework iteration.

35.6.1 Exercises

Exercise 35.31:

The graphical user interface introduced in the next iteration access and modify the HotGammon game's state through the Game interface.

- Identify the design pattern that the Game interface represents as seen from the perspective of a graphical user interface. Argue for benefits and liabilities of this design.

Exercise 35.32:

Expert players often analyze their games to learn and improve their game play. For this purpose they need a transcript of all actions made in the game, like e.g.:

```
Dice rolled: 3-1
RED moves (B1,B4)
RED moves (B1,B2)
Dice rolled: 2-4
BLACK moves (R1,R3)
...
```

1. Find a suitable design pattern to implement this requirement so any HotGammon variant can be transcribed. Your implementation must be purely *change by addition, not by modification*.
2. Describe the pattern you have chosen and outline why it is appropriate.
3. Implement your design.
4. Explain how can you turn transcribing on and off during the game.

Exercise 35.33:

A particular variant of backgammon is *shesh-besh*. The only difference in shesh-besh compared to backgammon is the roll 5-6 which is a joker roll: you are allowed to move two of your checkers to any two locations on the board irrespective of distance and direction.

1. Find a suitable design pattern to implement this requirement. Describe and argue for the resulting design.
2. Implement your design.

Exercise 35.34:

We want to enhance our HotGammon system to allow two players to play a game over some network. The game's state is stored on a central server and two players then access and modify the game's state using a user interface on their respective client computers: mobile phones, laptops, home computers, etc.

We envision a simple text/string based protocol to allow play using SMS/TXT messages, as exemplified by the following communication (the issuing computer shown in parentheses):

```
(client1) "ROLL DICE"
(server)  "3-1"
(client1) "B1,B4"
(server)  "OK"
(client1) "B1,B3"
(server)  "FAIL"
(client1) "B1,B2"
(server)  "OK"
(client2) "ROLL DICE"
(server)  "2-4"
...
```

That is, the first computer (client1) asks the server to roll the dice, and the server returns "3-1" to signal the outcome of the dice roll. Next, client1 moves a checker from B1 to B4, which the server accepts by replying "OK", etc.

Consider the implementation of the game on the client, for instance a mobile phone, which has graphical user interface that invokes methods on an implementation of the Game interface. This implementation must communicate with the server instead of doing the computations locally.

1. Find a suitable design pattern to support this requirement as seen from the client side with minimal changes into the existing design. Describe and argue for the resulting design.
2. Implement a partial solution to this problem. (Make server and client objects local and disregard networking, but ensure that server and client only communicate by exchanging strings.)

Exercise 35.35. Source code directory:
`library/minidraw`

MiniDraw contains a *boardgame* package. This experimental package provides hotspots for supporting graphical user interfaces specifically for board games. A demonstration application for the Breakthrough game can be found in the *minidraw.breakthrough* package.

1. Outline the design patterns used in the *boardgame* package to tie the graphical user interface to a game's domain code.

2. Describe how moving a figure representing a board game object, like a chess pawn in Breakthrough, can invoke the move method of a game: what design pattern is used? Argue why this pattern is necessary to achieve the necessary flexibility.

Exercise 35.36. Source code directory:
`project/hotgammon/patterns/gerry`

Tesauro (1995) has written a paper and developed a C function, pubeval.c, for computing moves for the black player in backgammon. I have converted it to Java and augmented it with a recursive move generator so a "best move" can be generated given the state of the board and dice: an *artificial intelligence (AI)* player. It is coded in the class Gerry. A simple JUnit test case for verifying black making a good move in response to die roll 1-6 in the opening position looks like this:

```
@Test
public void testOpening1() {
  move = gerry.play(openingboard, new int[] {1,6});
  // 6-1 -> B8-B7 + R12-B7
  assertEquals( move.getFrom(0), 17);
  assertEquals( move.getTo(0), 18);
  assertEquals( move.getFrom(1), 12);
  assertEquals( move.getTo(1), 18);
}
```

The play method takes two integer arrays, one encoding the state of the board (here the opening position), and one encoding the die values. The method returns a Move object which can be queried for the moves to make. The methods getFrom and getTo return simple integer values that uniquely identify a location on the board, like 17 for B8. Consult the source code for the encoding.

The present interface defines input and output using simple data structures and it is thus the responsibility of the client code that wants to use the AI player to, A) retrieve the state of a game and convert it into integer arrays, B) call the gerry.play method, and finally C) execute the moves that are returned in the move data structure.

An alternative design is based upon the ADAPTER pattern and add a method to class Gerry :

```
public class Gerry {
  public void play(GameAdapter game) { ... }
  [...]
}
```

In this revised design, the play method can implement all operations A–C once and for all but can play black in any backgammon implementation, not just your HotGammon system. That is, Gerry is the **client** role, playing the backgammon game via the GameAdapter interface (**Target** role), and your HotGammon system plays the **Adaptee** role in the ADAPTER pattern.

1. Describe the requirement of a GameAdapter in terms of the methods it must have and their responsibilities.

2. Write an adapter for the HotGammon system to allow Gerry to play black in a game.

Exercise 35.37:

Make a short oral presentation of two or three design patterns from the catalogue. Your team members/class act as opponents.

35.7 Frameworks

The learning objective of this small release is both practical and academic aspects of frameworks. You will get experience with specializing MiniDraw to a particular set of requirements. You will also explore aspects of several design patterns such as OBSERVER, FACADE and MODEL-VIEW-CONTROLLER, to do this integration. The product objective is to add a MiniDraw based graphical user interface, shown on Figure 35.1, to your HotGammon domain code.

The individual, practical, exercises below form increments that solved together develop a fully working user interface. However, other paths are possible to perform the integration so consider the sequence below a feasible path.

35.7.1 Integrating MiniDraw

As the graphics will be provided, the basic challenges you face when integrating your HotGammon domain code with a MiniDraw based user interface (GUI) is making information and control flow between the two units of software:

- *From GUI to HotGammon:* That is, when a user drags a checker from one location to another, or clicks a die to roll the dice, then the appropriate methods in the Game interface must be invoked.
- *From HotGammon to GUI:* That is, when the state changes in HotGammon, then the GUI must be updated to reflect this. For instance if a checker hits a blot, then two checkers must be graphically redrawn: the one the user moves as well as the one that goes to the bar.

This can be done in several ways, but in line with the compositional and design pattern oriented perspective, the exercises below describe an approach based upon patterns:

- *From GUI to HotGammon:* Already at the onset, all variants of HotGammon are accessed through the Game interface which thus serves as FACADE to the HotGammon system. MiniDraw hotspots associated with e.g. movement of the graphical checker figures will thus simply invoke the move method.

- *From HotGammon to GUI:* The GUI needs to be notified of state changes in HotGammon which is exactly the intent of OBSERVER. That is, MiniDraw must register itself as observer of the HotGammon domain and redraw the graphics whenever a relevant state change occurs, like dice rolled, checkers moved, etc.

The sequence diagram in Figure 35.4 outlines the overall protocol that the exercises below aim at. It shows the protocol from when a user moves a checker figure to the graphics has been properly updated.

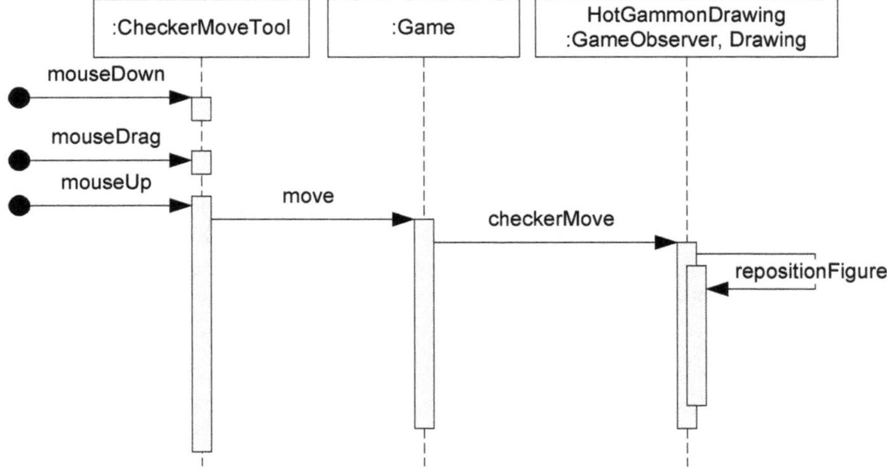

Figure 35.4: Protocol between HotGammon and MiniDraw.

The practical exercises below form the following set of functional increments that each add partial behavior to complete the GUI.

1. Augment the Game interface with **Subject** role methods for registering observers of state changes, as well as introduced state change notifications.
2. Implement the *from GUI to HotGammon* flow: introduce MiniDraw **tools** to move checkers and roll dice.
3. Implement the *from HotGammon to GUI* flow: ensure that MiniDraw redraws checkers and dice correctly based upon state changes in a Game instance.

35.7.2 Provided Code

In folder *project/hotgammon/frameworks* you will find production and test code as well as an initial Ant build management description to get you started building the graphical user interface.

Target `show` is a starting point, see Figure 35.5. It displays the graphical board, the dice, and two checkers but it is pure MiniDraw code as no attempt has been made to integrate the HotGammon domain code.

Furthermore, two helper classes are provided. hotgammon.stub.StubGame1 is a stub implementation of Game that you may use and extend as described in the

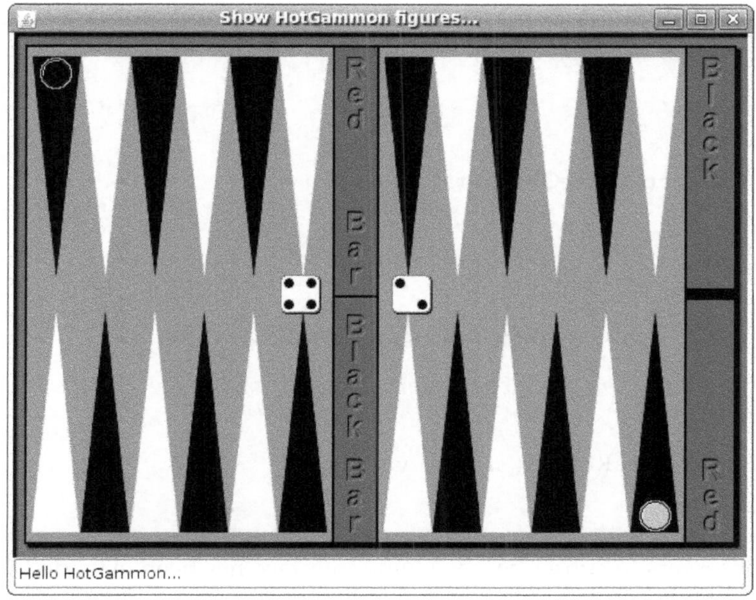

Figure 35.5: Executing the `show` target from the provided code.

exercises for developing partial aspects of the final integration. The class hotgammon.view.Convert contains static functions to help converting back and forth between the graphical coordinate system of the mouse (x,y) and the backgammon specific Locations (B1, B2, etc.) in the game.

35.7.3 Exercises

Exercise 35.38:

Analyze whether the HotGammon production code is a framework.

1. Contrast HotGammon with the characteristics of frameworks (Section 32.2).
2. Find examples of frozen and hot spots.
3. Find examples of *inversion of control*.
4. Find examples of TEMPLATE METHOD in its separation and unification variants.
5. Measure the reuse numbers (as in sidebar 32.1): how many lines of code are in your frozen spots and how many are in the hotspots, for your implemented HotGammon variants?

Exercise 35.39. Source code directory:
`project/hotgammon/frameworks`

Your HotGammon variants need to inform a GUI in case of state changes. The following interface defines an **Observer** role in the OBSERVER pattern.

Listing: project/hotgammon/frameworks/src/hotgammon/framework/GameObserver.java
```
package hotgammon.framework;

/** A game observer is notified whenever the state changes of the
 * Game. GameObserver is the observer role of the Observer pattern.
*/
public interface GameObserver {
  /** this method is invoked whenever a checker is moved from one
   * position to another
   * @param from the position the checker had before
   * @param to the new position of the checker
   */
  public void checkerMove( Location from, Location to );

  /** this method is invoked whenever the dice are rolled.
   * @param values the values of the two dice
   */
  public void diceRolled( int[] values );

}
```

To allow observers to subscribe, the Game interface has been extended with a subscription method:

```
  /** add an observer to this game
   * @param observer the observer to notify in case of state changes.
   */
  public void addObserver(GameObserver observer);
```

1. Implement the **subject** behavior in your HotGammon Game implementation using TDD such that all variants support observer behavior.

Note: you should not integrate with the MiniDraw user interface yet.

Exercise 35.40:

The MiniDraw GUI must enable moving checkers on the board. The standard role for enabling direct manipulation of the graphics in MiniDraw is **Tool**.

1. Develop a specialized tool to move checkers that invokes the move method of an associated Game instance. If a move is illegal, the checker must be moved back to its original position. The tool should not move die figures.

Hint: Instead of using one of your real HotGammon variants, you may use the provided (partial) stub implementation of the Game interface: *hotgammon.stub.StubGame1* in the *test* tree. This stub only has two checkers and defines all moves to be legal except moving to B3 and R3, and will print to the console whenever a move is made, for manual testing. Also, be sure to consult the Convert class for functions to help you identify locations based upon graphical (x, y) coordinates.

Exercise 35.41:

The MiniDraw GUI must enable rolling the dice to signal changing turn from red to black and vice versa. Again a tool is the obvious choice in the MiniDraw design.

1. Develop a specialized tool to roll the dice when clicked on a figure of a die. It must invoke the proper nextTurn method of an associated Game instance. The tool should not allow moving a die figure nor any checkers.

Note: updating the graphical die figures so they show the new values is the topic of the next exercise.

Exercise 35.42:

The tools implemented in the previous exercises modify the HotGammon domain state, but the MiniDraw graphics still do not respond to these state changes: the die figures do not show the proper graphics corresponding to the values of the thrown dice, checker figures are not properly aligned on the locations, and checker figures are not moved to the bar when hitting a blot.

1. Integrate MiniDraw with the HotGammon domain code so state changes in the game is properly reflected on MiniDraw's graphical interface.

Hints:

- MiniDraw stores its moveable graphics, the **Figures**, in its **Drawing** role, and therefore the most natural way to do this is by configuring MiniDraw with a special purpose Drawing implementation, and making special implementations of the Figure interface. The Drawing implementation's responsibility is to observe a Game instance and update its set of figures (that is, the visible checkers and dice) according to the state changes.
- Consult the Convert class for functions to help with aligning checkers properly on the locations.

Exercise 35.43:

A HotGammon game is basically a state machine that must alter between having the dice rolling tool and the checker move tool active.

1. Develop a tool that alternates between the two previously developed tools in response to the state of the game instance, to allow full play of the HotGammon variants.

Hint: The SelectionTool in MiniDraw can be an inspiration for a tool with a built-in STATE pattern.

Exercise 35.44:

MiniDraw provides a status line in the bottom of the windows. This can be used to write helpful messages to the user, like "Black: two moves left", "Red: Move illegal as it is in the wrong direction", etc.

1. Augment the Observer behavior of the HotGammon framework to notify when a game instance has some text information to display; and integrate it with the MiniDraw status line.

Exercise 35.45:

Document the design of your integration between your HotGammon framework and the MiniDraw framework.

1. Outline the variability points of MiniDraw that you have used to make your integration, and how you have used each to design and implement a usable graphical user interface.

2. Draw a class diagram that shows your design. Emphasis should be on the classes you have developed to inject into the variability points of MiniDraw.

3. Draw a sequence diagram that shows the protocol between your game framework and MiniDraw when the user drags a figure of a unit to move it.

Exercise 35.46:

Make a short oral presentation of *frameworks*. Focus on describing characteristics of frameworks and terminology (inversion of control, hotspots, etc.). Give examples of framework designs, like MiniDraw, and relate it to topics like design patterns and compositional design.

35.8 Outlook

The learning objective of this iteration is practical experience with configuration management and systematic black-box testing techniques.

For the systematic testing exercises, the unit under test is the move validation algorithm of your HotGammon system configured for standard backgammon, that is the method

```
public boolean move(Location from, Location to);
```

in the Game interface. As the rules of standard backgammon are complex with a lot of special rules, like moving off the bar, bearing off, etc., the exercises below are organized as a step-wise process to solve this problem. This section outlines some hints to your process.

Parameters for Move. While the move method only takes two parameters, the *from* and *to* location, remember that the game's state also influences the algorithm in the method. Thus the function to validate if a move is valid or not is actually a function of more parameters:

$$valid = v(\text{ from, to, player-in-turn, state-of-board, state-of-dice })$$

As an example, it is invalid to move a red checker when it is black's turn to move, thus "player-in-turn" is a parameter/condition to consider even though it is not a parameter to the move method. If a player has thrown 6-3 and already moved one checker 6, then only a move of distance 3 is valid, thus the "state-of-dice" influences the algorithm. Of course the state of the board is essential.

Classes of rules. Backgammon's rules for movement are actually a combination of different rules that apply under certain conditions. A plausible classification is

- *Standard moves.* Moving one checker from one normal location to another normal location. No checkers are in the bar, and the player is not bearing off. The focus here is whether the distance travelled matches an (unused) die value, if the proper player is in turn, if the "to" location is blocked by two or more opponent checkers, etc.
- *Bar moves.* A player has at least one checker in the bar and thus standard moves are all illegal, only moves from the bar to the opponent's inner table are allowed.
- *Bearing off.* Bearing off is a move from the inner table to the bear off location, and only allowed when a player has all his checkers in the inner table.
- *Special rules.* These are the tricky rules that compel a player to use the higher number or complete both die moves where possible. For instance if a player throws 6-3 but can only move either a 6 or a 3, then the 6 being the bigger number must be played.

Thus you can first generate test cases for the standard moves, ignoring the other classes. Next you can consider test cases for the bar moves while updating the test cases for the standard moves: the ECs and test cases for standard moves must obey the condition that the player has no checker in the bar for them to be legal. Next you consider bearing off that again requires a small addition to the standard and bar moves, etc.

35.8.1 Exercises

Exercise 35.47:

Establish a software configuration management environment for the development of your HotGammon source code and other documents.

1. Describe which tool you have chosen and how the environment has been set up.

2. Describe how you use the tool for collaborating with the team to develop the source code.

3. Describe how you use the tool to create stable versions to go back to in case you need to *Do Over* in your TDD process.

4. Purposely introduce a conflict in two workspaces and describe how the tool reports the conflict and how it helps to solve it.

Exercise 35.48. Source code directory:
`project/hotgammon/alphamon`

The Location class provided for the HotGammon project contains a distance method.

```
public static int distance(Location from, Location to) {
```

The specification of the method is defined in the source code file. Use the equivalence class partitioning technique and boundary value analysis technique to define quality test cases for this method.

1. Outline the EC table. Describe the analysis in terms of the conditions considered, the guidelines applied and argue for *coverage* and *representation*.

2. Outline the test case table based upon your EC analysis, and argue for the heuristics applied to generate them.

3. Augment the test cases with boundary values.

4. Compare your generated test cases with those in JUnit test class TestLocation. Are there any omissions? Are there any defects in the distance implementation?

Exercise 35.49:

Generate test cases using the equivalence class partitioning technique for the *standard moves* in Backgammon for the method move.

1. Outline the EC table. Describe the analysis in terms of the conditions considered, the guidelines applied and argue for *coverage* and *representation*.

2. Outline the test case table, and argue for the heuristics applied to generate them.

Exercise 35.50:

Add test cases to your test case table for the standard moves from the previous exercise based on a boundary value analysis. Argue for your decisions.

Exercise 35.51:

Generate test cases using the equivalence class partitioning technique for the *bar moves* in Backgammon, and potentially update your test cases for the standard moves.

Outline EC and test case tables as well as argumentation as outlined in exercise 35.49.

Exercise 35.52:

Generate test cases using the equivalence class partitioning technique for the *bearing off moves* in Backgammon, and potentially update your test cases for the standard and bar moves.

Outline EC and test case tables as well as argumentation as outlined in exercise 35.49.

Exercise 35.53:

Generate test cases using the equivalence class partitioning technique for the *special rules* in Backgammon.

Exercise 35.54:

Make a short oral presentation of key concepts and techniques in *equivalence class partitioning* and *boundary value analysis*.

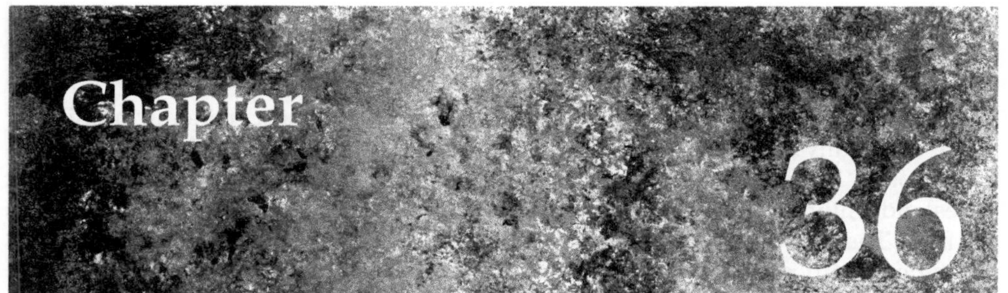

The HotCiv Project

Learning Objectives

This project is a progression of assignments that gives you hands-on experience with central techniques covered in the book. The assignments are grouped into learning iterations that roughly correlate to learning objectives of iteration 2–8 of the book. Each iteration also produces a small release of the final system. Combined, the iterations all add aspects to what becomes a framework and several configurations of it.

The framework's domain is a strategic computer game inspired by the seminal *Civilization* game designed by Sid Meier in 1991. In this game, several players control civilizations that compete to reach military and economic dominance.

> ☞ Search the internet for resources on strategy games like Civilization, Rise of Nations, Age of Empires, etc., to get an impression of the central game concepts and rules. You may also try out FreeCiv which is a free and open source implementation of more or less the original Civilization game.

36.1 HotCiv

HotCiv is a framework that allows you to design your own Civilization-like games. The framework will define a set of aspects that are in common for all variants. In this section, these general aspects of the game are described. In the assignments you will make variants of the game behavior which results in progressively more refined game play. You will also integrate a graphical user interface based on the MiniDraw framework.

36.1.1 Object of the Game

In HotCiv, as in Civilization, players compete to get the highest economic or military score—typically by eliminating all other players. The game takes place in an earth-like "board" or *world* consisting of various terrain. In this world, each player has cities and (military) units. The cities are stationary and may produce various types of units. The units are moveable and may attack opponent units and cities. A typical winning conditions is for one player to conquer all opponents' cities.

36.1.2 World

HotCiv is played on a *world* consisting of areas or *tiles* arranged in a 16 by 16 matrix, as shown in Figure 36.1. Tiles are indexed by a zero-based (row, column) coordinate system. Thus tile (2,3) is the tile in third row and fourth column.

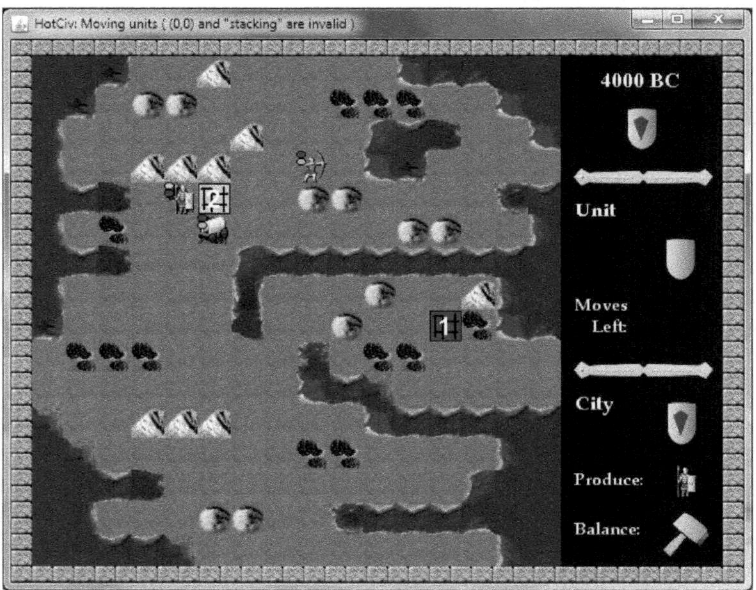

Figure 36.1: HotCiv world and a graphical user interface.

Each tile has a certain terrain type, like plains, forest, mountain, or ocean. Each type of terrain has its own characteristics as described in Table 36.1. An important aspect of a tile is what it can produce of resources. HotCiv defines two resources: *food* and *production*. Food is gathered to increase the population in cities while production is a resource used for building units in a city. In the table, the columns describe what the type of terrain may produce and in what number (food or production), how it looks on the graphical user interface, and whether units may move through the terrain or not.

Type	Production	Graphics	Movement
Plains	3 food		Yes
Oceans	1 food		No
Forests	3 production		Yes
Mountains	1 production		No
Hills	2 production		Yes
(City)	1 food + 1 production	1	Yes

Table 36.1: Data for terrain types.

36.1.3 Players

HotCiv is played by two to four players, each identified by a color, either red, blue, yellow, or green. Each player controls two things: the movement of his or her units, and the production in his or her cities. HotCiv is a turn based game like classic games such as chess, checkers, Stratego, etc. When it is a player's turn, he or she can move units, attack opponent cities, manage cities, etc. When a player is satisfied, the turn goes over to the next player, and so on. Red is the first player to take a turn, followed by blue, yellow, and green.

36.1.4 Units

Players control units that can be moved around in the world. The typical unit is a military combat unit that allow players to battle other units or invade cities. A unit of course belongs to a certain player and only that player is allowed to move the unit.

Types

A unit can only be produced in a city. If a city has gathered enough production resources a unit will be produced: the cost of the unit is simply deducted from the treasury of accumulated production. Example: A city has collected 13 production and is instructed to produce archers. As an archer unit costs 10 production, a new archer unit appears in the city tile and the city now has 3 production remaining in its production treasury. The basic set of unit types are shown in Table 36.2.

A unit may have a special associated *action* that the player can activate. An example is the settler's "build city" action. When this action is performed on a settler, it builds a new city and populates it with one population; the settler unit itself is then removed from the world. The archer's "fortify" action increases its defensive strength but makes it stationary.

Type	Cost	Distance	Graphics	Defense	Attack	Action
Archer	10	1		3	2	fortify
Legion	15	1		2	4	none
Settler	30	1		3	0	build city

Table 36.2: Data for unit types.

Movement

Units can be moved a certain distance depending on their type, see Table 36.2. Distances are measured by the amount of tiles, vertically, horizontally, or diagonally, that must be traversed to get from one tile, A, to another tile, B, excluding A but including B. Example: The distance between (2,2) and (3,3) is 1. The distance between (1,10) and (3,10) is 2, etc. Once a unit has been moved, it cannot move anymore in the current turn. When a new turn starts, all units have their movability restored. A unit cannot move into terrain that is marked with "no" in the movement column in Table 36.1, like ocean and mountains. Likewise a unit cannot be moved outside the world.

Battle

Attack occurs when a unit A, owned by a given player, tries to move into a tile that is occupied by a unit B, owned by an opponent player. An attack is resolved instantly according to rules that are particular for each HotCiv variant. Thus a player cannot withdraw a unit from a battle once it is started. If A wins then B is removed from the game world entirely, and A is moved to B's position (and its move count reduced by one). If B wins the battle, then A is removed, and B remains in its position.

In HotCiv, a unit has a *defensive* and *attacking strength*. These values are used in calculating who wins when one unit attacks another. Generally the higher a defensive (attacking) value is the higher is the probability that a unit will survive an attack (defeat an enemy unit). The exact rules for battles depend on the HotCiv variant, see the descriptions in the later sections.

36.1.5 Turns and Rounds

HotCiv is turn based like traditional board games: Red player moves his units and manages his cities, then it is blue's turn, and so forth. When all players have had a turn, the *round* ends, and a new round starts in which every player again take turns.

At the start of a round, all units are initialized to their maximal move counts. During each player's turn, the player may move any of his units (whose move count is larger than zero) in any order, but of course not any opponent units. Also during the player's turn he can inspect his cities and change the type of units to produce in the city, or the focus of the city's production.

Once a player neither wishes to move any more units nor do any more management of his cities, he must signal that his turn has ended. It is then the next player's turn. Note that a player does not need to move all his units in a turn. Thus all or some of the units' move count may be larger than zero when a player decides to end his turn. The move count, however, is not accumulated to the next round: an army cannot travel twice as long next month because it rests this month.

At the end of a round, each city collects food and production according to the size of the population (see description for cities below). Next, the world ages. The exact number of years that the world ages at the end of a round is defined by the particular game variant.

36.1.6 Cities

Cities are the "factories" of a HotCiv game. Citizens from the city collect production resources from the surrounding tiles and produce units. They also gather food which eventually leads to an increase in the population—which again means more people to collect resources.

Cities are owned by one of the players. A unit that is located at the same tile as a city is defending the city. If an opponent attacking unit defeats the defending unit, then the city changes ownership when the attacking unit moves into it.

The player decides two parameters for each city he owns (though they are not relevant for all variants). These are:

- *Production:* A city is constantly working on producing a specific unit. The player chooses what type of unit the city is currently producing from the list of potential units.
- *Workforce balance:* The player decides whether the focus of the workforce is on *gathering food* (to increase the size of the city as fast as possible) or on *production* (to produce units as fast as possible.)

The size of the population in a city is indicated by an integer number. This number indicates the number of tiles in the immediate vicinity of the city that the workforce can work on. Example: A population of 1 means that all workers work on the tile with the city itself. A population of 3 means that the city tile as well as two other tiles at distance 1 from the city are being worked upon. Thus a city with a large population and a workforce balanced towards production will select tiles like forest and hills to be worked upon, as the most production resources can be gathered there. The relation between food gathering and population size is described in the section on variants.

36.1.7 Initial Setup

The setup of terrain, units, and cities at the beginning of a game depends on the variant, and is described in the respective sections.

36.2 Test-Driven Development of AlphaCiv

The learning objective of this iteration is practical experience with and academic reflection over test-driven development. The product goal is to develop *AlphaCiv* that is an extremely simple HotCiv variant.

The requirements follow the general description in the previous section except for the following requirements that simplify the game and thus the development task significantly. (Admittedly the AlphaCiv game is less interesting from a gamer's point of view.)

- *Players.* There are exactly two players, Red and Blue.
- *World Layout.* The world looks exactly like shown in Figure 36.2. That is the layout of terrain is fixed in every game, all tiles are of type "plains" *except* for tile(1,0) = Ocean, tile (0,1) = Hills, tile (2,2) = Mountains.
- *Units.* Only one unit is allowed on a tile at any time. Red has initially one archer at (2,0), Blue has one legion at (3,2), and Red a settler at (4,3).
- *Attacking.* Attacks are resolved like this: The attacking unit always wins no matter what the defensive or attacking strengths are of either units.
- *Unit actions.* No associated actions are supported by any unit. Specifically, the settler's action does nothing.
- *Cities.* The player may select to produce either archers, legions, or settlers. Cities do not grow but stay at population size 1. Cities produce 6 production per round which is a fixed setup. Red has a city at position (1,1) while blue has one at position (4,1).
- *Unit Production.* When a city has accumulated enough production it produces the unit selected for production, and the unit's cost is deducted from the city's treasury of production. The unit is placed on the city tile if no other unit is present, otherwise it is placed on the first non-occupied adjacent tile, starting from the tile just north of the city and moving clockwise.
- *Aging.* The game starts at age 4000 BC, and each round advances the game age 100 years.
- *Winning.* Red wins in year 3000 BC.

36.2.1 Provided Code

The starting point for this and following exercises is the production and test code skeletons provided in folder *project/hotciv/alphaciv*. The provided supporting classes are shown in the UML class diagram in Figure 36.3[1]. The Game interface is the central interface allowing any client to access any state of the game as well as modify the game's state through user oriented methods, like move a unit, change city production, etc. Therefore Game has quite a long list of responsibilities:

[1]Please note that the associations shown in the diagram are *conceptual* relations and need not be coded literally in your production code.

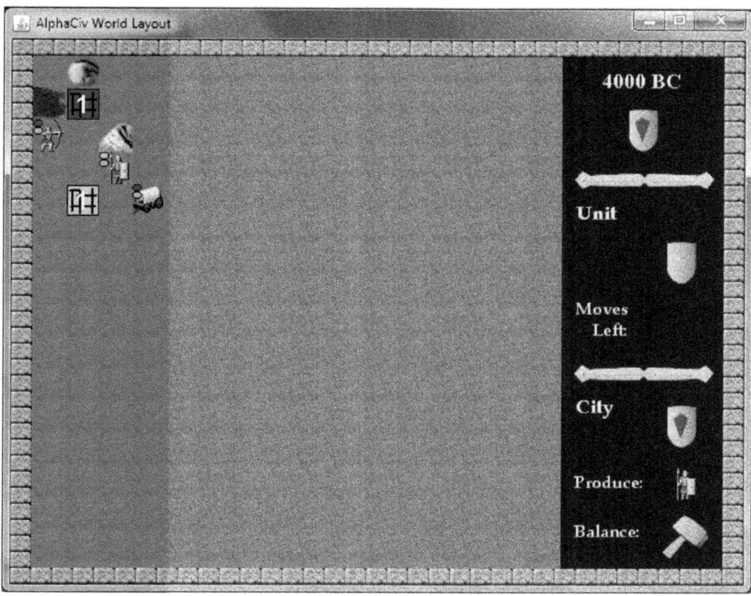

Figure 36.2: AlphaCiv game world.

Game
• Knows the world, allows access to individual tiles • Allows access to cities • Allows access to units • Knows which player is in turn • Allows moving a unit, handles attack, and refuses invalid moves • Allows performing a unit's associated action • Allows changing production in a city • Allows changing workforce balance in a city • Determines if a winner has been found • Performs "end of round" (city growth, unit production, etc.)

The Game interface is central for understanding how a graphical user interface may manipulate the game. Please study the documentation comments in the interface carefully.

The Tile, Unit, and City interfaces provide *read-only* interfaces for accessing properties of tiles, units, and cities like their type, move count, etc. Player is special as its only relevance is existence—there is no real interesting behavior nor data associated with a player seen from the perspective of the game. Therefore Player is an enumeration type identifying the colors of up to four players.

Finally, Position is a concrete class that allows storing (row, column) values used in queries for the Game interface, like for instance:

```
public Tile getTileAt( Position p );
```

So, an assert in a JUnit test case may look like

```
assertNotNull( game.getTileAt( new Position(2,3) );
```

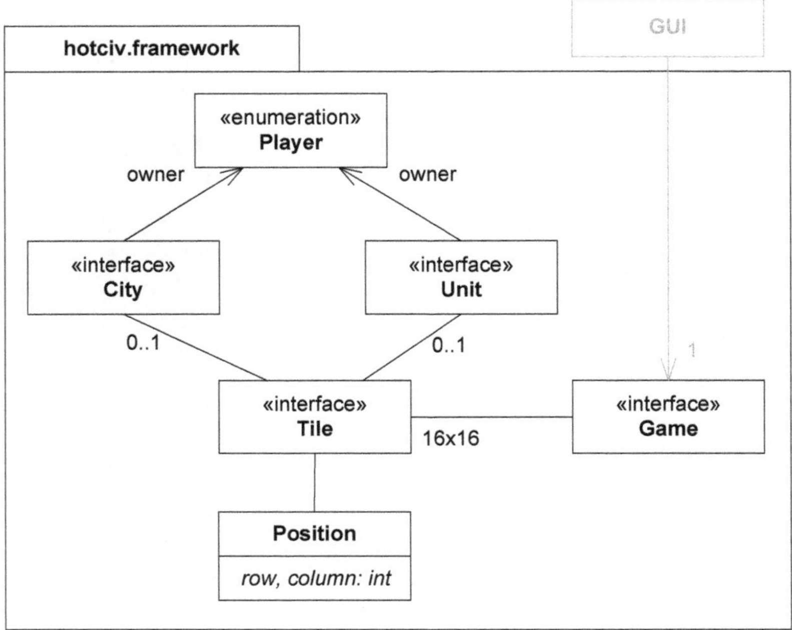

Figure 36.3: HotCiv central abstractions.

The GameImpl class is an empty skeleton implementation of Game to make the test case class, TestAlphaCiv, compile.

36.2.2 Design Decisions

Keep interfaces intact. You may add methods to the provided interface and the standard implementations as you like, but the signatures and responsibilities of the provided ones are used in the provided code for the graphical user interface introduced later. Thus radical changes to the interfaces will make it harder to take advantage of this code.

Read-only interfaces. Why are there no mutator methods on Unit and City? Well, you are free to add them in your TDD process. The reason they are absent is that if you include them, then the client (like the GUI) has two different ways to, say, move a unit: through the Game method and through the Unit interface. As explained in the FACADE chapter this is problematic and I advise to stick to the rule that only the Game interface contains public methods for modifying the game's state.

String based types. Why not use enumeration types for defining the different types in the game, like terrain type or unit type? Surely, enumeration type errors are caught by the compiler and thus leads to better reliability compared to using strings. However, it limits the valid set to that of the predefined enumeration type and we want to keep HotCiv open to adding new types in new variants without rewriting and recompiling existing code. The GameConstants in *hotciv.standard* defines constants for the type strings used in the set of HotCiv assignments: use these to lessen the problem of mistyping type strings.

Preconditions on Game methods. Several methods in the Game interface have associated rather strict preconditions. For instance consider moveUnit:

```
/** move a unit from one position to another.
 * Precondition: both from and to are within the limits of the
 * world.  Precondition: there is a unit located at position from.
 * @param from the position that the unit has now
 * @param to the position the unit should move to
 * @return true if the move is valid (no mountain, move is valid
 * under the rules of the game variant etc.), and false
 * otherwise. If false is returned, the unit stays in the same
 * position and its "move" is intact (it can be moved to another
 * position.)
 */
public boolean moveUnit( Position from, Position to );
```

These two preconditions state that the client code calling moveUnit must have the error handling code that handles that A) the unit is going to be moved outside the world (say to position (-2,-3)) and that B) there actually is a unit located on the from position. The reason that these are sensible preconditions is that the later graphical user interface will do that error handling. *It also means that you should not make test cases that violate these preconditions.*

No World abstraction? The UML class diagram as well as the supplied code skeleton do not include a World interface nor implementation class though it seems to have a rather prominent position in the HotCiv description. This is not a fixed design decision, but rather a consequence of the skeleton code being developed by my own TDD process where I could manage without it: *"Simplicity–the art of maximizing the amount of work not done"*. Feel free to introduce it if and when your TDD process tells you that the production code will become more maintainable and easier to read by having it.

36.2.3 Exercises

Exercise 36.1. Source code directory:
`project/hotciv/alphaciv`

> *Based upon the skeleton code develop the AlphaCiv variant using the test-driven development process.*

In this exercise, the learning objective is practicing the TDD process: the rhythm, the principles, and the values of *taking small steps, keep focus,* and *speed.* Do not design ahead in anticipation of future requirements (in the later learning iterations), but remember *simplicity.* Please consult sidebar 35.1 on page 430 on how to organize your team work. To get you going, the following incomplete test list is given as inspiration:

* Red is the first player in turn
* Red's city is at (1,1)
* there is ocean at (1,0)
* units cannot move over mountain
* Red cannot move Blue's units
* cities produce 6 'production' after a round has ended
* cities' population size is always 1
* after Red it is Blue that is in turn
* Red wins in year 3000 BC
* Red's unit attack and destroy Blue's unit
* ...

1. Develop production and test code for AlphaCiv using TDD.
2. Write a report that includes
   (a) The final test list.
   (b) An outline of two or three *interesting* TDD iterations in detail, outlining the steps of the rhythm, testing principles used, and refactorings made.
   (c) A reflection of observed benefits and liabilities of the TDD approach.

Hint: The specification does contain ambiguities (as any real world specification will). You may resolve them by talking to your "customer": the course instructor. Alternatively you may decide on an appropriate interpretation with your team mates.

Exercise 36.2:

Try to swap your team's developed test cases with another team and execute them on your production code.

1. Classify the reasons for test cases failing. Potential classes are 1) changed interface(s), 2) defects in the production code that your own test cases did not find, 3) defects in the test code, 4) vague specification of AlphaCiv that has led to different interpretations in the teams, etc.
2. Consider/count the number of test cases and number of asserts. Do more test cases (asserts) find more defects?

Exercise 36.3:

Refactor the development environment for your developed AlphaCiv to use the Ant build management tool.

Introduce the build management environment using *the rhythm* and *taking small steps.*

1. Develop Ant targets to compile production and test code and execute your developed tests.

2. Refactor your targets to split the source and build tree, and further split the source tree into a production code and test code tree.

3. Use Ant to create JavaDoc for the production tree code.

4. Write a report that includes

   (a) A short outline of iterations made.

   (b) A reflection of observed benefits and liabilities of using the rhythm and small steps in refactoring the build environment.

Exercise 36.4:

Make a short oral presentation of key concepts and techniques in *test-driven development* for your team members/class, acting as opponents. The opponents should give constructive critique on correctness and presentation technique.

36.3 Strategy, Refactoring, and Integration

The learning objective of this iteration is practical experience with and academic reflection over introducing a compositional design (notably the STRATEGY pattern) by refactoring the existing AlphaCiv design. Also the topics of integration testing and coupling and cohesion are treated. At the same time it is a small release whose product goal is to develop the *BetaCiv*, *GammaCiv*, and *DeltaCiv* variants that each add features to make HotCiv more playable.

36.3.1 BetaCiv

BetaCiv is identical to AlphaCiv, except for the following change in the requirements:

- *Winner.* The winner is the player that first conquers all cities in the world.
- *World aging.* The world ages using the following algorithm:

Between 4000BC and 100BC	100 years pass per round.
Around birth of Christ	the sequence is -100, -1, +1, +50.
Between 50AD and 1750	50 years pass per round.
Between 1750 and 1900	25 years pass per round.
Between 1900 and 1970	5 years per round.
After 1970	1 year per round.

36.3.2 GammaCiv

GammaCiv is identical to AlphaCiv (note: **not BetaCiv**), except for the following requirements:

- *Settler action.* When a settler is told to perform its action (build city), the settler unit itself is removed from the world and replaced by a city of population size one. Of course, the owner of the city is the same player as the one who owned the settler.
- *Archer action.* When an archer is told to perform its action (fortify), its defensive strength is doubled, however, it cannot be moved. If an archer is already fortified, invoking this action removes its fortification.

36.3.3 DeltaCiv

DeltaCiv is identical to AlphaCiv (note: **not BetaCiv nor GammaCiv**), except for the following requirement:

- *World layout.* The world's layout is that shown in Figure 36.1 on page 454. Red must have a city at position (8,12) and blue a city at (4,5). Furthermore, it should be easy for programmers to write their own algorithms for generating a world layout to be used in DeltaCiv without any source code changes in the HotCiv production code.

The world is still restricted to a 16×16 grid.

36.3.4 Exercises

Exercise 36.5:

Develop the BetaCiv variant using TDD by refactoring the AlphaCiv production code. Both variants must be maintained.

1. Sketch a compositional design for the HotCiv system that supports the variants.
2. Refactor the AlphaCiv production code to implement your design. Ensure your AlphaCiv passes all test cases before starting to implement BetaCiv. I advise to put common code into a package, like *hotciv.common,* and variant code in some other package, like *hotciv.variants.*
3. Implement the BetaCiv variant using TDD.

Exercise 36.6:

Develop the GammaCiv variant using TDD by refactoring the HotCiv common production code. All variants must be maintained.

1. Sketch a compositional design for HotCiv to support the new variant.
2. Refactor the existing HotCiv production code to support the new design while all existing variants pass their test suites.
3. Implement the GammaCiv variant using TDD.

Exercise 36.7:

Develop the DeltaCiv variant using TDD by refactoring the HotCiv common production code. All variants must be maintained.

1. Sketch a compositional design for HotCiv that supports the DeltaCiv variant.
2. Refactor the existing production code to support the new compositional design while all existing variants pass their test suites.
3. Implement the DeltaCiv variant using TDD.

Note: The DeltaCiv requirement exemplifies something that is rather tedious to test in full detail: that every tile is in the proper place. You may decide instead to do spot checks, that is, select 8–10 positions and verify that their tile types are correct, and/or count the number of each specific tile type and match them against the required number. The primary purpose of the exercise is compositional design, the precise world layout is less interesting.

Exercise 36.8:

The BetaCiv, GammaCiv, and DeltaCiv variants could of course be implemented using other variability techniques. Sketch designs and/or code fragments that represent:

1. A source code copy proposal.
2. A parametric proposal.
3. A polymorphic proposal.

Exercise 36.9:

After you have introduced several HotCiv variants, your testing code will consist of test cases that test features shared by all HotCiv variants as well as test cases for features particular to specific variants, BetaCiv, GammaCiv, etc.

1. Analyze your testing code with respect to cohesion and with respect to unit/integration testing. Are test cases that test features particular to a specific variant assembled in a properly named test class or are test cases mixed? Has the testing code been separated into unit and integration tests?

2. Refactor your test code and the folder and package structure so unit testing code is put into properly named, cohesive, test classes and integration tests in other test classes.

Exercise 36.10:

Analyze the compositional solution for the variants with respect to coupling and cohesion. Argue why coupling is low or high. Argue why cohesion is low or high.

Exercise 36.11:

One approach to implement the GammaCiv variant is to make SettlerUnit and ArcherUnit classes that are either implementations of the Unit interface or perhaps subclasses of AbstractUnit or StandardUnit. In this approach, the Unit interface is extended with an action() method that is responsible for the particular action associated with the unit. Consider the coupling aspect of this solution in contrast to a STRATEGY based solution for encapsulating the "unit action" algorithm directly in the Game instance:

1. Count the number of relations between instances of Unit and other abstractions in your design for the two solutions.

2. How and in which abstraction is the "destroy settler unit" responsibility handled in the two solutions?

3. How and in which abstraction is the "create city at position" responsibility handled in the two solutions?

Exercise 36.12:

Make a short oral presentation of the STRATEGY pattern and different implementation techniques for handling variable behavior.

36.4 Test Stubs and Variability

The learning objective of this iteration is to get practical experience and academic reflection over variability management using a compositional design, specifically by introducing test stubs and refactoring your design to encapsulate object creation in an ABSTRACT FACTORY. The product goal is to develop *EpsilonCiv*, *ZetaCiv*, and *EtaCiv* that each elaborate on features of the HotCiv game.

36.4.1 EpsilonCiv

EpsilonCiv is identical to AlphaCiv except for the following requirements:

- *Winner.* The winner is the first player to win three attacks. Successful defenses do not count, only successful attacks.
- *Attacking.* Attacks are resolved based upon an algorithm that determines the battle outcome based on *combined attack strength* of the attacking unit and *combined defense strength* of the defending unit. The combined strength is calculated based upon A) the unit's own strength, B) support from adjacent friendly units, and C) terrain factor.

The battle outcome is defined in terms of the combined strength:

> The combined attack strength, A, is first the attack strength of the unit itself. To this value, a supporting strength of +1 is added for each adjacent tile that has a friendly unit. This number is then multiplied by the terrain factor: the terrain factor is 2 if the unit is on a tile of type *forest* or type *hill*; or multiplied by 3 if the unit is in a city.

Example: A legion (attack strength 4) is in a city and two friendly units are located on adjacent tiles. The combined attack strength of the legion is $(4 + 1 + 1) \times 3 = 18$.

For the defending unit a combined defensive strength, D, is calculated using the same formula, except that it is of course based upon the unit's defensive strength. Example: An archer (defensive strength 3) is located on a hill with a single adjacent friendly unit. The combined defensive strength is $(3 + 1) \times 2 = 8$.

The outcome, O, of a battle is a boolean function—if O is true then the attacker wins otherwise the defender wins. Remember that if an attacking unit wins, the defender is removed and the winner unit moved to the position of the defender; if the defender wins then the attacking unit is simply removed from the game world.

O is calculated based upon the combined attack strength and the combined defensive strength using this formula

$$O = \begin{cases} \text{true} & \text{if } A \times d_1 > D \times d_2 \\ \text{false} & \text{otherwise} \end{cases}$$

where d_i is the outcome of rolling a six sided die, that is, a random integer value in range $1 \ldots 6$.

36.4.2 ZetaCiv

ZetaCiv is identical to AlphaCiv except for the following requirements:

- *Winner.* The winner is the player that first conquers all cities in the world (like BetaCiv). However, in case the game lasts more than 20 rounds then the winner is the first player to win three attacks (like EpsilonCiv). The counting of attacks won does not start until the 20th round has ended.

36.4.3 EtaCiv

EtaCiv is identical to AlphaCiv except for the following changes in the requirements:

- *City workforce focus.* The player can establish either a production focus or food focus in a city. If the balance is on production then population counts above 1 are distributed so the population works on adjacent tiles that produce the most production resources. Example: if the 8 adjacent tiles for a city are 5 plains, 2 mountains, and one forest, then a size 4 city will let people work on the city tile (mandatory), on the forest, and the two mountains (totaling 4 tiles) as this is the configuration that will produce the most production resources. If the balance is on food, then the population is of course distributed to maximize food gathering. Example: the same city as above would distribute the remaining three populations on the plains to maximize food generation.
- *City population.* Population size in the city increases by one once the total collected food in the city exceeds 5+(city size)*3. That is a city of size 4 will go to size 5 once the total food in the city exceeds 17. When the city population increases, the food total is reset to 0. Cities cannot exceed size 9.

36.4.4 Exercises

Exercise 36.13:

Develop the EpsilonCiv variant using a compositional approach by refactoring the existing HotCiv production code. As much production code as possible must be under automated testing control.

1. Sketch a design for EpsilonCiv and discuss it using the terminology of test stubs.
2. Implement the variant using TDD by refactoring the existing HotCiv system.

Exercise 36.14:

Develop ZetaCiv by refactoring the existing HotCiv production code.

1. Describe and analyze a pattern based solution for handling the ZetaCiv requirement.
2. Implement the ZetaCiv variant.

Exercise 36.15:

Consider the ZetaCiv specification. Clearly the requirement forces us to consider some responsibilities

Some Abstraction 1

- know the number of attacks won for a given player.

Some Abstraction 2

- increment the number of attacks won for a given player.

that has to be assigned to two (or one?) abstractions in the production code.

1. Identify candidate abstractions that may implement these responsibilities i.e. "which class can hold this integer?", "which class contains the incrementAttacksWonCounter method?"
2. Evaluate each candidate design with respect to coupling and cohesion.
3. Evaluate each candidate design with respect to ISO qualities: analyzability, changeability, and stability.

Exercise 36.16:

Develop EtaCiv by refactoring the existing HotCiv production code.

1. Describe a design for handling the EtaCiv requirement.
2. Implement the EtaCiv variant.

Exercise 36.17:

Refactor your present HotCiv design to use ABSTRACT FACTORY *for creating delegates (like strategies for setting up the world layout, battles, winner determination, etc). All your existing variants, Alpha, Beta, ..., should be represented by concrete factories.*

1. Describe a design based on ABSTRACT FACTORY.
2. Refactor your HotCiv production code to implement the new design.
3. Outline your experience with introducing ABSTRACT FACTORY.

Exercise 36.18:

Consider the following statement

The software unit that defines the world layout for AlphaCiv is a test stub.

1. Use the definition and properties of test stubs to verify if this statement is true.

Exercise 36.19:
Your HotCiv system will contain a number of test stubs at present.

1. Analyze and describe coupling and cohesion of your test stubs with respect to naming and position within the package and folder structure.
2. Refactor your production and test code so test stubs are properly named and cohesive classes and located into packages and folders that express their testing purpose nature.

Exercise 36.20:
Make a short oral presentation of key concepts and techniques for *test stubs*.

Exercise 36.21:
Make a short oral presentation of the STATE and ABSTRACT FACTORY patterns.

36.5 Compositional Design

The learning objective of this iteration is exploring the compositional design approach and its ability to handle multiple dimensions of variability. The product goal is *SemiCiv* that combines all advanced aspects of the previous variants and thus is more interesting from a gamer's perspective.

36.5.1 SemiCiv

SemiCiv is a variant of HotCiv that combines all the advanced requirements detailed so far. Specifically, SemiCiv augments the base requirements of AlphaCiv with the following requirements:

- *World aging.* The algorithm of BetaCiv is used.
- *Unit actions.* The settler can build cities like defined by GammaCiv.
- *World Layout.* The world layout is as specified by DeltaCiv.
- *Winner.* The winner is defined as outlined by EpsilonCiv.
- *Attacking.* Attacks and defenses are handled as defined by EpsilonCiv.
- *City workforce focus and population increase.* These aspects are handled like specified in EtaCiv.

Note: If you have not developed all the particular variants, then just make your SemiCiv the combination of all the advanced features that you *have* developed.

36.5.2 Exercises

Exercise 36.22:

Develop the SemiCiv variant.

1. Produce a configuration table (see Section 17.2) outlining all variants and their variability points.
2. Analyze the amount of modifications in the HotCiv production code that are necessary to configure the SemiCiv variant. Analyze if any design changes are necessary.
3. Implement the SemiCiv variant.

Exercise 36.23:

Consider a purely parametric design of the AlphaCiv, BetaCiv, ..., EtaCiv variants. That is, all variable behaviors are controlled by if's and switches in a single large implementation of Game containing code for all the requirements.

1. Analyze this solution with respect to the amount and type of parameters to control variability.
2. Sketch the code of a few Game methods with emphasis on the variant handling code.

Exercise 36.24:

Consider a purely polymorphic design of the Alpha, Beta, ..., Eta variants. That is, a design in which variants are created by subclassing the original AlphaCiv implementation, like shown in Figure 36.4.

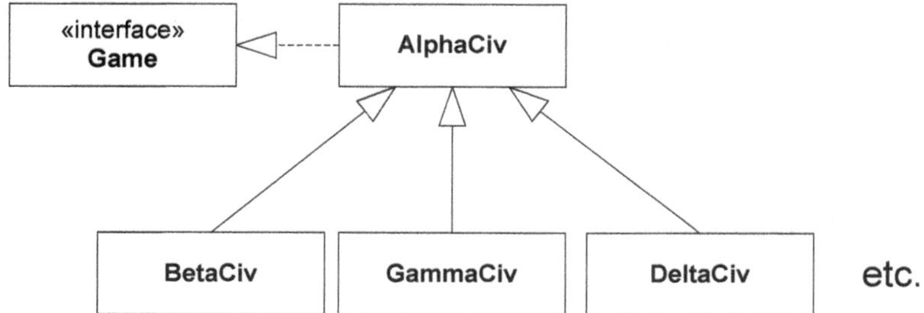

Figure 36.4: HotCiv variants handled by a polymorphic design.

For instance, the BetaCiv world aging algorithm would be handled by overriding the getAge method in class AlphaCiv, etc.

1. Sketch two different design proposals for how to implement SemiCiv based upon a purely polymorphic design. You may consider a design in a language that supports multiple implementation inheritance, like C++.
2. Discuss benefits and liabilities of the polymorphic design in comparison with the compositional design.

Exercise 36.25:

Draw a *role diagram* (see Chapter 18) showing the part of the HotCiv design that handles finding a winner of the game. The diagram must include all winner variants.

Exercise 36.26:

Relate your design to the concepts of behavior, responsibility, role, *and* protocol.

1. Find examples of abstractions, objects, and interactions in your HotCiv system that are covered by each of the concepts above.

Exercise 36.27:

Relate your design to the three compositional design principles.

1. Find examples in your design where you have used the first, the second, and the third principle. Describe aspects of your design that fit the ③-①-② process.

Exercise 36.28:

Make a short oral presentation of key concepts and techniques in compositional design, including definitions of role, responsibility, and protocol, and discuss the challenges of multi-dimensional variance.

36.6 Design Patterns

The learning objective of this iteration is to apply specific design patterns for solving additional requirements to HotCiv.

Note: The assignments in this iteration are not a prerequisite for the next framework iteration. Also note that some design patterns are treated in detail in the framework iteration.

36.6.1 Exercises

Exercise 36.29:

The graphical user interface introduced in the next iteration access and modify the HotCiv game's state through the Game interface.

1. Identify the design pattern that the Game interface represents as seen from the perspective of a graphical user interface. Argue for benefits and liabilities of this design.

Exercise 36.30:

At a HotCiv tournament, a transcript of each game is required for later analysis. A transcript is a text list of all actions made in the game, like e.g.

```
RED moves Archer from (2,0) to (3,1).
RED changes production in city at (1,1) to Legion.
RED ends turn.
BLUE changes workforce focus in city
  at (4,1) to food focus.
...
```

1. Find a suitable design pattern to implement this requirement so any HotCiv variant can be transcribed. Your implementation must be purely *change by addition, not by modification.*
2. Describe the pattern you have chosen and outline why it is appropriate.
3. Implement your design.
4. Explain how you can turn transcribing on and off during the game.

Exercise 36.31. Source code directory:
`project/hotciv/patterns/fractal`

A third party company has released a fractal generator to generate random maps. A fractal generator uses a recursive technique to generate maps, you may search the web for descriptions of the technique.

The map generator is not open source but comes in the form of a Java jar library and a simple demonstration of its usage in the form of a Java class. The interface for the generator is simple with only a single "interesting" method, getLandscapeAt:

```
public class ThirdPartyFractalGenerator {
  /** construct a 16x16 fractal landscape.*/
  public ThirdPartyFractalGenerator() {
    landscape = makeFractalLandscape();
  }

  /** get a character that indicate the type of landscape at
   * the given (row, column).
   * @param row the row of the landscape to inspect.
   * @param column the column of the landscape to inspect.
   * @return a type character defining the type of terrain
   * a the given (row, column).
   * Five types of terrain are possible:
   * '.' is ocean, 'o' is plains, 'f' is forest, 'h' is hills,
   * while 'M' is mountains.
   */
  public char getLandscapeAt( int row, int column ) {
    return landscape[row].charAt(column);
  }
  [...]
}
```

That is, once an instance of ThirdPartyFractalGenerator has been constructed, you can inspect the generated terrain type by invoking getLandscapeAt: it returns 'o' for plains, 'f' for forest, etc.

1. Find and describe a suitable design pattern that will allow you to integrate it into HotCiv for generating fractal maps. Your implementation must be purely *change by addition, not by modification*. Specifically you are not supposed to modify the developed production code for DeltaCiv.

2. Implement your design.

Exercise 36.32:

Several algorithms used by various variants need to iterate over all the eight positions around a given tile, *t*. This is called tile *t*'s *eight neighborhood*.

1. Implement a method get8neighborhood(Position p) that returns an iterator over Position instances for a given position.

Exercise 36.33:

As the HotCiv design is at the moment, each unit can only be associated a single action. In some Civilization games certain units (often called *engineers* or the like) can do many different actions on a tile: build a road, clean up pollution, change terrain from plains to forest, etc.

1. Find a design pattern that will support developers of HotCiv variants to associate multiple and custom developed actions to be associated with units.

2. Refactor your HotCiv production code to integrate this behavior.

Exercise 36.34:

The Game interface contains methods that are basically mutators: they change the state of the game by moving units, change production in cities, etc. However, once a state change has happened it is difficult to undo it.

1. Find a design pattern that will support undo of game actions in HotCiv.
2. Discuss if the Game interface should be refactored to use this pattern.
3. Discuss how actions like "move unit", "change production", "end of turn" would be called using this design.
4. Implement your design.

Exercise 36.35:

Make a short oral presentation of two or three design patterns from the catalogue. Your team members/class act as opponents.

36.7 Frameworks

The learning objective of this small release is both practical and academic aspects of frameworks. You will get experience with specializing MiniDraw to a particular set of requirements. You will also explore aspects of several design patterns such as OBSERVER, FACADE and MODEL-VIEW-CONTROLLER, to do this integration. The product objective is to add a MiniDraw based graphical user interface, similar to Figure 36.1, to your HotCiv domain code.

The individual, practical, exercises below form increments that solved together develop a fully working user interface. However, other paths are possible to perform the integration so consider the sequence below a feasible path.

36.7.1 The User Interface

The expected user interface that is the goal of this release is shown visually in Figure 36.1 on page 454. The requirements to the interfaces are that by using the mouse, the user can invoke all relevant state changing methods of the Game interface, and of course all state changes are correctly reflected by the graphics the user can see. The requirements to the user interface are:

1. moveUnit is invoked when a user drags a unit from one tile to another.
2. endOfTurn is invoked when the user clicks the top shield with the player's color on in the age section of the status panel.

3. changeProductionInCityAt is invoked when the user first has clicked on one of his/her cities and next clicks on the unit symbol, marked "Produce", in the city section of the status panel. Clicking the symbol iterates between (archer, legion, settler) and back.

4. changeWorkForceFocusInCityAt is invoked when the user first has clicked on one of his/her cities and next clicks on the hammer (production focus) or apple (food focus) icon in the city section marked "Balance." Clicking the symbol toggles between the two types of focus.

5. performUnitActionAt is invoked when the user clicks on a unit while holding down the shift key.

Furthermore the status panel should be updated according to the user clicking on icons on the user interface:

- Clicking on a city in the world: the icons in the city section is updated to reflect owner (shield color), production (show unit icon), and workforce balance (hammer or apple icon).
- Clicking on a unit in the world: the icons in the unit section is updated to reflect owner (shield color) and moves left (number to the right of the "moves left" text).
- Clicking on a tile with no city or with no unit clears the icons in the city or unit sections of the status panel respectively.

Furthermore, at each end of turn, two aspects of the age section of the status panel (uppermost part) should be updated: the world age must be written in text and the color of the shield updated to show which player is presently in turn.

36.7.2 Integrating MiniDraw

The basic challenges you face when integrating your HotCiv domain code with a MiniDraw based user interface (GUI) is making information and control flow between the two units of software:

- *From GUI to HotCiv:* That is, when a user drags a unit from one tile to another, or clicks a hammer icon to change work force focus in a city, then the appropriate methods in the Game interface must be invoked, as outlined in the previous section.
- *From HotCiv to GUI:* That is, when the state changes in HotCiv, then the GUI must be updated to reflect this. For instance if the turn ends then the age section icons and text must be updated, etc.

This can be done in several ways, but in line with the compositional and design pattern oriented perspective, the exercises below describe an approach based upon patterns:

- *From GUI to HotCiv:* Already at the onset, all variants of HotCiv are accessed through the Game interface which thus serves as FACADE to the HotCiv system. MiniDraw hotspots associated with e.g. movement of the graphical unit figures will thus simply invoke the moveUnit method, etc.
- *From HotCiv to GUI:* The GUI needs to be notified of state changes in HotCiv which is exactly the intent of OBSERVER. That is, our MiniDraw hotspot associated with the contents of the graphical model must register itself as observer of the HotCiv domain and update the graphical model whenever a relevant state change occurs, like age changes, units moved, etc.

The sequence diagram in Figure 36.5 outlines a plausible protocol to illustrate the dynamics: a user clicks the "end of turn" shield and the game instance notifies the **Drawing** of MiniDraw to update the turn shield figure of the status panel with the proper image, to display a blue or red shield.

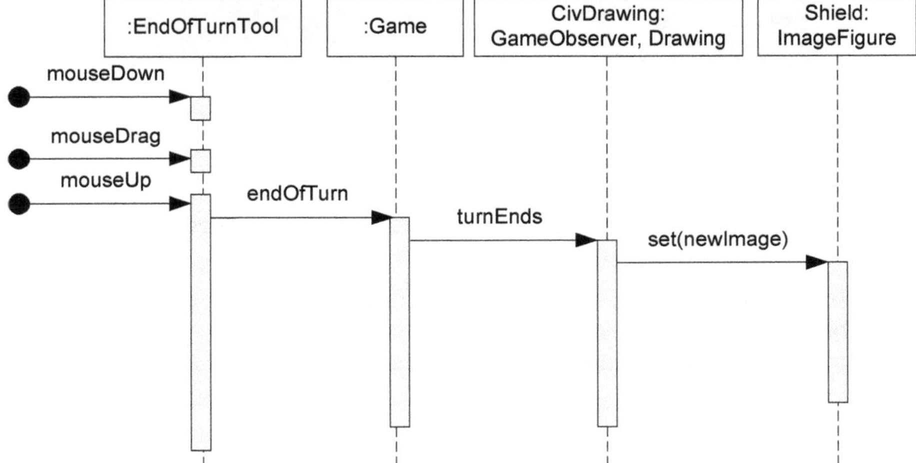

Figure 36.5: Example protocol between HotCiv and MiniDraw.

The practical exercises below form the following set of functional increments that each add partial behavior to complete the GUI.

1. Augment the Game interface with **Subject** role methods for registering observers of state changes, as well as introduced state change notifications.
2. Implement the *from GUI to HotCiv* flow: introduce MiniDraw **Tools** to move units, change city aspects, etc.
3. Implement the *from HotCiv to GUI* flow: ensure that MiniDraw redraws units and icons correctly based upon state changes in a Game instance.

36.7.3 Provided Code

You will find code relevant for the exercises below provided in folder *project/hotciv/frameworks.* You will find production and test code as well as an initial Ant

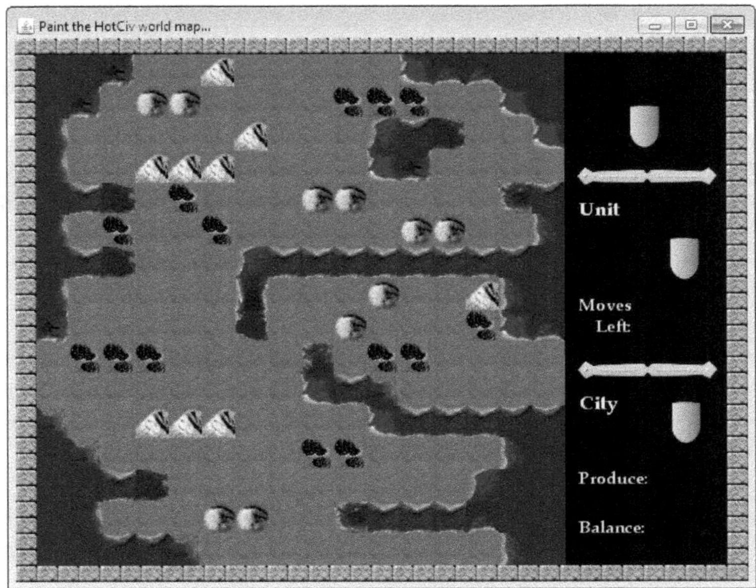

Figure 36.6: Executing the `show` target.

build management description to get you started building the graphical user interface.

Interface changes The Game interface has been extended with two additional methods: addObserver and setTileFocus. The addObserver allows registration of an observer on the game instance and will be explained in more detail in exercise 36.37. The second method is

```
/** set the focus on a specific tile. This will
 * result in an event being broadcast to all
 * observers that focus has been changed to
 * this tile.
 * @param position the position of the tile that
 * has focus.
 */
public void setTileFocus(Position position);
```

This methods adds a new responsibility to a game instance, namely to *know the tile in focus*. The GUI must display information for units and cities located on the *tile in focus* in the status panel on the right. The user typically clicks a tile to make it in focus and thus update the display to see what a city produces, its balance, etc.

Visual testing targets The provided code comes with some targets for manual, visual, testing. Target `show`'s main purpose, see Figure 36.6, is visual testing of the provided MapView class that implements the **DrawingView** role of MiniDraw. It draws a background image containing the brick border, the fixed text and graphics of the status panel; and draws the world map of a given game instance, using terrain graphics for every type of tile.

Target `text` demonstrates two aspects: first, the provided TextFigure is used to show how text (the world age) in the status panel can be displayed and updated; second, it demonstrates how a local **Tool** implementation is coded simply to test the updating of the text figure.

Target `city` demonstrates the provided CityFigure which is a **Figure** to represent a city on the world map: the color identifies the owner and its size is overlaid. Clicking anywhere forces the city instance (just a test stub) to change state and demonstrates how to update the graphics. Note how changed is invoked on the CityFigure instance

```
public void mouseDown(MouseEvent e, int x, int y) {
  [force a change in the state of the city]
  cityFigure.changed();
}
```

which tells MiniDraw to redraw the city figure.

Graphics positions The positions of all graphics in the status panel are defined as constants in the GfxConstants class.

36.7.4 Exercises

Exercise 36.36:

Analyze whether the HotCiv production code is a framework.

1. Contrast HotCiv with the characteristics of frameworks (Section 32.2).
2. Find examples of frozen and hot spots.
3. Find examples of *inversion of control.*
4. Find examples of TEMPLATE METHOD in its separation and unification variants.
5. Measure the reuse numbers (as in sidebar 32.1): how many lines of code are in your frozen spots and how many are in the hotspots, for your implemented HotCiv variants?

Exercise 36.37. Source code directory:
`project/hotciv/frameworks`

The graphical user interface must of course always reflect the state of the game instance, and an OBSERVER pattern is ideal for this purpose. The *hotciv.framework* package has therefore been extended with a GameObserver interface defining an **Observer** role.

Listing: project/hotciv/frameworks/src/hotciv/framework/GameObserver.java

```
package hotciv.framework;

/** Defines the Observer role for a Game.
 *
 */
public interface GameObserver {
  /** invoked every time some change occurs on a position
```

```
   * in the world - a unit disappears or appears, a
   * city appears, a city changes player color, or any
   * other event that requires the GUI to redraw the
   * graphics on a particular position.
   * @param pos the position in the world that has changed state
   */
  public void worldChangedAt(Position pos);

  /** invoked just after the game's end of turn is called
   * to signal the new "player in turn" and world age state.
   * @param nextPlayer the next player that may move units etc.
   * @param age the present age of the world
   */
  public void turnEnds(Player nextPlayer, int age);

  /** invoked whenever the user changes focus to another
   * tile (for inspecting the tile's unit and city
   * properties.)
   * @param position the position of the tile that is
   * now inspected/has focus.
   */
  public void tileFocusChangedAt(Position position);
}
```

To allow observers to subscribe, the Game interface has also been extended with a subscription method:

```
  /** add an observer on this game instance. The game
   * instance acts as 'subject' in the pattern.
   * @param observer the observer to notify in case of
   * state changes.
   */
  public void addObserver(GameObserver observer);
```

1. Using TDD and JUnit test cases, implement the **subject** behavior in your HotCiv Game implementation such that all variants support observer behavior.

Note: you should not integrate with the MiniDraw user interface yet.

Exercise 36.38:

The exercise above implemented the **subject** behavior in your game variants but the user interface of course must observe state changes and update the graphics accordingly to display the proper information to the user.

1. Integrate MiniDraw with the HotCiv domain code so state changes in the game is properly reflected on MiniDraw's graphical interface.

Hints:

- MiniDraw handles its moveable and changing graphics, the **Figures**, in its **Drawing** role, and therefore the natural way to do this is by configuring MiniDraw with a special purpose Drawing implementation and make special implementations of the Figure interface. An important responsibility of the Drawing implementation is to observe a Game instance and update its set of figures (that is, the visible units, city images, and status panel icons) according to the state changes of the game instance.

- As you do not yet have any means of making state changes in the game using MiniDraw itself, I advise you define a special testing tool that forces specific state changes upon every mouse click in a game test stub. You can find inspiration in the following code fragment:

```
class UpdateTool extends NullTool {
  private Game game;
  [...]
  private int count = 0;
  public void mouseUp(MouseEvent e, int x, int y) {
      switch(count) {
      case 0:
        System.out.println("Moving a unit...");
        game.moveUnit(new Position(2,0), new Position(1,1));
        break;
      [...]
      case 3:
        System.out.println("end of turn...");
        game.endOfTurn();
        break;
      [...]
      case 7:
        System.out.println("inspect position 2,3 (blue city)");
        game.setTileFocus( new Position(2,3));
        break;
    [...]
```

- Consult the GfxConstants class for functions and constants to help graphically aligning units, cities, and status icons properly.

Exercise 36.39:

The MiniDraw GUI must enable moving units in the world. The standard role for enabling direct manipulation of the graphics is **Tool**.

1. Develop a specialized tool to move units that, once a graphical unit image has been moved, invokes the moveUnit method of an associated Game instance. If a move is illegal, the unit must be moved back to its original position. The tool should not allow moving any other type of figures, like status icons, city figures, etc.

Exercise 36.40:

The MiniDraw GUI must enable inspecting the status of cities and units.

1. Develop a specialized tool to set the focus on a specific tile (invoking the setTileFocus method) only when a tile is clicked.

Exercise 36.41:

The MiniDraw GUI must enable changing a city's production and work focus.

1. Develop a specialized tool to change production and workforce focus for a specific city (the changeProductionInCityAt and changeWorkForceFocusInCityAt methods) only when the appropriate icon is clicked.

Exercise 36.42:

The MiniDraw GUI must enable handing over the turn to the next player.

1. Develop a specialized tool to end the turn (the endOfTurn) only when the top shield in the age section is clicked.

Exercise 36.43:

The MiniDraw GUI must enable invoking a unit's associated action.

1. Develop a specialized tool to invoke a unit's action when clicked while holding down the shift key.

Exercise 36.44:

Finally, a tool must be developed that intelligently combines all tools developed above so the user can interact with all game figures and icons smoothly.

1. Develop a tool that combines all developed tools to provide smooth interaction with the user.

Hint: The SelectionTool in the MiniDraw framework provides inspiration for how to make a complex tool by a compositional technique.

Exercise 36.45:

Document the design of your integration between your HotCiv framework and the MiniDraw framework.

1. Outline the variability points of MiniDraw that you have used to make your integration, and how you have used each to design and implement a usable graphical user interface.
2. Draw a class diagram that shows your design. Emphasis should be on the classes you have developed to inject into the variability points of MiniDraw.

3. Draw a sequence diagram that shows the protocol between your game framework and MiniDraw when the user drags a figure of a unit to move it.

Exercise 36.46:

Make a short oral presentation of *frameworks*. Focus on describing characteristics of frameworks and terminology (inversion of control, hotspots, etc.). Give examples of framework designs, like MiniDraw, and relate it to topics like design patterns and compositional design.

36.8 Outlook

The learning objective of this iteration is practical experience with configuration management and systematic black-box testing techniques.

36.8.1 Exercises

Exercise 36.47:

Establish a software configuration management environment for the development of your HotCiv source code and other documents.

1. Describe which tool you have chosen and how the environment has been set up.
2. Describe how you use the tool for collaborating with the team to develop the source code.
3. Describe how you use the tool to create stable versions to go back to in case you need to *Do Over* in your TDD process.
4. Purposely introduce a conflict in two workspaces and describe how the tool reports the conflict and how it helps to solve it.

Exercise 36.48:

> *Define a minimal set of test cases for method* moveUnit *using the systematic black-box testing technique* equivalence class partitioning. *You should ignore attacks in this exercise.*

In AlphaCiv the unit types are only allowed to move a distance of one tile, and cannot pass certain types of terrain. Furthermore, it is not allowed to "stack" friendly units, i.e. a unit cannot move onto a tile that is already occupied by a unit. They are moved by invoking the Game's method moveUnit.

```
public boolean moveUnit(Position from, Position to)
```

1. Describe a list of the relevant conditions that influence moveUnit.
2. Document an *equivalence class table* that enumerates all your found equivalence classes and briefly argue for the representation property and the set's coverage property.
3. Outline a *test case table* of concrete test cases defined from the previous analysis, and argue for the heuristics applied to generate them.
4. Present a short comparison to your previously developed TDD test cases from the moveUnit method. Did TDD by itself produce adequate testing?

Hint: Consider the representation property carefully and repartition when you are in doubt. For instance, the algorithm to calculate the distance of the move may incorrectly leave out taking the absolute values, like e.g.:

```
int rowDistance = to.getRow() - from.getRow();
```

Exercise 36.49:

Augment your analysis in 36.48 with a *boundary value analysis*. Does boundary value analysis improve the strength of the test cases significantly for this particular problem?

Exercise 36.50:

> *Define a minimal set of test cases for the EpsilonCiv attack function O using the systematic black-box testing technique* equivalence class partitioning.

In EpsilonCiv the method

```
public boolean moveUnit(Position from, Position to)
```

must include implementation of behavior to evaluate the outcome of an attack in case there is an opponent unit on tile *to*. We can formulate this behavior as a function, O, that returns a boolean value, *true* in case the attacking unit wins the attack, and *false* otherwise.

$$\text{won} = O(u_{from}^{type}, u_{to}^{type}, t_{from}, t_{to}, s_{from}, s_{to}, d_1, d_2)$$

where u_{from}^{type} is the type of unit (legion, archer, settler) on tile *from*, t_{from} is the type of terrain on tile *from*, s_{from} is the support the unit on tile *from* gets from friendly units, and finally d_1 is the value of the first die thrown. The other parameters are similar but for the *to* tile. A systematic testing effort must verify that function O's output is identical to the expected value won.

1. Outline a list of the relevant conditions that influence O.

2. Document an *equivalence class table* that enumerates all your found equivalence classes and briefly argue for the representation property and the set's coverage property.
3. Document a *test case table* of concrete test cases defined from the previous analysis, and argue for the heuristics applied to generate them.
4. Make a short comparison to your previously developed TDD test cases from the EpsilonCiv exercise. Did TDD produce adequate testing?

Hints: Do not include invalid equivalence classes that are invalid due to preconditions and postconditions in the production code. For instance, an invalid equivalence class is $d_1 < 0$ but as the production code does not produce die values outside the 1..6 range it is irrelevant to produce test cases covering this class.

Consider the representation property carefully and repartition when you are in doubt. For instance, the s_{from} is at first glance just the range $0, 1, .., 7$. However, think carefully if 0 is really a good representative for this range. No, it is not because if all test cases uses $s_{from} = 0$ then no tests will validate if the method to calculate support is correct or added correctly. Thus, this set must be repartitioned. Next, you may consider if enemy units are by mistake added as attacker's support.

The output should be partitioned as well.

Exercise 36.51:

Augment your analysis in 36.50 with a *boundary value analysis*. Does boundary value analysis improve the strength of the test cases significantly for this particular problem?

Exercise 36.52:

Make a short oral presentation of *black-box testing* with emphasis on *equivalence class testing*.

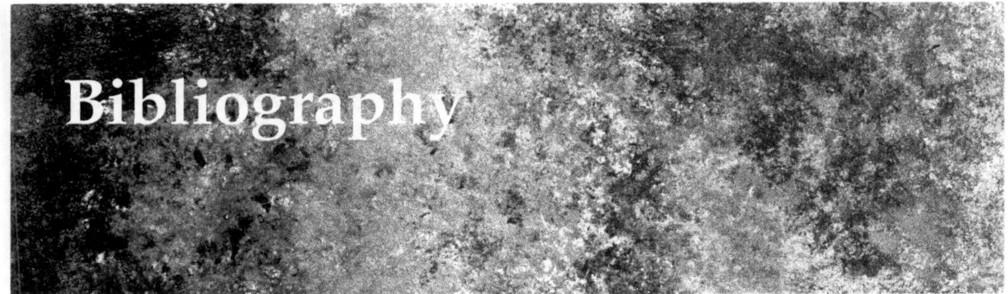

Bibliography

Alexander, C. (1964). *Notes on the Synthesis of Form*. Cambridge, Massachusetts: Harvard University Press.

Alexander, C. (1979). *The Timeless Way of Building*. Oxford University Press.

Alexander, C., S. Ishikawa, and M. Silverstein (1977). *A Pattern Language: Towns, Buildings, Construction*. Oxford University Press.

Alexander, C., M. Silverstein, S. Angel, S. Ishikawa, and D. Abrams (1975). *The Oregon Experiment*. Oxford University Press.

Ant (2009). Apache ant. http://ant.apache.org/, Accessed March 2009.

Bardram, J. E. and H. B. Christensen (2007). Pervasive Computing Support for Hospitals: An Overview of the Activity-Based Computing Project. *Pervasive Computing* 6(1), 44–51.

Barnes, D. J. and M. Kolling (2005). *Objects First with Java: A Practical Introduction Using BlueJ, 2nd ed.* Prentice Hall.

Bass, L., P. Clements, and R. Kazman (2003). *Software Architecture in Practice, 2nd ed.* Addison-Wesley.

Beck, K. (2000). *Extreme Programming Explained–Embrace Change, 1st ed.* Addison-Wesley.

Beck, K. (2003). *Test-Driven Development—By Example*. Addison-Wesley.

Beck, K. (2005). *Extreme Programming Explained–Embrace Change, 2nd ed.* Addison-Wesley.

Beck, K., J. O. Coplien, R. Crocker, L. Dominick, G. Meszaros, F. Paulisch, and J. Vlissides (1996). Industrial Experience with Design Patterns. In *Proceedings of 18th International Conference on Software Engineering (ICSE-18)*.

Beck, K. and W. Cunningham (1987). Using Patterns Languages for Object-Oriented Programs. In *Proceedings of the 1987 Conference on Object-Oriented Programming, Systems, Languages, and Applications (OOPSLA-87)*.

Beck, K. and W. Cunningham (1989). A Laboratory for Teaching Object-Oriented Thinking. In *Proceedings of SIGPLAN International Conference on Object-Oriented Programming, Systems, Languages, and Applications*, Volume 24 of *SIGPLAN Notices*, pp. 1–7.

Berliner, B. (1990). CVS II: Parallelizing Software Development. In *USENIX*, Washington D.C.

Binder, R. V. (2000). *Testing Object-Oriented Systems*. Addison-Wesley.

BlueJ (2009). BlueJ – The Interactive Java Environment. http://www.bluej.org/.

Booch, G., J. Rumbaugh, and I. Jacobson (1999). *The Unified Modeling Language User Guide*. Addison-Wesley.

Brown, W. H., R. C. Malveau, H. W. McCormick, and T. J. Mowbray (1998). *AntiPatterns: Refactoring Software, Architectures, and Projects in Crisis*. John Wiley and Sons.

Budd, T. (2002). *An Introduction to Object-Oriented Programming*. Addison-Wesley.

Burnstein, I. (2003). *Practical Software Testing*. Springer-Verlag.

Buschmann, F., R. Meunier, H. Rohnert, P. Sommerlad, and M. Stal (1996). *Pattern-Oriented Software Architecture – A System of Patterns*. John Wiley and Sons.

Christensen, H. B. (2005, June). Implications of Perspective in Teaching Objects First and Object Design. In *Proceedings of 10th Annual Conference on Innovation and Technology in Computer Science Education*, Lisbon, Portugal.

Christensen, H. B. (2009). A Story-Telling Approach for a Software Engineering Course Design. In *ITiCSE '09: Proceedings of the 14th annual ACM SIGCSE Conference on Innovation and Technology in Computer Science Education*, New York, NY, USA, pp. 60–64. ACM.

Christensen, H. B. and H. Røn (2000, November). A Case Study of Framework Design for Horizontal Reuse. In *Proceedings of 37th International Conference on Technology of Object-Oriented Languages and Systems*, Sydney, pp. 278–289. IEEE Computer Society Press.

Collins-Sussman, B., B. W. Fitzpatrick, and C. M. Pilato (2004). *Version Control with Subversion*. O'Reilly Media.

Eclipse (2009). Eclipse Development Platform. http://eclipse.org/.

Ernst, M. D., G. J. Badros, and D. Notkin (2002). An Empirical Analysis of C Preprocessor Use. *IEEE Transactions on Software Engineering 28*(2), 1146–1170.

Fayad, M. E., D. C. Schmidt, and R. E. Johnson (1999a). *Application Frameworks*, Chapter 1. Volume 1 of Fayad, Schmidt, and Johnson (1999b).

Fayad, M. E., D. C. Schmidt, and R. E. Johnson (1999b). *Building Application Frameworks*. John Wiley and Sons.

Feldman, S. I. (1979, April). Make – A Program for Maintaining Computer Programs. *Software – Practice and Experience*.

Fowler, M. (1999). *Refactoring*. Addison-Wesley.

Fowler, M. (2004, January). Inversion of Control Containers and the Dependency Injection Pattern. http://martinfowler.com.

Fowler, M. (2005, December). The New Methodology. http://martinfowler.com.

Fraser, S., K. Beck, G. Booch, J. Coplien, R. E. Johnson, and B. Opdyke (1997). Beyond the Hype: Do Patterns and Frameworks Reduce Discovery Costs? (Panel). In *Proceedings of the 1997 ACM SIGPLAN Conference on Object-Oriented Programming Systems, Languages & Applications*, pp. 342–344.

Freeman, S., T. Mackinnon, N. Pryce, and J. Walnes (2004). Mock Roles, Not Objects. In *OOPSLA '04: Companion to the 19th Annual ACM SIGPLAN Conference on Object-Oriented Programming Systems, Languages, and Applications*, New York, NY, USA, pp. 236–246. ACM Press.

Gamma, E., R. Helm, R. Johnson, and J. Vlissides (1995). *Design Patterns: Elements of Reusable Object-Oriented Software*. Addison-Wesley.

GCC (2009). GCC, the GNU Compiler Collection. http://gcc.gnu.org/, Accessed March 2009.

Grand, M. (1998). *Patterns in Java, Volume 1, A Catalog of Reusable Design Patterns*. John Wiley and Sons, Inc.

ISO/IEC International Standard (2001). *ISO/IEC 9126-1: Part 1: Quality model*. ISO/IEC International Standard.

Jeffries, R., A. Anderson, and C. Hendrickson (2001). *Extreme Programming Installed*. Addison-Wesley.

Johnson, R. E. and B. Foote (1988). Designing Reusable Classes. *Journal of Object-Oriented Programming 1*(2).

Kaner, C., J. Falk, and H. Q. Nguyen (1993). *Testing Computer Software, 2nd ed*. International Thomson Computer Press.

Kay, A. (1977). Microelectronics and the Personal Computer. *Scientific American 237*(3), 230–244.

Larman, C. (2005). *Applying UML and Patterns*. Prentice Hall.

Lieberherr, K. and I. Holland (1989, September). Assuring Good Style for Object-Oriented Programs. *IEEE Software*, 38–48.

Madsen, O. L., B. Møller-Pedersen, and K. Nygaard (1993). *Object-Oriented Programming in the BETA Programming Language*. Addison Wesley.

Martin, R. C. (1996, May). The Dependency Inversion Principle. *C++ Report 8*.

Meszaros, G. (2007). *xUnit Test Patterns: Refactoring Test Code*. Addison-Wesley.

Meyer, B. (1988). *Object-Oriented Sofware Construction*. Prentice Hall.

Myers (1979). *The Art of Software Testing*. John Wiley and Sons.

Pree, W. (1994). Meta Patterns–A Means for Capturing the Essentials of Reusable Object-Oriented Design. In *Proceedings of the 8th European Conference on Object-Oriented Programming*, Volume 821 of *Lecture Notes in Computer Science*, pp. 150–162. Springer-Verlag.

Pree, W. (1999). *Hot-Spot-Driven Development*, Chapter 16. Volume 1 of Fayad et al. Fayad, Schmidt, and Johnson (1999b).

Reenskaug, T. (1978). MVC XEROX PARC 1978-79. http://heim.ifi.uio.no/~trygver/themes/mvc/mvc-index.html, Accessed March 2009.

Savitch, W. (2001). *Java: An Introduction to Computer Science and Programming*. Prentice Hall.

Shalloway, A. and J. R. Trott (2004). *Design Patterns Explained: A New Perspective on Object-Oriented Design, 2nd ed*. Addison-Wesley.

Snyder, A. (1986). Encapsulation and Inheritance in Object-Oriented Languages. In *Proceedings of SIGPLAN International Conference on Object-Oriented Programming Systems, Languages, and Applications*, Portland, Oregon, pp. 38–45. ACM Press.

Sommerville, I. (2006). *Software Engineering, 8th ed*. Addison-Wesley.

Tesauro, G. (1995). Temporal Difference Learning and TD-Gammon. *Communications of the ACM 38*(3).

Tichy, W. F. (1985, July). RCS – A System for Version Control. *Software – Practice & Experience 15*(7), 637–654.

Tichy, W. F. (1988, January). Tools for Software Configuration Management. In Jurgen F. H. Winkler (Ed.), *Proceedings of the International Workshop on Software Version and Configuration Control*, Grassau, West Germany. B. G. Teubner, Stuttgart.

Wirfs-Brock, R. and A. McKean (2003). *Object Design – Roles, Responsibilities, and Collaborations*. Addison-Wesley.

Wolf, B. (1997). In R. Martin, D. Riehle, and F. Buschmann (Eds.), *Pattern Languages of Program Design 3*, Chapter Null Object, pp. 5–18. Addison-Wesley.

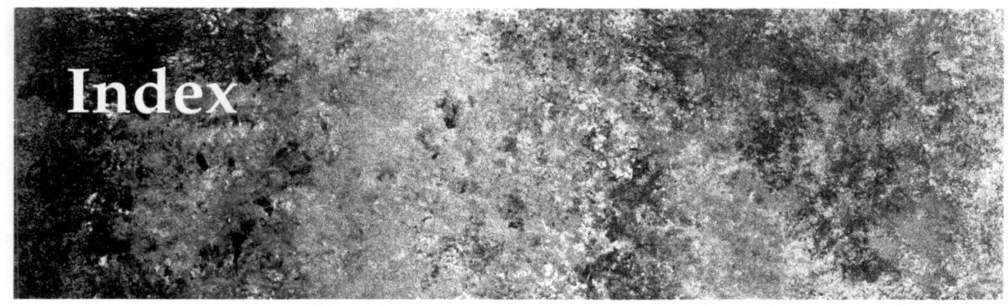

Index

Index of Sidebars/Key Points

Compositional Design Principles

Principles for Flexible Design:

1. Program to an interface, not an implementation.
2. Favor object composition over class inheritance.
3. Consider what should be variable in your design. (or: Encapsulate the behavior that varies.)

Design Pattern Index

Note: The page number refers to the page of the pattern overview box, not the first page of the chapter in which the pattern first appears.

ABSTRACT FACTORY: Provide an interface for creating families of related or dependent objects
without specifying their concrete classes. Page 217.

ADAPTER: Convert the interface of a class into another interface clients expect. Adapter lets
classes work together that couldn't otherwise because of incompatible interfaces. Page 295.

BUILDER: Separate the construction of a complex object from its representation so that the
same construction process can create different representations. Page 301.

COMMAND: Encapsulate a request as an object, thereby letting you parameterize clients with
different requests, queue or log requests, and support undoable operations. Page 308.

COMPOSITE: Compose objects into tree structures to represent part-whole hierarchies. Composite
lets clients treat individual objects and compositions of objects uniformly. Page 322.

DECORATOR: Attach additional responsibilities to an object dynamically. Decorators provide
a flexible alternative to subclassing for extending functionality. Page 289.

FACADE: Provide a unified interface to a set of interfaces in a subsystem. Facade defines a higher-level interface that makes the subsystem easier to use. Page 282.

ITERATOR: Provide a way to access the elements of an aggregate object sequentially without exposing its underlying representation. Page 312.

MODEL-VIEW-CONTROLLER: Define a loosely coupled design to form the architecture of graphical user interfaces having multiple windows and handling user input from mouse, keyboard, or other input sources. Page 342.

NULL OBJECT: Define a no-operation object to represent null. Page 325.

OBSERVER: Define a one-to-many dependency between objects so that when one object changes state, all its dependents are notified and updated automatically. Page 335.

PROXY: Provide a surrogate or placeholder for another object to control access to it. Page 317.

STATE: Allow an object to alter its behavior when its internal state changes. Page 185.

STRATEGY: Define a family of business rules or algorithms, encapsulate each one, and make them interchangeable. Strategy lets the algorithms vary independently from clients that use it. Page 130.

TEMPLATE METHOD: Define the skeleton of an algorithm in an operation, deferring some steps to subclasses or delegates. Template Method lets the behavior of certain steps of an algorithm be varied without changing the algorithm's structure. Page 366.

For Product Safety Concerns and Information please contact our EU representative GPSR@taylorandfrancis.com
Taylor & Francis Verlag GmbH, Kaufingerstraße 24, 80331 München, Germany

www.ingramcontent.com/pod-product-compliance
Ingram Content Group UK Ltd.
Pitfield, Milton Keynes, MK11 3LW, UK
UKHW030828080625
459435UK00005B/53